The New Peplum

The New Peplum

*Essays on Sword and Sandal
Films and Television Programs
Since the 1990s*

Edited by NICHOLAS DIAK
Foreword by DAVID R. COON
Afterword by STEVEN L. SEARS

McFarland & Company, Inc., Publishers
Jefferson, North Carolina

LIBRARY OF CONGRESS CATALOGUING-IN-PUBLICATION DATA

Names: Diak, Nicholas, 1982– editor. | Coon, David R., 1974– writer of foreword. | Sears, Steven L., writer of afterword.
Title: The new peplum : essays on sword and sandal films and television programs since the 1990s / edited by Nicholas Diak ; foreword by David R. Coon ; afterword by Steven L. Sears.
Description: Jefferson, North Carolina : McFarland & Company, Inc., Publishers, 2018 | Includes bibliographical references and index.
Identifiers: LCCN 2017052923| ISBN 9781476667621 (softcover : acid free paper) ∞
Subjects: LCSH: Peplum films—History and criticism.
Classification: LCC PN1995.9.P37 N49 2018 | DDC 791.43/658—dc23
LC record available at https://lccn.loc.gov/2017052923

BRITISH LIBRARY CATALOGUING DATA ARE AVAILABLE

**ISBN (print) 978-1-4766-6762-1
ISBN (ebook) 978-1-4766-3150-9**

© 2018 Nicholas Diak. All rights reserved

No part of this book may be reproduced or transmitted in any form or by any means, electronic or mechanical, including photocopying or recording, or by any information storage and retrieval system, without permission in writing from the publisher.

Front cover: scene from *Hercules*, 2014, *shown from left:* Aksel Hennie, Ingrid Bolso Berdal, Dwayne Johnson (as Hercules), Reece Ritchie, Rufus Sewell (Paramount Pictures/MGM/Photofest)

Printed in the United States of America

*McFarland & Company, Inc., Publishers
Box 611, Jefferson, North Carolina 28640
www.mcfarlandpub.com*

To Mithras and the Unconquerable Sun

Acknowledgments

First and foremost, I must express gratitude to Michele Brittany, my partner who has been the biggest supporter for all my projects. This is my first edited collection I've spearheaded, and her encouragement and advice through the process have been crucial for its success. My best friends Adam and Alan Handford, parents Stan and Tina Wrona, Aunt Rose and Grandpa Joseph have all been encouraging as well.

I'd like to recognize the professors and other academics who have mentored or inspired me over the years: Rob Weiner (Texas Tech University), David Coon (University of Washington), the late Philip Heldrich (University of Washington), and James Barnard (Arizona State University).

Appreciation and thanks are due to Barbra and Bryant Dillon, Sage Weatherford, Alex Wieser and Elliott Hewitt, who all have given me writing opportunities and outlets to keep honing my craft. I appreciate the support and encouragement from Adam Crowley and Jule Schlag (my colleagues from the H.P. Lovecast Podcast), the Los Angeles chapter of the Horror Writers Association, and Jacob Garner, a colleague from the Southwest Popular/American Culture Association.

I would like to pay homage to Christian Ryder, Lisa Duse, Robert Payne Cabeen, Beth Cato, Shaena Stabler, Madison Brunoehler, Nicholas Tesluk and Gary Myers. These folks are my role models, and I strive to be as accomplished as they.

Finally, but most important, appreciation must be given to the essayists in this book. Their wisdom and insight is inked on these pages. They are all amazing scholars and academics, and their endeavors here demonstrate this.

Table of Contents

Acknowledgments   vi

Foreword
    David R. Coon   1

Introduction
    Nicholas Diak   4

**Part One: Crossing the Rubicon:
Expanding the Neo-Peplum Boundaries**

Adapting to New Spaces: Swords and Planets and the Neo-Peplum
    Paul Johnson   21

Hercules: Transmedia Superhero Mythology
    Djoymi Baker   44

From Crowds to Swarms: Movement and Bodies in Neo-Peplum Films
    Kevin M. Flanagan   63

**Part Two: Wisdom from the Gods:
Mythological Adaptations**

There Are No Boundaries for Our Boats: *Vikings* and the Westernization of the Norse Saga
    Steve Nash   79

Sounds of Swords and Sandals: Music in Neo-Peplum BBC Television Docudramas
    Nick Poulakis   95

Hercules, Xena and Genre: The Methodology
  Behind the Mashup
    VALERIE ESTELLE FRANKEL 115

Part Three: The "Glory" of Rome: Depictions of the Empire

Male Nudity, Violence and the Disruption of Voyeuristic
  Pleasure in Starz's *Spartacus*
    HANNAH MUELLER 135

Sex, Lies and Denarii: Roman Depravity and Oppression
  in Starz's *Spartacus*
    JERRY B. PIERCE 155

In the Green Zone with the Ninth Legion: The Post-Iraq
  Roman Film
    KEVIN J. WETMORE, JR. 178

Part Four: Sculpted in Marble: Gender and Representation

Laughing at the Body: The Imitation of Masculinity
  in Peplum Parody Films
    TATIANA PROROKOVA 195

Queering the Quest: Neo-Peplum and the Neo-Femme
  in *Xena: Warrior Princess*
    HAYDEE SMITH 208

Afterword
  STEVEN L. SEARS 219

About the Contributors 223

Index 225

Foreword

DAVID R. COON

Popular culture is often dismissed as disposable entertainment that does not merit serious attention. As a scholar and teacher of popular media and culture, I often get questions and comments like "Why would you study that?" or "Well, that sounds like a lot of fun!" Don't get me wrong—I do think studying popular culture is fun, but there is much more to it. As Stuart Hall, Angela McRobbie, John Fiske, and many others associated with and influenced by the British Cultural Studies movement have demonstrated, popular culture is not something that should be dismissed or written off as inconsequential, because it has the power to reinforce, question, or challenge the values and ideals of the society that produces and consumes it. Working from the belief that textual meanings are not fixed, scholars generally view popular culture as a site of struggle, where creators and consumers negotiate the meanings of individual texts as well as the broader values they represent. This book engages with those negotiations by exploring a set of popular culture texts identified as neo-peplums—recent films and television programs typically set in Greek, Roman, or Biblical antiquity and featuring gladiators, mythological monsters, and heroic quests. The selected texts often contain epic battles and other physical manifestations of struggle, but the essays collected in this book highlight the ideological struggles over ideas and meanings that exist at the heart of these stories.

Films and series that fall into the neo-peplum category are situated at an interesting set of intersections, which makes them particularly rich texts for analysis. For example, they represent the intersection of high and low culture. The stories, after all, are frequently drawn from the history and mythology of ancient Greek, Roman, and Norse civilizations. These stories have previously been adapted in literary and visual art forms, collected in libraries and museums, taken up as objects of study and canonized by scholars and critics in classics departments, as well as programs in literature, art, and history. All of this associates the content of neo-peplums with forms and traditions that have been enshrined as high culture. At the same time, the distribution and marketing of neo-peplums—as summer action films and syndicated television shows, for example—places them closer to what has been considered lowbrow or mass culture.

In addition to bringing together high and low culture, neo-peplums offer the intersection of past and present and occasionally future. Although the stories are generally set in a fantasy or mythological version of the past, they frequently comment on events of the present or engage in some other way with the contemporary moment in which they are produced. As many of the essays in this collection demonstrate, this intersection of past and present enhances the complexity of the texts and the relationship between those texts and the audiences that consume them. Kevin M. Flanagan's essay, for example, demonstrates how stories of the past are repeatedly updated and reimagined with the help of technological advances in the present. And Djoymi Baker's essay considers how contemporary stories are always influenced by intertextual knowledge that draws on myths, legends, and other cultural artifacts from both the past and present.

Along with the intersections that exist within individual neo-peplums, there are intersections that come from juxtaposing the essays that have been collected in this book. For example, this collection brings together studies of many media formats, as these stories have made their way through folklore, literature, and art to graphic novels and comics, film, television, video games, and the internet. While each incarnation offers something unique based on the particular form it takes, many of the themes from these stories transcend their delivery format to reflect broader aspects of the culture in which they circulate, sparking ideas that echo throughout the essays in this book.

Additionally, as is the case with most anthologies, this book brings together scholars and critics from various disciplines, each shedding light on a different aspect of neo-peplums, helping to paint a more complete picture of their significance in our culture. Though the authors' backgrounds and their chosen objects of study may differ, a number of trends and common threads emerge when the essays in this collection are brought together. For example, many of the following essays explore issues related to storytelling in neo-peplums, examining details of narrative form, the process of adaptation, or the implications of genre categories. Other essays focus more on aesthetics, such as the visual and aural surface of the texts or the technical innovations that have expanded the possibilities neo-peplums. Still others emphasize questions of representation, focusing on specific treatments of gender, sexuality, and class or considering how particular characters and events reflect contemporary political events and figures. The dialogue created by these essays reveals a complexity in neo-peplums that is often overlooked by casual fans and dismissive reviewers.

Neo-peplum films and series provide fertile ground for detailed analyses, and the essays that follow certainly engage in such discussions. But of course neo-peplums are not produced for scholars and critics—the are produced for the fans who enjoy them. This is not to say that criticism and fandom need to be mutually exclusive. Indeed, this collection encourages readers/viewers not only to examine neo-peplums as objects of critical analysis but also to engage with them on their own terms, as popular entertainment, showing how criticism and fandom can, and frequently do, go hand in hand.

David R. Coon is an associate professor at the University of Washington, Tacoma, teaching film, media, and popular culture. He wrote *Look Closer: Suburban Narratives and American Values in Film and Television* (2013) and has published in the *Journal of Popular Film and Television*, *Feminist Media Studies*, and *The Journal of Homosexuality*.

Introduction
NICHOLAS DIAK

In the *xkcd* webcomic titled "Standards," two stick figure people ponder the nature of competing standards. Their solution to create an all-encompassing standard to supersede the others only leads to yet another competing standard.[1] While the comic is referring to standards for technologies, it is still applicable when depicting any scenario in which related but conflicting categories, labels, classifications or other identifiers are attempted to be corralled under a unifying banner.

In the realm of film genres, this situation is a bit of a rarity. For the most part, a western is a western, a horror film is a horror film, a sci-fi film is a sci-fi film and so on. These genres of course can be broken down into subgenres, such as the Italian *giallo* films being a type of horror film and space operas being a type of sci-fi film. Then there are mixed genres, such as splatterpunk being a combination of horror and comedy and weird westerns which are the fusion of westerns and other genres such as sci-fi.

There is an exception when it comes to peplum films, which has a plethora of synonyms, subgenres, related genres, and other parallel terms. Typically, when an individual refers to a peplum film, he or she is usually referring to a genre of Italian films made during the late 1950s through the 1960s that focused on ancient Greek, Roman, Biblical or other Mediterranean antiquity stories that featured gladiators, arena combat, mythological monsters, feats of strength, and legendary quests. These include films such as *Hercules* (1958, Pietro Francisci), *The Colossus of Rhodes* (1960, Sergio Leone) and *Ursus* (1960, Carlo Campogalliani). Another term that is used to describe these films, Italian produced or not, are "sword and sandal" films, while in his foundational work on Italian film studies, scholar Peter Bondanella refers to pepla as "neomythological" films.[2] Yet another term that is used to denote these films in a formal fashion, particularly for American made films, is the "historic epic." This term is normally reserved for more prestigious titles, such as *Ben-Hur* (1959, William Wyler), *Spartacus* (1960, Stanley Kubrick) and *Cleopatra* (1963, Joseph L. Mankiewicz).

Within these labels there are discrepancies on their usage. In the introduction to *Of Muscles and Men: Essays on the Sword & Sandal Film*, editor Michael G. Cornelius classifies peplum films into different categorical waves: the First Wave in the 1920s, the Second Wave in the 1950s and 1960s, the Third Wave in the early 1980s, and the Fourth Wave after the release of *Gladiator* (2000, Ridley Scott).[3] Scholars Caroline Eades and Françoise Létoublon mirror this logic of peplum waves when they refer to the peplum films of the 1960s as "neo-peplum" films,[4] implying the run of films in the 1920s should be referred to as the original pepla. On the other hand, Robert A. Rushing labels Cornelius' Fourth Wave of films as neo-pepla, because they are "new versions of the peplum film" and they are "linked in interesting ways to American neo-conservatism."[5]

There are of course related subgenres to the peplum formula. Sword and sorcery films were popular in the 1980s and included films such as *Conan the Barbarian* (1982, John Milius), *Hundra* (1983, Matt Cimber), and *The Beastmaster* (1982, Don Coscarelli), which per Coscarelli was inspired by the Steve Reeves sword and sandal films.[6] The sword and planet subgenre is predominately found in the literary world (particularly with Edgar Rice Burroughs' Barsoom/John Carter books), but films such as *Gor* (1988, Fritz Kiersch) and *Masters of the Universe* (1987, Gary Goddard) can be considered cinematic examples of the subgenre. Then there are a multitude of other historic epic subgenres as well, such as Viking films, barbarian films, ancient Egyptian films, Biblical films, pirate films, Arthurian films and so on.

Cornelius recognized this scenario of different classifications of peplum films and that critics and scholars are not necessarily in agreement on the genre's codification, particularly regarding pre–1950s Italian films.[7] Despite this, when it comes to these overlapping or competing labels for peplum films, scholars and fans are considered to be in alignment with each other. In the case of pre–1990 peplum films, the cinematic language remains intact despite the numerous terms.

However, peplum films produced after 1990 are fundamentally different in critical ways than peplum films from before. Post–1990 pepla, which include noteworthy films such as *300* (2006, Zach Snyder), *Clash of the Titans* (2010, Louis Leterrier), and the aforementioned *Gladiator*, need a proper and distinct classification, a new standard in which to address a new type of historic epic film and to explicitly differentiate from the epics of yesteryear. The argument must be made to either coin a new term or to re-appropriate an existing term to accomplish this feat. Much in the same vein as the term neo-noir came into currency to establish its own identity when compared to the original wave of noir films of the 1940s and 1950s, the term neo-peplum is the most appropriate verbiage to categorize peplum films made after 1990.

As referenced previously, neo-peplum films are fundamentally different in key ways than peplum films produced before 1990. There are five distinct factors surrounding neo-pepla that need to be recognized: the advent of pepla on television; rapidly improving technology and filming techniques; transmedia storytelling in other forms such as comics, video games and music; the establishment of fan culture and communities; and the fluidity and adaptability of what constitutes a neo-peplum film.

Television

Perhaps the singular, most important distinction that makes neo-pepla fundamentally different than other terms is the recognition of television as a medium to create peplum stories. Prior to the 1990s, historic epics were first and foremost produced for theater consumption with some films later being edited and cropped to be shown on television and cable, such as *The Sons of Hercules* edits of various Italian sword and sandal films. Pepla-themed television shows were a rarer phenomenon. Few attempts to bring original pepla to the small screen were made with miniseries such as *The Caesars* (1968), *I, Claudius* (1976), *Masada* (1981), *The Last Days of Pompeii* (1984), and *Quo Vadis?* (1985).

The 1980s did see the emergence of sword and sorcery television cartoons, no doubt due to animated productions which could be created at a much cheaper budget when compared to their live action counterparts. Examples include *Galtar and the Golden Lance* (1985–1986) from Hanna-Barbera and *Thundarr the Barbarian* (1980–1982) from Ruby-Spears along with sword and planet cartoons such as *Blackstar* (1981), *He-Man and the Masters of the Universe* (1983–1985) and its spinoff *She-Ra: Princess of Power* (1985–1987) all from Filmation. Two decades prior, Hanna-Barbera had also flirted with the sword and planet formula with *The Herculoids* (1967–1968).

The 1990s marked the turning point for peplum television shows as the genre was able to establish itself both economically and critically. The peplum genre as a whole was given a resurgence via *Mystery Science Theater 3000* (1988–1999). Thirty-year-old Italian peplum films, such as *Hercules* and *Hercules Against the Moon Men* (1964, Giacomo Gentilomo), were rediscovered and appreciated by a new generation of television viewers. The lampooning nature of *MST3K* presented these older films in a more palpable format, giving them a renewed interest or even a cult status.

While *MST3K* made strides at repurposing old films into a new medium, it was the unequivocal success of both *Hercules: The Legendary Journeys*

(1995–1999) and its spinoff *Xena: Warrior Princess* (1995–2001) that truly established the practicality of live action pepla on television. The success of both shows inspired many other pepla-esque shows in the nineties, such as television versions of *BeastMaster* (1999–2000) and *Conan: The Adventurer* (1997–1998) along with *Jack of All Trades* (2000) which was produced by Renaissance Pictures, which had also produced *Hercules* and *Xena*. Both *Hercules* and *Xena* had a profound cultural impact as well, with *Xena* being particularly praised for its positive portrayal of women protagonists and laying the groundwork for the female characters in *Buffy the Vampire Slayer* (1997–2003), *Dark Angel* (2000–2002), *Alias* (2001–2006), and *Battlestar Galactica* (2004–2009).[8]

The practicality of television pepla as established by *Xena* and *Hercules*, combined with renewed vigor in the subject matter from the unprecedented success of *Gladiator*, was enough to permanently open the gates for pepla on television. The advent of Netflix and premium cable channels willing to take the risk on higher production values for their own shows greatly contributed to the proliferation of the genre. This new wave of peplum programming includes shows such as *Empire* (2005), *Rome* (2005–2007), *Roman Mysteries* (2007–2008), *The Tudors* (2007–2010), *Spartacus* (2010–2013), *The Pillars of the Earth* (2010), *Camelot* (2011), *Vikings* (2013–present), *Black Sails* (2014–present), *Barbarians Rising* (2016), *Son of Zorn* (2016–2017) and *Troy: Fall of a City*, currently in production for BBC One and Netflix.

With such a cornucopia of small screen offerings, peplum stories are no longer confined to the large screen. Storytellers can take advantage of the medium to tell complex stories over multiple episodes, and as with the advancement of filming technologies, can depict special effects and ancient locales within practical budgets. Such fare on television with production values comparable to filmic counterparts would have been near impossible prior to the nineties.

Technology

In order to realize the fantastic settings, mythic creatures and dazzling magic, pepla films have always been dependent on special effects and evolving filming technologies. For example, the Italian sword and sandal films of the 1950s and 1960s borrowed "American technologies of new colour processes and widescreen filming."[9] This is best evidenced in the 1958 version of *Hercules* which was shot in Eastmancolor and in widescreen.[10] The iconic scene of Hercules (Steve Reeves), with outstretched chained arms, could not be depicted as powerful or grandiose with any lesser means.

For the various mythical beasts and monsters, stop motion effects were commonly employed. Legendary craftsman of the art Ray Harryhausen brought to life Talos and the sword-wielding skeletons in *Jason and the Argonauts* (1963, Don Chaffey) and the Rocs and the Cyclops in *The 7th Voyage of Sinbad* (1958, Nathan H. Juran). Matte paintings would provide the scenic, historic backgrounds for these films.

The nineties and beyond brought unparalleled advances in filmmaking technology, having a profound effect on sword and sandal cinema, in effect creating significantly different films and conveying new stories. The bluescreen was replaced by greenscreen and *The Matrix* (1999, the Wachowskis) introduced the world to bullet time cinematics. CGI, which had been previewed or showcased sparingly (and effectively) in films such as *The Abyss* (1989, James Cameron) and *Terminator 2: Judgment Day* (1991, James Cameron), became the staple for Hollywood blockbusters.

For neo-peplum examples, consider the tremendous leap in the depictions of the various stop motion monsters to digital means, such as the Kraken in the original *Clash of the Titans* (1981, Desmond Davis), and compare them to the 2010 remake which relied heavily on CGI. Matte painting of majestic lands of antiquity were also replaced by computer generated imagery. With the success of *Toy Story* (1995, John Lasseter), other films embraced computer-generated animation as their media of choice to create films. Neo-peplum animated films include *Beowulf* (2007, Robert Zemeckis) and *Gladiators of Rome* (2012, Iginio Straffi).

Avatar (2009, James Cameron) was a pivotal film in terms of technical influence on blockbusters due to its usage of 3D.[11] Eager to jump on the 3D bandwagon ushered in by *Avatar*'s success, many films, including neo-pepla, quickly followed suit and embraced the practice. Some films, such as *Beowulf*[12] and *The Legend of Hercules* (2014, Renny Harlin),[13] were shot in 3D, while others such as *Clash of the Titans* (2010, Louis Leterrier),[14] its sequel *Wrath of the Titans* (2012, Jonathan Liebesman)[15] and *Conan the Barbarian* (2011, Marcus Nispel),[16] were shot in 2D and then converted to 3D.

Choice of film formats also expanded significantly. While original pepla benefited from widescreen formats, such as CinemaScope, neo-peplum films such as *300*, *300: Rise of an Empire* (2014, Noam Murro), *Beowulf*, *John Carter* (2012, Andrew Stanton), *Prince of Persia: The Sands of Time* (2010, Mike Newell), and *Wrath of the Titans* have all had the benefit of being shot on 70mm for IMAX, creating the most bombastic viewing experiences possible.

The production aspect of neo-peplum films was not the only element greatly impacted by advanced technologies, but the viewing experiences of these films as well. Prior to the 1980s, peplum and historic epics films were mostly confined to first and second run theaters. At times, some of these films would be shown on television, but in both the theatrical and small screen scenarios, their availability to be seen was limited and not in control of the consumer. Beginning in the 1980s, the means to distribute these films to fans was greatly enhanced by the proliferation of not only VHS and movie rentals (and laserdiscs in a more niche capacity), but premium cable services such as Showtime and Cinemax as well. Don Coscarelli, the director of *The Beastmaster*, quipped that comedians had joked that HBO was an initialism for "Hey! Beastmaster is on!"[17] in reference to the film's frequent showings on the network.

In the 1990s and beyond, the means to watch neo-pepla expanded even further. Physical media transitioned from VHS to DVD and then to Blu-ray, so films often would be released multiple times. To entice fans to purchase a newer version, they would be bundled with commentaries, gag reels, documentaries, alternate cuts or even packaged in an ornate fashion. Outside physical media, digital means to watch films also gained wider acceptance as online streaming could be done through services like Netflix and Hulu. Films could now be enjoyed via one's personal computer, mobile device, and even gaming console.

The accelerated technical advances in both film creation and consumption have greatly altered the filmic landscape, and this is certainly felt with the historic epic genre. Stories can be realized now that simply could not before due to technical limitations, and they can be viewed by audiences in a myriad of formats.

Transmedia

While this collection focuses on neo-peplum films and television, the neo-peplum moniker can be applied to other media as well, such as comic books, music and video games, becoming a true transmedia term. In this regard, establishing neo-peplum as a transmedia term recognizes the intertextuality of different neo-pepla media to each other, allowing broader and more multifaceted scholarship to occur.

For example, film texts rarely exist by themselves anymore as a number of supplemental media is generated to coincide with its release. Sometimes these are simply promotional items, sometimes they are a continuation of the story or perhaps they add new narratives or dimensions to the film narrative. The film version of *300* probably cannot be analyzed without at least acknowledging the original *300* graphic novel created by Frank Miller eight years prior. In tandem to the film and graphic novel versions, there also exists a video game on the PlayStation Portable handheld system called *300: March to Glory*. What does this video game text contribute to the dialogue surrounding *300* the film or graphic novel, and in turn what do those media contribute back? An intertextual approach to these three distinct but related incarnations of the same story is applicable, and the concept of neo-peplum recognizes this narrative dynamic.

Outside adaptations of a story across multiple platforms, peplum elements exist in other art forms as well. In the realm of music, many bands incorporate peplum elements into their output. Power metal bands are mainly associated with fantasy and Tolkien elements, but many bands within this subgenre unabashedly flirt with elements of antiquity, penning many epic songs and ballads. Viking metal and folk metal bands also compose songs with peplum themes, though less so with Greek and Roman elements. These bands often adorn their releases with elaborate and beautiful cover art to glorify the subject matter. Examples can be found on *Giants of Canaan* by Attacker, *The Curse of Crystal Viper* by Crystal Viper, *Iron* by Ensiferum and *Caligvla* by Ex Deo.

Though not as common as in the metal scene, post-industrial acts also explore pepla subject matter. *Pro Liberate Dimicandum Est* from the Austrian black-ambient project Hrossharsgrani is an ancient Greece and Rome concept album that samples dialogue from *Gladiator* in the song "Pro Liberate Dimicandum Est" and from *300* in the songs "Never Surrender" and "The Victory." The song "Lord of Ages" by American neofolk band Blood Axis is a reworking of the Rudyard Kipling poem "A Song to Mithras" and is about Roman soldiers expressing adoration to the god Mithras.[18] The album *Veritas* by the Italian military pop band Lupi Gladius incorporates peplum inspired artwork on its cover.

Comic books and graphic novels are another medium that reinterprets peplum themes and stories. Examples include Michael Kogge's miniseries *Empire of the Wolf* that combines Roman history with werewolves, the aforementioned graphic novel *300*, the long running Franco-Belgian comic *Asterix* by René Goscinny, the DC superhero The Olympian who wore the Golden Fleece, the two Hercules graphic novels by Steve Moore (*The Thracian Wars* and *The Knives of Kush*), and Valiant Comics' sword and planet *X-O Manowar* series.

Red Sonja (originally from Marvel but currently with Dynamite Entertainment) is another sword and sorcery character that originated in comic book form, but has gone on to appear in a variety of other media, such as being portrayed by Brigitte Nielsen in *Red Sonja* (1985, Richard Fleischer), and appearing in the animated film *Red Sonja: Queen of Plagues* (2016).

Next to Red Sonja, though, perhaps the most iconic and important comic book character to touch upon peplum elements is without a doubt Wonder Woman. Wonder Woman has gone through different incarnations, (her origin story changes multiple times), but a consistent characterization of the character is her relationship with antiquity, such as receiving powers from Olympic gods, being the daughter of Queen Hippolyta (sometimes shaped from clay), and herself being the princess of the Amazons. As with Red Sonja, Wonder Woman is also a transmedia phenomenon, having had a television show, figurines, cartoon appearances and finally in the summer of 2017, a big budget film adaptation.

Finally, the advent of video gaming is a crucial media that needs recognition as part of the transmedia aspect of neo-peplum. Video games began to take foothold in the 1980s as a source of entertainment, and a handful of peplum-themed games were certainly made, such as *Prince of Persia* originally for the Apple II and *The Battle of Olympus* on the Nintendo Entertainment System.

With improving hardware and software came better graphics and new ways to explore the video game medium to tell stories. Cut scenes, immersive gameplay, realistically rendered worlds, and multiplayer capabilities all contributed to gaming becoming much more enriched and oftentimes cinematic. Prior generations of gaming consoles (Xbox and PlayStation in particular) featured pepla games such as *Rise of the Argonauts*, *Darkest of Days* (which entails time traveling back to the eruption to Mt. Vesuvius), *Ryse: Son of Rome*, *Shadow of Rome*, *Rome: Total War*, and perhaps the most iconic and influential, *God of War* from Sony which spawned an impressive franchise. On the PC market, real time strategy games proliferated, with *Age of Empires* being one of the longest running and respected series.

Though cinema remains neo-pepla's foundational base, its stories are suited across a broad range of (often connected) media. Neo-peplum is a truly transmedia genre of film, more so when compared to its predecessor genres.

Fanbases and Communities

Fandom has always been an important part of pop culture phenomena even before the nineties. Per Columbia University comics librarian Karen Green, the "sixties and seventies were the beginning of the fandom"[19] and juggernauts such as *Star Trek* and Star Wars certainly had their fair share of conventions, fan clubs, and cosplayers, creating different ways for fans to interact with each other. Pepla films during this time also had their devoted following who celebrated the genre. For example, Wendy Pini, one of the creators of the comic series *Elfquest*, entered a Red Sonja look-a-like contest at the behest of Frank Thorne (*Red Sonja* illustrator), won and would go on to appear at various other comic book conventions in her outfit.[20]

With the 1990s though, fandom was radically altered with the arrival of the internet. Instead of relying on mail-centric fan clubs and conventions, fans now had a plethora of other means to seek out and interact with each other, but also provide the gateways and means to entice new fans into their fold. *Xena* was one of the early neo-peplums that took advantage of the burgeoning world wide web. An unofficial *Xena* website appeared sometime in 2008 at xena.com[21] and operated until 2006[22] while online forums at the *Xena Online Community* are still in operation.[23] *Xena* fanfiction continues to be written online at FanFiction.net.[24] Pop culture conventions continued to proliferate as well, with *Xena* having its own devoted convention from 1999[25] up until 2015.[26]

With the advent of Web 2.0 in the later 2000s, the online means of fan interaction shifted again, becoming more centralized from homemade webpages to social media instead. On Facebook, production companies can make official Facebook pages to not only distribute news of their shows, but to invite fan interaction as well. For example, the official *Spartacus* Facebook page has 3.5 million likes, though since the show has concluded, regular posting has ceased.[27] Films, television shows and even movie stars oftentimes use Twitter to not only communicate directly to their followers, but engaged with them too. Popular neo-peplum actor Gerard Butler (Set from *Gods of Egypt* [2016, Alex Proyas], Leonidas from *300*, Beowulf from *Beowulf & Grendel* [2005, Sturla Gunnarsson], and Attila from the television miniseries *Attila the Hun* [2001]) has 456,000 followers on his official Twitter account.[28] Though the concept of web forums has fallen out of fashion, fans group together under other websites as well, such as Reddit which has subreddits devoted to neo-pepla such as *Spartacus* (3.5K subscribers),[29] *Xena* (1.3K subscribers),[30] and *Conan the Barbarian* (300 subscribers).[31] With the advent of Wikipedia, devoted fans may band together to create their own wikis to correlate information about their favorite shows, as can be seen in the *Spartacus Wikia*[32] and the *Hercules & Xena: The Legendary Wikia*.[33]

All these outlets allow fans to congregate and digest/process/disperse the flow of information from these productions. Fans not only engage in the consumption process from watching these films and television shows, but they also engage in the creation process as well by penning fan fiction, creating artwork, and continuing cosplay tradition. In turn, production companies may incorporate fan feedback into their programming. This feedback loop created by the large scale and near-instantaneous fan configurations is a facet of neo-pepla that did not exist pre-internet era, and this attribute is certainly an important and distinctive facet of the genre.

Fluidity of Neo-Pepla

The final defining aspect of what makes neo-pepla unique from other historic epic genre labels is how liberal and accepting it is when considering what films are part of its canon, eschewing focus on stories set in the Greco-Roman era of antiquity and embracing other historic time periods and other countries. With the television medium open for stories and evolving technologies allowing new types of narratives to be realized, filmmakers are exploring pepla concepts outside the genre boundaries, and that is being reflected in neo-peplum films. Examples of films that carry a distinct pepla feel to them that are outside traditional antiquity include *Apocalypto* (2006, Mel Gibson) which is set in pre–Columbian Mesoamerica, the anachronistic *A Knight's Tale* (2001, Brian Helgeland) set in medieval Europe, and *10,000 BC* (2008, Roland Emmerich) which concerns prehistory mammoth hunters. Neo-pepla also encompasses non-occidental peplum films as well, such as the Indian historic epics *Baahubali: The Beginning* (2015, S.S. Rajamouli), its sequel *Baahubali 2: The Conclusion* (2017, S.S. Rajamouli), and *Veeram* (2016, Jayaraj).

Post-modern and even avant-garde elements have appeared in neo-pepla as well, with quite a few films subverting, honoring or even parodying the genre. For example, *Hail, Caesar!* (2016, Joel Coen and Ethan Coen) takes place primarily in an early 1950s Hollywood studio that attempts to film a fictitious historic epic called *Hail, Caesar! A Tale of the Christ*. The film's lead actor, Baird Whitlock (George Clooney), is abducted off the set while still wearing his Roman military costume, which he spends the entirety of the film wearing. As with many Coen brothers' films, *Hail, Caesar!* is a multifaceted movie, with one of its intentions being a love song to genre films of the Golden Age of Hollywood, including the historic epic.

On the small screen, another example of a neo-peplum taking on experimental elements is *Son of Zorn*. The sitcom features animation inserted into live-action, similar to *Who Framed Roger Rabbit* (1988, Robert Zemeckis) and *Cool World* (1992, Ralph Bakshi). The animated components that are mixed into the sitcom draw heavily from 1980s sword and sorcery cartoons. The story follows Zorn, a He-Man-esque character, as he attempts to reconnect with his live-action suburban ex-wife and son. Though the show was cancelled after one season, it demonstrates the how malleable the genre is to different creative reworkings.

Another reworking of the genre can be found in the *Percy Jackson* series of young-adult films, *Percy Jackson & the Olympians: The Lightning Thief* (2010, Chris Columbus) and *Percy Jackson: Sea of Monsters* (2013, Thor Freudenthal). Based on Rick Riordan's *Percy Jackson & the Olympians* books, providing another example the transmedia nature of the genre, these films repurpose Greek mythology into new, present day stories. While the setting may be contemporary, all the core elements of a sword and sandal film are present.

Finally, with the increased instances of remakes, sequels, prequels and reboots, programming that was once sword and sandal or sword and sorcery have transitioned into neo-pepla as well. For example, the classic *Ben-Hur* film was remade in 2016 by Timur Bekmambetov. The *Conan* films of the 1980s were resurrected into a new film in 2011, but they also continue to thrive in other transmedia formats as well, such as comic books from Dark Horse, the video game *Conan* from THQ, and even the table top roleplaying game *Conan: Adventures in an Age Undreamed Of* from Modiphius Entertainment.

While historic epics and sword and sandal films are traditionally relegated to the distant past, the neo-peplum genre acknowledges that these types of stories can be retold in other fashions, such as setting them modern times or by flirting with experimental narratives. While the bulk of sword and sandal films are American and European in origin, neo-pepla does not discount that other countries also have their own variations on the genre.

Understanding Neo-Pepla

Critically and commercially, occidental neo-peplum films have been in a slump, with *The Legend of Hercules, Hercules, Pompeii* (2014, Paul W.S. Anderson), *Gods of Egypt*,[34] *Ben-Hur*[35] and *King Arthur: Legend of the Sword* (2017, Guy Ritchie) all faltering.[36] Failing to recreate the success of *Gladiator* and *300*, the genre seems to have lost its impact. Yet this does not seem to factor in the blockbusting successes of India's wave of recent neo-pepla,[37] the proliferation of new neo-pepla on television, or that neo-peplum elements continued to be incorporated into other film genres, such as the muddling of neo-pepla and the superhero genre in *Wonder Woman* (2017, Patty Jenkins) and *Thor: Ragnarok* (2017, Taika Waititi). While the big-budget, blockbuster neo-pepla may remain elusive for the time being, the genre has anything but lost its impact, and remains a rich and integral part of both cinema and television.

The importance and influence of neo-pepla can certainly benefit from academic reconsideration, and the goal of this collection aims to lay the foundation for this dialogue to occur. The essays in this book have been divided into four parts of related themes and subject matter. However, even outside these parts, many reoccurring elements throughout all these neo-peplum films, particularly regarding the human body, such as the role of masculinity and sexuality, become manifest. The first part, "Crossing the Rubicon: Expanding the Neo-Peplum Boundaries," builds upon the main points of this introduction by elaborating on the unique properties of the neo-peplum genre. Paul Johnson's "Adapting to New Spaces: Swords and Planets and the Neo-Peplum" builds upon the fluidity of the neo-peplum genre by focusing on sword and planet neo-peplum films, specifically *John Carter*, *Jupiter Ascending* (2015, the Wachowskis), and *Tron: Legacy* (2010, Joseph Kosinski). This is a rarer subset of the neo-peplum genre, but has become en vogue again as is evident in recent films such as *Transformers: The Last Knight* (2017, Michael Bay) and *Thor: Ragnarok*. Djoymi Baker's "Hercules: Transmedia Superhero Mythology" expands on the transmedia aspect of neo-peplum films by looking at the character of Hercules, his Dwayne "The Rock" Johnson incarnation in *Hercules* (2014, Brett Ratner), and the relationships from the comic book source material and paratexts such as trailers and Twitter posts. As stated before, more and more superhero films have been leveraging neo-peplum elements. Kevin M. Flanagan's "From Crowds to Swarms: Movement and Bodies in Neo-Peplum Films" explores the technology that neo-peplums embrace, especially how crowd scenes operate and their impact on the narrative (especially in action sequences) when they are realized via digital means.

Since neo-peplum films often draw from mythology and stories of antiquity, adaptation is a crucial element to them. The second part, "Wisdom from the Gods: Mythological Adaptations," explores the barriers, challenges and liberties involved when realizing old worlds as new. Steve Nash's "There Are No Boundaries for Our Boats: *Vikings* and the Westernization of the Norse Saga" dives into immaculate detail of how the television series reconfigures itself from the *Eddas* and the sagas to be told in a fashion palpable to Western audiences. Nick Poulakis takes a technical approach by looking at how music of antiquity is created and used in his essay "Sounds of Swords and Sandals: Music in Neo-Peplum BBC Television" which focuses on the docudramas *Pompeii: The Last Day* (2003, Peter Nicholson) and *Atlantis: End of a World, Birth of a Legend* (2011, Tony Mitchell). Finally, in "Hercules, Xena and Genre: The Methodology Behind the Mashup," Valerie Estelle Frankel celebrates the historical inaccuracy that both programs embraced and employed to their narrative advantages.

Part Three, "The 'Glory' of Rome: Depictions of the Empire," analyzes the nefarious pop culture depictions of the nation. Both Hannah Mueller and Jerry B. Pierce in their respective essays "Male Nudity, Violence and the Disruption of Voyeuristic Pleasure in Starz's *Spartacus*" and "Sex, Lies and Denarii: Roman Depravity and Oppression in Starz's *Spartacus*" analyze the gritty and ultraviolent television series, with emphasis on contrasting corrupt and debaucherous Roman politicians and citizens to the more noble slaves and gladiators. Mueller focuses on the exploitative elements while Pierce focuses on representations. Kevin J. Wetmore Jr.'s "In the Green Zone with the Ninth Legion: The Post-Iraq Roman Film" analyzes how the three ninth legion films, *The Last Legion* (2007, Doug Lefler), *Centurion* (2010, Neil Marshall), and *The Eagle* (2011, Kevin Macdonald), are analogous to the Iraq War,

16 Introduction

with the Roman soldiers being representative of American soldiers during the conflict.

The final part, "Sculpted in Marble: Gender and Representation," focuses on how sex and gender are portrayed in neo-peplum films. Tatiana Prorokova discusses how the peplum parody *History of the World, Part I* (1981, Mel Brooks) and neo-peplum parodies *Hail, Caesar!* and *Meet the Spartans* (2008, Jason Friedberg and Aaron Seltzer) portray masculinity as a source of mockery in her essay "Laughing at the Body: The Imitation of Masculinity in Peplum Parody Films." On the other hand, Haydee Smith's "Queering the Quest: Neo-Peplum and the Neo-Femme in *Xena: Warrior Princess*" discusses at length the virtues that *Xena* brought to the dialogue of feminist media studies and the positives aspects arising from the relationship between the series' titular character and her companion.

A foreword and an afterword by David R. Coon and Steven L. Sears respectively bookend this book, with Coon providing pop cultural contextualization for the genre while Sears gives a personal touch by musing on growing up with sword and sandal films and the nature of heroism in neo-pepla.

This collection takes only a small excursion into the realm of neo-peplum films, as the catalog is vast and constantly expanding. It is hoped that by the collection's end, with these essays put into practice, that other scholarship will follow suit, and that neo-pepla, in accordance to the five pillars that make it distinct (television, technology, transmedia, fandom and fluidity), will become solidified as its own unique definition.

Notes

1. Randall Munroe, "Standards," *xkcd*, accessed August 26, 2016, https://xkcd.com/927/.
2. Peter Bondanella, *Italian Cinema: From Neorealism to the Present* (New York: Continuum, 2007), 159.
3. Michael G. Cornelius, introduction to *Of Muscles and Men: Essays on the Sword & Sandal Film*, ed. Michael G. Cornelius (Jefferson, NC: McFarland, 2011), 4–5.
4. Caroline Eades and Françoise Létoublon, "From Film Analysis to Oral-Formulaic Theory: The Case of the Yellow Oilskins," in *Contextualizing Classics: Ideology, Performance, Dialog*, ed. Thomas M. Falkner, Nancy Felson, and David Konstan (Lanham, MD: Rowman & Littlefield, 1999), 301.
5. Robert A. Rushing, "Memory & Masculinity in the Italian Peplum Film and Zach Snyder's *300*," in *Culture et Mémoire: Représentations Contemporaines de la Mémoire dans les Espaces Mémoriels, les Arts du Visuel, la Littérature et le Théâtre*, ed. Carola Hähnel-Mesnard, Marie Liénard-Yeterian and Cristina Marinas (Paris: Ecole Polytechnique, 2008), 239.
6. *The Saga of the Beastmaster*, directed by Perry Martin (2005; Troy, MI: Anchor Bay Entertainment, Inc., 2005), DVD.
7. Cornelius, 14.
8. Cathy Young, "What We Owe Xena," *Salon*, last modified September 15, 2005, http://www.salon.com/2005/09/15/xena_2/.
9. Mary P. Wood, *Italian Cinema* (New York: Berg, 2005), 71.
10. "Hercules (1958)," *IMDB*, accessed May 13, 2017, http://www.imdb.com/title/tt0050381/.

Introduction (Diak)   17

11. Ed Power, "Avatar: How the Biggest Film of All Time Got Left Behind," *The Telegraph*, last modified April 15, 2016, http://www.telegraph.co.uk/film/avatar/james-cameron-box-office-cultural-impact/.

12. Alex Billington, "From Motion Capture to 3D: The Technology of Beowulf," *First Showing*, last modified November 15, 2007, http://www.firstshowing.net/2007/from-motion-capture-to-3d-the-technology-of-beowulf/.

13. Kristy Puchko, "Renny Harlin Racing to Beat the Rock with His Own Hercules 3D," *Cinema Blend*, accessed May 15, 2017, http://www.cinemablend.com/new/Renny-Harlin-Racing-Beat-Rock-With-His-Own-Hercules-3D-35506.html.

14. Steven James Snyder, "Titans Director: 'Clash' Trilogy Already Written, Dying To Tackle Avengers," *Time*, last modified March 31, 2010, http://techland.time.com/2010/03/31/titans-director/.

15. Todd Gilchrist, "'Clash of the Titans 2' Will Be Converted to 3D, Says Director Jonathan Liebesman," *Moviefone*, accessed May 15, 2017, https://web.archive.org/web/20120405124200/http://blog.moviefone.com/2011/02/24/clash-of-the-titans-2-converted-to-3d.

16. Brendon Connelly, "New Conan Images Offer First Good Look at Several Characters, Location," *Bleeding Cool*, last modified October 11, 2010, https://www.bleedingcool.com/2010/10/11/new-conan-images-offer-first-good-look-at-several-characters-locations/.

17. *The Saga of the Beastmaster*, directed by Perry Martin.

18. Rudyard Kipling, "A Song to Mithras," in *Puck of Pooks Hill* (1996; Project Gutenberg, 2010), http://www.gutenberg.org/files/557/557-h/557-h.htm#mithras.

19. *She Makes Comics: The Untold Story of Women in Comics*, directed by Marisa Stotter (2014; Respect Films, 2014), DVD.

20. *Ibid.*

21. *Amphipolis Village*, accessed May 26, 2017, https://web.archive.org/web/19981201193835/http://www.xena.com:80/.

22. *Ibid.*, accessed May 26, 2017, https://web.archive.org/web/20060101062653/http://www.xena.com:80/.

23. *Xena Online Community*, accessed May 26, 2017, http://xena.yuku.com/.

24. *FanFiction.net*, accessed May 27, 2017, https://www.fanfiction.net/tv/Xena-Warrior-Princess/.

25. "Past Events," *Creation Entertainment*, accessed May 27, 2017, https://www.creationent.com/pastevents.htm.

26. "Creation Celebrates Xena: Warrior Princess," *Creation Entertainment*, accessed May 27, 2017, https://www.creationent.com/cal/xebur.htm.

27. *Spartacus* (Facebook), accessed May 27, 2017, https://www.facebook.com/Spartacus.starz/.

28. *Gerhard Butler* (Twitter), accessed May 27, 2017, https://twitter.com/GerardButler.

29. "Spartacus: TV Series," *Reddit*, accessed May 27, 2017, https://www.reddit.com/r/Spartacus_TV/.

30. "Xena: Warrior Princess," *Reddit*, accessed May 27, 2017, https://www.reddit.com/r/xena/.

31. "ConanTheBarbarian," *Reddit*, accessed May 27, 2017, https://www.reddit.com/r/ConanTheBarbarian/.

32. "Home," *Spartacus Wikia*, accessed May 27, 2017, http://spartacus.wikia.com/wiki/Spartacus_Wiki.

33. "Home," *Hercules & Xena: The Legendary Wikia*, accessed May 27, 2017, http://hercules-xena.wikia.com/wiki/Main_Page.

34. Pamela McClintock, "Box-Office Preview: Big-Budget 'Gods of Egypt' Imperiled," *The Hollywood Reporter*, last modified February 25, 2016, http://www.hollywoodreporter.com/news/box-office-deadpool-wont-have-869356.

35. Liz Calvario, "'Ben Hur' Critical Roundup: Reviews Shrug at Epic Remake," *IndieWire*, last modified August 18, 2016, http://www.indiewire.com/2016/08/ben-hur-review-roundup-timur-bekmambetov-remake-2016-1201718181/.

36. Jack Shepherd, "King Arthur: Legend of the Swords Review Round-Up: What the

Critics Are Saying about Guy Ritchie's Latest Movie," *Independent*, last modified May 10, 2017. http://www.independent.co.uk/arts-entertainment/films/news/king-arthur-legend-of-the-swords-review-round-up-guy-ritchie-critics-charlie-hunnam-a7728066.html.

37. "The Game Changer," *The Tribune*, last modified April 29, 2017, http://www.tribuneindia.com/news/trends/the-game-changer/399023.html.

Bibliography

Amphipolis Village. Accessed May 26, 2017, https://web.archive.org/web/19981201193835/http://www.xena.com:80/.

Amphipolis Village. Accessed May 26, 2017, https://web.archive.org/web/20060101062653/http://www.xena.com:80/.

"Attacker—Giants of Canaan." *Discogs.* Accessed May 25, 2017. https://www.discogs.com/Attacker-Giants-Of-Canaan/master/561275.

Billington, Alex. "From Motion Capture to 3D: The Technology of Beowulf." *First Showing.* Last modified November 15, 2007. http://www.firstshowing.net/2007/from-motion-capture-to-3d-the-technology-of-beowulf/.

Blood Axis. *Blót: Sacrifice in Sweden.* 1998 by Cold Meat Industry. CMI.X. Compact disc.

Bondanella, Peter. *Italian Cinema: From Neorealism to the Present.* New York: Continuum, 2007.

Butler, Gerard. *Gerard Butler* (Twitter). Accessed May 16, 2017. https://twitter.com/Gerard Butler.

Calvario, Liz. "'Ben Hur' Critical Roundup: Reviews Shrug at Epic Remake." *IndieWire.* Last modified August 18, 2016. http://www.indiewire.com/2016/08/ben-hur-review-roundup-timur-bekmambetov-remake-2016-1201718181/.

"ConanTheBarbarian." *Reddit.* Accessed May 27, 2017. https://www.reddit.com/r/Conan TheBarbarian/.

Connelly, Brendon. "New Conan Images Offer First Good Look at Several Characters, Location." *Bleeding Cool.* Last modified October 11, 2010. https://www.bleedingcool.com/2010/10/11/new-conan-images-offer-first-good-look-at-several-characters-locations/.

Cornelius, Michael G. Introduction to *Of Muscles and Men: Essays on the Sword & Sandal Film,* edited by Michael G. Cornelius. Jefferson, NC: McFarland, 2011.

"Creation Celebrates Xena: Warrior Princess." *Creation Entertainment.* Accessed May 27, 2017. https://www.creationent.com/cal/xebur.htm.

"Crystal Viper—The Curse of Crystal Viper." *Discogs.* Accessed May 25, 2017. https://www.discogs.com/Crystal-Viper-The-Curse-Of-Crystal-Viper/master/372710.

Eades, Caroline, and Françoise Létoublon. "From Film Analysis to Oral-Formulaic Theory: The Case of the Yellow Oilskins." In *Contextualizing Classics: Ideology, Performance, Dialog,* edited by Thomas M. Falkner, Nancy Felson, and David Konstan, 301–316. Lanham, MD: Rowman & Littlefield, 1999.

"Ensiferum—Iron." *Discogs.* Accessed May 25, 2017. https://www.discogs.com/Ensiferum-Iron/master/212371.

"Ex Deo—Caligvla." *Discogs.* Accessed May 25, 2017. https://www.discogs.com/Ex-Deo-Caligvla/master/654919.

FanFiction.net. Accessed May 27, 2017. https://www.fanfiction.net/tv/Xena-Warrior-Princess/.

"The Game Changer." *The Tribune.* Last modified April 29, 2017. http://www.tribuneindia.com/news/trends/the-game-changer/399023.html.

Gerhard Butler (Twitter). Accessed May 27, 2017. https://twitter.com/GerardButler.

Gilchrist, Todd. "'Clash of the Titans 2' Will Be Converted to 3D, Says Director Jonathan Liebesman." *Moviefone.* Accessed May 15, 2017. https://web.archive.org/web/20120 405124200/http://blog.moviefone.com/2011/02/24/clash-of-the-titans-2-converted-to-3d.

Hail, Caesar!. Directed by Joel Coen and Ethan Coen. 2016. Universal City, CA: Universal Pictures Home Entertainment, 2016. Blu-ray.

"Hercules (1958)." *IMDB.* Accessed May 23, 2017. http://www.imdb.com/title/tt0050381/.

Hercules. Directed by Pietro Francisci. 1958. Chatsworth, CA: Image Entertainment, 2009. DVD.

"Home." *Hercules & Xena: The Legendary Wikia.* Accessed May 27, 2017. http://hercules-xena.wikia.com/wiki/Main_Page.
"Home." *Spartacus Wikia.* Accessed May 27, 2017. http://spartacus.wikia.com/wiki/Spartacus_Wiki.
Hrossharsgrani. *Pro Liberate Dimicandum Est.* 2009 by Steinklang Industries. SKD 25. Compact disc.
Kipling, Rudyard. "A Song to Mithras." In *Puck of Pook's Hill.* 1996. Project Gutenberg, 2010. http://www.gutenberg.org/files/557/557-h/557-h.htm#mithras.
Kogge, Michael. *Empire of the Wolf #1.* Glendale, CA: Alterna Comics, 2013.
Lupi Gladius. *Veritas.* 2014 by Hau Ruck! SPQR. SPQR XXXIV. Compact disc.
McClintock, Pamela. "Box-Office Preview: Big-Budget 'Gods of Egypt' Imperiled." *The Hollywood Reporter.* Last modified February 25, 2016. http://www.hollywoodreporter.com/news/box-office-deadpool-wont-have-869350.
Munroe, Randall. "Standards." *xkcd.* Accessed August 28, 2016. Https://xkcd.com/927/.
Mystery Science Theater 3000 Collection Volume 7. Burbank, CA: Rhino Home Video, 2005. DVD.
Mystery Science Theater 3000 Volume XXXII. Los Angeles: Shout! Factory, 2015. DVD.
"Past Events." *Creation Entertainment.* Accessed May 27, 2017. https://www.creationent.com/pastevents.htm.
Power, Ed. "Avatar: How the Biggest Film of All Time Got Left Behind." *The Telegraph.* Last modified April 15, 2016. http://www.telegraph.co.uk/film/avatar/james-cameron-box-office-cultural-impact/.
Puchko, Kristy. "Renny Harlin Racing to Beat the Rock with His Own Hercules 3D." *Cinema Blend.* Accessed May 15, 2017. http://www.cinemablend.com/new/Renny-Harlin-Racing-Beat-Rock-With-His-Own-Hercules-3D-35506.html.
Red Sonja: Queen of Plagues. 2016. Los Angeles: Shout! Factory, 2016. Blu-ray.
Rushing, Robert A. "Memory & Masculinity in the Italian Peplum Film and Zach Snyder's *300.*" In *Culture et Mémoire: Représentations Contemporaines de la Mémoire dans les Espaces Mémoriels, les Arts du Visuel, la Littérature et le Théâtre,* edited by Carola Hähnel-Mesnard, Marie Liénard-Yeterian and Cristina Marinas, 239–245. Paris: Ecole Polytechnique, 2008.
The Saga of the Beastmaster. Directed by Perry Martin. 2005. On *The Beastmaster.* Troy, MI: Anchor Bay Entertainment, 2005. DVD.
She Makes Comics: The Untold Story of Women in Comics. Directed by Marisa Stotter. 2014. Respect Films, 2014. DVD.
Shepherd, Jack. "King Arthur: Legend of the Swords Review Round-Up: What the Critics Are Saying about Guy Ritchie's Latest Movie." *Independent.* Last modified May 10, 2017. http://www.independent.co.uk/arts-entertainment/films/news/king-arthur-legend-of-the-swords-review-round-up-guy-ritchie-critics-charlie-hunnam-a7728066.html.
Snyder, Steven James. "Titans Director: 'Clash' Trilogy Already Written, Dying to Tackle Avengers." *Time.* Last modified March 31, 2010. http://techland.time.com/2010/03/31/titans-director/.
Spartacus (Facebook). Accessed May 27, 2017. https://www.facebook.com/Spartacus.starz/.
"Spartacus: TV Series." *Reddit.* Accessed May 27, 2017. https://www.reddit.com/r/Spartacus_TV/.
Wood, Mary P. *Italian Cinema.* New York: Berg, 2005.
Young, Cathy. "What We Owe Xena." *Salon.* Last modified September 15, 2005. http://www.salon.com/2005/09/15/xena_2/.
Xena Online Community. Accessed May 26, 2017. http://xena.yuku.com/.
"Xena: Warrior Princess." *Reddit.* Accessed May 27, 2017. https://www.reddit.com/r/xena/.

PART ONE: CROSSING THE RUBICON:
EXPANDING THE NEO-PEPLUM BOUNDARIES

Adapting to New Spaces
Swords and Planets and the Neo-Peplum

PAUL JOHNSON

Examining cinema and its ability to transcribe the epic (particularly the Homeric), Martin Winkler notes: "the history of visual adaptations exhibits anything but faithfulness to its sources. But there is nothing bad or wrong about the lack of slavish adherence to the model provided by a revered master."[1] Ultimately such adaptations should hold "Homeric creativity in mind"[2] as their model and treat the text with some freedom. This leads to "neo-mythologism," a term coined by Italian director Vittorio Cottafavi and used by Winkler as a springboard to discuss how historical epic films are reimagined and reinvented. Rather than being historical and faithful, the neo-mythologism style took more "freewheeling liberties"[3] with narrative, characters and style, distinct from those made in America by Cecil B. DeMille et al. Commonly known as sword and sandal films, or peplum, (so named by French critics),[4] they became highly popular in the 1960s, and then again in waves during the 1980s and from the 2000s on. In each era peplums show a significant ability to consciously play with the components they are infused with, each time developing a new textual approach to their build, an approach that Pierre Leprohon saw characterized by "humour and irreverence."[5]

Such definitions form the cornerstone to the following analysis of another generic twist on the neo-mythological epic: sword and planet films. An adjunct to peplum films, as well as being a part of the neo-peplum genre that followed the 1990s wave, this essay will explore *John Carter* (2012, Andrew Stanton), *Jupiter Ascending* (2015, the Wachowskis), and *Tron: Legacy* (2010, Joseph Kosinski), investigating how they are positioned within this generic arena. Initially the films in question might seem at odds with certain obligatory traditions: *Ascending* and *Legacy* lack the expected sandy landscapes of traditional peplum films, and the situation of an overtly muscular hero is missing from all three. It is this essay's intention to chart how, and to what extent, the films bend and continue peplum traditions. The sword and planet film narrative traditions, main characters, *mise-en-scène* and style, and surrounding themes will be measured against prominent peplum productions by examining tenets of genre and adaptation study. By developing the notion of fluidity and adaptation, the following seeks to highlight how the sword and planet demonstrates "that there is no intrinsic set of properties which defines one or all genres in any one or all media for all time."[6]

Adapting to Life

Key to examining these films as peplum offspring is considering how the elements operate within the neo-peplum genre, but also how they might adapt and modify pre-existing elements to fit within. This follows Winkler's detail above about there being nothing wrong if an adapted text is lacking slavish detail. Adaptation studies has lately moved beyond questions of fidelity; away from bases of literature to film as its locus, considering broader extra-textual and intra-media issues. As Kate Newell notes: "Most fidelity-based evaluations assume that fidelity is the only goal of adaptation and neglect to consider that, while some adaptations are informed by an agenda of fidelity, others are informed by an agenda of *infidelity*."[7] A series of agendas can be in play, and though most discussions of adaptation tend to circulate around literature to cinema, the position of intra-media adaptation (such as cinema to cinema) is also key and infidelity a lock to be opened. Thomas Leitch's investigations into adaptation play with similar concepts to Newell's, examining aspects that appear at first sight to betray adaptation's notional intentions of fidelity. For Leitch "the most common approach to adaptation is *adjustment*, whereby a promising earlier text is rendered more suitable for filming by one or more of a wide variety of strategies."[8] These include compression, expansion, correction, updating, and superimposition (where outside influences are imposed by creators upon the text).[9]

In a similar vein, the ways in which genres themselves seek to flex and change is itself a significant adjunct. Though film genres have been critically discussed with "theoretical clarity,"[10] Rick Altman has also noted, "genre history offers crossbreeds and mutants."[11] He goes on to relate that in certain decades a genre classification might be placed upon a vast range of what might be seen as different films, in others it is used to specify a set of films due to conventions or iconography that enabled distinctions and the categorization of a multiplicity of types. However recent decades have seen a surfeit of "entirely new types"[12] of genres. This latter idea is a contentious issue, along with the possibility of cross-genres, genre-hybridity and other accordant options.¹³ But Altman does denote "genre films must not only be similar in order to succeed, they must also be different."¹⁴

Clearly then genre films can exhibit consistency, but simultaneously also some variability, allowing inflections to the corpus. It's a facet Altman sees akin to the way a human body operates: "Not a single molecule in my body today was present in my body even ten years ago, yet current notions of personhood make it easier for me to image myself as a continuous being, regardless of changes in my physical make-up."¹⁵ Though people remain essentially the same throughout their lives (made up of core elements, essential traits and so forth), they also undergo significant change. Similarly, academics often note film genres are living organisms that grow, and/or undergo a biological evolution.¹⁶

Both conceptions showcase fluid change as inherent to a genre's life. However, the growth idea showcases predictability, whereas the evolutionary stance favors mutation. This latter notion might be seen as more useful to this discussion, since it highlights how films, despite or perhaps because of their basis in "non-living" technology, are alive to myriad inputs that operate to modify their basis massively or disruptively. Altman cites *Jurassic Park* (1993, Steven Spielberg) and how the film's genetically modified dinosaurs mirror genres. Genres like the aforementioned filmic creatures are seen as infertile which "at any time be crossed with any genre that ever existed."¹⁷ This is the game that neo-peplum arguably plays, particularly when it comes to the basis of this trio of films. Herein Cottafavi's conception of freewheeling liberties comes into play, highlighting how films and genres develop. These films manage to "de(re)compose" into new forms via a further adaptation theory proffered by Kamilla Elliott, which cites aspects of infidelity as key. Such adaptations pick and choose what is necessary to build their overall text for an audience, rejecting what is unnecessary whilst retaining what is.¹⁸

The Peplum Core

Patrick Lucanio highlights that despite or on account of "various locutions, the peplum feature remains an easily recognizable genre if only for the sheer quantity of output that reveals a singular characteristic, the films exotic opulence."¹⁹ Such films are designed to be epic and bold, in both on-screen scope as well as their advertising and promotional presence.²⁰ The exotic—or foreign constituent—can be seen through the use of strange ancient settings, a villain's reliance upon "extra-natural resources," use of elaborate dance sequences with scantily clad women, a vamp-like female who seduces the hero, and of course the central hero's hyper-muscular build and ability.²¹

However, though this constitutes an abundance of riches, such opulence in design and extravagant visuals also creates difficulties in categorization.

Despite these core characteristics and due to opulence as a driving force, there is constant vacillation between critics as to which elements consistently feature. In Daniel O'Brien's overview peplum films don't always include the aforementioned muscular heroes, but the classical era and location is necessary for it to qualify as pepla.[22] However, O'Brien goes on to state others see fit to include pirate and swashbuckling films as peplum, so long as they *are* set in the aforementioned classical era.[23] Yet, ultimately for O'Brien this set of characteristics is "too broad and vague to be of practical use," and see him set the peplum films as "the cycle of mythologically/classical action films made in Italy from the late 1950s to the mid–1960s, centring on a muscular hero and his extraordinary exploits in an ancient or pre-historical setting."[24]

However, this indecision and difference of opinion begins to highlight how the peplum genre can be seen as possessing fluidity that can be expanded upon when situated within the surroundings of the neo-peplum. Since cinema, like all culture, is a constantly evolving medium, there is always a strong possibility of change occurring. Though films can be seen in isolation, their ability to adapt due to the imposition of new directors, aesthetic traits, and types of actors and technology, shows that they draw upon, include, and sometimes withhold numerous elements that influence and inform their make-up. A freewheeling and de(re)composing methodology of a pick and choose approach is therefore used, where adjustments to the constituent elements are developed, allowing evolution as well as expansion, updating and even a sense of subjective correction to the films' make up as each production is produced and received by spectators.

Julie Sanders notes an adaptation "most often signals a relationship with an informing source text."[25] In her work upon how texts use adaptation, Sanders carefully considers the position of appropriation which is effecting "a more decisive journey away from the informing text."[26] Furthermore, the appropriation that develops between the prior and new texts enables "a more wholesale redrafting, or indeed recrafting" through imaginative reworking of existing textual pieces.[27] Adaptation and appropriation working in harmony makes for a useful tool in examining both the peplum and the neo-peplum, since each branch of the genre begin to show appropriation techniques.

Sansone contro il corsaro nero/Hercules and the Black Pirates (1964, Luigi Capuano) for example features the "classic" muscular hero figure, which in its English version is Hercules but in its Italian version is Samson, consequently highlighting an initial adjustment of the film's text. But this hero is really only Samson in name. The character, played by the aptly named Alan Steel, is like so many other peplum heroes in that he is an extremely strong and noble figure, but has little connection to the Biblical namesake. Indeed,

Steel was just the performer's stage name, with his real name being Sergio Ciani. Already then this Samson is a series of adjusted versions of the character, a set of revisions which extend beyond the text to include the performer as well. The film also adds in the titular pirates for further flavor, highlighting another expansion to the already appropriated adaptation of the peplum genre, and a mutation to the generic tableaux. The film shows off Steel/Ciani's body to suitable effect, and features a series of matches to reflect and show his strength, along with a beautiful damsel who falls in love with as well as for him to save. But the style of the film is overall more akin to the swashbuckling genre, and its setting is seventeenth-century Spain, both of which are decided adjustments to the more ancient locales, aesthetics and time zones seen elsewhere in *Hercules/Le fatiche di Ercole* (1958, Pietro Francisci) or *Colossus of Rhodes* (1961, Sergio Leone).

When moving into the later neo-peplums, and most especially the sword and planet films, the concepts of de(re)composing, redrafting, recrafting and modification to the genre become more important, often allowing appropriation, adjustment to narrative, characters, and other aesthetic and formal elements, that show Sanders' decisive journey away from the informing text.

Freewheeling Neo-Mythologism

In his writing on myth adapted within cinema Martin Winkler discusses how aspects of Greek and other mythology have always had alternate versions in circulation, noting, "It is therefore difficult, not to say impossible, to maintain that certain accounts of a myth are the correct ones and that others are false."[28] Although Winkler develops his concept across numerous films outside of the peplum genre, its basis stems from the ways in which myth is malleable, and peplums themselves often made plastic the ancient stories of Greece and other cultures, including an adjusted (and possible reductive) retelling of Jason and his quest for the fleece within Francisci's *Hercules* that is added into the main character's own mythic labors of which the fleece narrative only forms a part. Winkler's wider point is that these myths are open to adaptation and adjustment outside of the prototypical type. Subsequently, sword and planet films develop similar mythological constructions.

Jupiter Ascending, for example, develops and adjusts aspects of Oedipus, the Greek myth that tells of the King who murdered his father and married his mother. Within *Ascending* the roles are somewhat redrafted; though the King's part remains essentially the same, both his character and those of his father and mother become adapted, adjusted (and perhaps "corrected"), and the marriage occurs through a temporal and fantastical twist. The Oedipal King is split between the characters of Titus Abrasax (Douglas Booth) and his brother Balem (Eddie Redmayne), with Titus coercing heroine Jupiter (Mila Kunis), who is in fact a reincarnation of their mother, to marry him. However, Titus aims to kill Jupiter afterwards in order to inherit the power and authority her title carries. This revises the adaptation of the myth by having the son not only marry his mother, but also adjusts patricide to become matricide. In his side of the Oedipal revision Titus also aims to kill the parental figure through the reincarnated Jupiter, also following the modernizing trend, but in addition we discover that Titus murdered his mother in the first place. This might appear anathema to purists, but it closely follows both Winkler's notion of alternate versions mythology. It reflects a diegetic world where the position of the mother and the female hold power and replace the patriarchal icon. It takes on board Winkler's own conceptual basis drawn from Cottafavi's freewheeling concept, and the associated redrafting possible in adaptation by Sanders. Furthermore it reflects the directors' own sensibilities surrounding the position of women, gender and sexuality within cinema, which has been extant from their debut *Bound* (1996, the Wachowskis) through *The Matrix* (1999, the Wachowskis), *Cloud Atlas* (2012, Tom Tykwer and the Wachowskis) and into *Jupiter Ascending* as well as their Netflix series *Sense8* (2015–present). In each the texts push forward a strong revisionist stance on who is in power and control within the diegetic world and surrounding culture, whilst drawing upon a range of cultural and mythical influences (as Winkler has noted above).

Similar mythological revisionism is also seen within *Tron: Legacy*, which most pertinently develops aspects surrounding the Sirens, and their status of drawing hapless men to their doom. Soon after hero Sam Flynn (Garrett Hedlund) enters the grid he is captured and sent to take part in the games, which leads to him entering an underground armory and being prepared for the forthcoming arena by a set of four women, who are directly cited as Sirens in the credits of the film. Each of these characters are played by female performers who are dressed in tight fitting, rubberized costumes that amplify their bodies in an arguably sexual manner, particularly their breasts and bottoms, accentuated by lighting. Their hair and make-up is also similarly styled to highlight cheekbones, lips and eyes, which are given prominence in framing. Two of the Sirens (Beau Garrett and Ya DaCosta) are played by former models, and all four use physical performance over dialogue in order to convey their characters' personas. This gives them a highly sexualized manner, aligned with Mulvey's gaze theory, which produces objectification of the female by the male characters and viewers.[29] But in using adaptation and revision, this basis also provides the "female" characters a sense of power. Of course, the Sirens are not purely female in mythology and neither are they here, being electronic in construction and basis, a facet seen in part due to the characters' uncanny robotic movement. This allows a playful adaptation with both the gaze and the Sirens' basis, using Winkler's neo-mythologism concept, to create an update of the tale and its characters.

Each of the Sirens looks furtively at one another as well as at Sam as they use lasers to remove his clothes, with one noting, "He's different."[30] Sam looks on agog at what is happening, transfixed at the sight of these four beautiful women undressing him both literally and figuratively with their eyes. His immobility and dumbfoundedness continues as he is re-dressed with his grid-wear and identity disk. Sam is fastened by his feet during the scene, but he doesn't struggle whilst being defrocked, ogled and pawed at; instead he stands curious and, perhaps, excited. The impression produced within Sam's character is definitely one of mesmeric and hypnotic ambience, and this signifies the Sirens' mythological standing and their power as beautiful females who cause, or at least incite, men's death. They are also the peplum's prerequisite vamps—those alluring, wanton, women who conspire for the hero's attention. The scene also adapts and adjusts the Sirens' use of song and their calling of men to their death. In this instance their song is actually from Daft Punk's soundtrack, which uses electronic music to create a mysterious, mesmeric and dangerous sonic atmosphere, as befits the Sirens' characteristics.

A key mythological character seen within *Jupiter Ascending* is an appropriated Hermes, the Greek god associated with speed and swiftness, often seen with winged boots or cap. He's seen as an emissary of sorts, travelling between the worlds of man and gods, a guide for souls, a protector and a trickster. *Ascending* situates Hermes within Caine Wise (Channing Tatum), a half-man, half-wolf soldier (enhanced beyond human capability, and therefore demonstrably god-like) sent to aid Jupiter. Caine's position as Hermes is perhaps most clear in how he is able to move from a veiled and unknown-to-humanity-realm, with its various alien races, intergalactic dynasties that reap entire populations from planets, and associated technology and characters, into Jupiter's mundane world. He is Jupiter's protector, saving her upon numerous occasions, whilst also acting as an emissary in providing information surrounding her regal position. Finally, he is also something of a trickster, using his cunning against adversaries during a rescue of Jupiter and elsewhere to deceive Balem and his henchmen. Throughout this and other action sequences Caine makes use of gravity boots that propel him rapidly across surfaces as well as through the air, analogous to Hermes and his ability to move swiftly.

In terms of plots, all of the sword and planet films under discussion use classic quest narratives that are often aligned with mythology: showing characters overcoming obstacles which reflect audiences overcoming their own lives' complications. Within *John Carter* there are certain narrative elements that echo and adjust Homer's *Odyssey*. John Carter (Taylor Kitsch) first becomes transported from Earth to Mars, wherein he has to triumph over numerous obstacles as he attempts to return to his home world. Towards the end of the film, which is told in flashback through a visualization of Carter's nephew reading his uncle's journal, it is discovered that Carter has been transported against his will back to Earth not long after marrying Dejah Thoris (Lynn Collins), the Princess of Mars, and has spent many years searching for a means to return to her and Mars. The combination of these two overlapping parts of the story, showing Carter's estrangement from the world he originally called home and the one that latterly becomes it, together with the woman who becomes his wife, begin to transpose the *Odyssey* story. In addition to the many tests on his journey "home," Carter also has to defeat a massive white ape, killing the creature that is essentially blind, which adjusts and appropriates aspects of Odysseus's battle against the cyclops.

"More relative than this—the story's the thing"

Scott Higgins states: "Melodrama may well inform other contemporary Hollywood genres, but in the action film, it flourishes."[31] Each sword and planet film, like their peplum forebears, use action as a strong locus of their narrative. The action film, particularly contemporary examples, are loaded with spectacle, opulence and excess. As noted earlier, the narratives of the peplum are also based upon opulent excess: exotic and spectacular settings, overt, hyper-muscular bodies, vampish and beautiful women vying for the attention of the hero, who strives to save people from an oppressive ruler. For Higgins action spectacle and the melodrama are collaborators while peplum films are often seen by critics as following a melodramatic tradition, though of a certain sort. It is not that of the "family melodrama" as denoted by Thomas Elsaesser,[32] though his highlighting of the import of emotion and heightened sensationalism still carries through in the peplum and sword and planet film. Instead, peplums are based in the antecedent and broad melodramatic generic trends. Patrick Lucanio quotes the Oxford English Dictionary (OED) description which positions melodrama as "characterized by a sensational incident and violent appeals to the emotions, but with a happy ending."[33] The OED website also denotes that "exaggerated characters" are vital, along with "emotionally exaggerated behaviour or language."[34] Furthermore, Peter Brooks notes that the melodrama "from its inception takes as its concern and *raison d'être* the location, expression, and imposition of basic ethical and psychic truths [re-enacting] the menace of evil and the eventual triumph of morality."[35] In each of the sword and planet films there are numerous elements that continue core peplum narrative and character traditions in this way, using the melodramatic basis whilst also making adjustments to it.

Sword and planet films are florid, colorful and spectacular, using a visual scale that is at once epic, but also a twist on the conventions therein. Though peplum films have a sense of scale, they have been positioned as "a box office ploy in spectacular bad taste."[36] Frank Burke makes note of them using papier-mâché boulders and ridiculous monsters, which suggests low costs, whereas *John Carter*, *Tron: Legacy*, and *Jupiter Ascending* have vast budgets, enabling decent production values. Each film arguably looks professional in comparison to earlier pepla, but there are numerous aspects surrounding these films that do impart a sense of melodrama, spectacular cartoon-like style,[37] and occasionally bad taste. *John Carter* offers an eclectic mix of characters that—perhaps due to its basis as a family film from Disney—often seems cartoon-like in its style. Carter's gravity defying leaps and strength, the dog-like CG animated character of Woola, the overwrought dialogue that permeates throughout, plus the romance between Carter and Princess Dejah is especially redolent of peplum's antecedent style. Moreover, much of the dramatic development of the film between the heroes and villains is overtly elaborate to the point of being difficult to follow, creating a sense of spectatorial disbelief at how bad the film is. It starts to become amusing, which might position spectators to become more visually biased and less interested in story and characters. The visual spectacle, both in terms of action and locations, plays out on a huge melodramatically-based scale to the base emotional core of audiences via visceral thrills, rather than character engagement. In consequence, *Carter* operates on a vertiginous cut and thrust *modus operandi*, moving between high spectacle and hijinks; from Carter and Princess Dejah swooning against (or swinging into) a backdrop of massed aliens, explosions and/or other extraordinary sensational action, to light comedy, sometimes all at once.

Jupiter Ascending and *Tron: Legacy* operate on similar levels, with each developing their narratives in melodramatic ways. Both, like *Carter*, use romantic entanglement as part of their basis, and both also devote much of their duration to using conventions of the family melodrama as well as more broad melodramatic aspects. In *Ascending*, the Abrasax dynasty siblings, trying to usurp the matriarchal power-set, sit alongside both genders dueling for the attention of the female lead. But there are other numerous sensational and exaggerated moments that once again suffuse the film throughout, working to engage spectators in basic emotional ways. These include the climactic duel between Caine and Balem within the Jupiter refinery's spectacular disintegration, and Caine's rescuing Jupiter from certain death. Perhaps more melodramatic and arguably excessively camp is the acting style of Eddie Redmayne, who provides a suitably exaggerated and scene-stealing performance as Balem. It falls back to the pictorial, pantomime style of performance that is traditionally melodramatic, and ostentatiously camp.

Tron: Legacy uses similar situations and moments, including the arena-set games that feature spectacular cliffhanger moments, and an overtly emotional climax that sees Sam being in part saved by Quorra (Olivia Wilde) whilst he watches his father take on the villainous Clu (John Reardon and Jeff Bridges) with a wave of exponential energy that destroys both of them. The film also makes tremendous use of Daft Punk's score which channels a melodramatic use of music to encourage emotional engagement. The score is grandiose in conveying the core themes of the bond between father and son, using a heightened version of Kevin Flynn's (Jeff Bridges) musical leitmotif at the point when he gives his life for his son. The score is used to tremendous effect throughout the picture, to the point of being perfectly overwrought in its enshrouding of the action sequences as well as in emotional scenes between the Flynns and others.

The melodramatic notion of morality is strongly conveyed in *Tron: Legacy*, as it is in both *Carter* and *Jupiter Ascending* as well, an idea Higgins keenly situates as part and parcel of the action film.[38] Like many classical films, the pepla set up clear lines of demarcation for the heroes and villains, and this idea is retained even in an age where morality is often blurred—perhaps as means of re-instilling spectatorial behaviors? Villains in these films act as peplas' despotic tyrants, albeit with varying effect. *Legacy*'s Clu is a de facto fascistic leader dressed in black while making speeches to hordes of assembled supporters à la Nuremberg, who faces off against the white-robed god-like Flynn. In *Ascending* a similarly characterized Balem Abrasax wants nothing more than to wipe out the populations of entire planets for the sake of a beauty product, whilst *John Carter*'s Therns sinuously operate like gods who are playing with Mars and other planets to similarly use up their population and resources for their own ends.

This morality forms a part of Ben Singer's "cluster concept," where "pathos, emotional intensification, moral polarization, sensationalism and ... 'nonclassical narrative structure,'"[39] are prevalent aspects of the melodramatic state. The scenes under discussion adjust such core tenets to function in an environment that is distinctive, whilst also affirming the adaptive intentions of the sword and planet neo-peplum. In particular, they strongly develop Singer's last point, the nonclassical narrative mechanics, which has a preference "for outrageous coincidence, implausibility, convoluted plotting, *deus ex machina* resolutions, and episodic strings of action that stuff too many events together to be able to kept in line by a cause and effect chain of narrative progression."[40] It is easy see the many "trials," which are essentially scenes of either action and/or showing off the hero's body and strength, undergone by Hercules, Maciste, Samson and others as setting such trends for the later science fiction tinged films to use. Like older peplums, the nature of the plots of *Carter*, *Legacy*, and *Ascending* all feature episodic narratives which move quickly from one scene to the next, often with little pause or sense. These include the multitude of action sequences that see the characters race into the fray to save heroines, or to survive perilous encounters. The aforementioned games section of *Legacy* is one such lengthy example, as is Carter's fight with the white ape in the Thark arena. Similarly, improbable moments include the sudden and easy fixing of Quorra after she's seemingly been mortally wounded by Clu's henchman Rinzler (Anis Cheurfa and Bruce Boxleitner) within *Legacy*, and *Ascending*'s many moments of Caine cheating death at the last moment, such as his being ejected into space, apparently without a spacesuit. As Higgins surmises, "Riding an action film means navigating from situation to situation, being repeatedly brought to the height of a dilemma and plunging out of it through luck, wit, and firepower,"[41] which peplums and these sword and planet films similarly exemplify.

Location, Location, Location

Like other peplum writers, Blanshard and Shahabudin highlight the ancient world settings containing the hero and his exploits that were primitive and bereft of technology[42] as key to the genre. Though these landscapes were vast and often desolate, there were often also impressive constructs, such as palaces with ornate stone columns and marble floors that featured classically dressed characters in appropriate pepla-style costumes. Of the sword and planet films under discussion, *John Carter* is seen as the most concordant in continuing this component, with the red sand landscapes of Mars strongly evoking ancient times and locales of the classic peplum. Even the opening sections lead into this milieu by introducing Carter's character as living in the American West, a similarly arid setting that is bereft of advanced technology, before the film journeys to the apparently even more primitive Mars via a portal within a cave. However, despite the primeval-like situation that permeates the film (from gladiatorial arenas, horse-like animals used for transportation by Carter and others, plus swords and other basic weapons used by the Tharks), the film also contains spaceships, and introduces more advanced weaponry used by adversaries. The inclusion of the weaponry and spaceships shows how even Carter manages to de(re)compose the genre, appropriating what is necessary from the already fluid existing peplum, whilst adapting and superimposing new elements onto the text.

Looking at the *mise-en-scène* of the other films, it initially seems that they are beginning to move too far away from the age-old sand and stone of pepla, with both *Tron: Legacy* and *Jupiter Ascending* presenting more technologically infused worlds. Advanced vehicles and spaceships feature prominently in both films, which have settings that are fantastic, but are lacking much sand and stone. *Tron: Legacy* strives to create a dark, foreboding and digitally tinged aesthetic, using strips of effervescent neon-like lighting to decorate the landscape, architecture, clothing and transportation. This high-contrast lighting detail also streams from the vehicles during movement, such as the bikes ridden by Flynn and others, leaving light traces in the air, akin to afterburners. This gives spectators a sense of being within an advanced digital grid, inside the machine world. Again, *Legacy*'s main setting is prefaced by initial scenes set within Sam Flynn's twenty-first-century home city as he rides through the night time streets on his motorbike and breaks into ENCOM to hack into their systems. These early scenes are eerily prescient of the grid, cleverly parroting the real world by showing a series of similar municipal locations, lighting and ambiance. The first scene where Sam is inside the machine world furthers this, showing the external façade of Flynn's arcade and the surrounding street, mimicking the film's real world. Furthermore, the moment when Sam is picked up by a Recognizer uses shot composition, camera movement, and other visual and sound elements to simulate the earlier segment when Sam is arrested by the police. This subsequently draws spectators into the apparently futuristic world, deftly adjusting perspective for the main narrative focus.

However, despite connections to modern and future worlds, *Legacy* also manifests the classic peplum in its locations and clothing. Alongside the hi-tech craft and weapons, *Legacy* takes pains to show a number of locations and elements that make reference to ancient times. The games in which Sam participates in are held in a huge arena that mirrors the gladiatorial stage the heroes of peplum-past entered. Mass crowds sit high above in seating, screaming excitedly as the players engage in a series of games that echo those of the Romans. The games include a discus variation which can literally cut through opponents, as well as a chariot race reconfigured with light cycles. This latter event echoes both the more standard historical epics, as well as highlighting the peplum hero's need to show off his strength and ability against his foes. Such melding of past and future in terms of narrative trope and aesthetic design reinforces the idea of crossbreeds and mutants engendered by Altman, whilst showing the fluidity of the film.

Furthermore, despite the manifestations of technology abound within *Legacy*, the film often shows stripped down and desert-like landscapes, with rocky outcrops that lend themselves to a de(re)composed ancient peplum location. The difference is the desert land is only seen at night. *Legacy* then is similarly stripped down, arid, barren and barbaric in its setting and action when compared to classic peplum. The film instills sensations of ancient worlds in the smooth marble-like constructs that form many of the world's buildings, and rock-based architecture such as Kevin Flynn's home that is cut into a mountainside.

This ancient architectural basis is also seen within *Jupiter Ascending*'s style, which also features numerous buildings and locations that strongly signpost its peplum forebears. Through the film features advanced technology, from huge intergalactic cruisers to people-harvesting refineries, the make-up of these are often infused with accents of the ancient world and its architecture. Balem's Jupiter base, where the refinery is situated, is an orange, reddish-brown colored world, whose basis as a gaseous planet is visualized in the film in ways that make it appear as a swirling desert. Scenes set on the planet make good use of atmospheric effects to enable a sense of perpetual dust storms that are churning around the refinery. The architecture itself echoes Grecian style, with huge columns that reach up stratospherically to the ceilings high above, akin to that culture's temples. Other scenes feature structures analogous to Macedonian architecture, including a vast palace owned by Kalique Abrasax (Tuppence Middleton) with a domed roof section and a series of columns, set atop a cliff-top and waterfalls, with a grandeur that strongly evokes the great library of Alexandria, created in the third century BC.

Technological Adjustments

The system of motor-only shooting (MOS) was keenly used within 1950/60s peplum films. As Sam Davies states, "in post-war Italian cinema, all dialogue—all sound—was overdubbed," which allowed for a simplification of shooting for the production.[43] In the films of Michelangelo Antonioni, Davies notes it created a sense of existential crises for his characters through the dislocation of the face and dialogue, allowing for creative manipulation of performance both during and after shooting had concluded.[44] Davies also notes MOS use within Dario Argento's *giallo* and horror films that used a multi-national cast, such as *Suspiria* (1977, Dario Argento). He sees MOS providing "wholesale mismatch between sound and picture, entirely in keeping with the lucid nightmare of his aesthetic."[45] Furthermore, *Suspiria* actress Jessica Harper "once described it as requiring a silent era style, in which the focus was entirely on the visual telegraphing of emotion and state of mind."[46] Such lurid sensationalism within *giallo* films is not too different from peplum's exotic opulence outlined earlier, with each sharing an ability to use florid visual aesthetics, such as color, elaborate and baroque set and costume design, and mannered performance. More importantly, Lucanio also notes that the dubbing of peplum films is the "most significant aspect of the films' exotic appeal."[47]

However, MOS performances become more visually pronounced, noticeable and arguably hammy and possibly distracting, particularly in peplum.

Bondanella cites the use of dubbing as "clumsy and often inadequate" which caused "vitriolic attacks on their artistic merits."[48] From a director's perspective, there is an ability to coerce physical and emotive performances from the veritable strongmen who played the heroes without worrying about them delivering their lines well at the same time. Indeed, the heroic body was a central factor for a spectator's attention, and in later neo-peplum films those stars with thicker accents could be re-dubbed by other vocal performers. This might be seen as re-unifying or making complete the overall performance. Simultaneously, it's arguable such performances operate more fully through imagery and is something that becomes adapted in the sword and planet films discussed here.

Watching *John Carter*, the situation of dubbing is used for key alien characters Tars Tarkus, Sola and Tal Hajus, as well as other minor characters from the Thark race. These are configured through motion-capture (mo-cap) technology based upon (respectively) William Dafoe, Samantha Morton, and Thomas Haden Church's performances. On-screen, the Tharks are green skinned, four-armed aliens, with a height that sees them towering over the human characters. They feature tusks on either side of their heads, with flat noses that take up considerable room on their faces, have smooth skulls and wear skins and pelts as clothing. Dafoe and company are distinctly different in their physical appearance, and were "captured" during their performance wearing skin tight grey suits and helmets adorned with sensors to enable the software to track movement. This information, initially appearing like stick men, is built up by effects personnel in layers to create muscle, skin, fabric and other details of the characters' physical manifestation. This allows the director to focus distinctly separately on the aural and physical processes of performance at different points in the production, in a similar fashion to archetypal peplums. It permits a conjuring of the physical nuances necessary to make individual Tharks visually work, without worrying too much about the vocals during production, which can be re-dubbed later on. In addition to the work done by the performers and director on set, further labor by effects and technical personnel in post-production also demonstrates the adjusted mismatch that focuses spectatorial attention.

Head of animation Eamonn Butler noted that *Carter* used numerous footage outside of the director's preferred take, further highlighting how the performances are built out of mismatched elements. He continues: "the animators could look through other takes and pick out nice little details or nuances that might make the scene more appealing. The animators really helped to contribute or augment what the actors had done."[49] This shows a continuance *and* adaptation of methods used in producing the sword and planet films, where physical performance is conjured as disharmonized from the vocal. Using this technical methodology with the alien characters produces something exotic from the human characters. Characters here are visually pronounced, enacting spectacular physical moments onscreen, not just as spectacular visual effects, but because they are peplum based.

Blanshard and Shahabudin remark that the post-synched sound of peplum films created "a slightly unnatural air, and in the English versions the effects can be truly comic,"[50] which further links mo-cap to sword and planet films. *Tron: Legacy*'s central villain is conceived and visualized using mo-cap, situated upon the mismatch of sound and image, quite unusual and perhaps in this case (unnecessarily) comic. Clu, a construct created by Kevin Flynn, uses John Reardon for physical action and Jeff Bridges to drive the facial performance which then uses a digitized face of Bridges from the early 1980s mapped onto it. Though it is a technological marvel to see, it also stumbles into similar territory of older peplums that developed a more comical slant to their dubbed characters. When Clu utters the words "Your move Flynn,"[51] it should provide a sense of menace, and Bridges' vocalization does move towards this. But the intersection of the vocal soundtrack to facial performance does not quite fully connect, and instead of something that induces anxiety in the viewer it looks odd. The mouth looks as if it doesn't quite match the rest of the face, and this non-synchronization invokes a sense of absurdity. Conversely it also suggests a continuance of Masahiro Mori's "The Uncanny Valley," which posits a sense of eeriness in seeing and interacting with an artificial construct, such as a robot, that clearly doesn't look like a machine, but is also not quite human.[52] This in-between-ness situates the viewer in the aforementioned valley, but despite its possible farcical overtones, both the eeriness and humorous sensation manage to make the audience readily notice the character yielding a visual telegraphy of emotion, which continues the previously noted melodramatic condition.

Though it doesn't use mo-cap for any of its characters, the situation of dubbing is still in place for *Jupiter Ascending*'s lizard/dragon-like characters, the Sargorns, who are henchman for villain Balem Abrasax. These characters are realized using the more traditional animation technique of automated key frame animation to give them life. Nonetheless as with other animation, these characters, particularly Sargorn leader Greeghan, used dubbing from Ariyon Bakare to provide on-screen dialogue, and the characters' design made for an interesting adaptation of the MOS technique. Animation Supervisor Max Solomon states: "Their long, lizard skulls made dialogue interesting, especially as their teeth are fused to their lips. 'We had to find the right balance of flexibility within the constraints of that, so we made them talk out of the side of their mouths where there are fewer teeth.'"[53] It is this use of vocal dubbing which moves the characters out of traditional site of animation and instead into the peplum sphere via any dialogue which they deliver. Though a fantastical creature, with detailed attention towards creating a level of realism that might befit such creatures within the genre, they can instead be viewed as cartoon-like, similar to the self-referential and bad-taste excesses of *The Loves of Hercules/Hercules vs. the Hydra* (1960, Carlo Ludovico Bragaglia) or the multi-monster *Goliath Against the Giants* (1961, Guido Malatesta). These examples, along with *Jupiter Ascending*, all provide a monster for the hero to fight and dispatch. Though each one is brought to life in a technically proficient manner, the end result is a pictorially based camp effect. The additional of the peculiar use of dialog augments the excessive mismatch and folds in nicely with peplum customs—adapting and adjusting them to fit in with the new offshoot incarnation of the filmic type.

Adapted Villainy and the New Heroic Body

Jerry Pierce notes the position of the male heroic body is key to sword and sandal films. Its place and signification of heteronormativity produce displays of "normality," "straightness" and aligned presentations of a cultural and social hegemony. Pierce establishes such heroes as being positive, masculine models presenting safe displays of the male body and "a physically active struggle against tyrants."[54] These are situated upon characters who are often fathers, husbands and adept warriors. To this end, peplum heroes such as Hercules (Steve Reeves) in *Hercules/Le fatiche di Ercole*, and more recently the characters of Maximus (Russell Crowe) in *Gladiator* (2000, Ridley Scott), King Leonidas (Gerard Butler) in *300* (2006, Zack Snyder) and Achilles (Brad Pitt) in *Troy* (2004, Wolfgang Petersen), all showcase hyper-muscular heroes that are actively expressing monolithic ideals of paternalism, heterosexuality, and moral and physical strength. In opposition to this are the villains who appear thin or physically weak, effeminate, and engage in activities which are deemed as "deviant" (sexually or otherwise).[55] An example of such a villain is *Gladiator*'s Commodus (Joaquin Phoenix), who incestuously lusts after his sister, acts in an effete manner, and is ineffectual in armed combat. More blatantly Pierce notes *300*'s Xerxes (Rodrigo Santoro) is visualized as a bejeweled and pierced, smooth bodied character. Wearing eye liner and speaking with a strange, feminized inflected voice, he does nothing in battle himself save for examining his forces from afar.[56] Pierce also notes the character frequents sexual behavior of a "deviant" nature, with his command tent full of deformed women kissing and practicing obscene behaviors with other similar women and men.[57] If we begin to examine the heroes and villains of the sword and planet films under consideration here a similar though again adapted representations come to light.

Tron: Legacy's central villain Clu might initially be seen as the equal of Sam and Kevin Flynn, showing skill in a light cycle battle between him and

Sam. However, there are certain visual cues that show Clu adopting villainous peplum attributes that follow Pierce's work. Perhaps the most visually bold of these is the first sight of Clu in his command post high above the gladiatorial arena. Clu's frame is of a svelte nature, a facet shared by others, which shall be addressed below, and most importantly is seen draped across a chair, his head coquettishly tilted to one side. For all intents and purposes he appears as though he is modeling clothes or appearing in a lifestyle magazine. Though he is overseeing his world from above, the effect is far removed from a position of strength and dominance that his dictator possesses within the film's world. This position itself is allied to the villains of previous peplum films, where the dictator relies upon an army of others to conduct their actions, whereas Hercules, Maximus and Sam Flynn are either working alone, or with the help of only a few comrades. One key person upon which Clu relies is that of subordinate Jarvis (James Frain), who fawns over Clu in a way that can be read as suggesting homoerotic tensions. Eager to please throughout the film, Jarvis—dressed like so many in tight black costumes, but also with a shaved head and clear-plastic face-mask—appears to represent Clu's aspiring lover. As noted, many of the film's programs under Clu's employ are dressed in skin-tight, rubber-looking black costumes, and with accouterments similar to Jarvis' (helmets and darkened visors), the effect is like that of a fetish night club. With Daft Punk's booming electronic score, Clu is the de facto manager of the club, and in this position, the villain as whole is readable as other, askew and distinctly deviant. In effect what is seen in Clu is, once again, a signification of otherness, and characteristics that show distinct difference from the manfulness Pierce sees within the hero.

Jupiter Ascending's Balem Abrasax correspondingly features visual cues and characteristics inherent with the deviant peplum villain. His costumes are highly stylized, verging upon female catwalk couture in their aesthetic connotations. One particular piece of clothing is a long cape-like outfit, black in color but festooned with gold flecks that glitter, matched to a pair of gold skinny trousers. The cape is fastened around Balem's neck, exposing his bare chest and abdomen. This shows off his muscular stomach while emphasizing Balem's waif-like frame. There are no bulging biceps, or over-developed pectoral muscles on show. Instead, the costume design and character's body blend to produce an effect closer to a skinny glam-rock character, whose situation certainly countered positions of gender and sexuality for male performers when they appeared during the 1970s. Such positions of androgyny diffuses or absolves the constituent of a set gender basis.

Titus Abrasax though less feminine or androgynous in appearance and less of an outright villain than his brother Balem, does feature his own "deviant" characteristics. Whilst Titus dresses in more masculine gender-centric suits, he also wears a deep red costume comprising mainly of a robe, which is decorated with ornate stitching on the epaulette area and front, as well as ruched cuffs. This feminine attire contrasts with hero Caine Wise's own outfit. Wise is seen dressed in a dark leather sleeveless vest, covered with tribal-like embossing, that match the tattoos on his hyper-masculine arms. Similarly embossed long-sleeved tops are worn in other scenes, with all such costumes referencing Pierce's notes on the earthier, dirtier costumes worn by Maximus in *Gladiator*.[58] Though the film plays with gender and exploits a more androgynous approach to themes of masculinity, monolithic and dominant codes are still in play that define sites of heroic peplum masculinity and heteronormativity against those of the decadent, effeminate, and deviant position of the villains.

The Therns might be forgotten as *John Carter*'s main villains due to a lack of screen time, but they too follow this deviant approach to masculinity. The Therns are shapeshifting characters, but their nominal form is principally human and always male. Though archetypal in being evil, they are also demonstrably effete in their appearance, wearing long silver robes and occasionally floating down from the sky. The Therns also have bald heads, and piercing blue eyes, which give them a strange abnormal look to their visual appearance. Their conduct has a refined feminine quality that augments their personas, which like their heads appear shorn of virile masculine strength.

The male heroes of these films (Sam Flynn, John Carter, and Caine Wise) are distinct in their appearance compared to earlier peplum and neo-peplum heroes. As noted, the peplum hero is traditionally presented as hyper-muscular and shows his abilities and prowess of extraordinary strength within training montages and key scenes to save others. Though to a degree muscular and well-toned, this trio of leading men are much less overt in their physiques than Steve Reeves' Hercules, Arnold Schwarzenegger's Conan in *Conan the Barbarian* (1982, John Milius), and Dwayne Johnson's recent incarnation of the titular demi-god in *Hercules* (2014, Brett Ratner). However, the representation of heroes in such films and within other genres, such as action films, now feature a body that is arguably toned down. The likes of Carter et al. are akin to other recent action heroes such as Neo (Keanu Reeves) in *The Matrix* trilogy (1999, 2003, 2003, the Wachowskis), or Jack Reacher (Tom Cruise) in *Jack Reacher* (2012, Christopher McQuarrie), and female action heroes such as Mallory Kane (Gina Carano) in *Haywire* (2011, Steven Soderbergh). Though seemingly no less strong than previous action incarnations, their appearance and engagement with enemies and environments is tempered to reflect the period of release, a factor that is also seen within the sword and planet films.

Carter, Flynn, and Wise are still distinctly strong, with Carter in particular falling back on the classic strength paradigm, showing off a muscular torso, but even he shows an adjustment in how his abilities are gained and used. Carter is provided with his hyper-strength that enables him to jump massive distances and throw great weight with force through Mars' different gravity. Sam Flynn is an able hero in certain respects, being street savvy and showing aptitude to changing events in the grid. Nevertheless, he is less capable in the games when compared to his father in the original *Tron* (1982, Steven Lisberger). He falls back on his father and Quorra's abilities to help him succeed. Finally, Channing Tatum's Caine Wise shows strength of will and ability in many respects, alongside a fairly muscular physique. But Tatum's physicality is better showcased in the film *Magic Mike* (2012, Steven Soderbergh). Like Sam Flynn and John Carter, Caine's heroism is aided by his gravity boots and augmented via gene splicing.

This demonstrates an up to date representation of the muscular form, although it still follows Pierce's citing of typical physical attributes of the heroic body that evoke strength and heterosexuality. All of the male heroes continue the trend of being "physically fit and toned, indicating their bodies' preparedness for immediate action,"[59] and create a sense of "proper masculinity" linked to traditional patriarchal roles that denote security and stability.[60] These heroes are still fathers, and/or heterosexual lovers, upholding morality to a strong degree, unlike their opposites. Although no longer showcasing extremes of physicality and pure Herculean strength, they do possess muscle and ability to get feats done. Like other action stars, their abilities are in bodies responding to the modern age. They are infused with assistance from their settings, reflecting cinema's own technological advances.

Conclusion

John Hartley states that "[genres] are constantly transformed by the addition of new examples, so that in the end you have to conclude that there's no such thing as a 'typical' [genre film]."[61] Examining the sword and planet films arguably reflects this proposition in regard of continuing neo-peplums. Each shows an ability to flex in order to present a new form of the genre, but they still manage to show adherences to the originating construct. New locations and aesthetic designs, with some obvious accentuation towards technology, appear alongside more extraterrestrial-like inflections. Nonetheless, these films consistently demonstrate an ability to feature feats of strength, a melodramatic narrative basis and style, as well as key representations of male heroism, deviant and despotic villainy, heroines to be saved, ancient era inflections, a use of dubbing and a flair for bad-taste and campness.

The key to their basis and success is adaptation, appropriation, and an ability to recombine, adjust and mutate the paradigm. As Gledhill states, "genres hang together as an integrated system of intersecting fictional worlds,"[62] and these films operate by developing concepts of intersection, but move to amalgamate the parts necessary for their operation. *John Carter* seems to be the most successful of the three, displaying enough qualities of the older peplum films for it to be deemed sword-like, whilst also drawing on key science fiction elements to enable the planet element as well. But *Tron: Legacy* and *Jupiter Ascending* also highlight an *adapted* continuance of the genre through adjustments of the aforementioned fundamentals. Each of these films manages to organize the elements required, harvesting what is needed to build the sword and planet film they see fit, adapting where necessary. This may seem at odds with how a genre works, since repetition—and therefore a sense of fidelity—is often cited as key. However, as consistently highlighted by genre theorists and the films themselves, infidelity to composition is just as important. Colin McArthur's notes on the gangster film as "a constantly growing amoeba"[63] are equally significant here, wherein the continuance of any film genre must show an appreciation and obligation to changing shape to continue. Indeed, the sword and planet examples here readily exhibit strength and fortitude in using a melange of the past, present, and future. In closing it seems apt to quote *Tron: Legacy*'s Clu, who manages to effectively affirm what these films have done for the neo-peplum: "Together we have achieved a great many things. We have created a vast, complex system. We've maintained it; we've improved it."[64]

Notes

1. Martin M. Winkler, introduction to *Troy: From Homer's Iliad to Hollywood Epic*, ed. Martin M. Winkler (Malden, MA: Blackwell, 2007), 14.
2. Ibid.
3. Ibid., 15.
4. Maggie Günsberg, *Italian Cinema. Gender and Genre* (Basingstoke: Palgrave Macmillan, 2005), 97.
5. Pierre Leprohon, *The Italian Cinema*, trans. Roger Greaves and Oliver Stallybrass (London: Secker-Warburg, 1972), 174.
6. John Hartley, "Genre," in *Key Concepts in Communication and Cultural Studies*, 2nd edition, ed. Tim O'Sullivan, et al. (London: Routledge, 1994), 128–129.
7. Kate Newell, "We're Off to See the Wizard (Again): Oz Adaptations and the Matter of Fidelity," in *Adaptation Studies: New Approaches*, ed. Christa Albrecht-Crane and Dennis Ray Cutchins (Madison, NJ: Fairleigh Dickinson University Press, 2010), 79. Emphasis in original.
8. Thomas M. Leitch, *Film Adaptation and Its Discontents: From Gone with the Wind to The Passion of the Christ* (Baltimore: Johns Hopkins University Press, 2007), 98.
9. Ibid., 99–101.
10. Rick Altman, *Film/Genre* (London: BFI, 1999), 16.
11. Ibid.
12. Ibid., 19.
13. Ibid.
14. Ibid., 21.
15. Ibid., 70.
16. Ibid., 21.

17. Ibid., 70.
18. Kamilla Elliott, *Rethinking the Novel/Film Debate* (Cambridge: Cambridge University, 2009), 157–161.
19. Patrick Lucanio, *With Fire and Sword: Italian Spectacles on American Screens 1958–1968* (Meutchen, NJ: Scarecrow Press, 1994), 12.
20. Ibid.
21. Alastair Blanshard and Kim Shahabudin, *Classics on Screen: Ancient Greece and Rome on Film* (London: Bristol Classical Press, 2011), 58.
22. Daniel O'Brien, "Peplum," in *Directory of World Cinema: Italy*, ed. Louis Bayman (Bristol: Intellect, 2011), 177.
23. Ibid.
24. Ibid.
25. Julie Sanders, *Adaptation and Appropriation*, 2nd edition (London: Routledge, 2016), 35.
26. Ibid.
27. Ibid., 37–38.
28. Martin Winkler, "Neo-Mythologism: Apollo and Muses on the Screen," *International Journal of the Classical Tradition* 11, no. 3 (Winter 2005), 385.
29. Laura Mulvey, "Visual Pleasure and Narrative Cinema," *Screen* 16, no. 3 (Autumn 1975): 6–18, accessed October 2, 2016, doi:10.1093/screen/16.3.
30. *Tron: Legacy*, directed by Joseph Kosinski (2010; Burbank, CA: Walt Disney Studios Home Entertainment, 2011), Blu-ray.
31. Scott Higgins, "Suspenseful Situations: Melodramatic Narrative and the Contemporary Action Film," *Cinema Journal* 47, no. 2 (2008): 75, accessed November 15, 2016, http://www.jstor.org/stable/30137703.
32. Thomas Elsaesser, "Tales of Sound and Fury: Observations on the Family Melodrama," in *Imitations of Life: A Reader of Film and Television Melodrama*, ed. Marcia Landy (Detroit: Wayne State University Press, 1991), 68–91.
33. Lucanio, *With Fire and Sword*, 29.
34. "Melodrama," OEDwww, last modified 2016. http://www.oed.com/view/Entry/116226?rskey=PzEi75&result=1#eid.
35. Peter Brooks, *The Melodramatic Imagination: Balzac, Henry James, Melodrama, and the Mode of Excess* (New Haven: Yale University Press, 1995), 15.
36. Frank Burke, "The Italian Sword-and-Sandal Film from *Fabiola* to *Hercules and the Captive Women* Text and Contexts," in *Popular Italian Cinema: Culture and Politics in a Postwar Society*, ed. Flavia Brizio-Skov (London: I.B. Tauris, 2011), 18.
37. Ibid., 17.
38. Higgins, "Suspenseful Situations," 78.
39. Ibid.
40. Ben Singer, *Melodrama and Modernity: Early Sensational Cinema and Its Contexts* (New York: Columbia University Press, 2001), 46.
41. Higgins, "Suspenseful Situations," 93.
42. Blanshard and Shahabudin, *Classics on Screen*, 58.
43. Sam Davies, "Misread My Lips," *Sight and Sound* 26, no. 10 (2016): 52.
44. Ibid.
45. Ibid.
46. Ibid.
47. Lucanio, *With Fire and Sword*, 14.
48. Peter Bondanella, *A History of Italian Cinema* (New York: Continuum Press, 2009), 162.
49. Ian Failes, "A World Away: John Carter," *fxguide*, last modified, March 12, 2012, https://www.fxguide.com/featured/a-world-away-john-carter/.
50. Blanshard and Shahabudin, *Classics on Screen*, 59.
51. *Tron: Legacy*, directed by Joseph Kosinski.
52. Masahiro Mori, "The Uncanny Valley," *Spectrum IEEE*, last modified 2012, http://spectrum.ieee.org/automaton/robotics/humanoids/the-uncanny-valley.

42   Part One: Crossing the Rubicon

53. "Jupiter Ascending," framestorewww, last modified 2016, https://www.framestore.com/jupiterascending.
54. Jerry B. Pierce, "'To die or die manfully': Performing Heteronormativity in Recent Spectacle films," in *Of Muscles and Men/Essays on the Sword and Sandal Film*, ed. Michael G. Cornelius (Jefferson, NC: McFarland, 2011), 52.
55. *Ibid.*, 41.
56. *Ibid.*, 53.
57. *Ibid.*
58. *Ibid.*, 51.
59. *Ibid.*, 42.
60. *Ibid.*
61. John Hartley, "Genre," in *Key Concepts in Communication and Cultural Studies*, 2nd edition, ed. Tim O'Sullivan, et al. (London: Routledge, 1994), 128.
62. Christine Gledhill, "Rethinking Genre," in *Reinventing Film Studies*, ed. Christine Gledhill and Linda William (London: Edward Arnold, 2000), 224.
63. Colin McArthur, "Iconography and Iconology" (BFI Education seminar paper, London, 1973).
64. *Tron: Legacy*, directed by Joseph Kosinski.

Bibliography

Altman, Rick. *Film/Genre*. London: BFI. 1999.
Blanshard, Alastair, and Kim Shahabudin. *Classics on Screen: Ancient Greece and Rome on Film*. London: Bristol Classical Press, 2011.
Bondanella, Peter. *A History of Italian Cinema*. New York: Continuum Press, 2009.
Bound. Directed by the Wachowskis. 1996. Radlett, Hertfordshire, UK: Arrow 2014. Blu-ray.
Brooks, Peter. *The Melodramatic Imagination: Balzac, Henry James, Melodrama, and the Mode of Excess*. New Haven: Yale University Press, 1995.
Burke, Frank. "The Italian Sword-and-Sandal Film from *Fabiola* to *Hercules and the Captive Women* Text and Contexts." In *Popular Italian Cinema: Culture and Politics in a Postwar Society*, edited by Flavia Brizio-Skov, 17–52. London: I.B. Tauris, 2011.
Cloud Atlas. Directed by Tom Tykwer and the Wachowskis. 2013. Burbank, CA: Warner Home Video, 2013. Blu-ray.
Colossus of Rhodes. Directed by Sergio Leone. 1961. MGM. Film.
Davies, Sam. "Misread My Lips." *Sight and Sound* 26, no. 10 (2016): 52–53.
Elliott, Kamilla. *Rethinking the Novel/Film Debate*. Cambridge: Cambridge University, 2009.
Elsaesser, Thomas. "Tales of Sound and Fury: Observations on the Family Melodrama." In *Imitations of Life: A Reader of Film and Television Melodrama*, edited by Marcia Landy, 68–91. Detroit: Wayne State University Press, 1991.
Failes, Ian. "A World Away: John Carter." Fxguidewww. Last modified March 12, 2012. https://www.fxguide.com/featured/a-world-away-john-carter/.
Le fatiche di Ercole/Hercules. Directed by Pietro Francisci. 1958. Warner Bros. Film.
Gladiator. Directed by Ridley Scott. 2003. Universal City, CA: Universal Home Video, 2010. Blu-ray.
Gledhill, Christine. "Rethinking Genre." In *Reinventing Film Studies*, edited by Christine Gledhill and Linda William, 221–243. London: Edward Arnold, 2000.
Goliath Against the Giants. Directed by Guido Malatesta. 1961. Filmar Compagnia Cinematografica. Film.
Günsberg, Maggie. *Italian Cinema. Gender and Genre*. Basingstoke: Palgrave Macmillan, 2005.
Hartley, John. "Genre." In *Key Concepts in Communication and Cultural Studies*, 2nd edition, edited by Tim O'Sullivan et al., 127–129. London: Routledge, 1994.
Haywire. Directed by Steven Soderbergh. 2011. Relativity Media. Film.
Hercules. Directed by Brett Ratner. 2014. Paramount/MGM. Film.
Higgins, Scott. "Suspenseful Situations: Melodramatic Narrative and the Contemporary Action Film." *Cinema Journal* 47, no. 2 (2008): 74–96. Accessed November 15, 2016. http://www.jstor.org/stable/30137703.

John Carter. Directed by Andrew Stanton. 2012. Burbank, CA: Walt Disney Studios Home Entertainment, 2012. Blu-ray.
Jupiter Ascending. Directed by the Wachowskis. 2015. Burbank, CA: Warner Home Video, 2015. Blu-ray.
"Jupiter Ascending." framestorewww. Last modified 2016. https://www.framestore.com/jupiterascending.
Jurassic Park. Directed by Steven Spielberg. 1993. Universal City, CA: Universal Home Video, 2015. Blu-ray.
Leitch, Thomas M. *Film Adaptation and Its Discontents: From Gone with the Wind to The Passion of the Christ.* Baltimore: Johns Hopkins University Press, 2007.
Leprohon, Pierre. *The Italian Cinema.* Translated by Roger Greaves and Oliver Stallybrass. London: Secker-Warburg, 1972.
Lucanio, Patrick. *With Fire and Sword. Italian Spectacles on American Screens 1958–1968.* Meutchen, NJ: Scarecrow Press, 1994.
The Loves of Hercules/ Hercules vs the Hydra. Directed by Carlo Ludovico Bragaglia. 1960. Paris Interpoductions (PIP). Film.
Magic Mike. Directed by Steven Soderbergh. 2012. Warner Bros. Film.
The Matrix. Directed by the Wachowskis. 1999. Burbank, CA: Warner Home Video, 2008. Blu-ray.
The Matrix Reloaded. Directed by the Wachowskis. 2003. Burbank, CA: Warner Home Video, 2008. Blu-ray.
The Matrix Revolutions. Directed by the Wachowskis. 2003. Burbank, CA: Warner Home Video, 2008. Blu-ray.
McArthur, Colin. "Iconography and Iconology." BFI Education seminar paper, London, 1973.
"Melodrama." OEDwww. Last modified 2016. http://www.oed.com/view/Entry/116226?rskey=PzEi75&result=1#eid.
Mori, Masahiro. "The Uncanny Valley." *Spectrum IEEE.* Last modified 2012. http://spectrum.ieee.org/automaton/robotics/humanoids/the-uncanny-valley.
Mulvey, Laura. "Visual pleasure and narrative cinema." *Screen* 16, no. 3 (Autumn 1975): 6–18. Accessed October 2, 2016. doi:10.1093/screen/16.3.
Newell, Kate. "We're Off to See the Wizard (Again): Oz Adaptations and the Matter of Fidelity." In *Adaptation Studies: New Approaches,* edited by Christa Albrecht-Crane and Dennis Ray Cutchins, 78–97. Madison, NJ: Fairleigh Dickinson University Press, 2010.
O'Brien, Daniel. "Peplum." In *Directory of World Cinema: Italy,* edited by Louis Bayman, 176–178. Bristol: Intellect, 2011.
Pierce, Jerry B. "'To die or die manfully': Performing Heteronormativity in Recent Spectacle Films." In *Of Muscles and Men: Essays on the Sword and Sandal Film,* edited by Michael G. Cornelius, 40–57. Jefferson, NC: McFarland 2011.
Sanders, Julie. *Adaptation and Appropriation,* 2nd edition. London: Routledge, 2016.
Sansone contro il corsaro nero/Hercules and the Black Pirates. Directed by Luigi Capuano. 1964. Romana Film. Film.
Sense8. Directed by the Wachowskis, James McTeigue, Tom Tykwer, and Dan Glass. 2015. Netflix. Web.
Singer, Ben. *Melodrama and Modernity: Early Sensational Cinema and Its Contexts.* New York: Columbia University Press, 2001.
Suspiria, Directed by Dario Argento. 1977. London: Nouveaux Pictures, 2010. Blu-ray.
300. Directed by Zack Snyder. 2006. Burbank, CA: Warner Home Video, 2006. Blu-ray.
Tron. Directed by Steven Lisberger. 1982. Burbank, CA: Walt Disney Studios Home Entertainment, 2011. Blu-ray
Tron: Legacy. Directed by Joseph Kosinski. 2010. Burbank, CA: Walt Disney Studios Home Entertainment, 2011. Blu-ray.
Troy. Directed by Wolfgang Petersen. 2004. Warner Bros. Film.
Winkler, Martin. Introduction to *Troy: From Homer's Iliad to Hollywood Epic,* edited by Martin M. Winkler, 1–19. Malden, MA: Blackwell, 2007.
_____. "Neo-Mythologism: Apollo and Muses on the Screen." *International Journal of the Classical Tradition* 11, no. 3 (Winter 2005): 383–423.

Hercules
Transmedia Superhero Mythology

DJOYMI BAKER

Brett Ratner's 2014 film *Hercules* starts appropriately enough with a version of Hercules' origin story, an as-yet unnamed narrator declaring, "You think you know the truth about him? You know nothing."[1] The film nonetheless relies on the fact that the audience will already have expectations around Hercules built up from popular culture, as well as the paratexts surrounding the film itself. Ratner's *Hercules* is both a direct adaptation of the graphic novel *Hercules: The Thracian Wars*, as well as a transmedia expansion of Heracles' mythic tale as it has played out across millennia from Greek oral epic, theater, and vase paintings to comic books, television and film incarnations.[2] This essay examines the 2014 film as an instance of the inherently intertextual nature of myth, but one that is specifically situated within twenty-first-century reference points. The film and its paratexts—among them the film poster, trailer, and interviews—meld myth with the sword and sandal film and the popular superhero genre of which Hercules has always been a part, while also harnessing actor Dwayne "The Rock" Johnson's star persona. *Hercules* playfully deconstructs the mythic figure of Hercules only to ultimately reinstate his exceptional, semi-divine physicality. The result is a newly articulated Hercules as a mythic superhero hybrid.

The film's opening establishes a familiar mythic backstory to Hercules (Dwayne Johnson), only to undermine this account. The narrator informs the audience that Hercules is born "half human, half god," having been fathered by the god Zeus (not shown on screen), and his mortal mother, Alcmene (Karolina Szymczak).[3] Alcmene names the boy Hercules, or "glory of Hera," in an unsuccessful attempt to assuage the jealousy of Zeus' wife, who sends serpents to kill the young boy.[4] Hercules triumphs, but once fully grown "the gods commanded him to perform twelve labors … if he completed them all and survived, Hera agreed to finally let him live in peace."[5] On screen, we see Hercules battle with the Lernaean Hydra, the Erymanthian Boar and the Nemean Lion. But the scene cuts suddenly to an unknown, rough-looking man who declares, "What a load of crap!"[6] At this point, viewers discover that the narrator, the young Iolaus (Reece Ritchie), is not addressing the film audience directly at all, but rather is trying to impress and intimidate a rough band of pirates who have him tied up over a stake. He is soon rescued by his uncle Hercules, who confirms that he killed the Nemean Lion—whose pelt he now wears—with his "bare hands."[7] While this is indeed what the opening scene has shown, Hercules adds, "or so they say," immediately casting doubt on this version of events.[8] The rescue itself makes it clear that the pirate's proclamation is correct, for Hercules' seemingly superhuman feats actually come courtesy of a support crew of mercenaries.

In this respect, *Hercules* follows on from Wolfgang Petersen's *Troy* (2004) in rationalizing myth and removing the overt presence of the gods. Certainly, Julie Christie appears as Achilles' mother Thetis in *Troy*, but there is absolutely nothing to suggest that she is the immortal and ageless sea goddess of the Greek mythic tradition (Homer *Iliad* 15.76, 18.35–147).[9] The demythologizing move is ultimately questioned in *Hercules*. By the end of the film, Hercules' band and even Hercules himself begins to wonder if his preternatural strength may indeed come from divine heritage.

Classicists are often dismayed with film adaptations of myth, given that they keep—as Mary Beard terms it—"f***ing about with the plot" in the manner of *Troy* and *Hercules*, but it is the specific way that contemporary culture refashions myth that keeps it alive for new generations.[10] Classicist Martin M. Winkler speaks for many scholars in his field in dismissing the 2014 *Hercules* along with the recent batch of neo-peplum films, including *Clash of the Titans* (2010, Louis Leterrier), *Immortals* (2011, Tarsem Singh Dhandwar), *Wrath of the Titans* (2012, Jonathan Liebesman), and *The Legend of Hercules* (2014, Renny Harlin), accusing them of having only a "weak and puerile … understanding of and feeling for ancient myth."[11] In his review of Ratner's *Hercules*, Josho Brouwers notes the many historical discrepancies in the film, but then sensibly acknowledges that "*Hercules* is clearly not meant to be historical."[12] Eleonora Cavallini further argues that to become concerned with a film's "unfaithfulness" to ancient sources is to ignore the fact that any given myth "was told by many poets and writers in different ways, from different points of view, and at different times in different ancient cultures."[13] Before Petersen reimagined Thetis in his film, Homer's own version of her in the *Iliad* was itself a variation of the earlier mythic stories.[14] Winkler for his part also acknowledges that the Greeks themselves changed their mythic stories.[15] What he takes issue with is changes in tone and context in the recent films. It is precisely these changes that keep a myth relevant for any given era, the paratexts for Ratner's *Hercules* situating it within the currently popular superhero genre. In other words, when Winkler focuses exclusively on an "understanding of and feeling for ancient myth," it comes at the expense of an "understanding and feeling for" contemporary culture.[16]

Mythic Intertexts and Paratexts

Both ancient and contemporary audiences have a myriad of associations surrounding Hercules that vary from era to era and generation to generation. Mikhail Bakhtin suggests that when we read older works, we risk misreading them, inadvertently flattening out their meaning when we lack knowledge of their context.[17] As Henry Jenkins argues, students of Greek myth today struggle with their lack of contextual knowledge that would have given mythic tales their depth in antiquity.[18] The Greek audience would not need to be told of Achilles' divine parentage when listening to Homer's *Iliad*. It would simply be known and assumed. Indeed, the *Iliad* starts part way into the story and ends before it is completed. The rest of the tale is told elsewhere. Similarly, Homer is the earliest remaining textual reference for Heracles in 750 BCE, but he appears only briefly, and again there is a clear assumption that the audience will already know his backstory. Jenkins notes that in the present era, any given *X-Men* film may feel flat without the broader knowledge of its transmedia tale, the way its storytelling "unfolds across multiple media platforms, with each new text making a distinctive and valuable contribution to the whole."[19] Jenkins is ultimately cautious in making this comparison, arguing that overall, ancient storytelling traditions had a greater "depth of incrusted meanings" than contemporary culture.[20] As such, he stresses that heightened intertextuality and transmedia expansion are not new to the current era, but rather have new media to give them expression.

Classicist Ken Dowden argues that Greek myth is itself "an 'intertext,' because it is constituted by all the representations of myths ever experienced by its audience."[21] Sarah Iles Johnston by contrast prefers the term "plurimedial" over intertextual, for while she notes the way that the tragedians would deliberately toy with audience expectations by contradicting the narrative arc from epic, overall she argues that

> the point is not to trace particular traits of a character back to an earlier source or sources (with which a given audience member may or may not be familiar), but rather to understand how new figurations emerge and re-emerge against the background of a *range* of earlier treatments, never fully obligated to any of them.[22]

Ultimately, despite the difference in terminology, Dowden and Johnston both focus on the way that each new version of myth gains its meaning from the entire backlog of retellings coexisting through memory.

Writer Steve Moore's aim with the graphic novel *Hercules: The Thracian Wars* was to create Bronze Age tales of Hercules "which leave the original stories intact, but develop them further."[23] This, then, is both transmedia storytelling over the timespan of millennia and a new addition to the intertext of the Hercules myth as it was built up by the Greeks themselves and then played with by subsequent cultures. Jim Collins argues that contemporary audiences retain both old and new versions of a story in their minds simultaneously as part of their "cultural memory."[24] Audience members may each vary in their knowledge or appreciation of that complex textual and cultural backstory, but it comes into play regardless when they encounter a new text.[25] New stories about mythic heroes evoke both ancient and contemporary intertextual memories, even if, as Bakhtin suggests, many will only have partial and most likely inaccurate understanding of older stories. The 2014 *Hercules* film is an adaptation of the transmedia *Hercules: The Thracian Wars* graphic novel, but then alters and adds to the story, both by drawing on preexisting associations around Hercules, and by creating new ones.

The Greek Heracles (as he was known before the Romans changed his name to Hercules) is a rapist (Apollodorus 2.7.2, Pausanias 8.47.4), murderer, drunkard, and glutton, yet also capable of great deeds.[26] As a member of the older generation of heroes, the Heracles of Homer's *Odyssey* is described in terms that emphasize his rather more savage form of heroism as a point of contrast to the tale's hero, the cunning Odysseus (11.601–626).[27] He kills his children and in some accounts also his wife Megara in a fit of rage induced by the goddess Hera (Apollodorus 2.4.12, Euripides *Hercules* 950ff, Pausanias 9.11.2).[28] Heracles' labors appear to have been expanded upon over time, as are the stories of his youth.[29] Heracles was adopted as a cult hero across Greece, often replacing "local heroes whose exploits promptly were absorbed into his mythological baggage."[30] As Johnston notes of Greek myth more broadly, "interesting prequels, sequels, midquels, and paraquels could emerge, keeping the stories and their characters vigorously alive."[31] In the fifth century BCE, Heracles gets reinvented as an ethical hero. For example, in "The Choice of Heracles" by Prodicus, retold in the *Memorabilia* of Xenaphon (2.1.21-34), Heracles must choose between virtue or vice. He decides to reject the very excesses that had once defined him.

This is, then, a type of mythic reboot for Heracles. As Emma Stafford notes, from the early fifth century, Heracles' physicality became the basis of an athletic ideal, leading to a general "clean up" of his heroic image, such that he eventually becomes, somewhat improbably, an exemplar for philosophers, and an image of "supposed self-control."[32] Moore's graphic novel in some respects returns to the earlier, bestial, morally-ambiguous Hercules, as well as reintroducing the bisexuality that is clearly present in the Greek myths (Therocritus *Idyll* 13) only for the film to remove the bisexuality, and relieve

Hercules of responsibility for his family's death.[33] In both ancient and contemporary times, we have a continuing process of reinvention.

Greek epics and other forms of myth frequently make intertextual references to other heroes and other stories, helping the audience to situate any given story within a larger mythic network.[34] In the contemporary era, paratexts such as trailers, titles, credits, reviews and interviews, help to inform the way audiences situate a mythic story. Jonathan Gray, building on the work of Gérard Genette, argues that paratexts such as reviews "are not only forms of intertextuality, but they can control the menu of intertexts that audiences will consult or employ when watching or thinking about a text."[35] In the case of Ratner's *Hercules*, the film's different paratexts create different associations, aligning the film with the superhero genre, the sword and sandal film, and the star persona of wrestler and bodybuilder Dwayne 'The Rock' Johnson, drawing upon but also reconfiguring the hybrid transmedia mythic figure of Hercules.

Hercules and the Superhero Tradition

The late graphic novelist Steve Moore was keen to distance his work on *Hercules: The Thracian Wars* from the superhero tradition, but the *Hercules* film adaptation was actively promoted and received along these lines, harnessing the superhero genre's current popularity at the cinema.[36] In his review of the 2014 film, *Los Angeles Times*' Gary Goldstein calls Hercules an "ancient superhero," and MTV's Zalbenal calls him "the original superhero," while the UK *Express*' Henry Fitzherbert terms the film a "muscular myth-meets-superhero movie."[37] Lead actor Dwayne Johnson also entered the fray, albeit in a clearly tongue-in-cheek fashion, by declaring Hercules the "original and best superhero" who would easily beat Superman in a contest, or rather in Johnson's own words, "whoop Superman's ass."[38] These paratexts are obviously playful in tone and yet place the *Hercules* film within a superhero intertextual array, helping to expand the audience's perceptions of the story-world of Hercules beyond ancient mythology. In this respect, then, paratexts can make intertextual connections that re-map and expand the fictional world of the text in new directions. In this specific case (but certainly not all) paratexts can therefore be seen as transmedia extensions as well. Such paratexts have the potential to "deepen ... audience engagement," one of the many possible functions of transmedia according to Jenkins.[39]

Moore pointedly notes that the only other Hercules comic he ever read was a 1959 Dell comic adaptation of the famous Steve Reeves *Hercules* film (1958, Pietro Francisci) that he owned as a child.[40] He explicitly proclaims his own graphic novel to be completely independent of any knowledge of other Hercules comics.[41] His readers, however, may differ in this respect from

Moore, for everyone brings their own distinct selection of shared cultural memories.⁴² The paratexts for Ratner's *Hercules* film actively remind its potential audience of affinities between Hercules and the superhero tradition, encouraging the connections that Moore himself was eager to sever.

Hercules was in fact the inspiration for the figure of the superhero—or alternatively the antagonist to the superhero—since its inception. The earliest example, *Hugo Hercules*, was an American newspaper comic strip by Wilhelm H.D. Körner that had a brief run in the *Chicago Tribune* from September 7, 1902, to January 11, 1903. The barrel-chested Hugo Hercules uses his extraordinary strength to help in both minor and life-threatening situations with the repeated catch-phrase "Just as easy." While more of a traditional strongman than a superhero per se, he is nonetheless seen as a foundation figure in the development of the superhero.⁴³

Hercules was also a primary figure in the development of Superman, even if this mythical connection did not make its way into the comics themselves, in favor of an alien origin.⁴⁴ Co-creator Jerry Siegel recalls that the idea for Superman came to him back in 1934: "I am lying in bed counting sheep when all of a sudden it hits me. I conceive a character like Samson, Hercules, and all the strong men I have ever heard tell of rolled into one. Only more so."⁴⁵ Hercules was reincarnated as Marvel Boy in *Daring Mystery Comics* #6 June 1940 by Joe Simon and Jack Kirby, then reimagined by Bob Oksner in *USA Comics* #7 February 1941, in which little Martin Burns gains the strength of Hercules after an accident with (of all things) Hercules' mummy at a museum.⁴⁶ Other figures took on the mantle of Marvel Boy in subsequent decades.

Hercules was the nemesis of the Amazons in Wonder Woman's backstory, both in her original appearance in *All Star Comics* in December 1941 and again when she got her own title in 1942.⁴⁷ Indeed, it is Hercules who prompts the withdrawal of the Amazons from what they call "the man-made world."⁴⁸ In the opening pages to *Sensation Comics*, and in *Wonder Woman* comics through to the 1960s, Wonder Woman is touted as being as strong as Hercules, and in some cases is even said to be "stronger than Hercules."⁴⁹

Over at Marvel comics, Hercules made a brief appearance in *Avengers* #10 November 1964, but became a rival to the Norse god Thor in Stan Lee and Jack Kirby's *Journey into Mystery Annual 1*, October 1965, appearing regularly in *Thor* from #126 March 1966 onwards.⁵⁰ He eventually became part of the Avengers, and in the 1970s had his own group called the Champions which featured the god of the Underworld as antagonist.⁵¹ Hercules even had futuristic adventures, becoming a hero of a post-nuclear world in DC's *Hercules Unbound* #1–12 November 1975–September 1977, and at Marvel writer/artist Bob Layton transported him to the twenty-fourth century for *Hercules* #1–4 September–December 1982.⁵²

Even from this cursory and incomplete overview we can see that Hercules has been a superhero or supervillain in comic books since the beginning of superhero history, reappearing in various guises. As a non-copyrighted hero, he has been used by numerous comic companies. Many outings were overtly transmedia, with Gold Key Comics publishing just two issues of *The Mighty Hercules* to accompany the children's animation of the same name in 1963, notable in being the first U.S. television series to have myth as its foundation (as opposed to individual specials or episodes based on myth) but nonetheless more strongly aligned with superhero tropes.[53] Thor and Hercules continued their stand-off from the *Thor* comic over into the animated television program *Marvel Superheroes* in 1966. Starting with *Hugo Hercules*, the mythic figure of Hercules has been a transmedia superhero for over a century. In both the mythic *and* the superhero tradition, the figure of Hercules is one that has been subjected to continued reinterpretation.[54] More generally, both mythic heroes and superheroes exist in a type of perpetual present being continually told and retold.[55]

Because only a niche audience would have knowledge of this specific history of Hercules as a comic book superhero, ultimately the paratextual connections between the 2014 *Hercules* film and superheroes rely more on an attempt to expand the genre associations of the film beyond the sword and sandal film, and attract superhero film viewers. Director Brett Ratner and actor Dwayne Johnson both call Hercules "the first superhero" in several different interviews.[56] While Richard Reynolds argues that comic book creators have a history of emphasizing the similarities between their superheroes and mythic heroes as a form of cultural legitimization, here it is seemingly the opposite—cementing the importance of Hercules by stressing his role as the forefather of the current wave of immensely popular superhero films.[57]

Demythologizing and Remythologizing

Director Brett Ratner comments that he read Moore's "graphic novel and thought the story of demystifying the myth really is a great interpretation of this story."[58] The pirate's proclamation in the opening scenes that the traditional stories of Hercules' labors are just "a load of crap" alerts the audience to this demythologizing approach seemingly at the outset.[59] In practice, however, just as reviews and interviews can shape the intertextual network that audiences connect with a specific film, so too trailers attempt to shape and influence audience expectations prior to seeing the film itself.[60] The first trailer for *Hercules* proclaims in text, "Before he was a legend.... He was a man," and yet the highlights from the film emphasize the heroic encounters with mythic beasts that the film will later either call into question or overtly debunk.⁶¹ The three-headed hound Cerberus, who guards the Underworld, leaps towards the camera. The Hydra rears up out of the water. The Nemean Lion attacks Hercules, and its pelt is then seen in close-up on Hercules' head. The audience is thereby encouraged to expect a story that follows Hercules' most famous mythic exploits. In the second trailer, Hercules is seemingly pitted against "the descendants of Hades" sent by "the gods."⁶² In the film itself, this proclamation turns out to be mere propaganda, and while Hercules and his team imagine these painted warriors to be the aggressors in a local war, they later realize that their benefactor is to blame. Similarly, the image of Cerberus that haunts Hercules throughout the film turns out to be a hazy, drug-affected memory of three separate hounds that killed his family. The other encounters with mythic beasts in the opening, shown on screen only to illustrate Iolaus' fanciful narration, are briefly referenced in the comic book style closing credits as being the work of his entire team. Mythic traditions are set up only to be undercut.

As Klecker notes, among their many functions, trailers can "establish associations with other movies," attempting to harness a similar audience.⁶³ The early release poster for *Hercules* mirrors those of *300* (2006, Zack Snyder), *Clash of the Titans*, and *Immortals*, all of which feature buff men brandishing weapons while yelling something along the lines of "Aaarrrggghhh!" So too, the trailers for *Hercules* invite audiences to make connections with these recent neo-peplum films. In contrast with *Troy*, where the gods exist only in the minds and beliefs of its human characters, films such as *Clash of the Titans* and *Immortals* have the gods appear on screen.⁶⁴ *300*, although ostensibly about the historical battle of Thermopylae in 480 BCE, omits the gods but has fantastical beasts more at home in the mythic tales.⁶⁵ By emphasizing Hercules' battles with mythic beasts—some more fantastical than others—the trailers for *Hercules* prime the audience to expect the film to follow these recent trends. Indeed, Moore's *Hercules* graphic novel was commissioned precisely to cash in on the commercial success of Snyder's adaptation of *300*.⁶⁶ This is also underscored aesthetically in the trailer for *Hercules* in the use of sudden and extreme slow motion in the action scenes, a trend initiated in the current era of pepla by *300*. *Hercules'* opening seemingly confirms these expectations by expanding on these specific scenes, only to have them summarily cut short and discussed as "a load of crap," after which the rather more prosaic means of Hercules' victories is made clear.⁶⁷

Although *Hercules* follows the graphic novel by removing the overt presence of the gods, and exposes the mythic, heroic deeds of Hercules as deliberate propaganda designed to further his mercenary career, by the end of the film this demythologizing move is ultimately questioned. In a completely different genre setting, Jane Feuer argues that the musical can show how a musical number is put together and staged, but will then reaffirm the fantasy it initially exposed.⁶⁸ Thus the "You Were Meant for Me" romantic musical number in *Singin' in the Rain* (1952, Stanley Donen and Gene Kelly) "demystifies only in order to restore illusion. Although [Gene] Kelly gives us a look at the hardware behind movie magic (the wind machine, the soft lights) in an introduction to the song, the camera arcs around and comes in for a tighter shot of the couple during the central portion of the number, reframing to exclude the previously exposed equipment. We regress from an exposé of romantic duets to an example of a romantic duet."⁶⁹

Ratner's *Hercules* ultimately performs a similar sleight of hand, albeit through different methods. The opening's cynical, self-reflexive humor seemingly declares Hercules' divine parentage and his usual mythic feats to be ridiculously unrealistic. Despite this, towards the end of the film the audience, and indeed Hercules himself, is asked to reconsider his heroic and possibly semi-divine status. Hercules is bound in chains as his new love interest Ergenia (Rebecca Ferguson) is about to be slain at the order of her own father, Lord Cotys (John Hurt). Hercules' seer companion Amphiaraus (Ian McShane) rouses Hercules to action, asking him, "Are you only the legend, or are you the truth? ... Who are you?"⁷⁰ The hero responds by yelling, "I am Hercules!" straining on his chains and breaking free, saving his love, and, of course, everyone else as well.⁷¹ By this point in the film, the intertextual references have shifted from the neo-peplum film to its most famous progenitor—the original Steve Reeves peplum *Hercules*, at the end of which the hero strains on heavy chains to pull down a set of palace columns and ward off his enemies.⁷² Ratner has returned, then, to the mythic and filmic tradition that the film originally dismisses as nonsense. If it is not confirmed that Hercules is indeed the son of Zeus, it is at least heavily implied, and his bodily strength clearly marks him as different—and better—than other mere mortals.

To showcase the action of the hero's muscles, his chained body is paradoxically (if momentarily) still, a contradiction found in both Greek artistic representations of heroic action and the emergence of the silent sword and sandal film from proto-cinematic roots. Robert A. Rushing notes that the peplum returns again and again to this type of scene, in which the hero is immobilized, "his arms outstretched," his muscles straining.⁷³ In Greek art, Heracles is often captured mid-action, as is the case for the first evidence for all twelve labors together, at the temple of Zeus at Olympia of 460 BCE, where marble metopes included depictions of the hero about to club the Lernaean Hydra and Cretan Bull, and wrestling with the Ceryneian Hind.⁷⁴ Heracles was a prominent subject in red and black figure vase painting by Attic artists, with his fight with the Nemean Lion being the most popular.⁷⁵ Greek and Roman art in turn became the inspiration for pre- and early cinematic forms. Maria Wyke notes that the proto-cinematic photographic studies by Eadweard

Muybridge in 1879 included athletes in poses taken from classical sculptures.[76] In the 1894 Edison actualities of Eugen Sandow, a bodybuilder who was promoted as having modeled himself on a Hercules statue, the body itself became the central spectacle as part of what Tom Gunning famously termed "cinema of attractions."[77] Sandow displayed a series of poses, or "tableaux vivants," that mirrored the transition from photograph to moving image.[78] The sword and sandal film's focus on "the male body in stasis and motion" followed directly on from these earlier trends.[79]

This tension between movement and stillness is also of central concern to films based on comic books. As Liam Burke points out, adaptations of comics and graphic novels frequently use time and framing to emphasize their origins. As such, the "bullet-time" technology developed for *The Matrix* (1999, the Wachowskis) to capture "near-frozen moments" has been taken up extensively in film adaptations of comics, as "an appropriate equivalent of comics' static imagery," even as it has since been used in other genres as well.[80] This trend becomes particularly heightened in *300*, which, Rushing notes, is almost entirely shot in slow motion.[81] Rushing connects this with the peplum tradition, and Burke to graphic novel adaptations, but *300* has *both* the sword and sandal genre and the comic book adaptation intersecting in their shared aesthetic interest in action and stasis, which can also be seen in the case of *Hercules*.

If this aesthetic of paradoxically frozen action is employed in the trailer and opening to *Hercules*, it is seemingly bound up in all that is derided as "crap" soon after.[82] Despite this, just as Hercules is reclaimed in all his mythic glory by the film's end, so too the slow-motion aesthetic comes center stage once more for the closing credits. The animated end credits to the film resemble those of *300* but with a more restricted color palate, its character treatment closer to Admira Wijaya's artwork in Moore's graphic novel, and its sepia-toned browns and black on terracotta harking back to Attic red and black figure vases. Both the mythic and filmic traditions are aesthetically reinscribed, even as the credits also confirm the film's departure from myth, by depicting Hercules' entire team undertaking the labors. By this stage in the film, however, this is less a demotion of Hercules than an elevation of his team.

Despite this, the paratexts circulating around the film are predominantly focused on the figure of Hercules as embodied by lead actor Dwayne "The Rock" Johnson. Hercules is, after all, the best-known character, and lends his name to the film itself. In turn, Hercules as a mythic superhero hybrid becomes intimately bound up with the star persona of Johnson. The WWE World Heavyweight Champion launched a TeamHercules.com diet and workout based on his preparation for the film, so that viewers could also get the physique of "the world's first superhero."[83] Richard Dyer has written on how the peplum film puts on display a male body that has been strenuously worked for, built up through diet and exercise and suffering, or as Johnson himself tweeted, "Epic results take epic effort."[84] The fact that this is filtered through Johnson's biracial hyper-masculine body in the case of *Hercules* nonetheless goes against the prevailing racial trends of the genre, where black bodybuilders only rarely appear, and then only as villains or ineffectual sidekicks.[85] Johnson's invitation to his fans to build their own Hercules body is therefore seemingly more egalitarian, playfully asking his fans (and 7.3 million Twitter followers) to yell, "I am Hercules!" as they workout at the gym (echoing the famous "I am Spartacus!" scene from Stanley Kubrick's 1960 film).[86] This nonetheless requires the expense of either gym membership or gym equipment ownership, the leisure time to devote to "the Greek superhero workout," and money for a special diet.[87] Johnson's colleague Rufus Sewell, who plays the acerbic Autolycus in the film, comments: "We were all eating our own versions of the Dwayne Johnson diet.... But no matter how much you work out, it's quite easy to develop dysmorphia because if you stand next to Dwayne Johnson, you're always going to look like there's not enough going on."[88]

While Johnson prepared for the role and tweeted his fans, "Become the man you were born to be," TeamHercules—both in the film and in real life—is overshadowed by the body of Johnson/Hercules, emphasizing the exceptionality of the mythic hero that the *Hercules* film initially disavows only to reaffirm.[89]

Conclusion

The 2014 *Hercules* film and the paratexts surrounding it simultaneously retell, expand, and reconfigure numerous different storytelling traditions around the myth of Hercules, the sword and sandal film genre, and the superhero genre. Myth has always existed precisely at this juncture between tradition and innovation, or the retelling and the already told, even if the media used and the precise intertexts that the audience is invited to recall have shifted significantly.[90] As Shapiro notes, "in Greece, when a myth reached a version that was no longer open to reinterpretation or variant forms, it was dead."[91]

While classicists such as Beard may repeat the common lament that films too frequently get their ancient myth wrong, similarly they in turn fail to recognize the complexity of Hercules as a figure of popular contemporary imagination, as indeed does Moore. A new version of any given myth may make specific references to older variants, or more vaguely draw upon an entire accumulated cultural history that has become blended in popular memory. The 2014 film itself and the paratexts around it playfully understand the way that the transmedia figure of Hercules is a mythic superhero hybrid, whose meaning depends upon a complex array of associations, an anachronistic meld of both the ancient and contemporary, from which he can never be divorced.

NOTES

1. *Hercules*, directed by Brett Ratner (2014; Hollywood: Paramount Pictures, 2014), DVD. I would like to thank Diana Sandars for her comments on this essay. A shorter version was originally presented at the Superhero Identities Symposium, Australian Centre for the Moving Image, December 2016. I would like to thank the participants for their comments and questions, particularly Jason Bainbridge.
2. Steve Moore and Admira Wijaya, *Hercules: The Thracian Wars* (Carpinteria, CA: Radical Books, 2008). The film adaptation became controversial when it was revealed after the author's death that Moore had not checked the details of his publishing contract closely enough, and would get no film royalties whatsoever from the adaptation, a fact that friend Alan Moore (no relation) was at pains to make public. Hannah Means Shannon, "Alan Moore Calls for Boycott of 'Wretched Film' Hercules on Behalf of Friend Steve Moore," *Bleeding Cool*, July 2014, http://www.bleedingcool.com/2014/07/17/alan-moore-calls-for-boycott-of-wretched-film-hercules-on-behalf-of-friend-steve-moore/.
3. *Hercules*, directed by Brett Ratner.
4. *Ibid*.
5. *Ibid*.
6. *Ibid*.
7. *Ibid*.
8. *Ibid*.
9. Martin M. Winkler, "Troy and the Cinematic Afterlife of Homeric Gods," in *Return to Troy: New Essays on the Hollywood Epic*, ed. Martin M. Winkler (Leiden: Brill, 2015), 116.
10. Mary Beard, quoted in Sam Leith, "The Return of Swords 'n' Sandals Movies," *Financial Times*, May 14, 2010, https://www.ft.com/content/b9161614–5ecb-11df-af86–00144feab49a.
11. Martin M. Winkler, "Introduction: *Troy* Revisited," in *Return to Troy: New Essays on the Hollywood Epic*, ed. Martin M. Winkler (Leiden: Brill, 2015), 6.
12. Josho Brouwers, "Hercules 3D (review)," *Ancient Warfare*, August 13, 2014, https://www.karwansaraypublishers.com/pw/ancient-warfare/blog/hercules-3d-review/.
13. Eleonora Cavallini, "In the Footsteps of Homeric Narrative: Anachronisms and Other Supposed Mistakes in *Troy*," in *Return to Troy: New Essays on the Hollywood Epic*, ed. Martin M. Winkler (Leiden: Brill, 2015), 67–68.
14. Laura M. Slatkin, *The Power of Thetis: Allusion and Interpretation in the Iliad* (Berkeley: University of California Press, 1991). Seth L. Schein, *Homeric Epic and its Reception: Interpretive Essays* (Oxford: Oxford University Press, 2016), 43.
15. Winker, "Introduction," 3, 6.
16. *Ibid.*, 6.
17. M. M. Bakhtin, *The Dialogic Imagination: Four Essays*, ed. Michael Holquist, trans. Caryl Emerson and Michael Holquist (Austin: University of Texas Press, 1981), 420.
18. Henry Jenkins, *Convergence Culture: Where Old and New Media Collide* (New York: New York University Press, 2006), 120.
19. *Ibid.*, 95–96.
20. *Ibid.*, 121.
21. Ken Dowden, *The Uses of Greek Mythology* (London: Routledge, 1992), 8.
22. Sarah Iles Johnston, "Narrating Myths: Story and Belief in Ancient Greece," *Arethusa* 48, no. 2 (2015): 205, 208, emphasis in original. Similarly, Johnston suggests there is a fundamental difference between decentralized plurimedial Greek myth, and the contemporary unified transmedia expansion from a main narrative such as the *Star Wars* films. Johnston, "Narrating Myths," 206, n. 54. Henry Jenkins makes the distinction in this respect between transmedia, which, if "used by itself, simply means 'across media'" (and which in *Convergence*

Culture he notes could be found in ancient myth), and contemporary "transmedia storytelling ... where integral elements of a fiction get dispersed systematically across multiple delivery channels for the purpose of creating a unified and coordinated entertainment experience." Henry Jenkins, "Transmedia 202: Further Reflections," *Confessions of an Aca-Fan* (blog), 2011, http://henryjenkins.org/2011/08/defining_transmedia_further_re.html. Jenkins, *Convergence Culture*, 121. While the distinction is worth making, it nonetheless becomes blurred when considering the multi-authored nature of transmedia storytelling, and the fact that Jenkins includes unauthorized fan activities such as fan fiction and even cosplay indicates that what begins as a centrally coordinated story world does not remain so. Jenkins, "Transmedia 202."

23. Steve Moore quoted in Mike Conroy, "An Interview with Steve Moore," in *Hercules: The Thracian Wars*, by Steve Moore and Admira Wijaya (Carpinteria, CA: Radical Books, 2008). For an analysis of the graphic novel and its sequel, see T. H. M. Gellar-Goad and John Bedingham, "Hercules the Brute, Hercules the Tactician in Steve Moore's The Thracian Wars and the Knives of Kush comics," *Electra* 3 (2014): http://electra.lis.upatras.gr/index.php/electra/article/view/2178.

24. Jim Collins, "Batman: The Movie, the Narrative, the Hyperconscious," in *The Many Lives of the Batman: Critical Approaches to a Superhero and His Media*, ed. Roberta E. Pearson and William Uricchio (New York: Routledge & London: BFI, 1991), 170–171.

25. *Ibid.*, 179–180.

26. Ruby Blondell, "How to Kill an Amazon," *Helios* 32, no. 2 (2005): 183.

27. Seth L. Schein, *Homeric Epic and its Reception: Interpretive Essays* (Oxford: Oxford University Press, 2016), 45.

28. How many children he had with Megara varies among the sources, three according to Apollodorus and Euripides (*Hercules* 995ff) and eight according to Pindar (4.63ff). The graphic novel features none of Hercules' family.

29. Emma Stafford, *Herakles* (Abingdon, Oxon: Routledge, 2012), 24.

30. G. Karl Galinsky, *The Herakles Theme: The Adaptations of the Hero in Literature from Homer to the Twentieth Century* (Oxford: Basil Backwell, 1972), 3.

31. Sarah Iles Johnston, "The Greek Mythic Story World," *Arethusa* 38, no. 3 (2015): 309.

32. Stafford, *Herakles*, 121–127. Blondell, "How to Kill an Amazon," 184, 188.

33. On Heracles' male lovers, see Stafford *Herakles*, 131, 134–136. Moore takes the virgin hunter Atalanta of Greek myth (Apollodorus 3.9.2) and portrays her as overtly lesbian in the graphic novel, only for this, too, to be omitted from the film version. The Greeks were notably silent on the topic of lesbianism. Lillian E. Doherty, *Gender and the Interpretation of Classical Myth* (London: Duckworth, 2001), 75.

34. Dowden, *The Uses of Greek Mythology*, 8. Johnston, "The Greek Mythic Story World," 293–294, 296–298, 300.

35. Gérard Genette, *Paratexts: Thresholds of Interpretation* (Cambridge: Cambridge University Press, 1997). Jonathan Gray, *Show Sold Separately: Promos, Spoilers, and Other Media Paratexts* (New York: New York University Press, 2010), 141.

36. Manolis Vamvounis, "Moore Talks 'Hercules: The Thracian Wars,'" *Comic Book Resources*, December 4, 2008, http://www.comicbookresources.com/?page=article&id=19043.

37. Gary Goldstein, "Dwayne Johnson's 'Hercules' Packs Action-Filled Punch," *Los Angeles Times*, July 25, 2014, http://www.latimes.com/entertainment/movies/la-et-mn-hercules-movie-review-20140726-story.html. Zalbenal, "'Hercules': The Reviews Are In," *MTV*, July 25, 2014, http://www.mtv.com/news/1878447/hercules-the-reviews-are-in/. Henry Fitzherbert, "Dwayne Johnson Beefs Up Hercules in Muscular Myth-Meets-Superhero Movie," *Express*, July 24, 2014, http://www.express.co.uk/entertainment/films/491359/Hercules-review-and-trailer.

38. Dwayne Johnson, quoted in Danny Walker, "Hercules Would 'Whoop Superman's A**' Says Dwayne Johnson," *The Mirror*, July 22, 2014, http://www.mirror.co.uk/tv/tv-news/hercules-would-whoop-supermans-a-3894155.

39. Jenkins, "Transmedia," 202.

40. Conroy, "An Interview with Steve Moore."

41. *Ibid.*

42. Collins, "Batman," 170–171.
43. Peter Coogan, "Comics Predecessors," in *The Superhero Reader*, ed. Charles Hatfield, Jeet Heer, and Kent Worcester (Jackson: University Press of Mississippi, 2013), 7–8.
44. Richard Reynolds, *Super Heroes: A Modern Mythology* (London: B.T. Batsford, 1992), 9–10, 53, 61.
45. Jerry Siegel quoted in Reynolds, *Super Heroes*, 9.
46. Gina Misiroglu with David A. Roach, eds., *The Superhero Book: The Ultimate Encyclopedia of Comic-Book Icons and Hollywood Heroes* (Canton, MI: Visible Ink Press, 2004), 228–229.
47. William Moulton Marston and H.G. Peter, *Wonder Woman Archives Volume 1* (New York: DC Comics, 1998), 10.
48. *Ibid.*, 10, 148–150.
49. Marco Arnaudo, *The Myth of the Superhero*, trans. Jamie Richards (Baltimore: Johns Hopkins University Press, 2013), 15. Moulton, Marston and Peter, *Wonder Woman*, 199.
50. C.W. Marshall and George Kovacs, "Introduction," in *Classics and Comics*, ed. George Kovacs and C.W. Marshall (Oxford: Oxford University Press, 2011), xx.
51. *Ibid.*
52. *Ibid.* This type of genre-blurring around Hercules had already been seen much earlier in the peplum film tradition, with *Hercules Against the Moon Men* (1964, Giacomo Gentilomo).
53. Djoymi Baker, "Broadcast Space: TV Culture, Myth and *Star Trek*" (PhD diss., University of Melbourne, 2005).
54. In his famous essay "The Myth of Superman," Umberto Eco contrasts the fixed heroes of myth with the surprise of the modern novel, positioning the superhero as somewhere in-between. Greek audiences would certainly have known how a mythic hero's life ended, but the example of Heracles indicates that mythic heroes are anything but fixed. Umberto Eco, "The Myth of Superman," *Diacritics* 2, no. 1 (1972): 14–22. Scholars have debated Eco's approach primarily to argue about his interpretation of the superhero tradition. Angela Ndalianis, "Enter the Aleph: Superhero Worlds and Hypertime Realities," in *The Contemporary Comic Book Superhero*, ed. Angela Ndalianis (New York: Routledge, 2009). Marc Singer, "The Myth of Eco: Cultural Populism and Comics Studies," *Studies in Comics* 4, no. 2 (2013): 355–366. Jack Peterson Teiwes, "Crisis of Infinite Intertexts! Continuity as Adaptation in the Superman Multimedia Franchise" (PhD diss., University of Melbourne, 2015).
55. Thus as Johnston argues, "the deeds described by the [Greek] myths existed on a continuum that flowed uninterruptedly into the time of the listeners." Johnston, "The Greek Mythic Story World," 307.
56. Victoria Bull, "THN Attends 'Hercules' Preview & Cast Q&A With Dwayne Johnson," *The Hollywood News*, July 2, 2014, http://www.thehollywoodnews.com/2014/07/02/thn-attends-hercules-preview-cast-qa-with-dwayne-johnson/. "Dwayne Johnson Becomes Hercules in First Look at 'Hercules,'" *Huffington Post*, March 24, 2014, http://www.huffingtonpost.com/2014/03/24/dwayne-johnson-hercules_n_5020555.html. "Sneak Peek: The Rock Becomes Hercules," *Radical Studios*, March 25, 2014, http://radicalpublishing.com/2014/03/sneak-peek-rock-becomes-hercules/.
57. Reynolds, *Super Heroes*, 53.
58. Brett Ratner quoted in Bull, "THN Attends 'Hercules' Preview."
59. *Hercules*, directed by Brett Ratner.
60. Gray, *Show Sold Separately*, 51. Daniel Hesford, "'Action! … Suspense! … Emotion!' the Trailer as Cinematic Performance," *Frames Cinema Journal* 3 (2013), http://framescinemajournal.com/article/action-suspense-emotion-the-trailer-as-cinematic-performance/.
61. "Hercules Official Trailer #1 (2014)—Dwayne Johnson, Ian McShane Movie HD," YouTube video, 1:25, posted by Movieclips Trailers, March 26, 2014, https://www.youtube.com/watch?v=GFqY089piQ4.
62. "Hercules Official Trailer #2 (2014)—Dwayne Johnson, Ian McShane Movie HD," YouTube video, 2:31, posted by Movieclips Trailers, June 3, 2014, https://www.youtube.com/watch?v=OwlynHlZEc4.
63. Cornelia Klecker, "The Other Kind of Film Frames: A Research Report on Paratexts in Film," *Word & Image* 31, no. 4 (2015): 409.

64. See Latacz, quoted in Cavallini, "In the Footsteps of Homeric Narrative," 66.
65. Djoymi Baker, "*300*," in *The Encyclopedia of Epic Films*, C. Santas, J. Wilson, M. Colavito and D. Baker (Lanham, MD: Rowman & Littlefield, 2014), 499.
66. Conroy, "An Interview with Steve Moore."
67. *Hercules*, directed by Brett Ratner.
68. Jane Feuer, *The Hollywood Musical* (London: Macmillan, 1993), 46.
69. Ibid.
70. *Hercules*, directed by Brett Ratner.
71. Ibid.
72. In the 1950s, popular films set in antiquity started to be called *les péplums* by French fans after the Greek *peplos*, and by the early 1960s the term was being used in the renowned French film journal *Cahiers du Cinéma* in the context of debates about how *auteur* directors could put their personal, artistic stamp upon otherwise formulaic genres. Robert A. Rushing, *Descended from Hercules: Biopolitics and the Muscled Male Body on Screen* (Bloomington: Indiana University Press, 2016), 1. That the *peplos* was an item of women's clothing is somewhat ironic for a genre so heavily focused on displaying the male body. It becomes particularly interesting when we note that Loraux identifies several instances of Heracles wearing women's clothing in stories and images, such as in Diodorus (4.14.3), in which Athena gives Heracles a *peplos* to wear. Nicole Loraux, "Herakles: The Super-Male and the Feminine," in *Before Sexuality: The Construction of Erotic Experience in the Ancient Greek World*, ed. D.M. Halperin, J.J. Winker and F.I. Zeitlin (Princeton: Princeton University Press, 1990).
73. Rushing, *Descended from Hercules*, 5, 41, 43.
74. Stafford, *Herakles*, 24–25. Beth Cohen, "From Bowman to Clubman: Herakles and Olympia," *The Art Bulletin* 76, no. 4 (1994): 705–714. Earlier representations featured only single or smaller groups of labors rather than twelve.
75. H. A. Shapiro, "Old and New Heroes: Narrative, Composition, and Subject in Attic Black-Figure," *Classical Antiquity* 9, no. 1 (1990): 122–3, 136. Shapiro notes that the depiction of Heracles in art does not follow the general shift during the sixth century away from animals and mythological monsters to human or at least anthropomorphic foes.
76. Maria Wyke, "Herculean Muscle! The Classicizing Rhetoric of Bodybuilding," *Arion* 4, no. 3 (1997): 56.
77. Wyke, "Herculean Muscle!" 54–56. Tom Gunning, "The Cinema of Attractions: Early Film, Its Spectator and the Avant-Garde," *Wide Angle* 8, no. 3/4 (1986): 63–70.
78. Charles Musser, "At the Beginning: Motion Picture Production, Representation and Ideology at the Edison and Lumière Companies," in *The Silent Cinema Reader*, ed. Lee Grieveson and Peter Krämer (London: Routledge, 2004), 19–20.
79. Jacqueline Reich, "Slave to Fashion: Masculinity, Suits, and the Maciste Films of Italian Silent Cinema," in *Fashion in Film*, ed. Adrienne Munich (Bloomington: Indiana University Press, 2011), 237.
80. Liam Burke, *The Comic Book Film Adaptation Exploring Modern Hollywood's Leading Genre* (Jackson: University Press of Mississippi, 2015), 197. Even earlier, however, the television program *Marvel Superheroes* (1966) used a somewhat static, cost-saving "limited animation" style developed in the 1950s, which had the effect of looking like comic book panels. Jason Mittell, *Genre and Television: From Cop Shows to Cartoons in American Culture* (New York: Routledge, 2004), 65. Baker, "Broadcast Space," 74.
81. Rushing, *Descended from Hercules*, 54–57. As Rushing notes, *300*'s aesthetic extremes are often overlooked in the face of its "homophobia, misogyny, ableism, and racism." Rushing, *Descended from Hercules*, 28. See Rushing for an excellent extended discussion of temporality and stasis in the contemporary sword and sandal film.
82. *Hercules*, directed by Brett Ratner.
83. AllStar, "The Rock Wants You to Join Team Hercules," *Extra Health and Fitness*, June 2014, http://extrahealthandfitness.blogspot.com.au/2014/06/the-rock-wants-you-to-join-team-hercules.html. Johnson's video invitation to his fans has been archived here and elsewhere, but the TeamHercules website itself is now defunct.
84. Richard Dyer, *White: Essays on Race and Culture* (Hoboken, NJ: Taylor and Francis, 2013), 153. Dwayne Johnson, "This'll be punishing. Our final #TeamHercules labor—LEGS.

Push yourself…. Epic results take epic effort. #B2A," *The Rock* (Twitter), July 3, 2014, https://twitter.com/therock/status/484844039343063041.
   85. Dyer, *White*, 148, 178–179.
   86. "Team Hercules," YouTube video, 1:28, posted by Hercules Movie, June 11, 2014, https://www.youtube.com/watch?v=CNMzD0UEQF4.
   87. Bryan Alexander, "Dwayne Johnson on His 'Hercules' Twitter Smackdown," *USA Today*, July 10, 2014, http://www.usatoday.com/story/life/movies/2014/07/09/dwayne-johnson-the-rock-twitter-team-hercules/12405713/.
   88. Rufus Sewell, quoted in Neala Johnson, "Rufus Sewell Addicted to 'The Rock' Diet After Beefing Up to Fight with Hercules," news.com.au, 31 July, 2014, http://www.news.com.au/entertainment/movies/new-movies/rufus-sewell-addicted-to-the-rock-diet-after-beefing-up-to-fight-with-hercules/news-story/db673017044206e53edd6c05bc009301.
   89. Dwayne Johnson, "Become the man you were born to be," *The Rock* (Twitter), March 24, 2011, https://twitter.com/therock/status/44818864507414937?lang=en. It is worth noting, however, that Johnson's comments are often clearly tongue-in-cheek, and in a more serious moment the actor clarified that what people may aspire to through the Hercules workout relies less on emulating his specific (super)body than the effort to improve themselves: "From muscle gains, battling obesity to an overall healthier lifestyle—at the end of the day, people love saying that they faced their 'issue at hand' and kicked its ass. And we all know ass kickings are good for one's soul." This still aligns with the bodybuilding discourse around effort, expressed in terms that resonate with the Hercules role. Dwayne Johnson, quoted in Alexander, "Dwayne Johnson on his 'Hercules' Twitter Smackdown."
   90. Lowell Edmunds, "Myth in Homer," in *A New Companion to Homer*, ed. Ian Morris and Barry Powell (New York: Brill, 1997), 420. Baker, "Broadcast Space," 81.
   91. Shapiro, "Old and New Heroes," 148.

BIBLIOGRAPHY

Alexander, Bryan. "Dwayne Johnson on His 'Hercules' Twitter Smackdown." *USA Today*, July 10 (2014): http://www.usatoday.com/story/life/movies/2014/07/09/dwayne-johnson-the-rock-twitter-team-hercules/12405713/.
AllStar. "The Rock Wants You to Join Team Hercules." *Extra Health and Fitness*, June (2014): http://extrahealthandfitness.blogspot.com.au/2014/06/the-rock-wants-you-to-join-team-hercules.html.
Arnaudo, Marco. *The Myth of the Superhero*. Translated by Jamie Richards. Baltimore: Johns Hopkins University Press, 2013.
Baker, Djoymi. "Broadcast Space: TV Culture, Myth and *Star Trek*." PhD diss., University of Melbourne, 2005.
_____. "300." In *The Encyclopedia of Epic Films*, by C. Santas, J. Wilson, M. Colavito and D. Baker, 499–501. Lanham, MD: Rowman & Littlefield, 2014.
Bakhtin, M. M. *The Dialogic Imagination: Four Essays*. Edited by Michael Holquist. Translated by Caryl Emerson and Michael Holquist. Austin: University of Texas Press, 1981.
Blondell, Ruby. "How to Kill an Amazon." *Helios* 32, no. 2 (2005): 183–213.
Brouwers, Josho. "Hercules 3D (review)." *Ancient Warfare*, August 13 (2014): https://www.karwansaraypublishers.com/pw/ancient-warfare/blog/hercules-3d-review/.
Bull, Victoria. "THN Attends 'Hercules' Preview & Cast Q&A With Dwayne Johnson." *The Hollywood News*, July 2 (2014): http://www.thehollywoodnews.com/2014/07/02/thn-attends-hercules-preview-cast-qa-with-dwayne-johnson/.
Burke, Liam. *The Comic Book Film Adaptation Exploring Modern Hollywood's Leading Genre*. Jackson: University Press of Mississippi, 2015.
Cavallini, Eleonora. "In the Footsteps of Homeric Narrative: Anachronisms and Other Supposed Mistakes in *Troy*." In *Return to Troy: New Essays on the Hollywood Epic*, edited by Martin M. Winkler, 65–85. Leiden: Brill, 2015.
Cohen, Beth. "From Bowman to Clubman: Herakles and Olympia." *The Art Bulletin* 76, no. 4 (1994): 695–715.
Collins, Jim. "Batman: The Movie, the Narrative, the Hyperconscious." In *The Many Lives of*

the Batman: Critical Approaches to a Superhero and His Media, edited by Roberta E. Pearson and William Uricchio, 164–181. New York: Routledge & London: BFI, 1991.

Conroy, Mike. "An Interview with Steve Moore." In *Hercules: The Thracian Wars*, by Steve Moore and Admira Wijaya. Carpinteria, CA: Radical Books, 2008.

Coogan, Peter. "Comics Predecessors." In *The Superhero Reader*, edited by Charles Hatfield, Jeet Heer, and Kent Worcester, 7–15. Jackson: University Press of Mississippi, 2013.

Doherty, Lillian E. *Gender and the Interpretation of Classical Myth*. London: Duckworth, 2001.

Dowden, Ken. *The Uses of Greek Mythology*. London: Routledge, 1992.

Dyer, Richard. *White: Essays on Race and Culture*. Hoboken: Taylor and Francis, 2013.

Eco, Umberto. "The Myth of Superman." *Diacritics* 2, no. 1 (1972): 14–22.

Edmunds, Lowell. "Myth in Homer." In *A New Companion to Homer*, edited by Ian Morris and Barry Powell, 414–441. New York: Brill, 1997.

Feuer, Jane. *The Hollywood Musical*. London: Macmillan, 1993.

Fitzherbert, Henry. "Dwayne Johnson Beefs up Hercules in Muscular Myth-Meets-Superhero Movie." *Express*, July 24 (2014): http://www.express.co.uk/entertainment/films/491359/Hercules-review-and-trailer.

Galinsky, G. Karl. *The Herakles Theme: The Adaptations of the Hero in Literature from Homer to the Twentieth Century*. Oxford: Basil Backwell, 1972.

Gellar-Goad, T. H. M., and John Bedingham. "Hercules the Brute, Hercules the Tactician in Steve Moore's The Thracian Wars and the Knives of Kush Comics." *Electra* 3 (2014): http://electra.lis.upatras.gr/index.php/electra/article/view/2178.

Genette, Gérard. *Paratexts: Thresholds of Interpretation*. Cambridge: Cambridge University Press, 1997.

Goldstein, Gary. "Dwayne Johnson's 'Hercules' Packs Action-Filled Punch." *Los Angeles Times*, July 25 (2014): http://www.latimes.com/entertainment/movies/la-et-mn-hercules-movie-review-20140726-story.html.

Gray, Jonathan. *Show Sold Separately: Promos, Spoilers, and Other Media Paratexts*. New York: New York University Press, 2010.

Gunning, Tom. "The Cinema of Attractions: Early Film, Its Spectator and the Avant-Garde." *Wide Angle* 8, no. 3/4 (1986): 63–70.

Hercules. Directed by Brett Ratner. 2014. Hollywood: Paramount Pictures, 2014. DVD.

"Hercules Official Trailer #1 (2014) - Dwayne Johnson, Ian McShane Movie HD," YouTube video, 1:25, posted by Movieclips Trailers, March 26, 2014. https://www.youtube.com/watch?v=GFqY089piQ4.

"Hercules Official Trailer #2 (2014) - Dwayne Johnson, Ian McShane Movie HD," YouTube video, 2:31, posted by Movieclips Trailers, June 3, 2014. https://www.youtube.com/watch?v=OwlynHlZEc4.

Hesford, Daniel. "'Action! … Suspense! … Emotion!' The Trailer as Cinematic Performance." *Frames Cinema Journal* 3 (2013): http://framescinemajournal.com/article/action-suspense-emotion-the-trailer-as-cinematic-performance/.

Huffington Post. "Dwayne Johnson Becomes Hercules in First Look at 'Hercules.'" March 24 (2014): http://www.huffingtonpost.com/2014/03/24/dwayne-johnson-hercules_n_5020555.html.

Jenkins, Henry. *Confessions of an Aca-Fan* (blog). http://henryjenkins.org.

_____. *Convergence Culture: Where Old and New Media Collide*. New York: New York University Press, 2006.

Johnson, Dwayne. *The Rock* (Twitter). https://twitter.com/TheRock.

Johnson, Neala. "Rufus Sewell Addicted to 'The Rock' Diet After Beefing Up to Fight with Hercules." news.com.au, 31 July (2014): http://www.news.com.au/entertainment/movies/new-movies/rufus-sewell-addicted-to-the-rock-diet-after-beefing-up-to-fight-with-hercules/news-story/db673017044206e53edd6c05bc009301.

Johnston, Sarah Iles. "The Greek Mythic Story World." *Arethusa* 38, no. 3 (2015): 283–311.

_____. "Narrating Myths: Story and Belief in Ancient Greece." *Arethusa* 48, no. 2 (2015): 173–218.

Klecker, Cornelia. "The Other Kind of Film Frames: A Research Report on Paratexts in Film." *Word & Image* 31, no. 4 (2015): 402–413.
Loraux, Nicole. "Herakles: The Super-Male and the Feminine." In *Before Sexuality: The Construction of Erotic Experience in the Ancient Greek World*, edited by D.M. Halperin, J.J. Winkler and F.I. Zeitlin, 21–52. Princeton: Princeton University Press, 1990.
Leith, Sam. "The Return of Swords 'n' Sandals Movies." *Financial Times*, May 14 (2010): https://www.ft.com/content/b9161614-5ecb-11df-af86-00144feab49a.
Marshall, C.W., and George Kovacs. "Introduction." In *Classics and Comics*, edited by George Kovacs and C.W. Marshall, vii-xiii. Oxford: Oxford University Press, 2011.
Miller, Frank, and Lynn Varley. *300*. Milwaukie, OR: Dark Horse Books, 1998, 1999, 2006.
Misiroglu, Gina, with David A. Roach, eds. *The Superhero Book: The Ultimate Encyclopedia of Comic-Book Icons and Hollywood Heroes*. Canton, MI: Visible Ink Press, 2004.
Mittell, Jason. *Genre and Television: From Cop Shows to Cartoons in American Culture*. New York: Routledge, 2004.
Moore, Steve, and Admira Wijaya, *Hercules: The Thracian Wars*. Carpinteria, CA: Radical Books, 2008.
Moulton Marston, William, and H.G. Peter. *Wonder Woman Archives Volume 1*. New York: DC Comics, 1998.
Musser, Charles. "At the Beginning: Motion Picture Production, Representation and Ideology at the Edison and Lumière Companies." In *The Silent Cinema Reader*, edited by Lee Grieveson and Peter Krämer, 15–30. London: Routledge, 2004.
Ndalianis, Angela. "Enter the Aleph: Superhero Worlds and Hypertime Realities." In *The Contemporary Comic Book Superhero*, edited by Angela Ndalianis, 270–290. New York: Routledge, 2009.
Radical Studios. "Sneak Peek: The Rock Becomes Hercules." March 25 (2014): http://radicalpublishing.com/2014/03/sneak-peek-rock-becomes-hercules/.
Reich, Jacqueline. "Slave to Fashion: Masculinity, Suits, and the Maciste Films of Italian Silent Cinema." In *Fashion in Film*, edited by Adrienne Munich, 236–259. Bloomington: Indiana University Press, 2011.
Reynolds, Richard. *Super Heroes: A Modern Mythology*. London: B.T. Batsford, 1992.
Rushing, Robert A. *Descended from Hercules: Biopolitics and the Muscled Male Body on Screen*. Bloomington: Indiana University Press, 2016.
Schein, Seth L. *Homeric Epic and Its Reception: Interpretive Essays*. Oxford: Oxford University Press, 2016.
Shannon, Hannah Means. "Alan Moore Calls for Boycott of 'Wretched Film' Hercules on Behalf of Friend Steve Moore." *Bleeding Cool*, July (2014): http://www.bleedingcool.com/2014/07/17/alan-moore-calls-for-boycott-of-wretched-film-hercules-on-behalf-of-friend-steve-moore/.
Shapiro, H. A. "Old and New Heroes: Narrative, Composition, and Subject in Attic Black-Figure." *Classical Antiquity* 9, no. 1 (1990): 114–148.
Singer, Marc. "The Myth of Eco: Cultural Populism and Comics Studies." *Studies in Comics* 4, no. 2 (2013): 355–366.
Slatkin, Laura M. *The Power of Thetis: Allusion and Interpretation in the Iliad*. Berkeley: University of California Press, 1991.
Stafford, Emma. *Herakles*. Abingdon, Oxon: Routledge, 2012.
"Team Hercules," YouTube video, 1:28, posted by Hercules Movie, June 11, 2014. https://www.youtube.com/watch?v=CNMzD0UEQF4.
Teiwes, Jack Peterson. "Crisis of Infinite Intertexts! Continuity as Adaptation in the Superman Multimedia Franchise." PhD diss., University of Melbourne, 2015.
Vamvounis, Manolis. "Moore Talks 'Hercules: The Thracian Wars.'" *Comic Book Resources*, December 4 (2008): http://www.comicbookresources.com/?page=article&id=19043.
Walker, Danny. "Hercules Would 'Whoop Superman's A**' Says Dwayne Johnson." *The Mirror*, July 22 (2014): http://www.mirror.co.uk/tv/tv-news/hercules-would-whoop-supermans-a-3894155.
Winkler, Martin M. "Introduction: *Troy* Revisited." In *Return to Troy: New Essays on the Hollywood Epic*, edited by Martin M. Winkler, 1–15. Leiden: Brill, 2015.

_____. "Troy and the Cinematic Afterlife of Homeric Gods." In *Return to Troy: New Essays on the Hollywood Epic*, edited by Martin M. Winkler, 108–164. Leiden: Brill, 2015.

Wyke, Maria "Herculean Muscle! The Classicizing Rhetoric of Bodybuilding." *Arion* 4, no. 3 (1997): 51–79.

Zalbenal. "'Hercules': The Reviews Are In." *MTV*, July 25 (2014): http://www.mtv.com/news/1878447/hercules-the-reviews-are-in/.

From Crowds to Swarms
Movement and Bodies in Neo-Peplum Films

KEVIN M. FLANAGAN

Part of the appeal of peplum films across different periods of production and subgenres is the way that they imagine or visualize the residue of ancient history through the staging of costumed bodies. Biblical epics, gladiatorial sword and sandal pictures, and even fantastic hybridizations like the sword and sorcery cycle of the 1980s are generically defined through clothed fashion and *mise-en-scène*. Like the gangster films of the 1930s, this is a type of film primarily realized through a recurrent armory of iconography, inclusive of weapons (swords, tridents, nets, boulders in the arms of strongmen), articles of clothing (the eponymous *pepla* skirts, sandals, diaphanous robes and loincloths of all sorts), and the plunder of the past (goblets, jewels, religious idols made of precious metals).[1]

But, there are other visual conventions that locate the genre as well, sometimes un- or subconscious displays/interactions of people that typify the sensate of peplum films. Crowd scenes, and the imagination and creative display of crowd formations, are also bread and butter to the genre, often underscoring the most lavish and narrative-punctuating moments in these films. This is true across the whole history of peplum films, from early examples like *Cabiria* (1914, Giovanni Pastrone) to their prestige era in the 1950s and 1960s with films like *Ben-Hur* (1959, William Wyler), through Italy's exploitation and deconstruction of the genre through the mid–1960s in films such as *Hercules Unchained* (1959, Pietro Francisci), all the way to the genre's renewed ascendance across the global mainstream with *Gladiator* (2000, Ridley Scott). Yet, if the centrality of crowds is a foundational conceit of this type of film that remains consistent, then the conceptualization, staging, and function of those crowds is anything but rote. Technological shifts (broadly defined through a shift from analog, physical, and indexical imagery to a widespread embrace of computer generated imagery produced at a remove from specific referents) and shifting cultural anxieties (as refracted through changing modes of warfare and weaponry that characterize the bloody twentieth century) prompt different embedded meanings for the massed bodies of this genre.

This essay begins by locating the historical importance of crowds and spectacles to people in Greco-Roman antiquity, noting their function as a means of entertainment, a distillation of cultural anxieties, and as a means of social control. It examines these tendencies through ideas about crowd experience, as outlined by twentieth-century cultural commentators, especially Elias Canetti, whose book *Crowds and Power* (1960) provides a topography for the meanings inherent in different crowd types. Next, this essay explores how peplum films like *Hannibal* (1959, Carlo Ludovico Bragaglia and Edgar G. Ulmer) anchor their narratives and sense of history in crowd scenes, including sequences of political oratory, spectating at gladiatorial games, battle scenes, and so on, noting the largely static nature of such sequences, which seem to posit a kind of recovered grandeur through slowness, tableaux vivant arrangements, solidity, and histrionic posturing. This essay then contrasts this treatment of bodies and crowds with what is enabled by the CGI of newer films, taking care to keep those effects more to the internal generic development of peplum films (most writing on new modes of visualization look for trends outside of genre specificity).

The crux of the argument is that newer films in the genre such as *300* (2006, Zach Snyder), *Immortals* (2011, Tarsem Singh), *Wrath of the Titans* (2012, Jonathan Liebesman), and *300: The Rise of an Empire* (2014, Noam Murro) are less interested in revising the narrative or ideological terrain of earlier films—which remain largely conservative in their restoration-of-order narratives and their overlay of neoliberal themes onto historically incongruent material—and more concerned with pioneering new forms of bodily representation whose power as spectacles derives less from rootedness in Greco-Roman cultural milieus and more from sensations like speed and the impression of overwhelming force.[2] In particular, this essay examines how many of these recent films invest less importance in crowd scenes of the old sort, and instead imagine massed bodies as swarms, in the process engaging with the one of the most important technological/natural metaphorical images in contemporary thought. Neo-peplum films use contemporary audience anxieties about networks and multitudes to thrill, scare, and impress. While the crowds of old may find temporary expression in new peplum films, especially in moments of audiences listening to inspirational oration, emphasis has decidedly shifted to exploiting the dangerous and suprahuman valences of these groups.

Crowd Spectacles: The Greco-Roman Inheritance

Crowds are integral to traditional understandings of public communication and entertainment. In antiquity, crowds listened to oratory in the agora, marched in formation in anticipation of battle, and attended theatrical events in amphitheaters that allegorized their lives in relation to the gods. More specifically, crowds function as a necessary component of spectacle. On the one hand, a large crowd, is in and of itself, a sight to behold (this is a recurrent fascination championed by early cinema); on the other, crowds are what gather to look at spectacular entertainments. In the Roman world, for instance, spectacles included everything from watching Greek athletic contests (Zahra Newby discusses this fascination by way of Roman visual culture, specifically mosaics in Ostia and Rome) to engaging in spirited banqueting (which John Stephenson characterizes in performative and participatory terms as spectacles of engaged living that owe as much to the artifacts, objects, and opulence associated with spectacle forms as to the pleasures of experiencing).[3] Roland Auguet has outlined an anatomy of Roman spectacles as traditionally understood, noting the primacy of chariot races, gladiatorial combats, *venatio* (hunts), *naumachie* (sea battles), mythological dramas and tableaux, and theatrical representations as central forms.[4] The similarities between these events are self-evident: they are sights to behold, that intensify or expand the thrills and viscerality of everyday life.

According to Auguet, spectacles like this were "a sort of public service" that fulfilled an essential role in public life.[5] They yielded equally positive and pessimistic benefits for citizens. Positively, they worked as a chimera for egalitarianism, a temporary leveling agent. Auguet describes it as a "right" that prompted social mixing: "In Rome, the spectacles were free—one of the citizens' rights, and not a luxury, to be indulged in or not according to their tastes and means. The city, in short, assured its people their pleasures, even going so far as to organize banquets where anyone could take his seat near the rich or, if he so wished, at the rich man's table. Such a principle implies organization in the strict sense of the word. The spectacles as a whole were regular displays held at fixed intervals throughout the year and were not, if one may so put it, sufficient unto themselves."[6]

This recalls Mikhail Bakhtin's descriptions of the idea of carnival in the Middle Ages, a mix of "new" Christianity and the vestiges of residual paganism, in which, at set times in the year, social hierarchies were upended through mockery and grotesque mimicry in such celebrations as the "Feast of Fools" (a French liturgical holiday in which the people would elect leaders, like a fake Pope, from among lower orders in the Church).[7] Yet many forms of Roman spectacle also functioned negatively, as a mode of control that funneled tensions and transgressions into arenas of mass spectatorship and away from protest, uprising, or violent revenge. The Emperor Hadrian (who reigned from 117 to 138), for instance, consolidated power in this way while simultaneously propagating the reputation of Roman civilization. James Morwood writes that "the baths, the races and the bloody shows in the Colosseum gave Hadrian the opportunity to burnish the imperial image on both a small and large scale."[8] Gregory A. Borchard and Anthony J. Ferri describe the function as providing "illusions of stability" against the very real threat of enemies to ruling regimes, external and internal.[9] These two writers then proceed to compare this monumental mode of spectacle to the (sometimes overtly Greco-Roman) spectacles of contemporary Las Vegas, a move that brings to mind an analogous comparison. Like the spectacles of antiquity, cinema is a mode of mass entertainment *par excellence*, which moreover both visualizes the kinds of spectacular sights mentioned above, but also strives to find adequate aesthetic expression for their representation, such that the forms continue to embody the pleasures and anxieties that are meaningful to current audiences.

This was already a concern in the ancient world. Potentially spectacular forms such as narrative myths and architectural structures both strove for a sense of decorum, a matching of form and content that provided an alternative to official modes of literacy, in the sense that these modalities could be viewed or listened to instead of read. In her survey of Roman myths, Jane F. Gardner writes that "family legends" (outlining the family trees of the gods, from Jupiter on down) "appealed particularly to historical writers and also to orators like Cicero (even though they might sometimes express skepticism about them) because of their value as to what the Romans called *exempla*, illustrations of a particular moral truth ('what to imitate and what to avoid')."[10] On a practical level, at stake were values like familial loyalty, the learning of hierarchies, the dangers of jealousy, and so on. Put into context, these stories are fine-tuned vehicles for prioritizing the presumed social wellbeing of the context out of which they emerge. Gardner finds that the function of Roman myths is to "encourage acceptance of Roman moral priorities, in particular self-control and self-discipline, in the interests of the Roman state and its security."[11]

Drawing the abstract out of the particular was an especial talent of Greco-Roman architecture. Roland Auguet explores the symbolism of the Greek hippodrome via observations from the historian Pierre Wuilleumier: "The hippodrome was held to represent the world in miniature. The arena was the image of the earth. The *euripus* was the 'blue-green sea.'"[12] In other words, each element of the space held representative significance to the people who spectated there, whether they knew it or not. Auguet draws attention to the mad emperor Caligula (who ruled from 37–41) as particularly sensitive to the spatial qualities that make ideological or spiritual points:

As for Caligula, he had the most marked passion for creating eccentric buildings which were, so to speak, the "word for word" illustration of an abstract idea, of an expression or a phrase taken literally, in accordance with a procedure identical to that by which a legend is transformed into actuality on stage. For example, to give visual and palpable material form to symbolic identity established by his predecessors between the emperors and the gods, he had the Capitol, the temple of Jupiter (whose equal he was especially anxious to prove himself) connected to his own house by a bridge "which overtopped the temple of the divine Augustus."[13]

This was even pursued as a means of generating comedy: "Another obsession of the same prince consisted of devising 'live' anecdotes with the sole aim of deriving from them abstract expressions or entities to which their ostensibly accidental and artificial character gave a very particular humour."[14] Surprisingly, the notorious film *Caligula* (1979, Tinto Brass) actually gets at this obsession, especially in sequences that provide visual and didactic life to Caligula's (Malcolm McDowell) personal fantasies of power. For example, the blood-red wall that functions as a decapitation machine for victims who are buried in the ground up to their necks is an extreme visualization of the disjunction between state capacity for cruelty and the helplessness of the people.

In sum, spectacle in antiquity functioned in many ways, most notably as an organizing principle for gathering people and ideas into consuming entertainments that engaged the desires of the masses while serving the interests of those in power. Cinema, especially movies that reflexively look back at this period, have complementary functions. But, it is first crucial to expand on ideas about crowds and crowd formation that establish film as the main repository for group formations and anxieties.

Crowds and Cinema

If antiquity had a genius for producing crowds, then cinema proved equally adept at giving them a continued home of virtual relevance. Lesley Brill describes movies as "crowd machines," noting that "within moving pictures, indeed, the representation of crowds is commonplace, and the stories of many narrative films, like other stories, establish for the protagonists a central goal of joining, creating, or restoring a sympathetic crowd."[15] While it is perhaps most common to conceive of narrative cinema in terms of what it does to/for individual protagonists, Brill channels Elias Canetti in arguing for the absolute centrality of crowds to human experience. In *Crowds and Power*, Canetti describes the supra-individual attributes of crowds, which include density, ontological equality, and an urge to grow.[16] Humans join groups, form packs, and look to nature for ways to organize mass experience, a tendency that Canetti traces throughout history (through an anthropologically eclectic set of case studies) and that Brill finds to be intensified in cinema's burgeoning modernity. One strand of analysis that particularly interests Brill is the capacity of crowds to attack and smother oppression, in the process becoming something like crystallized social movements: "Transformation usually includes rejecting or escaping power. The authoritarian inflexibility of antagonists in movies of diverse genres embodies the hostility that power feels toward metamorphosis. Since metamorphosis is at the center of crowd formation, crowds resist power. Power, which desires isolation and uniqueness, in return opposes transformation and its attendant crowds, albeit that it may sometimes find using them expedient."[17] Crowds mutate to serve different purposes, sometimes rising to meet egalitarian or life-giving dictates.

In her book on digital effects, Kristen Whissel focuses on crowds in digital cinema. Whereas crowds for most of film history have been made from real bodies (Cecil B. DeMille's famous "cast of thousands" in *The Ten Commandments* [1956]), or their approximation (blobs on a distant matte painting), digital cinema produces new crowds with new powers: "Using a number of technologies (motion capture, 3D animation simulation programs such as MASSIVE [Multiple Agent Simulation System in Virtual Environment], digital split-screen techniques, crowd simulation engines, motion trees and libraries, and particle animation programs such as Dynamation), visual effects houses have created massive computer-generated armies, swarms, armadas, and hordes composed of as many as hundreds of thousands of digital beings—what might be called the 'digital multitude.'"[18]

For Whissel, digital "effects emblems" (similar to Canetti's "crowd symbols") "use the digital multitude to spatialize time and to emblematize their protagonists' relationship to sudden, often apocalyptic, historical change."[19] In broad strokes, digital cinema allows for new formations of grouped people and objects (some of which have no physical referent or direct indexical connection to the world) that supersede the scope and scale of analog precedent. So, while crowds can be said to remain relevant to all periods of the history of cinema, different types of crowds emerge at different moments. The internal development of the sword and sandal genre provides a compelling and historically justified location to analyze these visual developments and their attenuate anxieties.

Crowds and Movement in Earlier Peplum Films

A variety of crowd types have characterized peplum films since the genre's earliest days. In *Cabiria*, for instance, the famous Temple of Moloch scene provides an example of where cinematic spectacle dovetails with spectacle forms found in antiquity. The Carthaginian worshippers of Moloch are about to sacrifice the slave girl Cabiria (Carolina Catena) to their god, in an invocation carried out by a priest in front of a densely packed crowd of worshippers, who are bent over on the ground. Movement is supplied by flames flicking from torches, which contrasts with the large stillness of the state of their god. The sequence emphasizes its large number of bodies through the non-moving long shots common to "epic" works of silent cinema. The sequence builds to a fever pitch as Cabiria is placed on a sacrificial altar, whilst worshippers dance madly in front, their flailings contrast with the stillness of the other congregants. The sequence ends with Maciste (Bartolomeo Pagano) rescuing Cabiria. Visual attraction in *Cabiria* comes, in part, from the exaggerated facial contortions and operatic gestures of the actors. What counts is bigness and sweep, not naturalism or subtlety.

In early peplum films, there is often the sense that the crowds are destined to be subsumed to the awe-inspiring locales, settings, or set-pieces that constitute one of the primary attractions of the genre. For example, the primary spectacular appeal of the Ancient Babylonian sequences in D.W. Griffith's *Intolerance* (1916) is their capacity to overwhelm the audience by illustrating a contrast in scale. In the first sequence outside of Imgur Bel (the "Great Gate of Babylon"), the crowds are dwarfed by the architectural edifice they stand beside. This is emphasized by how the structure first enters the frame. The film cuts to a largely black screen with an iris in the lower right corner. That iris contains the part of the base of the wall. The iris then moves up and to the left, gradually revealing the size of the walls, before the iris itself opens and shows physical walls that dwarf the people below.

Examples from later in the genre's lifecycle highlight these different crowd functions to an even greater degree. In the moment of Italy's resumed flirtation with peplum films in the 1950s—Howard Hughes relates it to the inspiration provided by *Quo Vadis* (1951, Mervyn LeRoy) and *Helen of Troy* (1956, Robert Wise), both of which were filmed in Rome—the Italian film industry brought sword and sandal heroics to bear on everything from the Punic Wars to early tales of Christianity.[20] Some peplum films are outliers in their supernatural isolation of characters, like *Hercules in the Haunted World* (1961, Mario Bava), in which Hercules (Reg Park) and his companions make an expedition into Hades. Here, most of the locations are studio-based, with cavernous backgrounds (replete with Bava's famous mood lighting) and few characters in the frame at a given time.

A film like *Hannibal*, by contrast, shows the persistence of crowds to peplum films. Co-directed by Carlo Ludovico Bragaglia and Edgar G. Ulmer (whose next film, *L'Atlantide* [1961] was a costume epic about a journey to the lost underwater city, and was best described by Something Weird Video as "a sword and sandal gone screwy"), *Hannibal* engages all the prestige elements of Hollywood peplum films.²¹ A great example of one of the spectacles of crowds in "golden age" peplum films comes towards the beginning. Minitius (Franco Dominici) addresses the senate about rumors of Hannibal (Victor Mature) marching across the Alps, whereupon he is interrupted by a skeptical Fabius Maximus (Gabriele Ferzetti), who warns about imminent danger to Rome's borders. The exchange is further interrupted by soldiers entering and warning of first contact between the armies. What is so instructive about this relatively minor narrative sequence is that it appeals to slow pleasures of the genre. The senators are seated in costumed drapery. The oratory of the sequence is deliberately overblown, replete with the imagined grandeur of Roman rhetoric and civility. The visual appeal is of men dressed in a lush gloss of ancient fashion, behaving with a kind of unironic graveness and certitude that appeals to fantasies about the history of the time period. Put another way, what appeals about this sequence to audiences is the imagined fixity of the past: here are crowds of senators, grimly debating a coming war, in what now seems like a calm prototype for ideal democratic processes in periods to come.

Other films of the genre appeal to the pomp and splendor of the crowd. The Commodious parade in *The Fall of the Roman Empire* (1964, Anthony Mann), for example, combines idealized Roman costumes, a large reconstruction of the Roman forum that places bodies into an approximation of historical space, and a reliance on long shots that dwell on lines of colors that move through the streets at a slow march. The spectating crowds, including Lucilla (Sophia Loren) and Sohamus (Omar Sharif), watch in near-somnambulistic stupor. Part of the appeal for audiences of the time—something that is lost, in practice, in neo-peplum films—is the literal sense that this is a spectacle because so many people (real people) are visibly involved. Here, nearly five minutes of the film are absent of narrative movement; *The Fall of the Roman Empire* pauses to dwell on thousands of people approximating a visual display that allegorizes the glory that was Rome. A moment like this is reconstructed at the beginning of *Hail, Caesar!* (2016, Coen Brothers) as a parodic gesture of what appealed to audiences of the 1950s. Capitol Pictures star Baird Whitlock (George Clooney) appears in a lavish peplum film, that is first shown to the audience via a large-scale outdoor sequence of soldiers and captured slaves marching back to Rome. This entire pre-credit sequence shows the discipline of the legions, lets the audience delight in the detail of the costumes, and experience the imperial thrill of the brassy music. In narrative terms for the film-within-the-film, though, it does little other than to further explore the spectacle of the period, and to give with-it audiences of the 2010s some nice nods to antiquated forms of cinematic pleasure (watch for the smirk of one of the Legionnaires, which is a gesture to the kind of smug pomposity embodied by the histrionic acting styles preferred by the genre).

Hannibal also usefully illustrates how golden age peplum films visualize battle sequences. To be fair, the film excels at providing strategic justifications for the battles that it shows (the film's major battle is set up by Hannibal outlining his pincer attack plan with wine goblets on a table).[22] Much of the spectacle in this sequence comes from suspense and anticipation, the general extent to which the battle is prefigured by troop movements, discussions of strategy, and massed armies getting into position. The camera dwells on orderly Roman legions, which march toward a waiting Carthaginian army (the film cuts to shots offering well-composed tableaux of waiting Carthaginian irregular troops, posed in utter stillness, as if affixed on a decorative urn). When the clash of armies eventually does happen, the forces reach a curiously stilted parity. After charging at each other, the melee begins. While some medium shots have semi-skilled swordsmen in the foreground (with general mayhem in the background), long shots reveal a kind of stasis, with little movement beyond individual sword-fighting of paired groups. This may have to do with the film's shooting schedule. Filmed in Yugoslavia, this Battle of Cannae sequence was, according to Noah Isenberg, "shot in just five days instead of the twenty-three days that the shooting schedule called for," thus recalling Ulmer's earlier work on sub-B movies for the Producers Releasing Corporation.[23] That said, the sequence plays as representative of a common aesthetic approach to crowd spectacle in peplum films in that its principal attractions are its scale and its avowed connection to history, not its viscerality or its building of suspense. Robert A. Rushing suggests that this reliance on static posturing can be tied to mid-century peplum's reliance on bodybuilders for protagonists, and can be seen as a porting of the visual codes of bodybuilding performance to the confines of cinema.[24] More abstractly, this curious static quality also has to do with filmmaker and audience perceptions of history, which is herein ossified in all its supposed magnificence. But the representational codes and sense of faux-reverence in evidence for much of the history of peplum films gets reconfigured in the digital era.

From Crowds to Swarms

Crowd scenes of the older sort are not entirely absent from neo-peplum films. *300*, for instance, uses a crowd scene and its accompanying voice-over narration to recall its entire story. The movie is framed by Dilios' (David Wenham) speech to his soldiers, in which he both recalls the mythic history of Spartan King Leonidas (Gerard Butler) and then narrates his witnessing of the Spartan defense of the Thermopylae pass. Dilios addresses what seems to be a limited group of men (when they are first shown, it is night and only a few bodies are visible), but does so in a grandiloquent manner. The reveal of the sequence is that Dilios, a survivor of Thermopylae, is recalling his story of heroism to an assembled Greek army, who end the film claiming vengeance on the invading Persians.

Gladiator is an example of old-fashioned awe at spectating, while also looking forward to the new uses of multitudes in peplum films of the last fifteen years. The plot of *Gladiator* revolves around the pleasures of the crowd. Maximus (Russell Crowe) is a general of the Roman army ousted by new ruler Commodus (Joaquin Phoenix). Maximus regains his honor by fighting gladiatorial battles, eventually working his way back to Rome, where he faces Commodus (whose life succeeds or fails by the will of the crowd as much as Maximus') in a seemingly rigged match. Shot in 1999 and released in 2000, the film used computer generated "tiles" to multiply the number of spectating extras to become a massive crowd, a technique which Page duBois argues lends a sinister air to the film: "The vague, blurry sense of the crowd, then, experienced by the viewer, comes from this manipulation of a few thousand extras, who stand in for the masses, who are given bread along with their circus, and who are always potential enemies of the hero, in fact, to be swayed by the spectacle of death before them, unlike the real masses of *Spartacus*, which represents not just the opposing Roman legions, but also the individual faces and figures of the slave army and its accompanying slave community."[25] The threat suggested by digital crowds is an abiding obsession of neo-peplum films. There is an irony, of course: never have comparably so few physical bodies been used to represent or construct such overwhelming numbers.

Kristen Whissel argues that "the digital multitude enables these films to mediate recent geopolitical realities in a broad, polyvalent, and flexible fashion."[26] One of the threats that recent peplum films identify, and imagine in massed digital form, are crowds of enemy actors whose numbers, motives, and weaknesses are hard to parse. The fear that these films articulate—a fear as much based in social anxieties, or military problems, of the 2000s as a fear for characters in an imagined historical diegesis—is of swarms, collectivities of mutually enforced relations that almost spontaneously act as one, and of swarming, a focused kind of isolation and attack.[27] In their discussion of expanding forms of "netwar" (networked warfare), John Arquilla and David Ronfeldt describe swarming as "a seemingly amorphous, but deliberately structured, coordinated, strategic way to strike from all directions at a particular point or points, by means of a sustainable pulsing of force and/or fire, close-in as well as from stand-off positions."[28] It is a mode of waging war designed to make best use of what, historically, might have been seen as tactical disadvantages: "Swarming will work best—perhaps it will only work—if it is designed mainly around the deployment of myriad, small, dispersed, networked maneuver units. Swarming occurs when the dispersed units of a network of small (and perhaps some large) forces converge on a target from multiple directions. The overall aim is sustainable pulsing—swarm networks must be able to coalesce rapidly and stealthily on a target, then dissever and redisperse, immediately ready to recombine for a new pulse."[29] In contemporary conflicts, the swarm is the preferred form of terrorist cells and social activists, who group and disperse as circumstances warrant. While Arquilla and Ronfeldt ultimately advocate for conventional militaries to master the tactics of networked warfare (including swarming) so as to be able to stop them, films produced in Western contexts usually map the qualities of swarms onto enemy forces, the irrationally feared Other, or onto magical/non-human forces. What many neo-peplum films articulate is a fear of the swarm, often by pitting bulwarks of conventional military wisdom against this new and mysterious configuration of fighting.

300, again, uses this anxiety as part of its plot. While the official fear of the characters within the film is of the lumbering size of the invading army, their strategic setup is marked by a fear of swarms. The tactic on which the Spartans rely, which serves them well for as long as it can, is to funnel threats into a narrow field of battle—the mouth of the Thermopylae Pass—and use their ability to fight as a single, disciplined unit to their advantage. The fear is of being surrounded, of having to defend against multiple locations of attack, which eventually leads to their downfall thanks to the spurned Ephialtes (Andrew Tiernan) giving guidance to the Persians.

In *300: Rise of an Empire*, there is a visual motif throughout of atomized Greek soldiers that are surrounded and attacked by multiple assailants. A Greek spy that has been captured on one of Artemisia's (Eva Green) ships breaks free, but is pounced upon from all sides. During the Battle of Marathon, Themistocles (Sullivan Stapleton) is often surrounded, which provides an opportunity for him to display has prowess at handling multiple assailants, but which creates another dichotomy between the multitudinous horde and the valiant loner. During the opening portions of the sea-based Battle of Artemisium, Greek ships are encircled by the Persian armada, and it is only through the directional concentration of force (the ramming of the middle of enemy ships) that the Greeks live to fight another day.

Neo-peplum films frequently show how supernatural forces embody the qualities of the swarm. One example of combining a mythological tradition with a recent fear is in the sequence towards the beginning of *Clash of the Titans* (2010, Louis Leterrier) in which harpies commanded by Hades (Ralph Fiennes) attack soldiers who have just felled a statue of Zeus. They are surrounded, attacked in pulsing waves by harpies that swoop in and claw, bite, or carry away the offending soldiers. The camera encircles the soldiers and constantly changes position during the sequence to convey the disorientation being experienced by the men under attack. Sometimes, films even embody multiple (seemingly contradictory) kinds of threat into one figuration. In *Wrath of the Titans* "human" tactics of conventional warfare (the Greek phalanx, the measured advance of the disciplined hoplite) are pitted against Kronos, whose forces embody an alien hellscape. Kronos emerges from underground captivity with an eruption, a seemingly random bombardment of comet-like fireballs that transform into a cohort of multi-armed lava men, which immediately yield a sense of unpredictability in both protagonists and film audience. This sequence shows a fear of fluidity and shape-changing, as the human defenders are constantly facing new threats that render their instincts moot. These dangers come from all sides, with camera angles that once again accentuate the chaos. Most instructive is Kronos itself, the ultimate destructive force in the film, a single body made of multitudinous substances (lava, dust, absorptive obsidian). This suggests that, for all their anxiety about the non-hierarchical possibilities of swarms, most neo-peplum films still locate hierarchical responsibility somewhere, usually in something approximating a video game boss (from historical figures like Xerxes to mythological creatures to gods themselves).

Perhaps the film that best illustrates the newly spectacular dynamic of crowd scenes in peplum films is *Immortals*. The movie explicitly differentiates supernatural and human actants, often giving heavenly or supernatural forces a different relationship to time itself. Unlike in *300*, the manipulation of time as a means of conveying action is justified within the diegesis. The audience learns about this "magic time" early, for instance, when the Epirus Bow is first fired (there is what in analog cinema would have been called an undercranked frame rate and an accompanying artificial blur, to suggest that magical movement can slow down the rest of the world to achieve its ends).

The large battle sequence between the eponymous immortals and the imprisoned Titans is virtually the crystallization of the swarm anxiety. While men lead by Theseus (Henry Cavill) clash with the armies of King Hyperion (Mickey Rourke), gods clash with their physical equals. The Titans are a superhuman group of undifferentiated bodies, a fighting force that attacks in pulsing swarms with tenacity. Zeus (Luke Evans) and the rest of the gods fight the Titans to suppress them, in hopes that they do not escape their prison and invade the Earth. Despite each of the gods displaying unmatched skill in fighting, often attending to multiple Titans at once, and seemingly manipulating time and space at will, the threat of the Titan swarm (a seemingly endless attack that wears down the isolated defenders and exploits their weaknesses) is too much, and the situation can only be resolved through a minor apocalyptic gesture: Zeus destroys Mount Tartarus and teleports out with the wounded Poseidon (Kellan Lutz). In contemporary terms, only the equivalent to a missile or a bomb can suppress the threat of the swarm.

Conclusion

Despite a newfound reliance on digital technology, peplum films have always tried to engage audiences by giving them access to fantastic displays to which they can aspire or empathize. As Robert Rushing reminds, peplum films (then as now) are built around the display of bodies, in particular an audience's relationship to the bodies under threat.[30] More generally, audiences watch peplum films because they offer spectacles—not just spectacles of the trials and tribulations of people in antiquity or in its mythological equivalents, but also spectacles that engage the basic attractions of cinema. Cinema (in its dominant forms) supplies exotic locales, lavish costumes, impressively recreated buildings, comely actors, and most importantly for the purposes of this essay, crowds of all sorts. While crowds have always mattered to peplum films, digital crowds in particular induce new anxieties about stability and otherness. In particular, digital manipulations of speed and bodies echoes audience fears about new modes of warfare and protest that, far from being ossified into the ancient past, are alive in the headlines of the present.

NOTES

1. Colin MacArthur, *Underworld USA* (London: BFI, 1972), 23–35.
2. For a discussion of ideology in sword and sandal films, see Kevin M. Flanagan, "'Civilization ... Ancient and Wicked,': Historicizing the Ideological Field of Sword and Sandal Films," in *Of Muscles and Men: Essays on the Sword and Sandal Film*, ed. Michael G. Cornelius (Jefferson, NC: McFarland, 2011), 87–103.
3. Zahra Newby, "Greek Athletics as Roman Spectacle: The Mosaics from Ostia and Rome," *Papers of the British School at Rome* 70 (2002): 177–203, especially 180–186; John Stephenson, "Dining as Spectacle in Late Roman Houses," *Bulletin of the Institute of Classical Studies* 59.1 (June 2016): 54–56.
4. Roland Auguet, *Cruelty and Civilization: The Roman Games* (London: Routledge, 1994 [1972]), 17–18.
5. *Ibid.*, 184.
6. *Ibid.*, 17.
7. Mikhail Bakhtin, *Rabelais and His World*, trans. Helene Iswolsky (Bloomington: Indiana University Press, 1984 [1965]), esp. 74–81; Max Harris, "Feast of Fools," in *Oxford Bibliographies in Medieval Studies*, http://www.oxfordbibliographies.com/view/document/obo-9780195396584/obo-9780195396584-0078.xml (accessed 12 Dec. 2016).
8. James Morwood, *Hadrian* (New York: Bloomsbury Academic, 2013), 47.
9. Gregory A. Borchard and Anthony J. Ferri, "When in Vegas, Do as the Ancient Romans Did: Bread and Circuses Then and Now," *Journal of Popular Culture* 44.4 (Aug. 2011): 717.
10. Jane F. Gardner, *Roman Myths* (London: British Museum Press, 1993), 9.
11. *Ibid.*, 53.
12. Auguet, 143.
13. *Ibid.*, 105.
14. *Ibid.*, 106.
15. Lesley Brill, *Crowds, Power and Transformation in Cinema* (Detroit: Wayne State University Press, 2006), 1.
16. Elias Canetti, *Crowds and Power*, trans. Carol Stewart (New York: Continuum, 1981 [1960]), 29.
17. Brill, 189.

18. Kristen Whissel, *Spectacular Digital Effects: CGI and Contemporary Cinema* (Durham: Duke University Press, 2014), 59–60.
19. *Ibid.*, 60.
20. Howard Hughes, *Cinema Italiano: The Complete Guide from Classics to Cult* (New York: I.B. Tauris, 2011), 49, 55.
21. For a discussion of *L'Atlantide*'s paracinematic qualities and my source for the Something Weird description, see Kevin Heffernan, "'A Sword and Sandal Gone Screwy' or, Edgar G. Ulmer's Journey to the Lost City—*L'Atlantide*," in *Edgar G. Ulmer: Detour on Poverty Row*, ed. Gary D. Rhodes (Lanham, MD: Lexington Books, 2008), 263–271.
22. This is not necessarily to be taken as an accurate reflection of ancient military understanding. According to Victor Davis Hanson: "Few formal strategic doctrines have survived from antiquity. No college of military historians wrote systematic theoretical treatises on the proper use of military force to further political objectives. Although there are extant tactical treatises on how to defend cities under siege, the proper role of a cavalry commander, and how to arrange and deploy a Macedonian phalanx or a Roman legion, there are no explicit works on the various ways in which national power is to be harnessed for strategic purposes. Great captains did not write memoirs outlining strategic doctrine or military theory in the abstract." See Victor Davis Hanson, "Introduction: Makers of Ancient Strategy: From the Persian Wars to the Fall of Rome," in *Makers of Ancient Strategy: From Persian Wars to the Fall of Rome*, ed. Victor Davis Hanson (Princeton: Princeton University Press, 2010), 9. Though, to be fair, Howard Hughes likes the battle sequence that results: "The battle scenes are a mixture of large-scale location scenes, intercut with studio-bound re-enactments. Cannae is particularly impressive, with the Roman legions advancing across a yellowing grass valley when the Carthaginians spring their ambush, leading to a melee involving hundreds of extras." See Hughes, 56.
23. Noah Isenberg, *Edgar G. Ulmer: A Filmmaker at the Margins* (Berkeley: University of California Press, 2014), 240.
24. Robert A. Rushing, "Skin Flicks: Haptic Ideology in the Peplum Film," *Cinema Journal* 56.1 (Fall 2016): 101.
25. Page duBois, *Slavery: Antiquity and Its Legacy* (New York: Oxford University Press, 2009), 137.
26. Whissel, 88.
27. For more on the ontology of swarms, see Eugene Thacker, "Networks, Swarms, Multitudes: Part Two," *CTheory* (May 2004): http://www.ctheory.net/articles.aspx?id=423, accessed December 21, 2016.
28. John Arquilla and David Ronfeldt, *Networks and Netwars: The Future of Terror, Crime, and Militancy* (Washington, D.C.: Rand Corporation, 2001), 12.
29. *Ibid.*
30. Rushing, 100.

BIBLIOGRAPHY

Arquilla, John, and David Ronfeldt. *Networks and Netwars: The Future of Terror, Crime, and Militancy.* Washington, D.C.: Rand Corporation, 2001.
Auguet, Roland. *Cruelty and Civilization: The Roman Games.* London: Routledge, 1994 (1972).
Bakhtin, Mikhail. *Rabelais and His World*, trans. Helene Iswolsky. Bloomington: Indiana University Press, 1984 (1965).
Ben-Hur. Directed by William Wyler. 1959. Burbank, CA: Warner Home Video, 2004. DVD.
Borchard, Gregory and Anthony J. Ferri, "When in Vegas, Do as the Ancient Romans Did: Bread and Circuses Then and Now." *Journal of Popular Culture* 44.4 (Aug. 2011): 717–731.
Brill, Lesley. *Crowds, Power and Transformation in Cinema.* Detroit: Wayne State University Press, 2006.
Cabiria. Directed by Giovanni Pastrone. 1914. New York: Kino Video, 2000. DVD
Caligula. Directed by Tinto Brass. 1979. Hollywood: Image Entertainment, 2007. DVD.
Clash of the Titans. Directed by Louis Leterrier. 2010. Burbank, CA: Warner Home Video, 2010. DVD.

Canetti, Elias. *Crowds and Power*, trans. Carol Stewart. New York: Continuum, 1981 [1960].
duBois, Page. *Slavery: Antiquity and Its Legacy*. New York: Oxford University Press, 2009.
Fall of the Roman Empire. Directed by Anthony Mann. 1964. Santa Monica, CA: Genius Products, 2008. DVD.
Flanagan, Kevin M. "'Civilization ... ancient and wicked,': Historicizing the Ideological Field of Sword and Sandal Films." In *Of Muscles and Men: Essays on the Sword and Sandal Film*, edited by Michael G. Cornelius, 87–103. Jefferson, NC: McFarland, 2011.
Gardner, Jane F. *Roman Myths*. London: British Museum Press, 1993.
Gladiator. Directed by Ridley Scott. 2000. Universal City, CA: Dreamworks Video, 2000. DVD.
Hail, Caesar! Directed by Joel and Ethan Coen. 2016. Universal City, CA: Universal Studios Home Entertainment, 2016. Blu-Ray.
Hannibal. Directed by Carlo Ludovico Bragaglia and Edgar G. Ulmer. 1959. Tulsa: VCI Entertainment, 2004. DVD.
Hanson, Victor Davis. "Introduction: Makers of Ancient Strategy: From the Persian Wars to the Fall of Rome," in *Makers of Ancient Strategy: From Persian Wars to the Fall of Rome*, edited by Victor Davis Hanson, 1–10. Princeton: Princeton University Press, 2010.
Harris, Max. "Feast of Fools." In *Oxford Bibliographies in Medieval Studies*, http://www.oxfordbibliographies.com/view/document/obo-9780195396584/obo-9780195396584-0078.xml. Accessed 12 Dec. 2016.
Heffernan, Kevin. "'A Sword and Sandal Gone Screwy' or, Edgar G. Ulmer's Journey to the Lost City—*L'Atlantide*," in *Edgar G. Ulmer: Detour on Poverty Row*, edited by Gary D. Rhodes, 263–271. Lanham, MD: Lexington Books, 2008.
Helen of Troy. Directed by Robert Wise. 1956. Burbank, CA: Warner Home Video, 2004. DVD.
Hercules in the Haunted World. Directed by Mario Bava. 1961. Amazon Video.
Hercules Unchained. Directed by Pietro Francisci. 1959. West Conshohocken, PA, 2002. DVD.
Hughes, Howard. *Cinema Italiano: The Complete Guide from Classics to Cult*. New York: I.B. Tauris, 2011.
Immortals. Directed by Tarsem Singh. 2011. Los Angeles: 20th Century Fox Video, 2012. DVD.
Intolerance. Directed by D.W. Griffith. 1916. New York: Kino Video, 2002. DVD.
Isenberg, Noah. *Edgar G. Ulmer: A Filmmaker at the Margins*. Berkeley: University of California Press, 2014.
L'Atlantide/Journey Beneath the Desert. Directed by Edgar G. Ulmer. 1961. Seattle: Something Weird Video. DVD.
MacArthur, Colin. *Underworld USA*. London: BFI, 1972.
Morwood, James. *Hadrian*. New York: Bloomsbury Academic, 2013.
Newby, Zahra. "Greek Athletics as Roman Spectacle: The Mosaics from Ostia and Rome." *Papers of the British School at Rome* 70 (2002): 177–203.
Quo Vadis. Directed by Mervyn LeRoy. 1951. Burbank, CA: Warner Home Video, 2008. DVD.
Rushing, Robert A. "Skin Flicks: Haptic Ideology in the Peplum Film." *Cinema Journal* 56.1 (Fall 2016): 88–110.
Stephenson, John. "Dining as Spectacle in Late Roman Houses." *Bulletin of the Institute of Classical Studies* 59.1 (June 2016): 54–71.
The Ten Commandments. Directed by Cecil B. DeMille. 1956. Burbank, CA: Warner Home Video, 2011. DVD.
Thacker, Eugene. "Networks, Swarms, Multitudes: Part Two." *CTheory* (May 2004): http://www.ctheory.net/articles.aspx?id=423. Accessed 21 Dec. 2016.
300. Directed by Zach Snyder. 2006. Burbank, CA: Warner Home Video, 2008. DVD.
300: Rise of an Empire. Directed by Noam Murro. 2014. Burbank, CA: Warner Home Video, 2014. Blu-Ray.
Whissel, Kristen. *Spectacular Digital Effects: CGI and Contemporary Cinema*. Durham: Duke University Press, 2014.
Wrath of the Titans. Directed by Jonathan Liebesman. 2012. Burbank, CA: Warner Home Video, 2012. DVD.

PART TWO: WISDOM FROM THE GODS:
MYTHOLOGICAL ADAPTATIONS

There Are No Boundaries for Our Boats
Vikings *and the Westernization of the Norse Saga*

STEVE NASH

Mythology and mythmaking are crucial to navigating through an increasingly textualized world. Caught between texts, armed with only a schematic cognition of the narratives and metanarratives that have been inherited along the way to make sense of it all, critical reading forges ahead constructing new meaning and configurations. The following essay seeks to examine the reconfiguration of traditional Nordic modes of narrative to better fit a more clearly Western approach to storytelling, as is evident in the recent example of neo-peplum television series, *Vikings* (2013–present).

Utilizing the television show's source material: *Ragnar's Saga Loðbrókar*, and *Ragnarssona þáttr*, in addition to the *Poetic Edda* and *Prose Edda* of Snorri Sturluson, and with broader reference to the skaldic verse tradition, this essay will interrogate a possible major distinction between the authorial approaches to narrative. Deleuze and Guattari's notion of the rhizome (the unstructured and decentered, root-like, system of thought) is integral to the positing of a philosophy that distinguishes between these storytelling traditions, and it is difficult to underestimate the significance of the story, and the art of its telling, within the Nordic tradition. As Neil Price argues, "there is very good evidence to suggest that the Vikings lived in an intensely storied world."[1] A side-effect of both temporal distance and a culture so fixated on the telling of tales is that confronting the sagas and *Eddas* (whose dates of composition are, as shall be shown, uncertain) is to confront the dissolution of the border between myth and history. These stories may delve into fantasy, but they also describe some characters who certainly existed. The stories may have merged the actions of disparate figures into acts of individual heroism, and the bloodlines of some may be called into question (particularly the subjects of *Vikings* itself–Ragnar and his sons), but to acknowledge this is certainly not to disavow the significance of the stories and their role in the construction of a cultural identity. As Price suggests, "even when sources from such a wide diachronic and diatopic range are conflated, and even when subjected to the most rigorous critique, one is left with the unavoidable implication that the period they claim to describe was nevertheless filled with tales."[2]

The acknowledged conflation of the source material will be examined, as will the limitations of texts that have passed through generations of retellings both orally and through written translation, however the mobility and shapeshifting of the sagas can also be positively identified as a markedly appropriate aspect of their character. Price suggests that the attempt to even categorize the form of these texts is a fruitless task due to their nebulous nature: "Terminology is deceptive here, and in this light it is worth remembering that the Norse themselves did not know about 'the Norse myths.' It is important to understand that Viking-Age people need not have seen any reason to separate these categories and instead may have viewed them as a seamless whole."[3]

The Nordic sagas are presented in forms that reject clear delineation, chronology, borders, and boundaries. They are rhizomatic. The traditional Western mode of narrative is, what Deleuze and Guattari would define as, arborescent. It is structured, hierarchical, without a governing or organizing leader.[4] Therefore it would be reasonable to suspect that the shift that occurs, in the reconfiguring of the traditional Nordic tale, for a contemporary Western audience in the television narrative, is a shift from the rhizomatic to the arborescent. Even the title must be acknowledged as a remnant from an obsessive desire to categorize. While the title *Vikings* will be scrutinized in greater detail further on, it is worth acknowledging that it remains a highly reductive categorization of a broad and multifaceted culture. For now though, as Björn Sundmark suggests, "the Viking has ultimately become a deracinated and commodified symbol: a free-floating signifier and a wayward warrior."[5]

The rhizomatic represents a breakdown of the authoritarian structures that guide traditional Western narrative practice. Leonard Lawlor suggests that what Deleuze postulates in his theory of "the worst" is not the breakdown of these barriers, but the reaction to this breakdown.[6] If the barriers are transgressed, or are revealed to be illusory, then the reaction of the Western author is often to impose or reassert these barriers with greater force. This amounts to an act of authorial violence against the reader or viewer. In the context of *Vikings*, this presents a paradox. In this retelling of a history (that Deleuze and Guattari would term a "nomadology, the opposite to history") about a people obsessed with infinite passage and the rejection of boundaries, it is the freedom of the rhizomatic that has been eschewed in favor of structure.[7]

As will be argued, the original sagas and *Eddas* represent a nomadology but in their reconfiguration for the screen, has this become a history, with the figures navigating the tales no longer in passage, no longer in flight? Or to put it another way, is *Vikings* another evidentiary exhibit for Sundmark's claim, "Today we have only the horns?"[8]

Rites of Passage: The Nebulous Nature of "Viking"

The image of the Viking that most readily reveals itself is one of a seafaring folk, bent on ransacking villages in a bloodthirsty quest for riches and entertainment, their famously anachronistic horned helmets perched atop mounds of auburn hair. However, while it is evident that such an image is, at best, reductive or more likely, outright false, Erika Sigurdson notes that recently this generalizing image has become one of the choice Viking weapons in fighting back against the old received impression: "Rape and pillage acts as shorthand for any and all Viking crimes, whether real or purely fictional. Paradoxically, the phrase has become enshrined in the rhetoric of debunking, or at least problematizing, the simplistic notion of bloodthirsty Vikings."[9]

The image of the Viking then, and the meaning of the word, has clearly experienced considerable transformation over the past millennium, and seems yet to have found a suitable resting place. The sense of the nebulous extends far beyond the labeling of the people. Equally illusive is any universal consensus on the precise period of the Viking age. Sundmark, in addition to emphasizing the obscurity of the etymology of the term "Viking," regards the era as critically subjective, as she states that "the Viking Age is also difficult to pinpoint exactly; it depends on one's perspective. But the precondition for the Viking expansion was that new shipbuilding technology allowed young men to seek their fortune on the seas at a time when the population increased in the Scandinavian countries (8th and 9th centuries)."[10]

With the era itself being so elusive, it is little surprise then that the precise lifetime of the main protagonist of *Vikings*, Ragnar Lothbrok (Travis Fimmel), is similarly open to debate. Though texts such as *The Death Song of Ragnar Lodbrog*, and *Ragnar's Saga Loðbrókar*, have helped to provide a vague window regarding the show's erstwhile Viking King, attempts to date his existence precisely have proved fruitless. As Robert Rix has noted, "scholars differed widely when it came to the date of Ragnar's demise. Both the eighth and ninth centuries were offered as possibilities."[11] While terminology and chronology have provided an ambiguous basis for the recreation of Ragnar's saga for television, geography, one may think, should reveal some fixity in terms of place. Though there is acknowledgment of a vague Scandinavian setting, scholarship has revealed the Scandinavian Kings to have been an oddly placeless group. Each may have lain claim to the fealty of various clans but Scandinavia's Kings existed in a culture where "the custom of not having a fixed place of royal residence or single center of political power runs deep ... these individuals probably never were geographically static."[12] This rhizomatic sense of place is something that history has predictably attempted to arrest. This is evident in the region which Ragnar's son (a character of growing significance in the television show) Ivar (Alex Høgh Andersen) famously lay claim to: The Kingdom of York. It is now believed that Ivar's great army held a much more substantial area of land than that "evidence we have suggests that their English dominion in the tenth century consisted not simply of Northumbrian territory, but of Lincoln and (probably) the other five boroughs, perhaps periodically supplemented by some kind of related tributary overlordship in neighbouring Anglo-Scandinavian and English territory."[13] There is more to be productively gained from a closer look at Ragnar's televisual and (depending on the text) literary/historical sons. Ivar "The Boneless" is of particular significance for his historical importance, his name, and his infamous link with one particularly key scene from the television show: the rite of the blood eagle, which will be detailed further on in this essay. It would be imprudent however not to allow Ragnar himself to draw the initial focus.

It will be of little surprise to those familiar with the History Channel's original series that the Ragnar found in the skaldic verse of the death song and in the sagas is a character constructed through contradiction. From a serious-minded farmer and reluctant warrior, Rix suggests that, in the death song, "Ragnar is reconceived as a carousing character performing a merry drinking song."[14] In the death song, even whilst singing his final words, dying in a pit filled with snakes, Ragnar finds enough defiance and levity to laugh as he meets his end:

> I desire my death now.
> The desir call me home,
> whom Herjan hastens onward
> from his hall, to take me.
> On the high bench, boldly,
> beer I'll drink with the Gods;
> hope of life is lost now—
> laughing shall I die![15]

But whether or not Ragnar fits the archetype for the accepted image of the Viking, a figure that "often represents a very specific form of masculinity, one that encompasses notions of violence, dominance, and other aggressive traits," is certainly open to question.[16] One of the key complications here is that of translation. Continual reinvention, reinterpretation, and misunderstanding, has led to the representation of a figure folding inwards and outwards in a festival of multiplicity. The translatory misunderstandings have contributed to the creation of some of the most prevalent assumptions regarding the Viking figure. Even the image of halls of triumphant Viking warriors drinking from the skulls of their victims' heads, Rix claims, is owed to a single misinterpretation of skaldic verse.[17] For Ragnar though, it is perhaps his cultural reinvention, variously softened or sharpened to suit the wants of each translator's day, and reinvigoration of his character (of which *Vikings* can be considered simply the most recent variation) that has maintained his position as a figure of intrigue in the Western consciousness. As Rix states, "If Ragnar's ghost, as it came to haunt British imagination, looked somewhat different from his original incarnation in a Norse context, British translators and commentators had at least managed to acclimatize Ragnar, enabling him to wander into the midst of mainstream national culture."[18] Naturally, what is true of Ragnar is also true of the narratives themselves, and while Viking identity is demonstrably fluid, it is also important to acknowledge such fluidity in the source material and its creation. Slavica Rankovic outlines this rhizomatic nature of the sagas by suggesting: "In fact, the multilocal, decentralized production of the sagas of Icelanders ... supported the centrifugality of the traditional medium, allowing perspectives on past events and characters, accrued through time, to meet, compete, and negotiate."[19]

All Change: The Fluidity of Vikings' Source Material

It would be fairly innocuous to suggest that, due to such nebulous formation, the sagas, death song, and *Eddas* are chimerical creations, built by accretion, with each new interpreter or translator adding to an ever growing narrative. However, such a reading underestimates the complexity of the materials' history and heritage. Rankovic warns against such an interpretation by arguing that "the danger ... is that authorship of traditional texts would be conceived of in terms of mere adage, that is, it brings to mind a tidy string of individuals each making a definable contribution in this 'Chinese whisper' chain stretching back into the murky depths of unrecorded history."[20] Equally problematic for any attempt to create an authoritative representation of the history of Ragnar and his sons is the decidedly alien form of the original writings. Matthew Townend asserts that "skaldic verse ... is notoriously non-narrative," perhaps even rhizomatic, and any attempt to impose a more recognizably Western or linear form is a shift toward a coherent structure, a move toward the arborescent.[21] Stefanie von Schnurbein supports Townend's view of the complexity of skaldic verse by suggesting "these sources ... hardly demonstrate any coherence in and of themselves, as skaldic verse is itself a highly complex literary genre characterized by multi-coded metaphor."[22] It is not just within the plot or form of this source material that lines are blurred though. Wax and Wax argued as recently as the midpoint of the previous century that the sagas had, for the majority of readers, blurred the line been reality and fiction: "the sagas were long regarded by scholars as unique monuments of painstakingly correct recording, a misconception which has only recently been refuted."[23] The complexity of the source material and its origin, is analogous to the nebulous term and definition of Viking and this is made further evident through the sagas' conspicuously convoluted formation. Pernille Hermann explains that the word "saga" (i.e., "narrative") itself draws attention to this specific way of artificial organization, which clearly indicates that in the medieval period, it was fully accepted that memories could be mediated in narrative form.[24]

The *Poetic* and *Prose Eddas* of Snorri Sturluson present a particularly significant point of reference in this context. Wax and Wax give some useful background for Sturluson's work and *Vikings'* other source material: "Much of the *Poetic Edda*, the skaldic poetry, and some of the Family Sagas were composed in pre–Christian times, probably during the ninth, tenth, and eleventh centuries, and transmitted orally. Certain parts of the *Poetic Edda* may reach back as far as the fifth century, while the Family Sagas, for the most part were, relate events occurring in late pagan and early Christian times."[25]

Even here, though, in what can be reliably described as the most well-known (at least in to the western reader) of the Old-Norse literatures, issues of ownership and authorship are not as straightforward as one may expect. While the predictable misunderstandings and misinterpretations have contributed to the *Eddas* as much as the sagas, the legitimacy of Snorri Sturluson as author of the Eddas has been called into question.[26] Regardless of the thorny issue of authorship, there are further questions regarding the purpose of the original works. The *Eddas* in particular are multifaceted texts that tread a unique path between forms; between historical account, epic poem, and educational treatise, as Schnurbein outlines, "the Icelandic scholar, author, and politician Snorri Sturluson wrote the work as a textbook on the art of skaldic verse."[27] That a textbook should become the partial basis for a recent media narrative is appropriate considering the extent to which these texts blur the boundary between history and fiction. It would seem that the ambiguous nature of the *Eddas*, and their continued shapeshifting, is a trait shared by the sagas: "Skaldicists are becoming more aware that saga-authors did not always correctly interpret the early verses from which they quarried their historical information."[28]

It is at least clear then that any attempt to judge *Vikings* as a cultural artifact against its adherence to source material is misguided. Perhaps it would be more appropriate to discuss the approach to translation and interpretation as being accurate to a certain tone or atmosphere rather than the strict faithfulness to fairly arbitrary narrative details. Hollander gestures toward this valuable focus on feel rather than narrative precision: "Obviously, in the rendering of the sense of a passage it frequently may be necessary, owing to deep-going differences between archaic Old Norse and Modern English, to let whole stanzas go into the melting pot, to be entirely recast in conformity with English syntax. To do this, without serious damage to the spirit of the original, naturally is the hardest part of the translator's task."[29] This circumventing of narrative specificity in favor of tone, or general feel, merely presents further questions: How then should the tone of these diverse and nebulous texts be defined? What characterizes this notoriously difficult and ambiguous writing? A potential response can be found in the already noted placelessness of the characters that populate the tales. When Kevin Wanner argues that "there seems to me little warrant for situating them in a spatially central position or even for thinking that our sources for Norse myth posit any further any definite or absolute cosmological center," he is supporting a view of Norse identity that, despite its diversity, is characterized by one key trait: a rejection of centrality.[30] The space of Nordic history, it seems, is that of liminality and fluidity.

Two Journeys: Skaldic Verse and the Eddas

Skaldic verse may technically be a distinct mode of literature in its own right, but evidence suggests that the various forms that constitute the cultural understanding (and the television show's source material) share a great deal in terms of content and construction. They are individuated yet networked in their evolution, as Hermann explains: "the sagas and the whole of Old Norse literature is an intertextual whole ... any individual saga is intertextually connected to other sagas and to other Old Norse genres."[31] Part of the evolution of the texts has come through reinvention and translation, which has further perforated any boundaries between the original stories in addition to destabilizing the skaldic verses. Russell Poole, examining the translations of the skaldic verses argues that "often inconsistencies between verse and prose were allowed to stand, perhaps as a result of misinterpretation ... the result of all this is that the majority of poems can only be presented in modern editions as a jumble of stanzas, a few of which will only have dubious claims to the place which they occupy."[32] This has been partially acknowledged as an inevitable side effect of texts which have been so heavily influenced by, and constructed through, an oral medium or tradition. But, just as the boundary between history and fiction is revealed to be porous, so too the distinction between the oral and the written tradition is revealed to be fragile. It may ultimately be misleading to emphasize the significance of narrative in skaldic verse, because the form seems to be less concerned with expressing any sense of a recognizable narrative, than it is with upholding the fashion of the writer's or speaker's day: "the work *Edda* has its setting in Skaldic culture and that Skaldic poetry was full of obscure kennings, synonyms, etc., that were accepted because they were in vogue, not because their origin could be understood."[33]

As with skaldic verse and the sagas, there is a similar lack of consensus regarding much of the *Eddas*' origins. Le Roy Andrews' research offers a useful temporal window, but the specifics remain elusive: "Accepting ... the broad period of 800–1250 as that of the Eddic poems, we are at once confronted by the problem of dating them more exactly. Are they nearer 800 or 1250 or about half way between? ... Within the limits of several possibilities it cannot be said that scholarly opinion has yet reached any generally accepted agreement."[34] The texts themselves are certainly not straightforward subject matter for any reader, scholar, translator, or would-be adapter. Hollander describes the *Poetic Edda* as a text that "fairly bristles with difficulties of all kinds," and regardless of attempts to critically analyze and interpret the work, it appears that "they have not yet been entirely disentangled."[35,36] Yet, in spite of the various pitfalls and leaking boats awaiting the scholar of these Scandinavian texts, it seems that there is a definable shared ethos that unites them, and this can certainly be demonstrated through the Eddic texts. When Price argues that "although fully aware of genre and subject, he [Snorri Sturluson] did not make the same distinctions between 'heroic' and 'mythological' works that are common in critical traditions today," what is presented is a further example of the rhizomatic.[37]

The rhizomatic is also noted by Hermann with the emphasis on the surprising lack of distinction between the different sagas: "the textual repetitions, which would have been enforced and reorganized during transmission, are crucial when it comes to the intriguing question of how firm the boundaries between the different saga genres actually were."[38] What is revealed is a literature that evades capture whilst rejecting boundaries. Frank suggests that the usually distinct modes of writing and performance found themselves facing equally confronting frequent overlap; the border between the two rendered as porous as the limits between the sagas.[39] Even the instances of the appearance of skaldic song within the sagas seem to share an affinity with the rhizomatic. They are spontaneous, unbidden, and emphasize the fluidity of the form, "in key moments throughout the sagas the heroes break into improvised poems ... the focus is always on the interpretation of the present moment."⁴⁰ Ultimately the source material supports the image of the Vikings as a people hostile toward central control, whose history and mythology supports a philosophy of perpetual movement and flight. The question remains then, how does *Vikings* respond to this fluidity?

Boneless and the Brother's War: Vikings as a 21st Century Translation

Vikings (currently airing its fourth season at the time of writing) offers a lavish representation of the sagas of Ragnar and his sons, that opts for a historically authentic retelling of the elusive source material. Sigurdson suggests that "the series puts great attention into historicizing details, aiming for historical realism through the lavish use of dirt and blood as well as battle scenes."⁴¹ As with the retelling and constructing of history itself, this often results in the reducing of nebulous source details and dates into a singular, linear, timeline allowing for a straightforward chronology. Ragnar's death song is of particular significance to the series. Rix explains that the poem "was among the first Norse poems to receive attention and find translation into English ... the speaker in the poem is the semi-legendary Scandinavian King Ragnar Loðbrók, who recalls his warrior feats from a pit of poisonous snakes, into which he has been thrown by his enemy, King Ella of Northumbria."⁴²

In the death song Ragnar recounts his battles, talks of vengeance through his sons, and spares time for a final laugh at death. This version of Ragnar will certainly be recognizable in the permanently amused face of Ragnar as portrayed by Travis Fimmel on screen. Ragnar, as a character, is understandably difficult to pin down. He is serious, but prone to foolish behaviors; he is cool headed, but falls victim to great torrents of emotion. He is certainly multi-faceted and that is appropriate for a figure who has been reborn and reinvigorated over so long a period of time. The manner in which Rix describes the tendency to mold source material to each interpreter's desired model could be considered a model for the adaptation of literary material for film media in a broader sense, as he states that "parts of Ragnar's Death Song were foregrounded while others were neglected, if not omitted from translations."⁴³

One element of the sagas that has certainly not been left aside for this reinterpretation of the Nordic peoples is violence. There has been a resurgence of the focus on the more bloodthirsty aspects of Viking history, partially in an attempt to define them by such extreme behaviors. Frank argues that "new studies of the Scandinavian invaders of England seem determined to stress their demonic side, to expose the dark virulence and fanaticism of

Norse paganism."⁴⁴ That demonic side is brought out most clearly in the episode "Blood Eagle" which has its grounding in historical fact though it seems that the dates and characters involved may have experienced some transposition.⁴⁵ The sons commonly attributed to Ragnar are represented in the show—"Ivar 'the Boneless,' Björn 'Ironside,' and Sigurd 'Snake in the Eye.'"⁴⁶ The most recognizable, as noted earlier, is likely to be Ivar, who is focused upon here for two key reasons. The first is the interpretation of his name, and the second is for his historical link with the particularly gruesome rite that gives the episode its title. In the series, the reading of "Boneless" is that the child is born disabled, with a condition that renders his legs unusable, leading to Ragnar wishing to feed the new born infant to wolves. "Boneless" however, has been interpreted as a signifier of a diverse range of possibilities: "some have argued that 'boneless' is a mistranslation of 'childless' but the sagas recount how Ívarr was unable to walk and had to be carried on a shield. It has been suggested that he suffered from brittle bone disease."⁴⁷ While the recent proliferation of neo-peplum film and television can be viewed as the latest era of interpreters selecting their focus depending upon the wants of their readership/viewership, there has been a suggestion that the fetishistic use of violence reveals something more significant. There is certainly no lack of blood in *Vikings* and Sigurdson argues that this trend is linked to a certain authenticity with regard to critical perspectives of history, with directors "using the notion of historical accuracy as a powerful justification for the depicted violence."⁴⁸ If this is the case, and there is a tendency to embellish violence and brutality to create a tone of grim authenticity, then the rite of the blood eagle, which is explicitly recreated for the screen, would be an obvious example to interrogate more closely. The blood eagle was a form of ritual murder, and it is represented for the camera in an explicit manner that recalls Foucault's famous opening description of the disciplining of the body from *Discipline and Punish*. Here, Ragnar carves an eagle into his enemy's back, cuts away his ribs, and tears out his lungs so that they splay, like wings, in a particularly unsettling display. As is to be expected from such nebulous and uncertain source material, doubts have been cast over the specific details of the rite. That the rite existed though, does not seem to be in question as Frank attests: "even the pro-viking opposition has been forced to concede that the torture was unhappily no fiction."⁴⁹ The extreme version revealed on screen though, taken directly from the sagas, "has often been denounced as later folklore or mistranslation."⁵⁰ Through the disparate translations though it is possible to see varying levels of brutality within the ritual torture/murder: "The blood-eagling procedure varies from text to text, becoming more lurid, pagan, and time-consuming with each passing century."⁵¹ The rite variably has entailed the scratching of an eagle into an enemy's back, the rending of flesh, with variants including adding salt to the wound, to the full televised tearing of ribs from the spine. That the show opts for the most violent rendition possibly gives credence to Sigurdson's suggestion that extreme violence is a desirable quality in modern media representations of history. One of the most significant aspects of the occurrence of the rite in the sagas is who the character is that conducts the famous torture:

> And Ella's back,
> at had the one who dwelt,
> Ivarr, with eagle,
> York, cut.[52]

In *Vikings* the conflation of history offers the jouissance of a particularly shocking episode with the re-emphasis on Ragnar as a dangerous and formidable adversary, possibly even the demonic figure that Sigurdson alluded to.

A further trait used to emphasize the historical robustness of neo-peplum media, according to Sigurdson, is that of rape: "rape and the threat of sexual violence are portrayed as an unavoidable aspect of the violent life of a Viking."[53] While it may be the case that within the show this representation of extreme sexual violence is used to signify a particular archetypal character, for "it is only the marginal or unlikable characters who rape, and they are often punished for their actions." Despite the fairly clumsy manner with which the phrase "rape and pillage" is used to refer to the Viking figure, evidence suggests that "Vikings were not known to their victims in Frankia as notorious rapists."[54] Though it is impossible to be certain of the status of women in Viking civilization, it does seem clear that the representation of shieldmaidens fighting shoulder to shoulder with their male counterparts on the show is a reasonable presumption. However, in spite of characters such as Lagertha (Katheryn Winnick) being constructed in equal or superior terms to male characters, there is still a visible gender imbalance. Regardless of the actual ratio of female warriors to male, it is at least clear that women were not assumed to be passive objects.[55] In fact to fixate on gender binaries within the Viking period is to critically underestimate the complexity of gender roles in the era. Gender, like the literature and sense of place, was characterized by a sense of fluidity; a rejection of the fixed, as Schnurbein states, "femaleness was obviously not so rigid that it could not be superseded by other interests, for example, by honor or revenge."[56]

The rejection of fixity or centrality, and the disregard for borders can also be seen in the Norse refusal to accept limits, even for their boats. The limits of water did not necessarily signify the boundary of water-based travel. In another particularly notable scene from the episode "Portage," Ragnar, attempting his second breach of Paris, demands that his warband's boats be lifted from the water and carried over mountainous terrain to avoid Parisian sentries.[57] The episode follows similar accounts in the sagas detailing ships being carried over land or dragged across frozen seas. The water's boundary, like all other borders, it seems, was merely another porous and traversable obstacle waiting to be overcome.

The Last Ship: Vikings as Nomads/Vikings as a Nomadology?

When Deleuze and Guattari called for a nomadology "the opposite of a history," it is unlikely that the figure of the Viking would have offered itself as an obvious model.[58] However, as has been shown, the Viking represents a people obsessively preoccupied with a rejection of fixed narratives or boundaries. Where history attempts to arrest passage, to create a fixed linear narrative, the nomad stubbornly refuses to be contained. For Roberta Frank, the Viking always reveals borders to be illusory, "the boundary between Scandinavian and insular culture was porous, open to quick dance-steps of attraction and repulsion, conflict and curiosity."[59] The refusal to respect or even acknowledge geographical limits is similarly noted by Wanner who emphasizes this sense of placelessness, "it seems clear that those who produced and consumed Norse myths, and especially myths of Óðinn, were neither locative nor utopian mapmakers."[60] Even when close reading of the sagas begins to tempt the well-meaning scholar into generalizations about peoples from particular regions of Scandinavia, archaeology rejects the findings with increased support of the diversity of this nebulous and elusive culture, "revealing that individuals in any one region at any one time thought about and did things in a variety of ways."[61] Both the scientific and interpretive evidence then seem to agree on one factor at least: that any attempt to find a single authoritative narrative or account regarding the Vikings is futile. After all, as Price states, while "it might be possible to suggest the existence of these stories, perhaps in some instances even guess at their purpose ... we are unlikely ever to know their plots."[62]

With the stories themselves being revealed to be as elusive as their tellers it is understandable why Rankovic would suggest that these tales are, in a sense, eternally unauthored, and that "the story is telling itself."[63] These are shifting narratives that have become an echo, in a sense insisting upon their own reinterpretation to suit the audience or era across a millennium. In this context the television reimagining of the sagas becomes particularly significant and Hermann would suggest that they also represent another important stage in their cultural development, as "cultural memory is indebted to media, like writing, orality, and images. It needs media in order to be transmitted over time and to be externalized."[64] The creators of the History Channel's original epic, then, become the latest in a long tradition of distributed authors, the "trafficker[s] of a story that always already exists."⁶⁵ The imposition of a strict narrative structure does reflect a Western obsession with the arborescent, and reveals a concern when confronted with the nebulous rhizomatic, however this can also be interpreted as the latest in a broad and varied history of retellings of these tales. The Viking preoccupation with a rejection of central control ensures they will not be held in any rigid place for long; perpetually in flight and living in a liminal space, straddling borders, which, while elusive though the text may be, makes the final lines of the *Poetic Edda* particularly emphatic:

> I'll go quickly.
> For now I thought most of all that I was between worlds
> when these flames blazed all about me.⁶⁶

As Frank states, "the Vikings walked the line."⁶⁷ That line extends much further than a geographical border or a narrative thread. This line can be traced through to the mythology and cosmology beneath the intricate surface of the sagas and *Eddas*. Wanner confirms this by calling for a desire to reject traditional structured understandings of the culture: "the concentric model does not need to be corrected but jettisoned."⁶⁸ Even the maps in the stars then present too rigid a plot for these nomadic people.

Despite unclear origins, dubious translations (and authors), and a lack of historical consensus, Ragnar still "haunts the imagination."⁶⁹ While there may be some question over the appropriateness of the Westernized arborescent narrative mode of this latest reimagining of the sagas, at least there is scarcely a horned helmet in sight.⁷⁰

NOTES

1. Neil Price, "Passing into Poetry: Viking-Age Mortuary Drama and the Origins of Norse Mythology," *Medieval Archaeology* 54 (2008): 145.
2. Ibid.
3. Ibid., 149.
4. Gilles Deleuze and Felix Guattari, *A Thousand Plateaus* (London: Continuum, 1987), 23.
5. Björn Sundmark, "Wayward Warriors: The Viking Motif in Swedish and English Children's Literature," *Children's Literature in Education* 45 (2014): 197.
6. Leonard Lawlor, "There Will Never Be Enough Done: An Essay on the Problem of the Worst in Deleuze and Guattari," *Journal of Philosophy: A Cross Disciplinary Inquiry* 5, no. 11 (2010): 3.
7. Deleuze and Guattari, 25.
8. Sundmark, 209.
9. Erika Sigurdson, "Violence and Historical Authenticity: Rape (and Pillage) in Popular Viking Fiction," *Scandinavian Studies* 86, no. 3 (2014): 249.
10. Sundmark, 198.
11. Robert Rix, "The Afterlife of a Death Song: Reception of Ragnar Lodbrog's Poem in Britain Until the End of the Eighteenth Century," *Studia Neophilologica* 81 (2009): 54.
12. Kevin Wanner, "God on the Margins: Dislocation and Transcience in the Myths of Óðinn," *History of Religions* 46, no. 4 (2007): 342–343.

13. Neil Mcguigan, "Ælla and the Descendents of Ivar: Politics and Legend in the Viking Age," *Northern History* 52, no. 1 (2015): 23.
14. Rix, 55.
15. Ben Waggoner, *The Sagas of Ragnar Lodbrok* (New Haven, CT: Troth Publications, 2009), 83.
16. Sigurdson, 250.
17. Rix, 55.
18. *Ibid.*, 65.
19. Slavica Rankovic, "Who Is Speaking in Traditional Texts? On the Distributed Author of the Sagas of Icelanders and Serbian Epic Poetry," *New Literary History* 38, No. 2 (2007): 304.
20. *Ibid.*, 298.
21. Matthew Townend, "Pre-Cnut Praise-Poetry in Viking Age England," *The Review of English Studies* 51, no. 203 (2000): 355.
22. Stefanie Schnurbein, "The Function of Loki in Snorri Sturluson's Edda," *History of Religions* 40, no. 2 (2000): 110.
23. Rosalie Wax and Murray Wax, "The Vikings and the Rise of Capitalism," *American Journal of Sociology* 61, no. 1 (1955): 8.
24. Pernille Hermann, "Saga Literature, Cultural Memory, and Storage," *Scandinavian Studies* 85, no. 23 (2013): 344.
25. Wax and Wax, 2.
26. Kevin Wanner, "Off-Center: Considering Directional Valences in Norse Cosmography," *Speculum* 84, no. 1 (2009): 62.
27. Schnurbein, 111.
28. Roberta Frank, "Viking Atrocity and Skaldic Verse: The Rite of the Blood Eagle," *The English Historical Review* 99 (1984): 335.
29. Lee Hollander, "Concerning a Proposed Translation of the Edda," *Scandinavian Studies and Notes* 5, no. 6 (1919): 198.
30. Wanner, "Off-Center," 41.
31. Pernille Hermann, "Saga Literature, Cultural Memory, and Storage," *Scandinavian Studies* 85, no. 23 (2013): 336.
32. Russell Poole, "Skaldic Verse and Anglo-Saxon History: Some Aspects of the Period 1009–1016," *Speculum* 62, no. 2 (1987): 266.
33. Sivert Hagan, "On the Origin of the Term Edda," *Modern Language Notes* 19, no. 5 (1904): 134.
34. A. Le Roy Andrews, "The Criteria for Dating the Eddic Poems," *PMLA* 42, no. 4 (1927): 1046–1047.
35. Hollander, 199.
36. Andrews, 1044.
37. Price, 149.
38. Hermann, 336.
39. Frank, "Viking Atrocity," 335.
40. Brian Patrick, "Vikings and Rappers: The Icelandic Sagas Hip-Hop Across 8 Mile," *The Journal of Popular Culture* 41, no. 2 (2008): 284.
41. Sigurdson, 252.
42. Rix, 53.
43. *Ibid.*, 57.
44. Frank, "Viking Atrocity," 334.
45. "Blood Eagle," Season 2, Disc 2, *Vikings* (April 10, 2014; 20th Century Fox Home Entertainment, 2014), DVD.
46. Mcguigan, 22.
47. Julian Richards, *The Vikings: A Very Short Introduction* (Oxford: Oxford University Press, 2005), 73.
48. Sigurdson, 251.
49. Frank, "Viking Atrocity," 332.
50. Richards, 73.

51. Frank, "Viking Atrocity," 333.
52. *Ibid.*, 336.
53. Sigurdson, 252.
54. *Ibid.*, 253.
55. Rix, 59.
56. Schnurbein, 120.
57. "Portage," Season 4 part 1, Disc 3, Vikings (April 7, 2016; 20th Century Fox Home Entertainment, 2014), DVD.
58. Deleuze and Guattari, 25.
59. Roberta Frank, "Terminally Hip and Incredibly Cool: Carol, Vikings, and Anglo-Scandinavian England," *Representations* 100 (2007): 23.
60. Wanner, "God on the Margins," 345.
61. Frank, "Terminally Hip," 24.
62. Price, 148.
63. Rankovic, 296.
64. Hermann, 334.
65. Rankovic, 297.
66. Snorri Sturluson, *The Poetic Edda*, trans. Carolyne Larrington (Oxford: Oxford University Press, 2014), 273.
67. Frank, "Terminally Hip," 23.
68. Wanner, "Off-Center," 67.
69. Rix, 65.
70. Sundmark, 197.

BIBLIOGRAPHY

Andrews, A. Le Roy. "The Criteria for Dating the Eddic Poems." *PMLA* 42, no. 4 (1927): 1044–1054.
Deleuze, Gilles, and Felix Guattari. *A Thousand Plateaus*. Translated by Brain Massumi. London: Continuum, 1987.
Foucault, Michel. *Discipline and Punish: The Birth of the Prison*. Translated by Alan Sheridan. Harmondsworth: Penguin, 1975.
Frank, Roberta. "Viking Atrocity and Skaldic Verse: The Rite of the Blood Eagle." *The English Historical Review* 99 (1984): 332–343.
_____. "Terminally Hip and Incredibly Cool: Carol, Vikings, and Anglo-Scandinavian England." *Representations* 100 (2007): 23–33.
Hagan, Sivert. "On the Origin of the Term Edda." *Modern Language Notes* 19, no. 5 (1904): 127–134.
Hermann, Pernille. "Saga Literature, Cultural Memory, and Storage." *Scandinavian Studies* 85, no. 23 (2013): 332–354.
Hollander, Lee. "Concerning a Proposed Translation of the Edda." *Scandinavian Studies and Notes* 5, no. 6 (1919): 197–201.
Lawlor, Leonard. "There Will Never Be Enough Done: An Essay on the Problem of the Worst in Deleuze and Guattari." *Journal of Philosophy: A Cross Disciplinary Inquiry* 5, no. 11 (2010): 1–13.
McGuigan, Neil. "Ælla and the Descendents of Ivar: Politics and Legend in the Viking Age." *Northern History* 52, no. 1 (2015): 20–34.
Patrick, Brian. "Vikings and Rappers: The Icelandic Sagas Hip-Hop Across 8 Mile." *The Journal of Popular Culture* 41, no. 2 (2008): 281–306.
Poole, Russell. "Skaldic Verse and Anglo-Saxon History: Some Aspects of the Period 1009–1016." *Speculum* 62, no. 2 (1987): 265–298.
Price, Neil. "Passing into Poetry: Viking-Age Mortuary Drama and the Origins of Norse Mythology." *Medieval Archaeology* 54 (2010): 123–156.
Rankovic, Slavica. "Who Is Speaking in Traditional Texts? On the Distributed Author of the Sagas of Icelanders and Serbian Epic Poetry." *New Literary History* 38, no. 2 (2007): 293–307.

Richards, Julian. *The Vikings: A Very Short Introduction*. Oxford: Oxford University Press, 2005.
Rix, Robert. "The Afterlife of a Death Song: Reception of Ragnar Lodbrog's Poem in Britain Until the End of the Eighteenth Century." *Studia Neophilologica* 81 (2009): 53–68.
Schnurbein, Stefanie. "The Function of Loki in Snorri Sturluson's Edda." *History of Religions* 40, no. 2 (2000): 109–124.
Sigurdson, Erika. "Violence and Historical Authenticity: Rape (and Pillage) in Popular Viking Fiction." *Scandinavian Studies* 86, no. 3 (2014): 249–267.
Sturluson, Snorri. *The Poetic Edda*. Translated by Carolyne Larrington. Oxford: Oxford University Press, 2014.
———. *The Prose Edda*. Translated by Jesse Byock. London: Penguin, 2005.
Sundmark, Björn. "Wayward Warriors: The Viking Motif in Swedish and English Children's Literature." *Children's Literature in Education* 45 (2015): 197–210.
Townend, Matthew. "Pre-Cnut Praise-Poetry in Viking Age England." *The Review of English Studies* 51, no. 203 (2000): 349–370.
Wanner, Kevin. "God on the Margins: Dislocation and Transcience in the Myths of Óðinn." *History of Religions* 46, no. 4 (2007): 316–350.
———. "Off-Center: Considering Directional Valences in Norse Cosmography." *Speculum* 84, no. 1 (2009): 36–72.
Waggoner, Ben. *The Sagas of Ragnar Lodbrok*. New Haven: Troth Publications, 2009.
Wax, Rosalie, and Murray Wax. "The Vikings and the Rise of Capitalism." *American Journal of Sociology* 61, no. 1 (1955): 1–10.

Sounds of Swords and Sandals
Music in Neo-Peplum BBC Television Docudramas

NICK POULAKIS

> Docudrama is not a kind or type of story, but rather a means of representation, a way of offering argument about the past.
> —Steven Lipkin[1]

This essay is not meant to be an exclusive and extensive account on all neo-peplum BBC Television docudramas concerning their soundtracks and music manipulation. On the contrary, it focuses on specific programs that function as case studies with a twofold critical objective: to highlight particular aspects of the contemporary neo-peplum audiovisual representations as well as to open up a debate on the usage of music and sound in docudramas as a postmodern television genre. Subsequently, this study considers two BBC Television shows that fall into the docudrama category, specifically *Pompeii: The Last Day* (2003, Peter Nicholson) and *Atlantis: End of a World, Birth of a Legend* (2011, Tony Mitchell), which have been produced and broadcasted during the post-millennium era.[2] This essay also reflects on the way television docudramas can become vehicles for discussion about numerous issues that dominate up-to-date theoretical debates on audiovisual representation—particularly, the means through which sound and music enhance images with emphasis to the spectators' identification, the aestheticization of reality, in addition to issues of new age nostalgia and postmodern exoticization of antiquity.

This essay's opening statement by Steven Lipkin makes a perfect liaison between the docudrama television genre and the concept of "representation." Generally, representation is considered to be a channel of expression, rationalization and objectification of the real; that is, par excellence, the poetic (constructional) and rhetoric (legitimizing) mechanism of cultural description, signification and symbolization that create and validate practices, narratives, notions and behaviors of human beings. Not only social groups but also individuals heavily rely on representations, since through this way they become familiar with and further understand their surrounding domain—the world in which they live, act and exchange their experiences. Both linguistic and conceptual systems of representation are established by means of several types of signs, codes and conventions which are socio-culturally shaped through their intra-genealogical transmission. In fact, every representation is a performed discourse, which conveys certain ideological and philosophical viewpoints and, therefore, becomes a part of the continuous conflict over cultural power and control. Similar to verbal discourse, audio and visual (as well as their combination—the audiovisual) discourses express and communicate particular attitudes towards the cultural and institutional milieu, thus setting up a specific politics of representation.[3]

Representations are also important for another reason: they take part in both the identification and differentiation processes, which are essential for people to construct their notion of existence and presence and further create a sense of unity and communality with others—meeting the need for addressing their entity as well as for becoming a member of a group. Homi Bhabha considers that, habitually, defining oneself encompasses a differentiation from the others by signifying their similarities and dissimilarities.[4] Besides that, representations, even though unavoidable, are neither permanent nor unbiased; instead, they are adaptive, dynamic and spatiotemporally formed. Following the work of Bhabha, contemporary critical cultural theory rejects romanticized depictions of phenomena that delineate various cultures as static, ageless or ahistorical, eternally stuck on a "frozen" present—an imaginative space-time continuum, which is presented as "pure" but is completely authoritative as it is based on previous stereotypical representations.

Performing cultural representations is a continuous process between the mind and the body experience. In respect to the tradition of "visual hegemony" according to Alan Burdick, Westernized representations of identity are bound up with the authorization of sight as the main channel of perception and knowledge.[5] But, if seeing is believing, then hearing is empathizing. As John Dewey has long before mentioned, "vision is a spectator; hearing is a participator."[6] This comes to be a modern idea of experiencing reality through the means of audiovisually simulated representations in current mass media genres, such as video games, feature films and television shows, since present day societies have already established much of their existence on technologically mediated practices. However, since emphasis is usually given to visual narrative techniques, due to the long-lasting Western visu-centric tradition, the dynamics of music and sound in general (as non-representational systems, since they can hardly be comprehended without any contextualization) has not been particularly investigated within the framework of mass media production.

Considering musical practices of Western modernity in his essay on noise and musical sound, Jacques Attali makes a distinction between specific cultural networks of music production, dissemination and response.[7] In particular, apart from the network of the "sacrificial ritual," assigned to the pre-modern period, Attali talks about the relationship between the networks of "representation" and "repetition" and the way this leads to the next phase of musical and cultural practices—the network of "composition," which indicates the postmodern era. According to Attali, representation refers to the period of cultural history of the Western world in which the sacrificial dramatic ritual is transported into a theatrical stage show. On the other hand, the "repetition" network designates the state of the standardized imitation and systematic reproduction of music performances, which are mainly attributable to the development of new forms of information, technology and communication. There are parallel transition networks, similar with music practices, that can be located in the field of audiovisual media in general. The appearance of the medium of television in the middle of the last century as well as its rapid spread have changed to a great extent both the reception and the perception of the audiovisual spectacle and have contributed to the transformation of the audiovisual projection from a public task to a private matter that takes place at home, thus assigning representation with the quality of individualistic repeatability.[8]

Within the contemporary world, where modern mass media plays a significant role not only as vehicles but also as modulators of the globalized aspect of cultural and economic systems, television through its optical and visual apparatus launches the Western postmodern lifestyle as the dominant logic of the constitution of its flows. Regarding the challenge of cultural preconceptions, the systematic reproduction of stereotypes and their symbolic connotations with music and image is a commonplace in contemporary popular audiovisual genres. As musical and cultural stereotypes are part of broader social taxonomical systems, they acquire meaning in accordance to their specific representations and the context of their performances. Deriving from the long-standing, hegemonic film music tradition of Hollywood, the connection between music and image in Western popular culture is based on representations that, in most cases, create stable and predefined musical and cultural associations. James Buhler, David Neumeyer, and Rob Deemer label them as "style topics" (conventionally coded types of music).[9]

Music and sound in Western popular television shows usually do not function in a pioneering way to break any of the stereotypical cultural constructions created on the difference between the hegemonic Self and the subaltern Other as been audiovisually portrayed on small screen. On the contrary, although they enrich and establish some of these *clichés*, their dynamics have not been contextually analyzed. Compared to the film music academic literature, there is a limited number of books that deal with the relationship between music and the small screen, perhaps because of television's temporary and unsophisticated nature.[10] These studies complement that one of the primary disparities between film and television is that film favors the spectators' visual sense, while television privileges their acoustic perception. Recent television technological evolutions have led to the introduction of an assortment of practices already implemented in film music production, such as the utilization of the underscoring techniques in order to stress emotional states and boost narrative tension as well as the sound design procedure to draw the viewers' attention to the on-screen action by enhancing the levels of aurality.[11]

Correspondingly, televisual narratives share several more attributes. The most significant is that, as genuine expressions of postmodernity, they count on hybrid representations combining special advanced techniques and novel art forms within earlier and outdated conceptual frameworks. Television docudramas—also known as drama(tic) documentaries or dramadocs—are an example where reality and fantasy are mingled in new screen ecosystems via an intertextual reflection that sustains the blurring of classic genres through the fluidity of their boundaries as well as their functions. This controversial audiovisual genre has always been difficult to define as it encompasses a relationship between two dissimilar genres: the documentary and the (melo)drama. As Hayden White underlines: "What happens in the postmodernist docu-drama or historical metafiction is not so much the reversal of this relationship (such that real events are given the marks of imaginary ones while imaginary events are endowed with reality) as, rather, the placing in abeyance of the distinction between the real and the imaginary. Everything is presented as if it were of the same ontological order, both real and imaginary—realistically imaginary or imaginarily real, with the result that the referential function of the images of events is etiolated."[12]

During the 90s, it was this particular genre in the lightweight patterns of docusoap that offered a controlled escape from the economic and competition crisis of prime-time television production, providing a "value for money" solution.[13] Subsequently, docudramas in postmodern digital television depend on "faction"—the wittingly blending of fact and fiction—in order to create what Wolf calls "subjunctive documentaries" that focus on "what *could be, would be* or *might have been*" and frequently apply computer-generated simulation.[14]

Dramatized depictions of real facts from the real world concerning real people have always dominated human performances and representations from primitive practices and rituals to stage shows and modern media. Furthermore, narratives from the distance past, such as ancient myths, important events from Greece, Rome, Egypt, Babylon, Scandinavia, etc., as well as biblical and pirate stories have all been presented as modern epic costume dramas under the peplum (also sword and sandal or sword and sorcery) label, mainly in cinema but also in television and video games.[15] The most familiar style of television docudrama is the one that puts a historical/mythical event or era at the heart of the storyline and weaves dramatic elements within the plot. A close analysis and interpretation of specific neo-peplum BBC Television docudramas will highlight the ambiguous practice through which their sound and music operate in opposition to the theoretical properties of the television's audibility and, thus, will foster the idea of considering these shows to be treated like telefilms which aim mostly at melodrama rather than documentation, although "research suggests that viewers place more faith in the accuracy of these overtly dramatic performances than in the academic or expert performances provided by presenters and interviewees."[16]

In the earlier history of literature and stage, melodrama is portrayed as a conflation of music and drama, where drama is being exaggerated through the plentiful application of music. Contemporary theorists, like Linda Williams, define the "mode" of melodrama as a coherent aesthetic system that embodies modern (though utopian) sociocultural and psychological tensions to attain high emotional engagement and sentimentality "through a dialectic of pathos and action."[17] Melodramatic shows are based on the archetypal romantic narrative with stereotyped characters and intentional overacting, pointing towards an excess that would directly appeal to everyday audiences. As such, melodramas simplify obscure incidents and provide a sharp contrast between good and evil, ground their narratives in issues from the social world and transform these events into fictional stories, ensue an episodic form focusing on people's emotions and needs and, ultimately, feature plots that are unrealistic or implausible.

Epic television melodramas, in specific, just as sword and sandal films, usually refer to grandiose themes such as classic myths and legendary symbols, authoritative gods and supernatural heroes, wise kings and attractive princesses, important battles and love tragedies, great commanders and brave soldiers, sacred traditions and moral values, glorious victories and terrible catastrophes. They rely deeply on mass culture practices and encourage a universal concept of (Western) identity, by means of a postmodern nostalgia of the past, where "the archaic is a sign of an authentic common past, a home that soothes modernity's homelessness."[18] This is the way through which they can satisfy simultaneously, through their virtual high-tech representations, the needs and the demands, the feelings and the preconceptions of both the producers and the audiences in the context of an ambivalent global television marketplace.

Pompeii: The Last Day is a dramatized representation that reveals the life-stories of people residing in the ancient Italian cities of Pompeii and Herculaneum during the day that Mount Vesuvius erupted. It is a reconstructed mosaic with a scientific essence proceeding from the eyewitness letters of Pliny the Younger (Gaius Plinius Caecilius Secundus [Martin Hodgson]), a Roman administrator and poet. The story begins displaying the 24th of August 79 AD as an ordinary day in the city. The show monitors the routine of different persons, mainly Caius Julius Polybius ([Jim Carter] a rich businessman and prospective politician) and other members of his family (his wife Epidia [Chrissie Cotterill], his pregnant daughter Julia [Katherine Whitburn] and her husband Sabinus [Leigh Jones]), Stephanus the Fuller ([Jonathan Firth] a good-looking but egocentric man) and Fortunata ([Rebecca Clarke] Stephanus' gentle and decent wife), two famous gladiators (Africanus [Chad Shepherd] and Celadus [Robert Whitelock]), as well as the Roman writer, lawyer, naturalist, philosopher and military commander Pliny the Elder (Gaius Plinius Secundus [Tim Pigott-Smith]) and his relatives—his nephew (later adopted son) Pliny the Younger and his sister Plinia (Rachel Atkins).

At the first signs of Vesuvius erupting, the characters take different courses of action. As the phases of the volcano eruption proceed, some of them remain unswerving while others reevaluate their position enduring their cruel fate. Pliny the Younger's account links the past and the existing situation in Pompeii as the latest is demonstrated (mostly in a realistic depiction) during the closing half hour of the docudrama. Geologist, science writer and producer Victoria Bruce narrates the epilogue of the series in favor of creating a nostalgic yet almost frightening nexus between the easygoing present life, the heart-rending tragedy that struck the ancient city and the possibility of a forthcoming explosion of the Mount Vesuvius volcano in the near future.

Atlantis: End of a World, Birth of a Legend is about another colossal natural disaster, the Minoan eruption of Thera (Santorini) during the middle of the second millennium BC. In order to induce a hybrid mythical and scientific essence, the show tries to connect the archaeological, seismological and vulcanological evidence of the Minoan civilization with the legend of Atlantis as described by the ancient Greek philosopher Plato. The story involves an aspirant bull-leaper Yishharu (Reece Ritchie) and his wife Pinaruti (Stephanie Leonidas) who have just come back to Thera from Crete. When the pre-volcanic activity begins, only Yishharu feels something is amiss while others seem to not notice. The volcano soon erupts, throwing out tons of ash and lava that devastate the island. The two young companions manage to get through the first phases of the catastrophe, but later they are separated.

Yishharu is left behind while his wife and other people sail away from Thera. As a result of the titanic tsunami which was caused by the eruption, Pinaruti is washed up on the seashore of a nearby island.

The analysis of these two productions allows for useful assumptions that illuminate the ways in which modern popular media like television use both the artistic and the social dynamics of music and sound as performative events—i.e., as cultural constructs that refer to various experiential, expressive and communicative processes—in order to present and consolidate a specific policy of aestheticization and enculturation. Simply put, using to the 1960s BBC motto which still rings true today: "To make the good popular and the popular good."[19] This strategy is consistent with the postmodern lifestyle and highlights the state of the art qualities of the television phenomenon, especially those related to history, space and nature popularized-science docudramas, like *Pompeii* and *Atlantis*. Besides being BBC Television productions of the post-millennium era, these two docudramas additionally share four common attributes: their plot concerns ancient Mediterranean civilizations, therefore they could be both categorized as "neo-peplum" shows; they lean on a melodramatic plot that combines the sentimentality of a love story with the tragedy of a massive natural disaster, specifically a volcano eruption; they reconstruct ancient (built and natural) environments through digital computer-generated imagery (CGI) technology; and, finally, their music is entirely computer-performed and has been written by the same artist, Ty Unwin, a British composer who has scored several science-based television shows over the last fifteen years.

As listening is vital to any social information and communication, media ecologies and archaeologies heavily rely on the auditory perception to enable the emergence of social insight as the audiences interact and engage with each other. The attempt to impose meaning on image using sound is also a long-time concept. Originated from the earlier filmic framework, modern audiovisual practices are subject to the interactivity between the optic and the acoustic sphere to build some equally realistic and emotional representations. As Steven Feld has pointed out, "our era is increasingly dominated by fantasies and realizations of sonic virtuality."[20] *Pompeii* and *Atlantis* are both visual remakes of ancient, mythical, lost or fantastic worlds. But how do they represent the respective soundscapes of these imaginative worlds? And, furthermore, where do these interpretations originate from?

New age music and sound romanticism in contemporary pseudo-historical television docudramas is preoccupied with an artistic form of dual temporality, one that yearns for the "archaic," the "natural" and the "exotic," while embodying issues of postmodern nostalgia, ideological aestheticization, eclectic innovation and post-capitalistic consumption, therefore leading to what Timothy Taylor has already described as "armchair cosmopolitanism."[21]

This double-sided (imaginative/factual) audiovisual conception is clearly stated in the shows' construction of their audible environments. In correspondence with the sci-fi genre, where narrative advances "futurization" (i.e., the balance between making new worlds strange and readable at the same time),[22] historical docudramas storylines call for music and sound "archaization." Music in *Pompeii* and *Atlantis* operates mainly as a narrative element in the same way as it is used in fiction films; it is connected with the story and is designed according to the structure of the film. These docudramas use music and sound effects in an attempt to create an ambivalent sonic atmosphere that is heard as an encompassing filmic soundtrack occupied by both an exoticism and familiarity in relation to the postmodern audio culture of the West. Their voice-over, sound design and musical scores are quite unveiling.

Pompeii begins with a constant, underlying synthetic drone as the line "Pompeii 79 A.D." appears on the screen. A triangle breaks the music drone continuum and a humbled female voice starts repeating vowels in a melismatic style—something between a murmur and a song—accompanied by a deep, slight sound of a timpani. The sonorous voice of a male narrator begins reciting: "Frozen in time ... by an epic eruption."[23] Photographs depicting the fossilized bodies of the people of Pompeii are interspersed with images from the dramatized story that illustrate the pre-eruption phases. Present documentation is blended with the representation of the past not only pictorially but also aurally. The narrator shares the outline of the story whilst we listen to the voices of the inhabitants of Pompeii talking to each other. Gradually, this ambient background soundtrack—being simultaneously calm and exotic—fades out and the only sounds heard are the narrator's voice and the words spoken by an actor. This (almost silent) moment of the show's overture prepares the following audio and visual scenes of the volcanic activity since, all of a sudden, the loud sound of explosion interrupts the ostensible serenity of human dialogues. Screams, calls and moans along with epic music take over the sonic environment while the screen is visually occupied with catastrophic images of both destroyed nature and manmade buildings. "This is their story."[24]

From the beginning, it is obvious that the music in this docudrama is derived from synthetic (electronic or digital) musical instruments rather than actual, physical ones. This particular attribute of the show's soundscape conforms to its imagescape, with reference to the computer-generated sounds and images, respectively. Specifically, music simulates the grandiose sound of the strings *tutti* of a digital symphonic orchestra that play the uncomplicated melodic lines mostly in unison in contrast with the brass section of vertical/harmonic chordal homophony and the keyboard arpeggiated accompaniment, as well as the sharp but simple rhythmic motives played on the timpani.

The above remarks could be applied to the overall music score of the program, except that there are not any other melodies clearly heard and conceived as such in this docudrama. On the contrary, the series' soundscape is an improvised continuum that basically fuses a sweeping background instrumental score with enhanced natural, ambient, Foley and studio-generated sound effects. The show's volcanic explosion scenes confirm these premises. The juxtaposition of slow motion pans of people trying to escape their tragedy along with fast camera movements portraying a mixture of a real volcano eruption and a CGI pyroclastic flow attack enhance the dramatic tension. The visuals are accompanied by a mingle of (sci-fi) electronic and (virtual) orchestral ambient music, drum rhythms of anxiety and suspense, screams, thunderstorms and explosions. The following lethal pyroclastic surges, underscored with dynamic strings, brass and timpani tones, end up with simple melodious lines played by a synthesized harp or wind instrument and synth pads in order to create a melodramatic background to the murderous setting. The deceased characters of the show, their manner of death and their "voices" are visually linked with the skeletons and plaster casts of victims still in situ, as well as with the epistles of Pliny the Younger that describe the eruption of Mount Vesuvius and the remains of the city that have been brought to light. This scene is juxtaposed with the present-day life of Pompeii in the last part of the program, which is musically accompanied by a more pop-oriented, easy-listening background scored by Phil Sawyer, applying a rather differentiated approach as compared with the preceding soundtrack.

The opening sequence in *Atlantis* starts with the end of the story and, like *Pompeii*, it is also surrounded by a sustained drone soundscape. A *cliché* sound of a seagull interrupts this ambience and aurally establishes a coastal setting. A wretched girl (Pinaruti) is lying unconscious on a stack of hawsers on a boat. She opens her eyes and barely manages to get off the boat, when a mysterious female voice begins singing in an oriental-style mood. It is an unmeasured, wordless melody, reminiscent of traditional Balkan lament songs. This passionate vocalization keeps on, while the girl wanders around among ruins and dead bodies. The sound of splashing water from the young woman walking through a small pothole is intermingled with the following low-pitched melodic line played by synthetic cellos and double basses. After a *crescendo* with strings and cymbals, the sharply uttered words of an old man break the quietness of the scene: "The Gods have spared us, girl! It's time for a sacrifice."[25] Then, he starts laughing. His laugh gives way to an orchestral increase to climax strengthened by an "aahs" men's synth choir. When music reaches a peak, rhythmic timpani and snare-drums accompaniment, full-scale symphonic score and voice-over commentary unveil. It is at this point, when the main narrative begins.

Music and sound in *Pompeii* and *Atlantis* enhance epic spectacle, which underlines an assertive view of ancient civilizations based on modern audiovisual representation, especially through the simplistic and conventionalized way that it tries to sonically accompany (through denotative codes) the visuals. This promotes a moralistic Western-centric ideological attitude towards what appears to be ancient, exotic and unfamiliar with modern occidental culture. The lack of realistic (source) music, the use of a sweeping and lavish score, the intensification of sound design and amplified effects, as well as the incorporation of an authoritative voice-over narration are the main characteristics of the soundscapes of these two docudramas. Following Anahid Kassabian's dual model of music-image relation according to the spectators' perceptions, the shows' music clearly highlight an assimilating identification of the audience with their soundscapes.[26] The assimilating identification, in contrast to the affiliating identification, occurs when the viewers conceive the music and sound of an audiovisual situation as a strictly controlled condition. See, for instance, the background scores that reproduce aspects of the hegemony of the post-romantic and neo-classical Hollywood filmic tradition. On the other hand, through affiliating identification spectators relate to the music and sound by means of an open, subjective and emergent procedure. This association involves mainly the compilation scores that contain popular music and supports the creation of a multiform experience through various cultural projections.

At first glance, music and sound in these docudramas function in a complex mode, as the composer and the sound editors utilize affiliating identification techniques but in an assimilating identification way in order to formulate the constant framework of the necessary audiovisual representations. Both *Pompeii* and *Atlantis* use sound and music in an attempt to create attractive, encompassing and exotic—in relation to the Western culture—sonic environments. This neocolonial (aural) discourse is dominant for BBC Television docudramas; it conveys the new-age aesthetics and borrows elements from a mixture of magical realism, eco-philosophy, superhero culture and postmodern spiritualism. From a critical anthropological point of view, the entire concept is linked up with the question of the symbolic escapism of the "civilized" Self towards the "primitive" Other and the corresponding enculturation process as a route of cultural interventionism and nostalgic imitation—a case of an inverted "postcolonial mimicry,"[27] since it is the Western Self (through his own, egocentric, unsophisticated and decontextualized approach) who tries to visually and aurally represent the Noble Savage.[28] In fact, this reflection conceals the monolithic mode of audiovisual perception of both nature and culture, reality and imagination in contemporary television docudramas.

Music and sound effects in audiovisual media do not work autonomously. Their function is inextricably linked with another key-element of the medium, namely human speech. Both *Pompeii* and *Atlantis* apply a disembodied narrator voice-over, which is imposed upon all other audio elements of the shows. In these cases, the "voice of God" is (re)presented as the voice of the (pop-)scientist that should be audible, powerful, authoritative, grave and commanding. The narrators' voice-overs set up a didactic, educative and pedantic tone all over the episodes. With reference to the characters' dialogues, the docudramas use solely Modern English. Apparently, this anachronistic discrepancy in language does not serve as a deterrent since it corresponds to the earlier filmic tradition of Hollywood representations of ancient cultures and, therefore, makes the shows more accessible—as if all their protagonists are still present in the spectators' fantasies! Furthermore, although both shows elaborate diegetic sounds of the natural environment, i.e., sounds whose source is part (either on or off screen) of the docudramas' world, and their musical score gives the impression of a thoroughgoing atmospheric background, thus contributing to the subconscious psychoacoustic balancing with their digital illustrations, there is hardly any diegetic music embedded in their soundtrack. As opposed to the production's agony to systematically recreate the ancient imagescapes through visual effects, it seems that there is no equivalent approach for the diegetic music and dialogues to be "authentically" represented.

The end of both docudramas leads to heterotopic—dystopic or utopic—worlds that convey an ambivalence toward the past, a nostalgia that looks at the older times but from the safety of the present. This is about a postmodern standpoint that camouflages the need of the Self for a safe (yet voyeuristic) glance on the Other's catastrophe. Metaphorically speaking, both shows' music and sound tracks create a sense of politically correct auralism. *Pompeii* and *Atlantis* soundscapes adopt a postmodern video game music processing and orchestration which encompasses typical modulations, dense texture, dramatic contrasts and abrupt dynamics through a superfluous background score—a kind of new-age music that could be described as mesmerizing, entrancing or meditative. Music and sound, together with costumes and settings, are modeled on existing docudrama concepts. But this brings to light an inherent ambivalence of the genre. Although there is an effort to create a realistic visual sphere along with naturalistic sound effects (especially those of the volcanic eruptions), the production team sees no need to establish an essence of musical historical authenticity. In fact, both shows' music represents the type of scoring that puts the romantic television music style before audiovisual archaeology. The composer does not attempt to recreate a genuine ancient music soundscape but to provide a passionate ambience that fits the Western impressions of the past. In an analogous case, Stephen Meyer describes the attempt of regenerating the older audiovisual sphere in postwar biblical filmic epics as "authenticity anxiety": "The technological marvels and audiovisual grandeur of the epics are superficially attractive, but they do not convey any genuine or authentic truth. What we might call the 'authenticity anxiety' surrounding the epics—the sense that despite (or because of) their technological sophistication they remained fake—may help to account for one of their more curious features, namely, the extent to which producers, directors, and studio executives attempted to establish their historical credentials."[29] This stereotypical audiovisual representation carries a notion of quixotic, ahistorical and universal conception of ancient cultures closely related with the critique on the colonial politics of cultural identity.

The soundscapes of both docudramas unveil a fast, effortless, frugal and, at the same time, audience convincing choice for their non-diegetic musical ambiance. They make use of classical underscoring which emphasizes the romanticism of string melodies, the masculinity of brass harmonies, as well as the tension of rhythmic and pitched percussion according to the scenic performance. The programs' scores assign quite a few widely-used Hollywood musical *clichés*, such as the "stinger," an all-together-playing *sforzando* (sudden and strong musical emphasis), illustrating the dramatic moments of unexpected tensions on the screen and paralleling image and vision to music and sound. The above conventions are used to maintain structural sonic unity and highlight the content through an exact synchronization between music and visual action—a kind of contemporary "mickey-mousing" technique. Loose themes, conventional harmonies, alternating moods and standard orchestration, all these music elements are arranged by the composer and the sound editor into suites or longer cues (much the same as the freely improvised form of fantasy) to create an easy-listening, non-stop, instrumental medley and evoke an atmospheric, pleasurable and unobtrusive qualities. Thus, musically, any motivic materials, pure structures or recurrent patterns seem to be stuck to a completely haphazard aestheticization process.

The aestheticization of culture as the main component of the Western romantic ideal is based on the ambivalence between two poles: the direct contact with reality (i.e. the objective experience) and the detachment from it through subjective experience. However, the difference between the earlier concept of aestheticization and the current (postmodern) one is that the present procedure is not generated by and does not refer to a small, clearly defined group of a specific elite but is a generalized, massive policy covering almost all aspects of the postmodern lifestyle. Moreover, there is an additional key element that characterizes the above process, namely the degradation of the particular nuances of minor cultures and the emergence of a global rationale of representation. Local, subordinate, regional, minority, liminal and other non-standard aspects of contemporary culture are integrated in a hegemonic cultural model, which leaves no room for details that express its internal contradictions.

Through their music and sound environs, neo-peplum BBC Television docudramas validate the cultural politics of the postmodern condition that advances a digitized aestheticization of reality in the context of mainstream consumerism and new-age nostalgia of the older times that conceal a present crisis-driven distress, isolationism and fear for the future. These politics comply with the Western lifestyles and highlights the massive dimensions of the phenomenon of present day docudramas, as the philosophy of the postmodern dramatized reproductions of actual or mythical events is not limited to a symbolic and imaginary level but it is broadly realized and implemented in everyday life.

The CGI context of these two shows incorporates an extensive variety of narrative genres such as documentary, melodrama, romance and adventure into the hybrid form of postmodern docudrama. This pseudo-scientific reconstruction of ancient worlds counts on a naïve musicscape. But, as Holly Rogers has noted,

> our understanding of realism in relation to sound and music in the digital age has become highly complex. Ubiquitous music in our everyday lives, in shops, on TV and on mobile media has highly attuned our sonic awareness. In addition, the saturation of music in fiction cinema has formed audiences highly accomplished in processing images with the help of musical signification.... [M]usic in film is one of the most powerful illusory persuaders that what we are watching is, in fact, yet rather paradoxically, as real as possible.[30]

As docudrama creation is also an artificial process that includes fictitiousness and selectiveness, music offers a popular medium which may reinforce aspects of pseudo-realistic perception and develop an appealing spectacle under the perspective of contemporary Western exoticism. Their postmodern sonic layer makes it easier for the productions to develop an extensive diachronic representation. These connotations are reflected in the shows' background score, enclosing linkages with the Western impressions of primitive, mystical and emotional exoticism.[31]

Their overall sound design commissions an eclectic synthesis of new-age musical idioms and effects by means of up-to-date standards of spirituality and meditation, thus constructing an imagined non–Western ancient culture in the light of aestheticism and optimism. The episodes' historical, ethnic and cultural representations are harmonized primarily with present day Western ways of thinking and modern lifestyles (values, ideals and concerns) of mediated spectacle and economic reciprocity. Both series' music productions, broadcasting and promotion modus operandi is a reminder of the latest, new-age television music and docudrama practices that form their music entity as a homogeneous and standardized one, referring to motionless spatiotemporal state of affairs.

Both shows' music is given a distant, mysterious and often supernatural character. This framework is of particular importance because it follows a monological condition of music representation, an objectified and autonomized shaping of the performative processes of music addressed to the audience with the aim of creating a modern spectacle. Their music is presented as a phenomenon with underlying continuity, authenticity and purity, a sanctified, mechanical and stylized means of making the programs broadly accessible and comprehensible. This kind of homogenization and suppression of cultural, historical and performative particularities as well as the subsequent normalization of the information provided are symbolically and practically established through particular image-sound representations. In other words, communality is replaced by virtuality according to the stereotyped audiovisual representation of the non–Western ancient Other through a superficial new-age tele-aesthetics that combines "tele-education" and "tele-entertainment" in the form of "tele-film." These sorts of audiovisual informative techniques are popular today, as Russell Staiff explains in regards to *Pompeii*: "The way film reconstructs Pompeii effectively (and devastatingly) competes with other didactic forms of interpretation because of the unique power of visual culture and, in particular, of the moving image hitched to a soundtrack of mood-evoking music."[32] In fact, this is about a post-neoteric type of mediated communication that infuses entertainment with education into a new trend called "edutainment"—in this case, archeologically referred.[33] This gives music an impression of simultaneous contrasting feelings, specifically closeness and remoteness, convergence and divergence.

The stereotypical sound and music references used in these docudramas refer directly to the commercialized dimension of prevalent sound and music culture, since music and sound representations are determined by their relation to wider economic factors, thus become treated as plain consumer goods of the cultural production chain which includes the intentions of the creators, the framework of the production process, the artwork itself and its public appreciation. This decontextualization and dehistoricization of cultural phenomena becomes a fundamental component of the docudramas analyzed. Although the points made continuously throughout the shows relate their audiovisual representations to an enhanced experiential approach as a primary communicative mode of accessing "reality," eventually their context reveals a wide crisis of experience—an experience which seems to rest merely upon digital illusionism and postmodern commercialism. With reference to both the creative choices and the commercial conditions (as well as the expectations) of the production context of *Pompeii* and *Atlantis* in earlier interviews, Ty Unwin, the docudramas' music creator, has previously commented:

> Sometimes you can't avoid using a sound because it becomes associated with particular things in people's minds. On *Pompeii: The Last Day* I used the Bizarre Guitar sample as part of the volcano effects and although I was cautious about it the production

team loved it. Later I heard the same sample on another programme and swore to myself that I wouldn't use it again. When I came to do *Supervolcano* the producer kept referring to that particular sample; in a way it had become associated with the sound of a volcano, so I used it again.[34]

Musically I like what I did on *Supervolcano* and *Atlantis* even though both were nightmare projects schedule/deadline wise. *Space* was great in that it was my big break.[35]

Likewise, Fred Karlin and Rayburn Wright have already forewarned the specialists scoring or analyzing films and other media: "Don't assume that docudramas are necessarily any less dramatic than fictional films; it depends on the intention of the writer and the director."[36] Ty Unwin is an acknowledged television composer who has been working on a regular basis for BBC Television historical, space and nature "movie documentaries" and "mini-series documentaries." Coupling music creation with the television market, Steven Gordon reveals: "Licensing music for popular TV shows has become a lucrative source of income for the music business.... Needless to say, promotion of music on TV shows has become a phenomenon, and artists heavily rely on these shows to advance their careers."[37] Unwin got into music business at an early age, and after compiling characteristic musicscapes for numerous of television shows, he is now widely known as "Mr. BBC Doc."[38] He is also affiliated with Universal Publishing Production Music promoting his commercial videos jingles, orchestral scores, chill out tunes and other atmospheric music tracks and, as himself affirms, making his living out of his hobby: "Lots of composers for TV take themselves far too seriously.... At the end of the day we have the best job in the world: we sit on our arses, writing tunes, playing with loads of hi-tech stuff and get paid great money for it! The only problem is that directors always want miracles ... yesterday!"[39] In another interview, when he was called to comment on the juxtaposition between the use of real performance and virtual instrumentation for underscoring, Unwin stated that he is "something of a control freak," he finds "real orchestral sessions frustrating" and that, "in a perfect world, personally" he would "work completely with samples, [since] they don't answer back and eat less biscuits!"[40]

It is evident that the meaning of these shows' music and their relation to the visuals is settled neither in their background scoring nor in the music performance itself but in the musical outcome. In this way, both the beautification and the stabilization of the performative practices are used to stimulate the commodity dimensions of cultural audiovisual productions. In the standard signifying practices of television industry, music operates as a "hidden persuader" to grasp the audiences' attention and feelings.[41] In this case, music loses its interactive dialogical narrativity and becomes converted into an (apparently neutral) instrumental non-human activity that legitimizes and strengthens the existing hegemonic cultural politics of nostalgia and mimicry. As the deeper, essential and bidirectional exchange between cultural operators and the public disappears, the whole thing is transformed into a distant (virtual) audiovisual relationship. This is what John Richardson has indicated as the paradox of postmodern "acoustic music": "'Acousticness' obviously has a distinctive phenomenal imprint: a sonic quality arising from the performance of unamplified instruments in close proximity to listeners. That said, much of what passes today for acoustic music involves elements of unamplified instruments in close proximity to listeners."[42]

This experiential inconsistency in postmodern performing arts, which far too easily blend meditation with mediation, is closely linked to the technological evolution and often leads to a loss of the representations' symbolic dynamics and an extreme simplification of their performative dimensions. Given that experience is considered as a historically, culturally and spatiotemporally determined process, neo-peplum BBC Television docudramas may be distinguished not just for applying an aestheticization of politics, as described by Walter Benjamin,[43] but for imposing a specific politics of aestheticization as the dominant viewpoint of organizing and managing cultural representations in a globalized production sphere. What is more, this aestheticization is performed not only visually but also aurally, through their music and sound that match the contemporary aesthetic and commercial standardization of culture. To expand Steven Lipkin's initial remark, it can be argued that the docudrama is not only a means of representation, offering argument about the past; it also becomes a means of representation offering argument about the present—a means of self-reflection and introspection. In a (re)viewer's own words, "[t]hough I'm not too fond of the use of color filters, theatrical play behavior and blue screen CGI and pompous music, I found this interesting."[44]

Notes

1. Steven N. Lipkin, *Docudrama Performs the Past: Arenas of Argument in Films Based on True Stories* (Newcastle upon Tyne: Cambridge Scholars, 2011), 2.

2. *Pompeii: The Last Day*, directed by Peter Nicholson (London: British Broadcasting Corporation, The Learning Channel, Norddeutscher Rundfunk, and France 2, 2003), DVD; *Atlantis: End of a World, Birth of a Legend*, directed by Tony Mitchell (London: British Broadcasting Corporation, Discovery Channel, France Télévisions, and Prosieben, 2011), DVD.

3. For a comprehensive approach of the concept of "representation" and its politics through a cultural-studies perspective and case studies analyses, see Stuart Hall, Jessica Evans, and Sean Nixon, eds., *Representation* (London: Sage, 2013). For the relation between cinema, documentary and representation, see respectively Bill Nichols, *Representing Reality: Issues and Concepts in Documentary* (Bloomington: Indiana University Press, 1991).

4. Homi Bhabha, *The Location of Culture* (New York: Routledge, 1994), 45.

5. Alan Burdick, "Now Hear This: Listening Back on a Century of Sound," *Harper's Magazine* 303, no. 1804 (2001): 75.

6. John Dewey, *The Public and Its Problems* (New York: Holt, 1927), 219.

7. Jacques Attali, *Noise: The Political Economy of Music*, trans. Brian Massumi (Minneapolis: University of Minnesota Press, 1985).
8. John Ellis, *Visible Fictions: Cinema, Television, Video* (New York: Routledge, 2002), 275.
9. James Buhler, David Neumeyer, and Rob Deemer, *Hearing the Movies: Music and Sound in Film History* (New York: Oxford University Press, 2010), 195.
10. The most influential works on music and television include Philip Tagg, *Kojak, 50 Seconds of Television Music: Toward the Analysis of Affect in Popular Music* (New York: The Mass Media Music Scholars, 2000); Ron Rodman, *Tuning In: American Narrative Television Music* (New York: Oxford University Press, 2010); James Deaville, ed., *Music in Television: Channels of Listening* (New York: Routledge, 2011); Kevin J. Donnelly and Philip Hayward, eds., *Music in Science Fiction Television: Tuned to the Future* (New York: Routledge, 2013).
11. Kevin J. Donnelly, *The Spectre of Sound: Music in Film and Television* (London: British Film Institute, 2005), 112.
12. Hayden White, "The Modernist Event," in *The Persistence of History: Cinema, Television, and the Modern Event*, ed. Vivian Sobchack (New York: Routledge, 1996), 19.
13. Jonathan Bignell, "Docudramatizing the Real: Developments in British TV Docudrama Since 1990," *Studies in Documentary Film* 4, no. 3 (2010): 195–208.
14. Mark J. P. Wolf, "Subjunctive Documentary: Computer Imaging and Simulation," in *Collecting Visible Evidence*, ed. Michael Renov and Jane Gaines (Minneapolis: University of Minnesota Press, 1999), 274.
15. See, for example, Monica S. Cyrino, ed., *Rome, Season One: History Makes Television* (Malden, MA: Blackwell, 2008); Michael G. Cornelius, ed., *Of Muscles and Men: Essays on the Sword and Sandal Film* (Jefferson, NC: McFarland, 2011); Kevin J. Harty, ed., *The Vikings on Film: Essays on Depictions of the Nordic Middle Ages* (Jefferson, NC: McFarland, 2011); Adele Reinhartz, *Bible and Cinema: An Introduction* (New York: Routledge, 2013); Joanna Paul, *Film and the Classical Epic Tradition* (Oxford: Oxford University Press, 2013); Almut-Barbara Renger and Jon Solomon, eds., *Ancient Worlds in Film and Television: Gender and Politics* (Leiden: Brill, 2013); Matthew Wilhelm Kapell and Andrew B. R. Elliott, eds., *Playing with the Past: Digital Games and the Simulation of History* (New York: Bloomsbury Academic, 2013); Daniel O'Brien, *Classical Masculinity and the Spectacular Body on Film: The Mighty Sons of Hercules* (New York: Palgrave Macmillan, 2014); Monica S. Cyrino, ed., *Rome, Season Two: Trial and Triumph* (Edinburgh: Edinburgh University Press, 2015); Monica S. Cyrino and Meredith E. Safran, eds., *Classical Myth on Screen* (New York: Palgrave Macmillan, 2015); Robert A. Rushing, *Descended from Hercules: Biopolitics and the Muscled Male Body on Screen* (Bloomington: Indiana University Press, 2016); Roy Kinnard and Tony Crnkovich, *Italian Sword and Sandal Films, 1908–1990* (Jefferson, NC: McFarland, 2016).
16. Angela Piccini, "Faking It: Why the Truth is so Important for TV Archeology," in *Archaeology and the Media*, ed. Timothy Clack and Marcus Brittain (Walnut Creek, CA: Left Coast Press), 227.
17. Linda Williams, "Melodrama Revised," in *Refiguring American Film Genres: History and Theory*, ed. Nick Browne (Berkeley: University of California Press, 1998), 42.
18. Gerald Gaylard, "Postmodern Archaic: The Return of the Real in Digital Virtuality," *Postmodern Culture* 15, no. 1 (2004), accessed January 5, 2017, https://muse.jhu.edu/article/175222.
19. This phrase has been attributed to Huw Wheldon, a celebrated BBC Television managing director of the sixties, and it is quoted in Jonathan Bignell and Stephen Lacey, eds., *British Television Drama: Past, Present and Future* (New York: Palgrave Macmillan, 2014), 20.
20. Steven Feld, "A Sweet Lullaby for World Music," *Public Culture* 12, no. 1 (2000): 145.
21. Timothy D. Taylor, *Beyond Exoticism: Western Music and the World* (Durham: Duke University Press, 2007), 208.
22. Guido Held, "Schizophrenic Chords and Warm Shivers in the Stomach: The 'New Astronautic Sound' of *Raumpatrouille*," in *Music in Science Fiction Television: Tuned to the Future*, ed. Kevin J. Donnelly and Philip Hayward (New York: Routledge, 2013), 87.
23. *Pompeii*, Nicholson.

112   Part Two: Wisdom from the Gods

24. Ibid.
25. *Atlantis*, Mitchell.
26. Anahid Kassabian, *Hearing Film: Tracking Identifications in Contemporary Hollywood Film Music* (New York: Routledge, 2001).
27. For the concept of "postcolonial mimicry," see Bhabha, *The Location of Culture*, 122.
28. For a relevant appreciation of television gladiators as noble savages, see Michael G. Cornelius, "Introduction: Blood, Sand and Men," in *Spartacus in the Television Arena: Essays on the Starz Series*, ed. Michael G. Cornelius (Jefferson, NC: McFarland, 2015), 15–16.
29. Stephen C. Meyer, *Epic Sound: Music in Postwar Hollywood Biblical Films* (Bloomington: Indiana University Press, 2015), 10.
30. Holly Rogers, "Introduction," in *Music and Sound in Documentary Film*, ed. Holly Rogers (New York: Routledge, 2015), 3.
31. For an interpretation of the use of the exoticized "word music" practices in contemporary pseudo-historical television dramas, see Nick Poulakis, "Spotting Amazons, Scoring Demigods: Television, Music and the Reception of Greek Antiquity," in *Revisiting the Past, Recasting the Present: The Reception of Greek Antiquity in Music, 19th Century to the Present*, ed. Katerina Levidou and George Vlastos (Athens: Hellenic Music Centre, 2013), 42–49.
32. Russell Staiff, *Re-imagining Heritage Interpretation: Enchanting the Past-Future* (New York: Routledge, 2016), 90.
33. For an account of *Pompeii* and *Atlantis* as dramatized archeological documentaries, see Fiona Hobden, "The Archeological Aesthetic in Ancient World Documentary," *Media, Culture and Society* 35, no. 3 (2013): 366–381.
34. Kevin Hilton, "Ty Unwin," *Resolution Magazine* 4, no. 6 (2005): 49.
35. "Leading Television Composer Ty Unwin Talks about Hardware, Software and Staying Ahead of the Game," *Time+Space* (2012), accessed January 5, 2017, http://www.timespace.com/features/2373.
36. Fred Karlin and Rayburn Wright, *On the Track: A Guide to Contemporary Film Scoring* (New York: Routledge, 2004), 181.
37. Steve Gordon, *The Future of the Music Business: How to Succeed with the New Digital Technologies* (Milwaukee: Hal Leonard Books, 2005), 92.
38. Gary Rubio, "The Story of Science—Ty Unwin (Composer)," *Gary Rubio Music* (2013), accessed January 5, 2017, http://www.garyrubiomusic.com/the-story-of-science-ty-unwin-composer.
39. "Ty Unwin: Composing for Space and Beyond," *DV247* (2007), accessed January 5, 2017, http://www.dv247.com/news/Ty%20Unwin%20Composing%20for%20Space%20and%20Beyond/131462.
40. "Leading Television Composer Ty Unwin," *Time+Space* (2012).
41. James Deaville, "Selling War: Television News Music and the Shaping of American Public Opinion," *Echo: A Music-Centered Journal* 8, no. 1 (2006), accessed January 5, 2017, http://www.echo.ucla.edu/Volume8-Issue1/roundtable/deaville.html.
42. John Richardson, *An Eye for Music: Popular Music and the Audiovisual Surreal* (New York: Oxford University Press, 2012), 240.
43. Walter Benjamin, "The Work of Art in the Age of Mechanical Reproduction," in *Illuminations: Essays and Reflections*, ed. Hannah Arendt, trans. Harry Zohn (New York: Schocken Books, 1968), 217–251.
44. OJT, "Great as History Telling, Flawed as a Movie," International Movie Database (2013), accessed January 5, 2017, http://www.imdb.com/title/tt1744825/reviews.

Bibliography

Atlantis: End of a World, Birth of a Legend. Directed by Tony Mitchell. London: British Broadcasting Corporation, Discovery Channel, France Télévisions, and Prosieben, 2011. DVD.
Attali, Jacques. *Noise: The Political Economy of Music*, translated by Brian Massumi. Minneapolis: University of Minnesota Press, 1985.
Benjamin, Walter. "The Work of Art in the Age of Mechanical Reproduction." In *Illumina-*

tions: Essays and Reflections, edited by Hannah Arendt, translated by Harry Zohn, 217–251. New York: Schocken Books, 1968.
Bhabha, Homi. *The Location of Culture*. New York: Routledge, 1994.
Bignell, Jonathan. "Docudramatizing the Real: Developments in British TV Docudrama since 1990." *Studies in Documentary Film* 4, no. 3 (2010): 195–208.
_____, and Stephen Lacey, eds. *British Television Drama: Past, Present and Future*. New York: Palgrave Macmillan, 2014.
Buhler, James, David Neumeyer, and Rob Deemer. *Hearing the Movies: Music and Sound in Film History*. New York: Oxford University Press, 2010.
Burdick, Alan. "Now Hear This: Listening Back on a Century of Sound." *Harper's Magazine* 303, no. 1804 (2001): 70–77.
Cornelius, Michael G. "Introduction: Blood, Sand and Men." In *Spartacus in the Television Arena: Essays on the Starz Series*, edited by Michael G. Cornelius, 1–25. Jefferson, NC: McFarland, 2015.
_____, ed. *Of Muscles and Men: Essays on the Sword and Sandal Film*. Jefferson, NC: McFarland, 2011.
Cyrino, Monica S., ed. *Rome, Season One: History Makes Television*. Malden, MA: Blackwell, 2008.
_____, ed. *Rome, Season Two: Trial and Triumph*. Edinburgh: Edinburgh University Press, 2015.
_____, and Meredith E. Safran, eds. *Classical Myth on Screen*. New York: Palgrave Macmillan, 2015.
Deaville, James. "Selling War: Television News Music and the Shaping of American Public Opinion." *Echo: A Music-centered Journal* 8, no. 1 (2006). Accessed January 5, 2017, http://www.echo.ucla.edu/Volume8-Issue1/roundtable/deaville.html.
_____, ed. *Music in Television: Channels of Listening*. New York: Routledge, 2011.
Dewey, John. *The Public and Its Problems*. New York: Holt, 1927.
Donnelly, Kevin J. *The Spectre of Sound: Music in Film and Television*. London: British Film Institute, 2005.
_____, and Philip Hayward, eds. *Music in Science Fiction Television: Tuned to the Future*. New York: Routledge, 2013.
Ellis, John. *Visible Fictions: Cinema, Television, Video*. New York: Routledge, 2002.
Feld, Steven. "A Sweet Lullaby for World Music." *Public Culture* 12, no. 1 (2000): 145–171.
Gaylard, Gerald. "Postmodern Archaic: The Return of the Real in Digital Virtuality." *Postmodern Culture* 15, no. 1 (2004). Accessed January 5, 2017, https://muse.jhu.edu/article/175222.
Gordon, Steve. *The Future of the Music Business: How to Succeed with the New Digital Technologies*. Milwaukee: Hal Leonard Books, 2005.
Hall, Stuart, Jessica Evans, and Sean Nixon, eds. *Representation*. London: Sage, 2013.
Harty, Kevin J., ed. *The Vikings on Film: Essays on Depictions of the Nordic Middle Ages*. Jefferson, NC: McFarland, 2011.
Held, Guido. "Schizophrenic Chords and Warm Shivers in the Stomach: The 'New Astronautic Sound' of *Raumpatrouille*." In *Music in Science Fiction Television: Tuned to the Future*, edited by Kevin J. Donnelly and Philip Hayward, 87–110. New York: Routledge, 2013.
Hilton, Kevin. "Ty Unwin." *Resolution Magazine* 4, no. 6 (2005): 46–49.
Kapell, Matthew Wilhelm, and Andrew B. R. Elliott, eds. *Playing with the Past: Digital Games and the Simulation of History*. New York: Bloomsbury Academic, 2013.
Karlin, Fred, and Rayburn Wright. *On the Track: A Guide to Contemporary Film Scoring*. New York: Routledge, 2004.
Kassabian, Anahid. *Hearing Film: Tracking Identifications in Contemporary Hollywood Film Music*. New York: Routledge, 2001.
Kinnard, Roy, and Tony Crnkovich. *Italian Sword and Sandal Films, 1908–1990*. Jefferson, NC: McFarland, 2016.
"Leading Television Composer Ty Unwin Talks about Hardware, Software and Staying Ahead of the Game." *Time+Space* (2012). Accessed January 5, 2017, http://www.timespace.com/features/2373.

Lipkin, Steven N. *Docudrama Performs the Past: Arenas of Argument in Films Based on True Stories*. Newcastle upon Tyne: Cambridge Scholars, 2011.

Meyer, Stephen C. *Epic Sound: Music in Postwar Hollywood Biblical Films*. Bloomington: Indiana University Press, 2015.

Nichols, Bill. *Representing Reality: Issues and Concepts in Documentary*. Bloomington: Indiana University Press, 1991.

O'Brien, Daniel. *Classical Masculinity and the Spectacular Body on Film: The Mighty Sons of Hercules*. New York: Palgrave Macmillan, 2014.

OJT. "Great as History Telling, Flawed as a Movie." *International Movie Database* (2013). Accessed January 5, 2017, http://www.imdb.com/title/tt1744825/reviews.

Paul, Joanna. *Film and the Classical Epic Tradition*. Oxford: Oxford University Press, 2013.

Piccini, Angela. "Faking It: Why the Truth Is So Important for TV Archeology." In *Archaeology and the Media*, edited by Timothy Clack and Marcus Brittain, 221–236. Walnut Creek, CA: Left Coast Press.

Pompeii: The Last Day. Directed by Peter Nicholson. London: British Broadcasting Corporation, The Learning Channel, Norddeutscher Rundfunk, and France 2, 2003. DVD.

Poulakis, Nick. "Spotting Amazons, Scoring Demigods: Television, Music and the Reception of Greek Antiquity." In *Revisiting the Past, Recasting the Present: The Reception of Greek Antiquity in Music, 19th Century to the Present*, edited by Katerina Levidou and George Vlastos, 42–49. Athens: Hellenic Music Centre, 2013.

Reinhartz, Adele. *Bible and Cinema: An Introduction*. New York: Routledge, 2013.

Renger, Almut-Barbara, and Jon Solomon, eds. *Ancient Worlds in Film and Television: Gender and Politics*. Leiden: Brill, 2013.

Richardson, John. *An Eye for Music: Popular Music and the Audiovisual Surreal*. New York: Oxford University Press, 2012.

Rodman, Ron. *Tuning In: American Narrative Television Music*. New York: Oxford University Press, 2010.

Rogers, Holly. "Introduction." In *Music and Sound in Documentary Film*, edited by Holly Rogers, 1–19. New York: Routledge, 2015.

Rubio, Gary. "The Story of Science—Ty Unwin (Composer)." *Gary Rubio Music* (2013). Accessed January 5, 2017, http://www.garyrubiomusic.com/the-story-of-science-ty-unwin-composer.

Rushing, Robert A. *Descended from Hercules: Biopolitics and the Muscled Male Body on Screen*. Bloomington: Indiana University Press, 2016.

Russell Staiff. *Re-imagining Heritage Interpretation: Enchanting the Past-Future*. New York: Routledge, 2016.

Tagg, Philip. *Kojak, 50 Seconds of Television Music: Toward the Analysis of Affect in Popular Music*. New York: The Mass Media Music Scholars, 2000.

Taylor, Timothy D. *Beyond Exoticism: Western Music and the World*. Durham: Duke University Press, 2007.

"Ty Unwin: Composing for Space and Beyond." *DV247* (2007). Accessed January 5, 2017, http://www.dv247.com/news/Ty%20Unwin%20Composing%20for%20Space%20and%20Beyond/131462.

White, Hayden. "The Modernist Event." In *The Persistence of History: Cinema, Television, and the Modern Event*, edited by Vivian Sobchack, 17–38. New York: Routledge, 1996.

Williams, Linda. "Melodrama Revised." In *Refiguring American Film Genres: History and Theory*, edited by Nick Browne, 42–88. Berkeley: University of California Press, 1998.

Wolf, Mark J. P. "Subjunctive Documentary: Computer Imaging and Simulation." In *Collecting Visible Evidence*, edited by Michael Renov and Jane Gaines, 274–291. Minneapolis: University of Minnesota Press, 1999.

Hercules, Xena and Genre
The Methodology Behind the Mashup

VALERIE ESTELLE FRANKEL

Hercules: The Legendary Journeys (1995–1999) and *Xena: Warrior Princess* (1995–2001) delighted viewers with action-adventure and sword and sorcery. Sam Raimi and Rob Tapert formed Renaissance Pictures and made their dream project, the horror film *The Evil Dead* (1981, Sam Raimi) before moving on to their New Zealand based fantasy adventures. *Hercules*, starring Kevin Sorbo, launched with five made-for-television movies in 1994. The films' success inspired Universal to launch *Hercules: The Legendary Journeys* as a weekly series, arriving in January 1995. In September of the same year, the creators of *Hercules* premiered a spinoff about a strong action heroine, and no one could believe the story's instant popularity.

Like *Hercules*, *Xena* functions as a love letter to ancient Greece and Rome, celebrating their spectacle and luxury as the heroine wears fine silks and gold to seduce Caesar, or bathes in Cleopatra's famous milk bath. Nonetheless, the running joke is both shows' lack of historical accuracy—as characters chomp on American fast food, use modern slang, and have battles of the bands, there's a huge modern sensibility. Sidekick Joxer (Ted Raimi) dresses as a sloppy medieval knight, Aphrodite (Alexandra Tydings) wears lingerie, and no one in myth or history ever dressed like Xena (Lucy Lawless) and Gabrielle (Renée O'Connor). "*Xena* never has taken itself too seriously," says Steven Sears, co-executive producer, of its core appeal. "As realistic as it tries to be, we didn't write everything as a minor chord. The show has had its tongue in cheek from the beginning, and it's a comedy one week and a drama the next. That is really what separated it from the rest."[1]

Another more important reimagining is the feminist utopian twist in *Xena*, in which women can be anything they wish and needn't submit to men—Gabrielle can be a bard, and Xena a respected warrior. Even in *Hercules*, women can run off and join the Amazons to force men to respect them. The actual myths were far more sexist with Helen of Troy stuck as a prize for the strongest man, and Hercules slaughtering his own family in a fit of madness. Jason, Theseus, and Hercules met the Amazons, but generally raped and slaughtered them. In historical Greece and Rome, women didn't fare much better, as they were property, traded away in marriage by the family's men.

Xena clearly isn't bound by the constraints of history or traditional myth. Celebrating this freedom, she pops into many conflicting eras, meeting Paris, Helen, and Deiphobus from the Trojan War (estimated at 1300 BCE), Ulysses on his voyage, the Amazons (written about in 65–50 BCE), Euripides (480–406 BCE), Homer (c. 690 BCE), Hippocrates (c. 460–370 BCE), and Galen (c. 129 CE)—often in the same episodes! Sappho (625–570 BCE) writes a poem about Xena and Gabrielle, who hail from Poteidaia (founded 609 BCE) and Amphipolis (founded 437 BCE). At the same time, Xena feuds with Julius Caesar (100 BCE–45 BCE) and soon gets mixed up in the Ides of March. To cap it off, she goes exploring outside Greece, inserting herself into legends of Cleopatra (69 BCE–30 BCE), but also Genghis Khan (c. 1162–1227), Lao Tzu (died 531 BCE), Beowulf (written approx. 1000 CE), Boadicea (died 61 CE), Dahak the Zoroastrian dragon of darkness, the Indian myth of Indrajit, and the Chinese discovery of gunpowder (c. 800 CE). She also helps invent Santa Claus! Further, the fighting, especially Xena's, is more Asian than Greek. Showrunner Rob Tapert explains: "I've always been impressed with the Hong Kong cinema style of action, so with *Hercules*, we initially tried to emulate that style. In fact, when we pitched the idea for *Xena*, I made a demo reel of four Hong Kong movies to show the syndicators the kind of action sequences we wanted to do in the show. We also weren't afraid to break the rules of fight realism and go for action that's entertaining and something that the American television audience has never seen before."[2] Meanwhile, Sorbo trained with Douglas Wong, one of Bruce Lee's original students.[3]

In one of many of his own myth-mashes, Hercules kicks off the Olympic Games. Season three's "A Star to Guide Them" is a Christmas episode, complete with the birth of Jesus. There's a mummy episode and then dragon slaying before Herc heads to the crystal-powered Atlantis and on to meet Gilgamesh (c. 2100 BC), then interfere with Norse and Irish myth. The few historical figures are polarized, as there is also a Vlad the Impaler episode (c. 1428–c. 1476 CE) and one with Queen Nefertiti of Egypt (c. 1370–c. 1330 BCE).

This is the power of the subversion—placing the story in a fantasy world rather than a specific year in history. Viewers can accept ancient feminism by swordswomen in metal bikinis or a truly sensitive Hercules who cries and listens to women—why not throw in Rome and India too? That's the appeal of *Xena*'s fake Greece—the feminism safely set as fairytale.

Hercules the New Man

Sam Raimi describes *Hercules* as "the formula for *Army of Darkness*—a funny hero who speaks kind of modern in ancient times."[4] Further, he's sensitive—a pacifist who prefers to settle differences peacefully and is happy to listen to and respect his female partners. Chronicler Robert Weisbrot reports, "*Hercules: The Legendary Journeys* presents a hero of Olympian sensitivity well suited to America in the 1990s. Kevin Sorbo's Hercules is a romantic for the ages."[5] As such, he's the "new man" of television's nineties era, though surprisingly set in a time of violence, with the name of mythology's biggest brawler. This, like the feminist invention of Xena, romanticizes his story for nineties women (and men), creating the kind of lead they prefer. Once again, the historical mishmash sets his story as fantasy, not pure history or even traditional myth. Thus he needn't conform to his era.

His fellow actor Bruce Campbell adds, "Kevin Sorbo portrayed a good guy who always did the right thing, and I'm sure that sat well with parents who were nervous about the lack of 'morals' on TV."[6] This character wasn't just meant to be a role model for kids but an attractive figure for liberated female viewers as he courted warrior women with gentility. "The new sensitive man stood between the liberated woman and what television suggested were two unattractive extremes, spinsterhood and feminism," explains Judy Kutulas in her essay "Liberated Women and New Sensitive Men."[7] She adds:

> The new sensitive men added the final critical touch to the portrait of the liberated woman. He provided the legitimacy that equated her from the feminist. He modeled sensitivity for male viewers, reassuring them that there was still a place for them in liberated women's lives and teaching them how to treat female coworkers as friends and equals.... Together, the liberated woman and the new sensitive man carefully separated the most palatable aspects of feminism and packaged them into a neat consumer-friendly ideal. From the start, television's notion of liberation was fraught with contradictions, but a lot of its appeal was its complexity, which signified its realism. That complexity eased the frustrations and pleasures of real women's lived experiences—their uncertainty, their sense of being trapped between ideologies, their objectification, and their new consumer identities.[8]

In 1993, Sorbo almost landed the role of Superman in the TV show *Lois & Clark: The New Adventures of Superman* (1993–1997). While not a show about ancient times, it's absolutely one about nineties feminism with a butt-kicking career woman as Lois Lane (Teri Hatcher) and sensitive, gentle Clark Kent (Dean Cain). Like Hercules, Superman has godlike strength that he uses to protect mankind but prefers to settle differences with conversation and empathy. Like Xena, Lois can kick butt and call the shots during their team-ups, even as she finds herself intrigued by the man so much softer than herself. Both shows reimagined stories from a more traditional era, recasting its heroes as figures of the nineties.

The "New Man" of course is common in sitcoms as the sweet "nice guy"—Ross (David Schwimmer) or Chandler (Matthew Perry) from *Friends* (1994–2004), Frasier (Kelsey Grammer) from *Cheers* (1982–1993), or Eric (Topher Grace) from *That '70s Show* (1998–2006). This archetype continued with Ted (Josh Radnor) from *How I Met Your Mother* (2005–2014) and Raj (Kunal Nayyar) or Leonard (Johnny Galecki) from *The Big Bang Theory* (2007–present), among many others. Kutulas adds, "He was a media creation, a man himself liberated from gender stereotypes and open to his feelings, genuinely interested in women as people, nurturing and warm, a man not afraid to cry."[9] Disney movies of the time brought in feisty girls Ariel, Belle, and Jasmine, while their men—especially the Beast—grew into sensitive listeners who discovered the women's struggle. "The 'sensitive guy' increasingly became a cultural ideal during the late twentieth century, and the term became a buzzword," adds John Ibson in the "Sensitive Male" entry of *American Masculinities: A Historical Encyclopedia*.[10]

To create a similar hero, series creator Christian Williams looked at how Hercules had been presented in both the Greek myths and modern films, such as the Steve Reeves movie *Hercules* (1958, Pietro Francisci) with its manly hero. Other films include the hokey *Hercules at the Centre of the Earth* (1961, Mario Bava), one of many in an Italian-made series that sent Hercules to Atlantis, the Underworld, and other exotic adventures. With stock footage, reused sets, serious departures from myth and history, and implausible geography, these became more melodrama than historical epic.

Williams decided that the show should present Hercules with "a completely American persona" like American football star Joe Montana.[11] Thus friendly, all-American Herc was born. "He was a hero with considerable depth and congeniality, and the show, with its light, campy, and humorous turns, made for an interesting spin on the ancient hero."[12]

When Kevin Sorbo was cast, his look included long hair, an open shirt, and fake tan.[13] Continuing the glam look, producers asked Sorbo to shave his chest—something he argued Hercules wouldn't do. "When would he have the time for personal grooming," Sorbo quipped.[14] Nonetheless, their hero was well-groomed, and even objectified at times as he took off his shirt to do manual labor while women circled around him to stare and gush. In one famous episode, he posed for an art class wearing only a bunch of grapes.[15]

Nineties Hercules was also happy to take the softer role sometimes. "You're cute when you're nervous," the blacksmith/warrior Atalanta (champion bodybuilder Cory Everson) told Hercules in "Ares," hoisting the blushing hero high in the air. He also wasn't above doing the cooking when wimpy Salmoneus (Robert Trebor) did the hunting and the great warrior princess announced she wouldn't be doing it.[16] Producer Dan Filie said that Sorbo's Hercules seemed like "a guy you wanted to hang out with ... a regular, good guy."[17] He was actually so charming on set that he ended up wooing and marrying guest star Sam Jenkins.[18]

As Sorbo tells it, his original character was tougher. "As much as I liked the first script, it bothered me that the Hercules character was such a serious guy and a self-absorbed womanizer with a violent streak. He was so unlikeable; it was almost silly. I worried that people wouldn't want to watch the show."[19] He began adding jokes and lighter moments that stayed in.

Meanwhile, the first *Hercules* script (*Hercules and the Amazon Women* [1994, Bill L. Norton]), involved militant Amazons retraining macho Hercules out of his chauvinism. The story opens in classic, sexist Greece with the women washing the men's feet and evil stepmother Hera (Meg Foster) sending thugs to persecute Hercules. "She's a perfect example of what happens when a woman gets too much power," Hercules says.[20] He's sexist when asking his best friend Iolaus (Michael Hurst) what his new wife will do for him—cook, sew, provide free labor. However, this historical world soon gets a violent correction.

Bristling with spears, Queen Hippolyta (Roma Downey) and her Amazons capture the hero and tell him, "Just because we are not the kind of women you'd like us to be. Make no mistake, these are women. Women who will not be controlled by men. Not beaten down, not bought and sold like oxen. Men will never dominate these women."[21] Her sidekick, Lysia (Lucy Lawless), hurls Hercules to the ground scornfully. To the queen's surprise, Hercules puts up with a controlled regression to figure out the causes of his sexism and then volunteers to transform:

> HIPPOLYTA: Women need respect and loyalty just as much as you do. But you'll never understand that.
> HERCULES: What if I try to change?
> HIPPOLYTA: You can't change. You're a man.
> HERCULES: If I learned to be the way I am, I can learn to be another way.[22]

Hercules learns to respect the warrior women and passes on his lesson to their abandoned husbands in Gargarenthia. When one smirks, "Our clothes will be mended. We'll eat better. It'll be back to the way it should be," Hercules retorts, "What's wrong with you? Those attitudes are what got you in trouble in the first place. The women aren't the ones who have to work around here. It's you men. All of you."[23] He trains them in listening and helping with housework, until the Gargarenthian men and women are reunited.

As the films continue, he saves the ladies but also vulnerably confides his fears to a teenage girl and breaks down when his best friend is killed. He's also attentive to his mother. "The movies unexpectedly won fans among women as well as men, reflecting Sorbo's deft portrayal of Hercules as the world's most sensitive man as well as the strongest ... it was an apt training ground for [writer John] Schulian's new task: to show the vulnerable human side of the world's mightiest hero."[24]

Hercules Does Myth Mash-Ups

Hercules has few anchors to history, as his stories are more about battling gods and monsters than human adversaries. Commentary indicates that Xena got the warlord stories and Hercules got the god stories, at least in the beginning.[25] Mostly he bounces between classic myths, including those of Midas, Atalanta, Daedalus, Oedipus, Psyche, and Persephone. In these stories, he convinces Atalanta (Corinna Everson) she can be proud of her warrior skills and needn't hide in a dress. He defends Oedipus's daughter Antigone (Paige Moss) and helps her fulfill her potential as queen. He likewise talks Cupid (Karl Urban) down from becoming a jealous "green eyed monster" and makes a match between him and the naïve Psyche (Susan Ward). His skill here is listening to women instead of dictating to them as the arrogant gods do.

In the episode "The Other Side" he goes on a mission for Demeter (Sarah Wilson) to reclaim her lost daughter Persephone (Andrea Croton) from the underworld. This is a soul-wrenching trip as he meets his dead wife and children who embrace him joyfully, unaware that they're dead. "Are you crying, Daddy?" his little daughter Ilea asks.[26]

"No, no, it's the wind—just blew something in my eye," he insists.[27] Meanwhile, Hades (Erik Thomson) offers Hercules his family back if he'll leave Persephone there. Hercules finally must suffer through telling his wife that she's dead but has a chance at life—if they condemn mankind to eternal winter. "So people are starving and they're dying. And the little problems of our family just pale in comparison, don't they?" she notes sympathetically.[28] She releases him with a final "Seeing you brought me more joy than you could have ever dreamed of. But just promise me one thing.... That no matter how long it takes that you and I will be back together again."[29] More angst for the audience as he bids her and each child goodbye.

On the same quest, Hercules sympathetically negotiates with Persephone to return. As Demeter and Hades fight over her, Hercules bursts out, "Now hold on, both of you! I hear a lot about what you want and what you want, but I don't hear what she wants. Well, Persephone, what do you want?"[30] When she wishes for both of them, Hercules creates the famous compromise—"She wants both. She can have both. She ate half the fruit. That means she can stay half the year on the other side with Hades, half on Earth with her mother."[31] He restores her power, something rarely seen in the narrative—

even in more liberated forms, her only choice is a smothering mother or a devouring husband. This time, Herc helps Persephone call the shots. She even insists he save a farmer's beloved pig. "Why do I get myself into these things?" he mutters, but of course, he saves the cuddly pet too.[32]

The scaly monster-woman Echidna (Bridget Hoffman) blames Hercules for slaying her children the Hydra (*Hercules and the Amazon Women* [1994, Bill L. Norton]), the She-Demon ("The Wrong Path") and the Stymphalian Bird ("The Road to Calydon"). In revenge, Echidna kidnaps Hercules' mother. "He killed my children! He killed them one after another! No mother should have to endure that," she roars.[33]

Hercules rescues his mother but succumbs when Alcmene (Liddy Holloway) pleads for Echidna's life, saying, "We're better than that. We're not monsters. We're not instruments of death and destruction. We're human beings. And besides now I know how she felt when her children died. She felt the same way I would have."[34]

Hercules proves he was right to spare Echidna when she returns later that season. Hercules travels with the kindly giant Typhon (Glenn Shadix), only to discover he's Echidna's husband (both of these were fierce monsters in myth, now kinder and more misunderstood). He reunites gentle Typhon with his angry tentacled wife, smiling that it seems there's someone for everyone. Meanwhile, the pair resemble the fierce woman and sensitive man fictional couple so popular at the time. In fact, Typhon and Echidna make a sweet modern duo as he loves her despite her prickliness. Typhon tells her, "I know about the kids. It was all Hera's fault. She's the one who made them do bad things. Hercules was just trying to make the world a nice place."

> ECHIDNA: I've been such a fool. And I've done such horrible things!
> TYPHON: But I still love ya, Echidna.
> ECHIDNA You do? Then come here, lover-boy![35]

The hard-edged woman finds love from the sensitive man and all goes well—in time, Hercules not only saves their newest child, but finds them every modern couple's dream—a reliable babysitter.

As for Hercules' friends, all are repurposed to give Herc a sense of community. Iolaus is reimagined from the nephew of the myths to childhood companion, giving Hercules the loner hero a beloved partner. The opportunist Salmoneus is actually a character in Greek myth, a self-serving narcissist who tried to co-opt the gods' worship until Zeus wipes him out with a thunderbolt. Remaking him as a salesman is a much more modern take on the character that leaves him more humorously greedy than evil. Autolycus (Bruce Campbell), the King of Thieves from Greek myth, could fit, except that his grandson Ulysses (John D'Aquino) appears on *Xena* and the two are about the same age. The joke character Falafel (Paul Norell) begins by serving his namesake then goes on to offer hotdogs, tacos, ambrosia (specifically the marshmallow salad kind), a modern wedding cake, and boiled sea serpent with "eyes and fries." Herc cringes. "I am hungry, but I'm more interested in good food," he complains.[36] Donna Minkowitz explains in her essay, "Xena: She's Big, Tall, Strong—and Popular":

> The show thrives on anachronism. Actually, both *Hercules* and *Xena* utilize this at times to make humorous comments about contemporary life. In one episode of *Hercules*, a man at a roadside stand sells Hercules some "fast food." Hercules takes a bite and immediately spits it out. "This is horrible!" "Yes," answers the vendor, "but it's fast?" Salmoneus, more of a regular on *Hercules* than on *Xena*, seems to exist primarily for this purpose. At one point he says that Xena needs a "theme song" for herself which, of course, he would be happy to provide.[37]

All these flips emphasize a freedom for the producers to do what they wish with the characters—sensitive Herc is no stranger than Iolaus eating tacos. Likewise, their cronies come across as incredibly modern, especially in their attitudes. There's a series of modern ballroom dance and fashion adventures all starring Michael Hurst as the hilarious high-pitched Widow Twanky. This lets the actor show his own softer side in heels and skirts as he trains Hercules and an ugly duckling girl so they can win a dance competition. Other characters follow suit as Salmoneus and Autolycus cross-dress to understand the women's world—earning Autolycus a delighted girlfriend.

Season five is Hercules' great year of travel. Of course, his adventures are filled with a soul-aching loss that only makes him more attractive. In the later seasons "Hercules spins tales with new emotional power, as the world's strongest man must vanquish not only warlords and monsters but also the darkness in his heart."[38] After Gilgamesh (circa 2100 BC, played by Tony Todd) kills Iolaus, Hercules goes on an extended arc in the kingdoms of Norse myth, involving himself with the death of Balder (Rupert Cox), and also falls for the Morrigan (Tamara Gorski) in Irish lands (references for both mythic characters go back to the ninth century). Meanwhile, Hercules' companions Salmoneus and Autolycus do an *Arabian Nights* adventure in "Genies and Grecians and Geeks, Oh My." King Arthur (Neill Rea) stops in, but in this instance, Merlin (Tim Faville) specifically explains that he made him travel in time. This single anachronism has story logic, though it also highlights all the others that go unexplained. In a crossover with the *Xena* arcs paralleling his own show, Hercules tops all this off by encountering Julius Caesar (Karl Urban) and the Archangel Michael (Charles Measure). As he treats his new alt-world sidekick Iolaus 2 with compassion and continues flirting with powerful sorceresses and heroines, he's truly a hero of fantasy.

Alt-world episodes include making them all French during the Reign of Terror in "Les Contemptibles" and introducing the Sovereign (Kevin Sorbo), an evil Hercules from a parallel world. The modern "Yes, Virginia,

There Is a Hercules" suggests Herc and Ares (Kevin Smith) are really alive in Los Angeles and Hercules is *pretending* to be actor Kevin Sorbo, while the following "Porkules" transforms him into a barnyard animal. "For Those of You Just Joining Us" is another L.A. story with the real Herc pitching stories that become a season five clip show. All these re-envisionings emphasize Hercules as a true heartthrob, since the modern actor is all-powerful and divine.

Xena the Warrior Woman

Rob Tapert describes arguing with Universal for the right to do a women's action show and having the writer from previous generation's shows *The Bionic Woman* (1976–1978) and *Cagney and Lacey* (1982–1988) retorting that neither had made much money. However, a new era with a new type of feminism had arrived. "I'm really glad I got to get my foot in the door so that more would follow," he concludes. "It really led to a whole retooling of girl power."[39]

In fact, the phenomenon of girl power took off at just the right time for *Xena*. The genre was inspired by the lyrics of Madonna, Riot Grrrl, and the Spice Girls in the nineties. "Girlpower celebrities include such diverse subjects as Lara Croft, Tank Girl, Buffy the Vampire Slayer, Courtney Love, and the Spice Girls (whose own girlpower heroine was, famously, Margaret Thatcher). They are deemed to embody girlpower because they are outspoken, not afraid to take power, believe in themselves, and run their own lives."[40]

Thus in the nineties women like Sailor Moon, the Powerpuff Girls, and Buffy kicked butt. "Girl power heroines, while strong, are also thoroughly feminine, wearing short skirts and makeup not to please society but because they want to."[41] However in each case, the women were subtly reduced or made fantastical to leave the patriarchal structure in place. Buffy begins as a parody, and keeps the humor and girlish frivolity in place. Sailor Moon is another schoolgirl with schoolgirl interests. The Powerpuff Girls are not just superheroes but kindergarteners. All of them live in fantastical places. Thus, no female hero both as powerful and as serious as Superman ever arrives to provide real competition. Xena's self-parody helps keep her nonthreatening to male structure, as does her mismatched setting—it's a contemporary story and a historical one, but not really. Her storyline never actually happened, then or now.

In this new imagining of feminism, the heroines could wear sexy clothes, but they also saved themselves without male assistance. In this tradition, Xena is lovely and sexy—dressing provocatively and unabashedly using seduction as a tool. "With her distinctive leather outfit, swirling brass design on her breastplates, blue eyes, and dark, flowing hair, Xena redefined the conventions of action heroes and women warriors."[42] She's gorgeous and groomed but still an action woman. Her actress, Lucy Lawless, adds, "Xena's power doesn't come from her sexuality … it is not that she can seduce men, but that she can out-strategy them; that she is a great leader, and great sword person, and is inspirational to others."[43]

At the same time, she's undeniably strong. "Real warriors—hulking, muscle-bound men in pursuit of plunder and booty—quiver in fear when Xena strides onto the scene. She destroys them with ease, if they do not flee first."[44] Xena is nearly undefeatable. Before losing to an entire army in the final episode, she spends the series run defeating warlords and gods. "I'm thrilled the show has struck such a chord with women because it's been brought to my attention that an awful lot of women need that," Lawless concludes.[45]

Her sidekick Gabrielle is also a leader, training in season one to become an Amazon queen and an expert with her fighting staff. By the time of Xena's season five pregnancy, she's defending herself with a pair of sais and is such a warrior that Ares tries to appoint her his protégé. In that season, she chooses the "way of friendship" over the "way of peace," becoming a formidable force herself. At the series' end, she has mastered all of Xena's skills and takes on her role as the next lone warrior-adventurer. At the same time, she's still a "girl," innocent, sweet and blonde, even as she gradually loses the long hair and skirts. She's Xena's conscience and path to redemption, a girly girl as Xena is the tough one.

As these two women travel, critics assert that the series emerges as "a Hollywood corrective to the ancient world's sexism."[46] Xena and Gabrielle battle social injustice, defending the weak. The show makes "the traditionally male superhero genre cool for girls without hollowing out the strong message."[47] The characters also took a major step for gay rights. While they did not directly come out as lesbians on the show, the two women established themselves as soulmates who had no need of male husbands or long-term boyfriends—only each other.

Further, in this idealized world, no one ever insults Xena and Gabrielle's skill levels because they're female or tries to block them from being a traveling warrior or bard. Even when Gabrielle returns to her childhood village, no one uses words like "You're just a girl." Thus she becomes much more. Cathy Young explains in her essay, "What We Owe Xena": "Gender, in the Xenaverse, just wasn't a big deal: No one questioned Xena's ability to fight and command, or Gabrielle's desire to be a warrior, because they were girls."[48] Women can be damsels, ruling queens, villainesses. Whichever role they held, they were more nuanced than stereotyped. Even the Amazons were not an idealized sisterhood but tribes with internal conflict that introduced friends and enemies. Young concludes, "Women on *Xena* were simply human, no better or worse than men: feminism as it ought to be."[49]

Xena Subverts Myths

There's more than Xena's feminist role that's anachronistic. Her armor has Maori designs, she wields a Persian chakram. Her outfit is from the "chick in a brass bra" concept popularized in sword and sorcery but hardly in history. Xena also battles with mysticism from the female author of the *I Ching*, as well as Alti's Siberian shamanism and pressure points (a complete medical fantasy) from a mysterious Egyptian slave. Young comments: "The sense of mischievous, quirky, anything-goes fun was heightened by the setting: a pseudo-historical, kind of mythological world in which ancient Greeks wore medieval or Middle Eastern clothes and talked late-20th century American English (where else could you hear an Olympian god talk about someone's 'inferiority complex'?); in which Caesar and Pompey coexisted with Amazons, centaurs and gods; and in which the Trojan War, the Battle of Marathon and the death of Cleopatra were separated by just a few years."[50] Renée O'Connor adds: "We had animals shrinking. We had metaphors around Jesus, around Caesar. We had Roman battles. We traveled the world into all these different countries from India to China. There wasn't a lot that Rob and his staff didn't approach."[51] In fact, the show has so many myths inverted that a few representative ones will show much about the show's new message.

In "Cradle of Hope," Xena and Gabrielle meet Pandora (Mary Elizabeth McGlynn), who carries her grandmother's cherished box to keep hope safe. This reimagines the original legend with Pandora as a force of evil to a kinder guardian—as Xena discovers at the episode's end, "the box was empty, but Pandora was still carrying our hope: hope has been and always will be safe. It's inside every one of us."[52] She is no longer treacherous Eve, but a devoted protector.

"Beware of Greeks Bearing Gifts" presents the Trojan War (1184 BC), with its great heroes long dead. Meanwhile, chauvinist pigs Paris (Warren Carl) and King Menelaus (Ken Blackburn) consider Helen (Galyn Görg) a possession. Xena thus invents the Trojan Horse and catapults herself out of it, ending the siege. "What do you want to do?" she asks Helen. When the other woman replies, "No one's ever asked me that before!" Xena frees her to find her own destiny, no longer as princess or prize.[53] Melissa Meister explains in her essay, "*Xena: Warrior Princess* through the Lenses of Feminism": "In *Xena's* recreation of the story, Helen (who is also incidentally African-American in this rendition) is given a voice. She firmly expresses her desire and power by telling Xena that she left her husband for Paris because she was in love and she left of her own free will. Through *Xena*'s recreation of western fiction, Helen is given a responsibility in her own history. She is no longer the pawn of men, but an active player in her own destiny."[54] Following this, Xena helps Ulysses (with his jarring Roman name) get home, out-singing the Sirens, secretly bending his bow, and executing all the clever plans he invents in the books. Thus she becomes the true agent, though she lets the male hero take credit. "In influencing male mythical and historical icons, the series attempts to give credit to women for the great discoveries of time, yet at the same time acknowledges that males have received the credit in the annals of history."[55]

"How can Homer (of *Iliad* and *Odyssey* fame) tell the story of Spartacus ... when that particular slave revolt occurred at least seven hundred years later?" one critic protests.[56] Certainly, the Bardic school competition is quite a mishmash. Further, Gabrielle counsels the mythic Orion only to discover he's the future legend Homer (Dean O'Gorman) after she meets stuffy Euripides (Joe Manning), and engaging Stallonus (Patrick Brunton)—a Sylvester Stallone pun. None make misogynistic comments about competing with a female bard. Finally, Gabrielle coaches Homer and gives up her place to him, allowing him, like Ulysses, to claim credit.[57]

In "The Giant Killer," Xena sets up the David (Antony Starr) and Goliath (Todd Rippon) battle by counseling the Israelite hero in the weak spots Goliath is hiding well as human politics. Gabrielle, meanwhile, encourages him to keep writing psalms.[58] Sandra Falero explains in her essay, "Mything in Action: Re-envisioning Male Myth/History in the Xenaverse": "There is a design within the narrative that hints at the fact that the "real" credit goes to Xena for winning the battle, as well as for arriving at the idea that David's credibility as a leader needed to be cemented by the act of killing Goliath. This re-envisioned male mythical/historical event has carefully tread on sacred ground by exalting David as a good, kindhearted, and promising leader, while at the same time illustrating the power a woman used to get him there."[59] Showrunner R.J. Stewart quips, "We were always just telling it like it is. We were correcting the impression that centuries of sexism has created by taking credit away from Xena and giving it to all these pretender males."[60] Beowulf's legend follows the same pattern, replacing the heroes with Xena and Gabrielle. Beowulf (Renato Bartolomei) begs Xena's aid to battle Grendel, who in fact was the Valkyrie Grinhilda before Evil Xena forged the cursed ring and corrupted her with it. To fix her past mistake, Xena claims the ring and is struck with amnesia, while Gabrielle becomes Brunhilda sleeping in her ring of fire. Though Xena takes the role of "the noble and fair Wealthea," and submits to King Hrothgar (John Leigh) as gentle wife, she finally remembers her true self and saves her soulmate Gabrielle with a kiss. This is not a story of brawling Beowulf and a monster, but a story of Xena's sacrifice and Grinhilda's (Luanne Gordon) healing as her humanity is restored.[61]

Xena may have learned this strategy from her mentor. In fact, the Chinese book of Lao Tzu is not written by him—he is a vicious tyrant (died 531 BCE). Instead, his wife Lao Ma (Jacqueline Kim) keeps him perpetually comatose and writes the book in his name. As she tells Xena, "This wisdom comes from Heaven. What difference does it make who gets credit for it—Lao Ma or Lao Tzu?"[62] Thus one of China's greatest philosophers is recast as a woman. Further, Xena is the one to publish the book, spreading her friend's wisdom. Returning to China, Xena uses Lao Ma's teachings to destroy the entire army of Genghis Khan (c. 1162–1227) and with it the world-threatening recipe for black powder. Once again, she inserts herself into history. "The visual representation of thousands of soldiers turned to stone implies that Xena herself fashioned the famed earthenware burial army of the First Emperor of Ch'in (c. 210 BCE)."[63] This too becomes a story of redeeming kindness. Xena explains, "Today, I felt a kind of compassion that I've never felt before.... The power that I had today wasn't born out of anger. I wasn't even thinking about those men. I was thinking about the people that they wanted to hurt. So, I guess what I said before isn't true anymore. I have seen love end a war."[64] Lao Ma has taught her loving-kindness in the name of saving lives.

While sometimes she lets men take credit, other times Xena battles patriarchal thinking directly. "Is There a Doctor in the House" has Xena use tracheotomies, amputations, splints, and a respirator, and perform CPR as well. Meanwhile the head physician Galen (Ron Smith) is a misogynist and blustering control freak, insisting, "This is our temple! We decide who will be treated!"[65] She kicks out Galen and instead trains his caring apprentice Hippocrates (Andrew Robertt). The two were in fact not contemporary, and Hippocrates was older. "Hippocrates lived c. 460–370 BCE, while Galen was born later, c. 129 CE. Nonetheless, Hippocrates becomes involved in an intellectual relationship with Xena after noticing her mastery of poultices and herbal medicines."[66] Through her storytelling, gentle Gabrielle convinces General Marmax (Ray Woolf) to set aside the conflict—thus the women dismantle the patriarchal structure of war and medicine, remaking them as they wish.

"The Furies" sees Xena trapped in the conundrum of Orestes (Steve Farac Ciprian). Apparently her mother Cyrene (Darien Takle) murdered her father and the Furies are punishing her for not taking vengeance. When Xena discovers this, she supports Cyrene, saying flippantly, "So Mama killed Papa. Doesn't matter. You were trying to save my life, right? I should be grateful." Xena rejects the gods' commands, and insists on battling Ares instead—defeating him will prove she has a divine father and not a mortal murdered one. She wins, pummeling him humiliatingly and claiming victory while also protecting her beloved mother.[67]

Her great patriarchal nemesis from seasons two through four is Caesar himself. "Destiny" shows Caesar (100 BCE–45 BCE) betraying and crucifying Xena, beginning their feud. "Divide and conquer, my friend. You divide a woman's emotion from her sensibilities—and you have her," he smirks.[68] Thus this becomes a gender war, with the independent warrior woman taking on the greatest empire. "The Roman Empire here is a historicized monster against which Xena does battle, her efforts meant primarily to mitigate the effects of imperialism and to defend the weak."[69]

Soon enough, Xena visits Britannia and allies herself with its most famous warrior woman, Boudica (Jennifer Ward-Lealand). Together they humiliate Caesar. In "When in Rome," Xena sneaks into Rome to free the rebel Vercinix of Gaul (Tamati Rice) and return him to his loving family. She captures Crassus (Matthew Chamberlain), Caesar's equal in the First Triumvirate, to hold hostage. A Crassus–Vercinix exchange "expresses again the dichotomy between the Roman agenda and the domestic values Xena champions."[70] She then marches into Rome and Caesar's very palace, shocking Caesar with her boldness. "Xena—this is impossible. How can you j—this is Rome. You can't—you—" he babbles.[71]

With perfect control, she retorts, "There's a sentence in there just dyin' to get out. Huh. Sorry about your soldiers. We were playing tag in the forum, and I gotta tell ya, they don't lose well."[72] When Caesar tries to charm her Xena retorts, "I gotta go to the bathroom. Are we done yet?"[73] She swaps Crassus for Vercinix, and Caesar, caught looking foolish, publicly executes his ally. Xena has thus struck against Rome and caused a great historical figure's death.

She likewise manipulates Pompey (Jeremy Callaghan) and Caesar in "A Good Day" with the help of innocent villagers, and then executes Pompey in "Endgame." This time, Xena and Gabrielle's army of Amazons aid her in taking down Rome. Caesar rejects an alliance with them, eroding Brutus' trust. In fact, Xena subverts his faith in Caesar over and over, orchestrating the Ides of March. "I don't think she's been given full credit in the history books, which is one of the reasons we wanted to set the record straight," says co-executive producer Eric Gruendemann mock-seriously.[74]

The Crossovers

The team-up episodes continue to mash myths. "Prometheus" has Hera chain the episode's namesake up (an event also puzzlingly seen in the film *Hercules and the Circle of Fire* [1994, Doug Lefler]), and as a result mankind loses the gifts of healing and fire. The oracles say, blending Greek and Roman references, "If you want to free Prometheus, you must go to Vulcan Mountain, and enter the cave of Hephaestus."⁷⁵ Classically, Hercules freed Prometheus, but now Xena aids him, reclaiming part of the myth. Both generously try sacrificing their lives, emphasizing that this is altruism and mutual love, not a competition for acclaim. Hercules tells Xena he's thinking with his heart. "That means, I can't let you die, if I can do anything to stop it."⁷⁶

The story of the Golden Hind is greatly subverted as it's not an animal Hercules catches on his labors but a shy, beautiful young woman he marries. The gods kill her and frame Hercules, giving him another arc of soul-wrenching despair and audience sympathy. It's strong, self-assured Xena who comes to town to defend him when he's most vulnerable and can't bear to fight.⁷⁷

Together Hercules and Xena kill the entire Olympian pantheon (or nearly). Hercules begins by defending his dear friend Xena, who is giving birth to the chosen one—baby Eve. The female Fates warn Zeus he cannot escape:

> ZEUS: My dreams are dark. There's danger. Illuminate that section—there, my Fates. Tell me.
> CLOTHO: As it has been since time beyond remembering—you will continue to rule supreme among supreme—
> LACHESIS: —until such time, as a child not begotten by man is born—
> ATROPOS: —a time that's fast approaching.⁷⁸

King Zeus defies them, insisting, "Our dominion here—is eternal" and "I have always been the *master* of fate. I'm not about to become its servant."⁷⁹ He attacks Xena, and Hercules regretfully kills him. Now mankind can choose their destiny without the control of the gods. Hercules, however, does not take his place, turning his back on the rulership through murder that defined Zeus as well as his father and grandfather in classic myth.

Following this, Xena kills many more gods while defending her baby girl. At the end of season five, she slays a gigantic, roaring Poseidon, then decapitates Discord and hurls Hephaestus's own hammer into his chest. Even weaponless, she lights Hades on fire and squashes Deimos under the furniture. Up on Olympus, she kills Artemis and Athena. Suddenly Ares (who is becoming a New Man) sacrifices his immortality to heal Xena's beloved Eve and Gabrielle, though he knows this will cost him his divinity. Having fallen for the warrior princess, he is taking her values for his own.⁸⁰ She finally rewards him for his growth by restoring his powers and Aphrodite's, reinstating a pantheon of love and a more compassionate war, in place of the Christian archangels who were a bit too willing to sacrifice the innocent—more patriarchy she denies rulership.

As the heroes continue adventuring in comics and a single cartoon (*Hercules and Xena—The Animated Movie: The Battle for Mount Olympus* [1998,

130   Part Two: Wisdom from the Gods

Lynne Naylor]), they emphasize that they can co-opt the ancient myths, even while reimagining them as a world of modern equality.

The nineties era of assertive heroines and sensitive men synced well with classical times ... or rather, fake ones. The Herc- and Xenaverse was a silly, sexy world of American slang, fast food, leather and whips where anything was possible—even gender roles far removed from history. Thus the pair of heroes set a new standard, carrying the ancient legends into modern sensibilities.

NOTES

1. Rick Sherwood, "War Stories," *Hollywood Reporter—International Edition* 361, no. 8 (January 4, 2000): S-1, accessed December 17, 2016.
2. "What Puts the Punch into Hercules & Xena," *Black Belt*, September 1996.
3. Kevin Sorbo, *True Strength: My Journey from Hercules to Mere Mortal—and How Nearly Dying Saved My Life* (Boston: Da Capo Press, 2011), 30.
4. Bruce Campbell, *If Chins Could Kill: Confessions of a B Movie Actor* (New York: St. Martin's, 2002), 276.
5. Robert Weisbrot, *Hercules: The Legendary Journeys: An Insider's Guide to the Continuing Adventures* (New York: Taylor Trade, 2004), 252.
6. Campbell, *If Chins Could Kill*, 289.
7. Judy Kutulas, "Liberated Women and New Sensitive Men: Reconstructing Gender in the 1970s Workplace Comedies," in *The Sitcom Reader: America Viewed and Skewed*, ed. Mary M. Dalton and Laura R. Linder (Albany: State University of New York Press, 2005), 223.
8. Ibid., 224.
9. Ibid., 223.
10. John Ibson, "Sensitive Male," in *American Masculinities: A Historical Encyclopedia*, ed. Bret Carroll (New York: Sage, 2013).
11. Robert Weisbrot, *Hercules: The Legendary Journeys: The Official Companion* (New York: Doubleday, 1998), 2.
12. Gladys L. Knight, *Female Action Heroes: A Guide to Women in Comics, Video Games, Film, and Television* (Santa Barbara, CA: Greenwood, 2010), 321.
13. Sorbo, *True Strength*, 34.
14. Ibid., 30.
15. "If I Had a Hammer," Season 4, Disc 4, *Hercules The Legendary Journeys* (January 12, 1998; Universal City, CA: Universal Studios Home Entertainment, 2013), DVD.
16. "Unchained Heart," Season 1, Disc 3, *Hercules The Legendary Journeys* (May 8, 1995; Universal City, CA: Universal Studios Home Entertainment, 2010), DVD.
17. Weisbrot, *Hercules: The Legendary Journeys*, 83.
18. Sorbo, *True Strength*, 41.
19. Ibid., 33.
20. *Hercules and the Amazon Women*, directed by Bill L. Norton (1994; Universal City, CA: Universal Studios Home Entertainment, 1998), DVD.
21. *Ibid.*
22. *Ibid.*
23. *Ibid.*
24. Weisbrot, *Hercules: Continuing Adventures*, 4.
25. "The Furies," Season 3, Disc 1, *Xena: Warrior Princess* (September 29, 1997; Universal City, CA: Universal Studios Home Entertainment, 2012), DVD.
26. "The Other Side," Season 2, Disc 2, *Hercules The Legendary Journeys* (October 30 1995; Universal City, CA: MCA Television, 2003), DVD.
27. *Ibid.*
28. *Ibid.*

29. *Ibid.*
30. *Ibid.*
31. *Ibid.*
32. *Ibid.*
33. "The Mother of All Monsters," Season 2, Disc 2, *Hercules The Legendary Journeys* (October 16, 1995; Universal City, CA: MCA Television, 2003), DVD.
34. *Ibid.*
35. "Cast a Giant Shadow," Season 2, Disc 3, *Hercules The Legendary Journeys* (November 13, 1995; Universal City, CA: MCA Television, 2003), DVD.
36. "The Other Side."
37. Donna Minkowitz, "Xena: She's Big, Tall, Strong—and Popular," *Ms. Magazine*, July/August 1996.
38. Weisbrot, *Hercules: Continuing Adventures*, 91.
39. "Warrior Tales," 1996, On *Xena: Warrior Princess Season Two* (October 14, 1996; Beverly Hills, CA: Starz / Anchor Bay, 2003), DVD.
40. Anita Harris, *Future Girl: Young Women in the Twenty-First Century* (New York: Routledge, 2004), 17.
41. Valerie Estelle Frankel, *Buffy and the Heroine's Journey* (Jefferson, NC: McFarland, 2012), 12.
42. Carolyn Skelton, "Xena: Warrior Princess," *The Essential Cult TV Reader*, ed. David Lavery (Lexington: University Press of Kentucky, 2010), 329.
43. Varla Ventura, *Sheroes* (San Francisco: Red Wheel Weiser, 1998), 314.
44. Sherrie A. Inness, *Tough Girls: Women Warriors and Wonder Women in Popular Culture* (Philadelphia: University of Pennsylvania Press, 1999), 167.
45. Ventura, *Sheroes.*
46. "Why Greek Tunics Are Back." *The Economist*, May 17, 1997, 93.
47. Mark Kingwell, "Babes in Toyland: Xena versus Sailor Moon," *Saturday Night*, February 1997, 83.
48. Cathy Young, "What We Owe Xena," *Salon*, September 15, 2005.
49. *Ibid.*
50. *Ibid.*
51. Natalie Abrams, "An Oral Herstory the Untold Tale of Xena: Warrior Princess," *Entertainment Weekly* 1414 (May 13, 2016): 34, accessed December 17, 2016.
52. "Cradle of Hope," Season 1, Disc 1, *Xena: Warrior Princess* (September 25, 1995; Universal City, CA: Universal Studios Home Entertainment, 2010), DVD.
53. "Beware Greeks Bearing Gifts," Season 1, Disc 3, *Xena: Warrior Princess* (January 15, 1996; Universal City, CA: Universal Studios Home Entertainment, 2010), DVD.
54. Melissa Meister, "Xena: Warrior Princess through the Lenses of Feminism," *Whoosh* 10 (1997).
55. Sandra Falero, "Mything in Action: Re-Envisioning Male Myth/History in the Xenaverse," *Whoosh* 56 (2001).
56. Minkowitz, "Xena."
57. "Athens City Academy of the Performing Bards," Season 1, Disc 4, *Xena: Warrior Princess* (January 22, 1996; Universal City, CA: Universal Studios Home Entertainment, 2010), DVD.
58. "The Giant Killer," Season 2, Disc 1, *Xena: Warrior Princess* (October 14, 1996; Beverly Hills, CA: Starz / Anchor Bay, 2003), DVD.
59. Falero, "Mything in Action."
60. "Interview: The Ring," 2000, On *Xena: Warrior Princess Season 6* (November 20, 2000; Beverly Hills, CA: Starz / Anchor Bay, 2005), DVD.
61. "The Ring" (608).
62. "The Debt, Part 2," Season 3, Disc 2, *Xena: Warrior Princess* (November 10, 1997; Universal City, CA: Universal Studios Home Entertainment, 2012), DVD.
63. Karen Pusateri, "Xena: Warrior Princess: An Analytical Review," *Whoosh* 1 (1996).
64. "Back in the Bottle," Season 5, Disc 2, *Xena: Warrior Princess* (November 15, 1999; Beverly Hills, CA: Starz / Anchor Bay, 2004), DVD.

132   Part Two: Wisdom from the Gods

65. "Is There a Doctor in the House?" Season 1, Disc 5, *Xena: Warrior Princess* (July 29, 1996; Universal City, CA: Universal Studios Home Entertainment, 2010), DVD.
66. Falero, "Mything in Action."
67. "The Furies."
68. "Destiny," Season 2, Disc 3, *Xena: Warrior Princess* (April 21, 1997; Beverly Hills, CA: Starz / Anchor Bay, 2003), DVD.
69. Alison Futrell, "The Baby, the Mother, and the Empire: Xena as Ancient Hero," in *Athena's Daughters: Television's New Women Warriors*, ed. Frances Early and Kathleen Kennedy (Syracuse: Syracuse University Press, 2003), 22.
70. *Ibid.*, 23.
71. "Destiny."
72. *Ibid.*
73. *Ibid.*
74. "When in Rome..." Season 3, Disc 4, *Xena: Warrior Princess* (March 2, 1998; Universal City, CA: Universal Studios Home Entertainment, 2012), DVD.
75. "Prometheus," Season 1, Disc 2, *Xena: Warrior Princess* (November 6, 1995; Universal City, CA: Universal Studios Home Entertainment, 2010), DVD.
76. *Ibid.*
77. "Judgment Day," Season 3, Disc 5, *Hercules The Legendary Journeys* (February 17, 1997; Universal City, CA: Universal Studios Home Entertainment, 2013), DVD.
78. "God Fearing Child," Season 5, Disc 3, *Xena: Warrior Princess* (January 31, 2000; Beverly Hills, CA: Starz / Anchor Bay, 2004), DVD.
79. *Ibid.*
80. "Motherhood," Season 5, Disc 5, *Xena: Warrior Princess* (May 15, 2000; Beverly Hills, CA: Starz / Anchor Bay, 2004), DVD.

BIBLIOGRAPHY

Abrams, Natalie. "An Oral Herstory the Untold Tale of *Xena: Warrior Princess*." *Entertainment Weekly* 1414 (May 13, 2016): 34. Accessed December 17, 2016.
"Athens City Academy of the Performing Bards." Season 1, Disc 4, *Xena: Warrior Princess*. January 22, 1996; Universal City, CA: Universal Studios Home Entertainment, 2010. DVD.
"Back in the Bottle." Season 5, Disc 2, *Xena: Warrior Princess*. November 15, 1999; Beverly Hills, CA: Starz / Anchor Bay, 2004. DVD.
"Beware Greeks Bearing Gifts." Season 1, Disc 3, *Xena: Warrior Princess*. January 15, 1996; Universal City, CA: Universal Studios Home Entertainment, 2010. DVD.
Campbell, Bruce. *If Chins Could Kill: Confessions of a B Movie Actor*. New York: St. Martin's, 2002.
"Cast a Giant Shadow." Season 2, Disc 3, *Hercules The Legendary Journeys*. November 13, 1995; Universal City, CA: MCA Television, 2003. DVD.
"Coming Home." Season 6, Disc 1, *Xena: Warrior Princess*. October 2, 2000; Beverly Hills, CA: Starz / Anchor Bay, 2005. DVD.
"Cradle of Hope." Season 1, Disc 1, *Xena: Warrior Princess*. September 25, 1995; Universal City, CA: Universal Studios Home Entertainment, 2010. DVD.
"The Debt, Part 2." Season 3, Disc 2, *Xena: Warrior Princess*. November 10, 1997; Universal City, CA: Universal Studios Home Entertainment, 2012. DVD.
"Destiny." Season 2, Disc 3, *Xena: Warrior Princess*. April 21, 1997; Beverly Hills, CA: Starz / Anchor Bay, 2003. DVD.
"Endgame." Season 4, Disc 5, *Xena: Warrior Princess*. May 3, 1999; Universal City, CA: Universal Studios Home Entertainment, 2013. DVD.
Falero, Sandra. "Mything in Action: Re-Envisioning Male Myth/History in the Xenaverse." *Whoosh* 56 (2001).
Frankel, Valerie Estelle. *Buffy and the Heroine's Journey*. Jefferson, NC: McFarland, 2012.
"The Furies." Season 3, Disc 1, *Xena: Warrior Princess*. September 29, 1997; Universal City, CA: Universal Studios Home Entertainment, 2012. DVD.
Futrell, Alison. "The Baby, the Mother, and the Empire: Xena as Ancient Hero." In *Athena's*

Daughters: Television's New Women Warriors, edited by Frances Early and Kathleen Kennedy, 13–26. Syracuse: Syracuse University Press, 2003.
"The Giant Killer." Season 2, Disc 1, *Xena: Warrior Princess*. October 14, 1996; Beverly Hills, CA: Starz / Anchor Bay, 2003. DVD.
"God Fearing Child." Season 5, Disc 3, *Xena: Warrior Princess*. January 31, 2000; Beverly Hills, CA: Starz / Anchor Bay, 2004. DVD.
Harris, Anita. *Future Girl: Young Women in the Twenty-First Century*. New York: Routledge, 2004.
Helford, Elyce Rae. "Feminism, Queer Studies, and the Sexual Politics of *Xena: Warrior Princess*." In *Fantasy Girls: Gender in the New Universe of Science Fiction and Fantasy Television*, edited by Elyce Rae Helford, 135–162. New York: Rowman & Littlefield, 2000.
Hercules and the Amazon Women. Directed by Bill L. Norton. Written by Andrew Dettmann and Jule Selbo. 1994; Universal City, CA: Universal Studios Home Entertainment, 1998. DVD.
Ibson, John. "Sensitive Male." In *American Masculinities: A Historical Encyclopedia*, edited by Bret Carroll, 413–414. New York: Sage, 2013.
"The Ides of March." Season 4, Disc 5, *Xena: Warrior Princess*. May 10, 1999; Universal City, CA: Universal Studios Home Entertainment, 2013. DVD.
"If I Had a Hammer." Season 4, Disc 4, *Hercules The Legendary Journeys*. January 12, 1998; Universal City, CA: Universal Studios Home Entertainment, 2013. DVD.
Inness, Sherrie A. *Tough Girls: Women Warriors and Wonder Women in Popular Culture*. Philadelphia: University of Pennsylvania Press, 1999.
"Interview: Endgame." 1999. *Xena: Warrior Princess Season Four*. May 3, 1999; Universal City, CA: Universal Studios Home Entertainment, 2013. DVD.
"Interview: The Ring." 2000. On *Xena: Warrior Princess Season 6*. November 20, 2000; Beverly Hills, CA: Starz / Anchor Bay, 2005. DVD.
"Is There a Doctor in the House?" Season 1, Disc 5, *Xena: Warrior Princess*. July 29, 1996; Universal City, CA: Universal Studios Home Entertainment, 2010. DVD.
"Judgment Day." Season 3, Disc 5, *Hercules The Legendary Journeys*. February 17, 1997; Universal City, CA: Universal Studios Home Entertainment, 2013. DVD.
Kingwell, Mark. "Babes in Toyland: Xena versus Sailor Moon." *Saturday Night*, February 1997, 83ff.
Knight, Gladys L. *Female Action Heroes: A Guide to Women in Comics, Video Games, Film, and Television*. Santa Barbara, CA: Greenwood, 2010.
Kutulas, Judy. "Liberated Women and New Sensitive Men: Reconstructing Gender in the 1970s Workplace Comedies." In *The Sitcom Reader: America Viewed and Skewed*, edited by Mary M. Dalton and Laura R. Linder, 217–226. Albany: State University of New York Press, 2005.
Meister, Melissa. "*Xena: Warrior Princess* through the Lenses of Feminism." *Whoosh* 10 (1997).
Minkowitz, Donna. "Xena: She's Big, Tall, Strong—and Popular." *Ms. Magazine* (July/August 1996): 74–77.
"The Mother of All Monsters." Season 2, Disc 2, *Hercules The Legendary Journeys*. October 16, 1995; Universal City, CA: MCA Television, 2003. DVD.
"Motherhood." Season 5, Disc 5, *Xena: Warrior Princess*. May 15, 2000; Beverly Hills, CA: Starz / Anchor Bay, 2004. DVD.
"The Other Side." Season 2, Disc 2, *Hercules The Legendary Journeys*. October 30 1995; Universal City, CA: MCA Television, 2003. DVD.
"Prometheus." Season 1, Disc 2, *Xena: Warrior Princess*. November 6, 1995; Universal City, CA: Universal Studios Home Entertainment, 2010. DVD.
Pusateri, Karen. "Xena: Warrior Princess: An Analytical Review." *Whoosh* 1 (1996).
"Return of the Valkyrie." Season 6, Disc 3, *Xena: Warrior Princess*. November 27, 2000; Beverly Hills, CA: Starz / Anchor Bay, 2005. DVD.
"The Ring." Season 6, Disc 2, *Xena: Warrior Princess*. November 20, 2000; Beverly Hills, CA: Starz / Anchor Bay, 2005. DVD.
Sherwood, Rick. "War Stories." *Hollywood Reporter—International Edition* 361, no. 8 (January 4, 2000): S-1, accessed December 17, 2016.

Skelton, Carolyn. "Xena: Warrior Princess." In *The Essential Cult TV Reader*, edited by David Lavery, 329–336. Lexington: University Press of Kentucky, 2010.
Sorbo, Kevin. *True Strength: My Journey from Hercules to Mere Mortal—and How Nearly Dying Saved My Life.* Boston: Da Capo Press, 2011.
"Ulysses." Season 2, Disc 4, *Xena: Warrior Princess.* January 27, 1997; Beverly Hills, CA: Starz / Anchor Bay, 2003. DVD.
"Unchained Heart." Season 1, Disc 3, *Hercules The Legendary Journeys.* May 8, 1995; Universal City, CA: Universal Studios Home Entertainment, 2010. DVD.
Ventura, Varla. *Sheroes.* San Francisco: Red Wheel Weiser, 1998.
"Warrior Tales." 1996. On *Xena: Warrior Princess Season Two.* October 14, 1996; Beverly Hills, CA: Starz / Anchor Bay, 2003. DVD.
Weisbrot, Robert. *Hercules: The Legendary Journeys: An Insider's Guide to the Continuing Adventures.* New York: Taylor Trade, 2004.
_____. *Hercules: The Legendary Journeys: The Official Companion.* New York: Doubleday, 1998.
"What Puts the Punch in Hercules and Xena?" *Black Belt*, September 1996.
"When in Rome..." Season 3, Disc 4, *Xena: Warrior Princess.* March 2, 1998; Universal City, CA: Universal Studios Home Entertainment, 2012. DVD.
"Why Greek Tunics Are Back." *The Economist* (17 May 1997): 93ff.
Young, Cathy. "What We Owe Xena." *Salon*, September 15, 2005.

PART THREE: THE "GLORY" OF ROME:
DEPICTIONS OF THE EMPIRE

Male Nudity, Violence and the Disruption of Voyeuristic Pleasure in Starz's *Spartacus*

HANNAH MUELLER

"A guilty pleasure"

The *Washington Post* called it "deliciously, marvelously bad."[1] The *New York Times* described it as "fantastically soapy" and "fundamentally absurd."[2] Media studies scholar Christopher Vitale confessed to enjoying it as "a guilty pleasure" only after judging rather devastatingly: "The acting is second rate, the script is useless."[3]

The subject in question is the television show *Spartacus*, which aired over four seasons between 2010 and 2013 on the U.S. premium cable channel Starz. The show about history's most famous gladiator was Starz's first significant success with an original series, but the harsh criticism it faced from television critics suggested that it could not hold a candle to similarly opulent shows like HBO's *Rome* (2005–2007) and *Game of Thrones* (2011–present). In a direct comparison with *Rome*, the other sword and sandal show on twenty-first-century premium cable, the *New York Times* suggested that the similarities between the two series started and ended with their setting in Ancient Rome: "The two ventures are alike in togas only."[4]

This unfavorable comparison was not limited, however, to *Spartacus* as one individual series: rather, *Spartacus* was seen as symptomatic for the premium cable channel's failure to produce original "quality" programming. The *Hollywood Reporter* for example questioned Starz's ability to keep up with competitors HBO and Showtime, whose original programming has inspired critics and academics since the late 1990s to ecstatic claims about the so-called "golden age of quality television"[5]: "Can *Starz*, a premium pay-cable channel, even compete in a world where *HBO* and *Showtime* dominate from within while *Netflix* creates pressure from the without? After all, those three are working the same model that powers *Starz*, but you almost never hear anything about *Starz* in the zeitgeist."[6]

At first glance, this assessment is not surprising. Starz's *Spartacus* does not seem to fit easily into the same category with the slew of *auteur*-driven, polished quality dramas from HBO's *The Sopranos* (1999–2007) to *Westworld* (2016–present), which critics and academics like to compare to the highbrow aesthetics of "European art cinema"[7] and the nineteenth-century "Russian novel."[8] *Spartacus* looks for inspiration elsewhere. With its exaggerated slow-motion sequences, excessive CGI, a feast of gore and blood, and an ubiquity of nudity and sex, the show doesn't make any effort to hide how much it is indebted to the visual language of pulp and exploitation cinema. The very first scene, with its oversaturated colors, slow-motion effects, and graphic-novel inspired detail shots of splattering blood[9] make it clear that *Spartacus* is not trying to emulate the hyperrealism of HBO's *Rome*.

However, while *Spartacus* might differ from the stereotypical acclaimed "quality drama," critics who dismissed the program merely as Starz's failed attempt to compete with other premium cable channels on their own turf seem to have misunderstood the consistency of *Spartacus*' aesthetic vision, likely as a result of expectations shaped by their notion of "quality TV." In fact, Starz's "penchant for drawing on commonly derided genres"[10] and its turn toward the visual tropes of lowbrow culture in its original programming, from *Spartacus* to *Black Sails* (2014–present) and *Outlander* (2014–present), can be understood as part of a branding strategy with the goal to establish a niche that explicitly diverges from the canon of contemporary quality drama as represented by other subscription providers like HBO, Showtime, AMC, FX, and Netflix.

Consequently, this essay argues that *Spartacus* is worth a closer look *not despite* the show's affinity for exploitation aesthetics, but precisely *because* of its obvious references to genres like melodrama, horror, and porn. In particular *Spartacus*' representation of nudity, sexuality, and violence is in many ways more complex than the acclaimed "quality dramas" with their proclivity towards profanity for the sake of transgression[11] and strategies like "sexposition"[12] for the sake of titillation. Drawing on the film-theoretical concept of the cinematic gaze, as well as Linda Williams' theory of "body genres,"[13] this essay shows how *Spartacus* consciously uses the visual language of exploitation to consistently defy audience expectations in its representation of emotion, violence, and sex. On the one hand, the show uses its setting in a historical hypermasculine environment to undermine gender conventions regarding the voyeuristic gaze and the representation of naked bodies by associating control over the gaze with social status rather than gender, and by making the nude masculine body of the gladiator the object of the camera's gaze. On the other hand, the show breaks with genre-specific conventions by mixing visual tropes from lowbrow genres like melodrama, horror, and porn, and thus, in its most intriguing moments, radically disrupts voyeuristic pleasure by exposing the television spectator's complicity with the violent nature of the gaze.

"A fine specimen": The Male Body as Object of the Gaze

Spartacus' interpretation of its historical setting diegetically motivates much of the nudity on the show. The Roman Republic in the first century BC is represented as an era in which nudity and sex play a significant role in both private and public spaces. However, *Spartacus* establishes a clear difference between, on the one hand, the representation of casual nudity and consensual sex as essential parts of everyday life, and the abuse of power in scenes of forced nudity, coerced sex, and rape on the other.

The cinematography throughout the series creates the impression of a rather carefree attitude towards casual nudity, both among Romans and, later, the escaped slaves. In scenes of casual nudity, the camera neither lingers nor awkwardly obscures the viewer's gaze, and often uses panning shots to simulate a casual, almost disinterested glance at the naked bodies in the frame. In the first episode of *Blood and Sand*, for example, this strategy is used for the representation of a presumably plebeian audience at a lower-rate gladiator fight. Women are shown with partially or fully exposed breasts, but ostensibly given barely a second thought by the camera's gaze. Male casual nudity is treated in a rather similar way: when Spartacus (Andy Whitfield/Liam McIntyre) first arrives at Batiatus' (John Hannah) gladiator school in "Sacramentum Gladiatorum,"[14] the camera performs a similarly casual sweep over the fully exposed bodies of gladiators who are in the process of being cleaned with oil and strigil by the ludus slaves.

The camera also takes an "equal opportunity" approach in most of the consensual sex scenes, whose sheer frequency alone implies that both men and women in *Spartacus*' Roman Republic have strong sexual appetites, and that consensual sex, both for mere pleasure and as an expression of love and affection, is common and expected. Throughout the series, scenes of sexual encounters between loving couples like Crixus (Manu Bennett) and Naevia (Lesley-Ann Brandt/Cynthia Addai-Robinson), Spartacus and Mira (Katrina Law), Oenomaus (Peter Mensah) and Melitta (Marisa Ramirez), or

Agron (Dan Feuerriegel) and Nasir (Pana Hema Taylor) are usually shot in a specific and recognizable way that highlights the romantic nature of the act. The scenes generally use dimmed lighting and soft focus, showing the two bodies closely entwined. Despite the fact that the camera demonstratively lingers on the naked bodies, their arrangement in a tight embrace noticeably obscures the lovers' genitals, with the effect of making these love scenes appear relatively modest compared to other examples of nudity on the show. It also means that there is remarkably little difference between the representation of male and female bodies in these scenes, in a clear divergence from mainstream pornography and in fact most sex scenes in mainstream screen culture, which primarily expose the female body to the spectator.[15]

In contrast to these romantic love scenes, moments of coerced or violent sexual acts are depicted very differently, but they have this last aspect in common with representations of casual nudity and consensual sex: the camera does not significantly distinguish between male and female bodies. In this regard, *Spartacus* noticeably diverges from traditional cinematic (and televisual) conventions which usually put the man in control over the gaze, and stage the female body as its object.[16] On *Spartacus*, control over the gaze mirrors the diegetic imbalance of power, which does not occur so much along gender lines, but is rather based on social status. The most obvious hierarchy of power is the division between Roman citizens and their slaves, whose bodies, whether male or female, are constantly utilized and objectified by their masters. At a private celebration, a married slave is forced to have sex with her husband's best friend for the entertainment of the invited guests[17]; in another episode, a slave girl's virginity is gambled away for a political favor[18]; and a male gladiator is ordered to attend to a guest by his owner with the words: "If Varus wishes you to suck his cock dry, you will savor every drop."[19]

In this regard, Roman women are depicted as equally callous as Roman men, and are frequently shown to be in control of the voyeuristic gaze. They explicitly fetishize the gladiators' muscular physique and make use of their bodies as they please. Unlike the femme fatale in the classic Hollywood narrative,[20] who may transgress gender norms but is ultimately punished for adopting an active gaze, the Roman women's treatment of male slaves works within the social norms of their class standing, and thus, their active gaze remains unpunished. In contrast to mainstream pornography, their look at the men's naked bodies is also not automatically reverted into a form of masculine empowerment. As Peter Lehman has discussed, the camera's gaze at the male naked body in pornography may very well represent female desire, but that doesn't mean that this gaze simply mirrors the male cinematic gaze: "Equal time for men and women in pornography does not mean equal representational strategies."[21] In fact, one might say that the woman's gaze in pornography, captivated by the bigger-than-average erect genitals of the male porn star, ultimately reaffirms male prowess—it is merely an indicator of the man's ability to satisfy her. *Spartacus*, however, upholds the power imbalance between the Roman women and the enslaved gladiators. In scenes where Roman women contemplate men's bodies, they often keep the gladiators shackled and thus powerless and immobile, or they look down at them from an elevated position. The men, on the other hand, either bow their heads in submission or stare straight ahead into nothing—their gaze is empty, that is also, empty of power. The women's speech further enforces the men's visual objectification, as becomes obvious in a conversation between Lucretia (Lucy Lawless) and Ilithyia (Viva Bianca): "How do you live with the noise and the smell, surrounded by these ... animals?" Ilithyia asks, prompting Lucretia to respond: "Yes, they are wild and savage, aren't they?"[22] The women's habit of calling the gladiators "beasts" or "specimens" dehumanizes the men and stands in distinct contrast to the gladiators' perpetual talk about winning honor and glory in the arena when they are among themselves. This discrepancy makes it clear that the men's dreams of glory as gladiators are an illusion. They might put hope into their victories in the arena, but in fact they are barely more than livestock, literally kept to be slaughtered, and sometimes for breeding. When Batiatus' wife Lucretia fails to get pregnant from her husband, she decides to have a gladiator impregnate her. The first time she orders gladiator Crixus to have sex with her, she exercises her control over the gaze by denying it entirely when she demonstratively turns away from him during the act: "I would not look at you," she says. "The sight turns stomach."[23] Just as the Roman women's gaze on their naked bodies objectifies the gladiators, Lucretia's refusal to look at Crixus likewise dehumanizes him, and contributes to his realization that he is without power during the entire encounter, despite his active role in the sexual act.

Many of these scenes, in which Roman women—sometimes casually, sometimes deliberately and consciously—objectify the gladiators through their gaze, language, and physical/sexual transgressions, are clearly staged to create a sense of discomfort in the television spectator. While part of this discomfort is certainly due to the sense of helplessness on the side of the gladiators, to some extent it also stems simply from the show's blatant reversal of cinematic conventions in regard to the male gaze. Audiences are so used to having a man's gaze directed at a woman's body that for the most part it hardly registers, but *Spartacus*' demonstrative role-reversal stands out for the way it aggressively and consciously violates viewing expectations—the series clearly knows and purposefully plays with these conventions in order to generate specific emotional reactions, thus also exposing the audience's viewing expectations in the process.

"With what cock?" The Demystification of the Penis

The steering of the voyeuristic gaze, however, is not the only way in which *Spartacus* breaks common cinematic/televisual conventions. The show's frequent use of full frontal male nudity is another violation of viewing expectations, even for audiences accustomed to the more generous representation of nudity on premium cable. Ryan McGee notes that "neither male nor female audiences are particularly trained to handle viewing male frontal nudity in mass-market entertainment."[24] In hardcore pornography, the only genre where the penis is shown commonly and frequently, it is almost always larger-than-average, and usually shown only in its erect or semi-erect state[25]; but outside of hardcore pornography, as Lehman explains, "[t]he penis is almost always covered,"[26] because "the awe we attribute to the striking visibility of the penis is best served by keeping it covered up."[27] Hidden from view, that is, uncorrupted by the physical reality of the actual body, the penis more easily retains its phallic power, because it can always be imagined as erect and impressively large. Consequently, mainstream cinema and television across different cultural traditions have long used complicated strategies to obscure the audience's look at male genitals, as Lehman has shown in detail. Even in scenes when other characters direct their gaze at an exposed penis, the audience does not get to see it, leaving the spectacle up to the viewer's imagination. Within this framework set up to maintain phallic power, it would be fatal to show the penis—and reveal it to be a disappointment, unimpressive, flaccid, without power.

This, however, is precisely what *Spartacus* does, thus demonstratively undermining the established constellation of audience expectation and phallic representation. Erect genitals do make an appearance on *Spartacus*, but only in the form of replicas, and noticeably always in the hands of women: in "Shadow Games,"[28] Lucretia and Ilithyia use a candle in the shape of an erect phallus for a fertility ritual; in "Fugitivus," a prostitute wearing a strap-on dildo is shown penetrating a male customer in a brothel.[29] Still, the camera does not avoid the gaze at the actual naked male body, and in particular the gladiators' bodies are often fully bared. In fact, Dickson and Cornelius claim that "[n]ever before in the history of American television has ... the most private member of the male form, been so on display."[30] In contrast to pornography however, *Spartacus* generally shows the penis in its unaroused, flaccid state, with the curious result that precisely the gladiators' impressively muscular physique makes their genitals appear relatively small in comparison, regardless of whether they are actually average in size or not.[31] Thus, *Spartacus* severs the commonly assumed link between physical strength, sexual prowess, and control over the voyeuristic gaze by staging male genitals on screen not as phallus, but mostly just as penis.[32] Perhaps not so coincidentally, the full-frontal look at the "unimpressive" penis often also appears in a scenario in which the naked man is deprived of power, for example when Ilithyia studies the naked Crixus with scrutiny while his lover Naevia is forced to watch.[33] A similar dynamic is set up when Ilithyia saves her husband Glaber (Craig Parker) from Seppia's (Hanna Mangan-Lawrence) assassination attempt in the bath, and the camera shows the spouses next to each other in the aftermath of the carnage: her proudly upright in a blood-stained white dress, clutching the dagger; him looking strangely diminished next to her, completely naked and covered in his dead mistress' blood.[34]

But not only does *Spartacus* undermine the connection between masculine strength, male dominance, and phallic power, it further demystifies the phallus/penis by questioning the conventional association of physical penetration with dominance. Granted, this does not happen on the level of dialogue, where *Spartacus* seems to constantly reaffirm the connection between sexual penetration and power. The male characters in particular almost obsessively use metaphors of oral and anal penetration to comment on relationships of power. When he is displeased with the turn of his fate, ludus owner Batiatus frequently complains about getting "screwed" by the divine powers: "Once again the gods spread the cheeks and ram cock in fucking ass!"[35] The gladiators similarly tend to insult each other by referring to sexual penetration: "I will fuck your corpse," gladiator Gnaeus (Raicho Vasilev) threatens in expectation of his fight against Crixus, prompting Crixus to reply: "With what cock?"[36]

However, the perpetual reiteration of the relationship between penetration and power on the level of dialogue is consistently undermined in the representation of actual sexual encounters. The aforementioned brothel scene for example treats the television audience with the (for mainstream visual culture) rather unusual sight of a male customer being willingly penetrated by a female prostitute wearing a strap-on. The gaze of the camera does not dwell on the scenario, and none of the characters comment on it, indicating that the television audience is supposed to interpret it as a not particularly noteworthy occurrence. *Spartacus* also includes a considerable number of male characters involved in same-sex relationships or engaging in male/male sex, many of whom resist any stereotypical categorization in regard to social status, virility, and penetration. Gladiator Barca (Antonio Te Maioha) for example is, during the timeline of *Blood and Sand*, in an apparently monogamous relationship with Pietros (Eka Darville), a younger, more effeminate house slave, and shown to be the conventionally dominant partner both socially and sexually. In "The Thing in the Pit," Spartacus witnesses a sexual encounter between Barca and his lover, during which Barca penetrates Pietros from behind.[37] However, in the later-aired prequel *Gods of the Arena*, Barca's previous partner is revealed to be Auctus (Josef Brown), a fellow gladiator, who is presented as his equal in physical strength and social status. Whether there is a set dynamic to their sexual encounters is not revealed to the audience, leaving this aspect of their relationship up for speculation. In another episode of the same season, Barca is also shown being penetrated himself by a guest during an orgy at Batiatus' villa.[38]

Former house slave Nasir is another character who is depicted as flexible in his sexual encounters with other men. Once freed by the rebels, he enters a marriage-like union with gladiator Agron. While their relationship dynamic develops as one of equally strong-willed partners, their love scenes indicate that Nasir occupies the "passive" role in their sexual relationship. However, he is first introduced to the audience in a scene that shows him in a coerced threesome with his dominus and a female slave. In this scene, the patrician is penetrating the obviously bored woman who is sprawled on her back on the bed, and as he appears to get closer to climax, he orders Nasir to "place cock in ass,"[39] that is, to take him from behind. Both Barca and Nasir's shifting roles in different constellations undermine the assumption that sexual submission in same-sex relationships indicates a lack of either physical strength or social status, thus consistently negating the association of penetration with dominance and power.

Spartacus' representation of male homosexuality across a wide range of different physical and emotional constellations is remarkable among portrayals of male homosexuality in contemporary mainstream popular culture in and on itself, but it is even more noticeable considering the show's setting in a hypermasculine community. In their attempt to appeal to male straight audiences, which are usually thought of as the most desired "quality demographics" of subscription television, much of the original programming of premium cable channels such as HBO, Showtime, FX, and AMC, "utilizes masculinity as a site for distinguishing its quality brand and promoting the exclusivity it offers its clientele."[40] The result is that many of the shows now counted within the canon of "quality television drama" have focused on narratives set in hypermasculine societies, often mirroring the misogyny and homophobia that serve as stabilizing elements of the homosocial communities they depict.[41] As Lynne Joyrich argues, these televisual texts "construct a violent hypermasculinity, an excess of 'maleness' that acts as a shield"[42] against the presumed femininity of the medium television. These televisual environments usually don't offer much space for lived homosexuality, or only as an indicator of emasculation and/or a form of violence and punishment. *Spartacus*, however, portrays male homosexuality both as a normal expression of sexual desire *and* as an integral element of hypermasculine communities. On the one hand, the show normalizes encounters between same-sex lovers by staging them like any other sex scene: the similarities in regard to lighting, position of the actors, and camera angle/movement indicate that there is no significant difference between a romantic scene featuring heterosexual couple Crixus and Naevia or homosexual lovers Agron and Nasir. On the other hand, homosexual relationships are also shown to be firmly embedded within the homosocial community of the gladiators. In *Blood and Sand*, Barca and his lover Pietros first appear together in what might be called the Roman version of a locker room shower scene, where Pietros assists Barca in cleaning up after a training session the same way the rest of the gladiators are attended to by other slaves.[43] Since they are not revealed to be a couple until later, it is basically impossible for the audience to identify them as lovers in this scene where they are surrounded by other naked, oiled-up gladiators engaging in the same type of grooming. By making the lovers part of this homosocial practice without marking them clearly as homosexual, the show blurs the line between homoerotic homosociality and lived homosexuality in a way that destabilizes heteronormative assumptions of default heterosexuality. *Spartacus* further normalizes male homosexuality in a way that violates cinematic conventions by letting the television spectator experience encounters between male lovers through the eyes of a diegetic male, heterosexual observer. Since the gladiators live in extremely close quarters both before and after their revolt, sexual activity tends to happen in front of an audience, and *Spartacus* uses this set-up to steer the audience's gaze. Shortly after Spartacus' arrival at Batiatus' ludus in *Blood and Sand*, he witnesses Barca and Pietros engaging in intercourse as he walks past their cell[44]; a similar scenario plays out when Gannicus (Dustin Clare) watches Barca and Auctus kissing passionately in *Gods of the Arena*.[45] The way the camera directs the audience's gaze in these scenes is remarkable not only because it puts the viewer in the position of a heterosexual male character aiming his voyeuristic gaze at a display of male/male sex; but also because the observer's reaction in both situations is mostly a non-reaction. Neither Spartacus nor Gannicus seem perturbed or even embarrassed by what they see, thus signaling to the television spectator that what they are seeing is in fact neither unusual nor scandalous.

"It tears my heart to see him so": Melodrama, Horror, Porn

Thus, *Spartacus* consistently defies cinematic conventions regarding the gendering of the voyeuristic gaze and its traditional taboos. Throughout its four seasons, women are in control of the gaze, heterosexual men willingly watch two men have sex, male bodies are turned into a spectacle, and the phallus loses its symbolic power. Furthermore, the show also contradicts audience expectations in regard to the exploitation genres it borrows from so heavily. Linda Williams has defined melodrama, pornography, and horror as "body genres" because these genres subject both the fictional characters and the spectators in front of the screen to extreme bodily sensations: emotional despair, arousal/pleasure, and disgust/fear respectively. Williams understands this constellation as a form of contract between the spectator and the text. Audiences choosing to see a melodrama/porn flick/horror movie do so because they *expect* to feel these bodily reactions: "the success of these genres often seems to be measured by the degree to which the audience sensation mimics what is seen on the screen."[46] Williams also points out that the sensations experienced in body genres—the bodies subjected to extreme feelings both on- and off-screen—are typically gendered. Within the diegesis of the fictional text, all three body genres have in common that the body on screen subjected to extreme sensations is usually gendered as female: "[I]n each of these genres, the bodies of women figured on the screen have functioned traditionally as the primary *embodiments* of pleasure, fear and pain."[47] In melodrama, it is the grief-stricken body of the heroine; in splatter movies, it is the young female victim of the sadistic serial killer; and in pornography, it is the naked female body as the object of the gaze, consumed by the pleasure that she experiences under the ministrations of her male partner(s). *Spartacus* however replaces at once the melodramatic heroine, the sexually objectified porn star, and the female victim of sadistic violence with the hypermasculine body of the gladiator. Certainly, *Spartacus* shows women being objectified by men, but it is the male body of the gladiator that comes under scrutiny most frequently. It is constantly being studied and prodded, for assessment of its worth as much as for the pleasure of both other characters and the television audience. Of course women are tortured and killed on *Spartacus*, but it is the dismemberment of the male body that is staged as a spectacle over and over again—both in the arena for the entertainment of the Romans, and on the screen for pleasure of the television audience. Over the course of four seasons, the spectator gets to experience—often in close-up and slow-motion—a man's face being ripped off, his tongue cut out, his head severed, his genitals mutilated, his guts spilling out, his blood gushing. Finally, *Spartacus* tells stories of women who love and lose those they love, but it is the men that are shown wrecked and ruined by heartbreak, after losing their beloved through betrayal, infidelity, or death. When Crixus is told by Agron (falsely) that his lover Naevia has been killed, the camera lingers on his convulsing body as he is consumed by grief.[48]

But *Spartacus* does not merely offer a reversal of genre conventions by displaying the male body as the object of the gaze and subjecting it to the extreme sensations usually reserved for the female body in melodrama, horror, and porn. Instead, the show also toys with audience expectations by shifting abruptly and suddenly between modes relating to different genres. By invoking in short succession contradicting expectations and sensations, the show radically disrupts not only the characters, but also the spectator's voyeuristic pleasure, and exposes the spectator's complicity in the violence inflicted through the gaze.

Of course, one might argue that the sensations and pleasures associated with different body genres cannot be that clearly separated in the first place—and it is certainly true that the sensations evoked by these seemingly very different genres overlap in numerous ways. Feminist scholars have long discussed pornography as a form of sexual violence, arguing that the sexual pleasure experienced through pornography is tied to the repeated symbolic and physical violation of the female body.[49] Reversely, the violent murders in slasher movies have often been interpreted as a "displacement of sex into violence,"[50] once again tying sexual penetration to physical assault. Finally, Ann Douglas has linked melodrama to sexuality by calling Harlequin romance novels "[s]oft-core pornography, specifically designed for women."[51] At the same time, however, the social legitimation of the spectator's enjoyment of body genres relies very much disguising the connections between the desires or sensations that drive the different genres, on cultural assumptions about intended audiences, and therefore, on the viewer's expectations about the experience they subject themselves to. These expectations become part of the contract between spectators and the cultural texts they consume, and allow for the socially legitimate voyeuristic pleasure associated with these genres. Heterosexual men, for example, are permitted, or even expected, to experience sexual pleasure while watching porn, and it is similarly acceptable for them to enjoy the thrill of violent horror movies; whereas sexual arousal at the sight of torture, mutilation, or murder is generally frowned upon. Men are also not supposed to be emotionally moved by melodrama and romance, albeit for different reasons.

Spartacus explicitly draws on the visual and narrative repertoires of all three body genres, but also perpetually upsets and undermines genre and audience conventions, thus delegitimizing and disrupting the spectators' sensual experience and interfering with their viewing pleasure. The first episode of *Blood and Sand*[52] provides a good example for the disturbing effect created by the abrupt switching between genre-specific modes. The beginning of the episode shows a flashback to Spartacus' life before he is captured by the Romans. The scene in which he says goodbye to his loving wife before heading into battle is filmed as a backlit long-shot with oversaturated colors, eerily similar to a classic shot from a 1940s melodrama. In contrast, the following montage showing his transport from Thrace to Rome creates a fragmented, sinister atmosphere. By intercutting different detail shots with low-key lighting and a grey-to-black color scale, the sequence generates the surreal flicker effect typical for the horror genre, despite the fact that the flickering in horror films is usually associated with malfunctioning electronic technology, something that is for obvious reasons absent from the setting of *Spartacus*. A side-by-side comparison between the expository montage from *Spartacus'* first episode and the opening credits for *Murder House*, the first season of the FX show *American Horror Story* (2011–present)[53] which draws explicitly on various horror tropes, reveals the similar visual and acoustic strategies the two sequences employ. Both share the bleak color scheme, the flicker effect that is enforced by the intercut detail shots, and even the soundtrack. The static noise in the *American Horror Story* credits is mirrored in *Spartacus* by a similarly rhythmic background noise that is soon revealed to be the sound of waves rolling against the outside of the ship. In one of the following scenes, the horror theme from this montage sequence is picked up again when Spartacus waits for his turn to fight in the arena and stares at the fragmented, mutilated bodies of the slaughtered gladiators piled up next to him. However, his transport to Capua and the fight in the arena are connected through a scene during which Spartacus and other prisoners are presented at the villa of a Roman politician, where naked women perform in shallow pools for the entertainment of the guests. This scene borrows heavily from the language of softcore pornography: for once, the female body is displayed as object of the gaze, and the scene even includes the seemingly mandatory lesbian interaction for the sake of titillating a male straight audience. Yet Spartacus' traumatized gaze in this scene does not remain steadily fixed on the women's bodies; it keeps jumping from detail to detail. His flickering gaze and the camera's fragmentation of the female body not only mirror the fragmented images in the earlier montage sequence on the boat, but also foreshadow the fragmentation of mutilated bodies in the arena. Thus, the pornographic images in this scene are framed by scenes that utilize the visual language of horror, and connected to them through the shared element of fragmentation. Even more so, all this plays out after the spectator's viewing expectation has been shaped by the melodramatic coloring of the initial scenes between Spartacus and his wife. In this context, the naked bodies of the dancing women in the background, which regular audiences of premium cable drama have grown so accustomed to, take on a nightmarish quality that gets in the way of perceiving them as merely ornamental or titillating and thus disturbs the spectators' voyeuristic pleasure.

This strategy of contrasting genre-specific modes in order to disrupt the audience's voyeuristic pleasure is used repeatedly, and even more demonstratively, in subsequent episodes. In "Mark of the Brotherhood,"[54] the patrician woman Ilithyia chooses her own personal gladiator from a line-up of newly acquired slaves. Her gaze, and that of the camera, lingers on the men who are exposed to her look, and her elevated position on the balcony of the villa highlights the imbalance of power between her and her hosts on the one hand, and the gladiators on the sand down below on the other. Anise Strong, and rightly so, reads this scene as a demonstrative reversal of the male gaze, in which the male body becomes the spectacle: "the new recruits are merely a set of objectified male bodies."[55] But within the context of the entire episode, the scene takes on a much more complex meaning. At first glance, the encounter between gladiators and Romans appears to indicate a return to the idea of phallic power: despite the dominance of the female gaze, the attention of the spectators—including not only the Roman women and the other gladiators, but also the television audience—is directed at the impressively large penis of Gallic recruit Segovax (Mike Edward). Ilithyia's breathless fascination with his manhood, and therefore his apparent masculine prowess, appears to tilt the balance of power in his favor. However, Ilithyia's (and the audience's) belief in the correlation between penile size and masculine dominance is quickly revealed as naïve. Later in the episode, she commands Segovax to murder her enemy Spartacus, but he fails to carry out the plan, and Batiatus punishes the treacherous gladiator by having him publicly castrated and crucified, a gruesome spectacle that Ilithyia watches again from the balcony of the villa in a repetition of the previous scene, but this time in horror and disgust.

This final scene violently and demonstratively disrupts voyeuristic pleasure in a number of ways. On the narrative level, Batiatus' demonstration of power through a public execution marks the failure of Ilithyia's scheming. On a symbolic level, Segovax' castration and death disappoints the fantasy of the return of phallic power. Commonly, "penis size relates to castration anxiety"[56] in the sense that a large penis is assumed to provide reassurance against the threat of castration. In this case, however, it does in fact precisely the opposite: his large penis is what makes Segovax vulnerable to Ilithyia's gaze and consequently leads to his violent dismemberment and death. More importantly, the scene also disrupts voyeuristic pleasure in regard to the television audience's viewing expectations. When Ilithyia, faced with the lineup of enslaved recruits, calls them "spectacles," she speaks for the television spectators as much as for herself, and this early scene in the courtyard has a distinctly humorous element to it that legitimates the audience's appreciation of its erotic aspects. Just like the Romans on the balcony and the other gladiators down in the yard, the television spectator is permitted to gaze at the display of impressive masculinity with amused delight. But the resolution of the plot line in the final execution scene radically disrupts the viewer's pleasure. Not only is the television audience (just like Ilithyia) forced to watch as the sexualized object of their voyeuristic gaze, the enormous man with the enormous penis, is mutilated in the most gruesome way; the comic relief paired with erotic pleasure that the spectator got to experience during the earlier scene is also spoilt by the realization that it was precisely the eroticized gaze at the gladiator, which the audience had participated in, that ultimately led to the man's violent death.

A similar strategy of having pornographic imagery abruptly turn into horror is employed during "Empty Hands."[57] During a celebration at Glaber's villa, male and female slaves perform in the nude as living centerpiece for the entertainment of the guests. The slaves wear masks and garters resembling stylized genitals, which reinforce the appearance of the slaves as ornamental and decorative: they can be enjoyed as mere aesthetic objects, a work of art. Yet, the centerpiece is broken up—quite literally—when the captured rebels are led into the room. Framed by the naked dancers on both sides, the injured and thus much less decorative gladiators are displayed to the guests, and as another "party favor," the Romans proceed to torture one of them to death, by dismembering, skinning, and finally fatally stabbing him. Again, the erotic pleasure the television audience may have derived from the initial aesthetic display of naked slaves is brutally disrupted by the realization that slaves are not merely ornaments, but made from flesh and blood. The abrupt switch from pornographic spectacle to horror mode makes the flawless naked bodies in the background now appear uncanny, even revolting.

In both of these examples, *Spartacus* disrupts the spectators' voyeuristic pleasure by brutally destroying the object of the gaze. In other scenes, *Spartacus* is even more blatant in its interruption by also violating the spectator in control of the gaze. In "Fugitivus,"[58] the television audience is introduced to a brothel, where the gaze of the camera wanders from one group of characters to the next, akin to installations in an art exhibit. The gaze briefly lingers on the aforementioned customer being penetrated by a female prostitute with a strap-on, then moves on to a customer receiving oral sex from a male prostitute, to the image of two male clients manhandling a woman, and then to a scene of four men roughly (ab)using one woman. What starts as an extravagant erotic spectacle subtly turns increasingly violent with every following display, and the sex workers' participation in the performances appears less and less consensual. In the first scene, the prostitute is the active (penetrating) partner to a submissive male customer; in the last scene, the woman's screams as she is pushed around by the men sound decidedly more fearful rather than aroused. The spectator may have felt excited by the initial displays, but might grow more and more uncomfortable as the camera travels down the hallway. However, even if the spectator is still able to enjoy the pornographic, but rather violent display offered in the final scenario, this changes abruptly as the camera proceeds to take a 180-degree turn and focus on the unappealing image of the masturbating brothel owner, revealing to the television audience, like a look in the mirror, whose gaze they have been identifying with. The uncomfortable moment of self-recognition in the face of the brothel owner's (and therefore, the audience's) voyeuristic pleasure does not last, however—it quickly turns into terror as the man is stabbed to death by a sword through the throat. Once again, the visual mode shifts abruptly and radically; the camera transforms the spectator from the voyeur of a pornographic spectacle into the witness (and implicitly, victim) of a violent massacre, as Crixus and his group of fugitive gladiators proceed to slaughter all the male customers in the brothel, covering the aesthetically pleasing nude bodies of the prostitutes in spatters of blood.

"To what end?": Conclusion

Drawing on the language of exploitation cinema and body genres, *Spartacus* thus disrupts voyeuristic pleasure by building up expectations of sensations to be experienced by the audience, only to shift abruptly into a different generic mode in the most disturbing way.

This has several consequences for the reception of the show. On the one hand, it keeps spectators unsettled by constantly undermining expectations in regard to *Spartacus*' intended audience. The focus on the hypermasculine community of gladiators and the excessive use of violence seem to mark the show as a product geared at straight male audiences, similar to other hypermasculine dramas on premium cable, such as HBO's *Generation Kill* (2008). At the same time, it perpetually seems to reject the genre-specific conventions associated with that type of show. Romantic plots and love scenes follow the cinematic conventions of female-oriented genres like romance and melodrama; the erotization of the nude male body and the normalization of male homosexuality within the context of homosocial structures seem to appeal much more overtly to a gay male audience than a show like HBO's *Oz* (1997–2003), which was known for its inclusion of male nudity, but also represented male/male sexuality mostly in the form of sadistic rape or manipulative coercion. In contrast, *Spartacus*' demonstrative "messiness," both in regard to the copious amounts of blood and other bodily fluids spilled over the course of four seasons, and in regard to its convergence and blurring of genre categories, makes up a lot of the show's appeal. However, it also makes the series difficult to categorize, which might have contributed to the rather harsh reviews the show received from professional critics when it first aired on Starz. But this essay has shown that it would be a misunderstanding to measure *Spartacus*' aesthetics based on a direct comparison with more stereotypical "quality drama" series from *Oz* to *Breaking Bad* (2008–2013). *Spartacus* does not fail at emulating the highbrow cinematic aesthetic that HBO and Showtime have established as quasi-canonical over the past two decades, but rather demonstratively employs the visual tropes of lowbrow exploitation genres in order to offer a rather complex and self-referential treatment of on-screen nudity, sex, and violence. Unlike other premium cable shows set in a historical and/or hypermasculine setting, *Spartacus* does not use its setting as a justification to perpetuate genre conventions regarding the representation of nudity and sexuality, such as the continuous objectification of the female body or the conflation of male homosexuality with rape. Instead, *Spartacus* exposes those conventions by delegitimizing the audience's enjoyment of specific scenes and revealing the spectator's compliance in the violent nature of the voyeuristic gaze.

Notes

1. Hank Stuever, "TV Preview: Starz's 'Spartacus' Offers up a Bloody, Good Time on Friday Night TV," *Washington Post*, January 22, 2010, http://www.washingtonpost.com/wp-dyn/content/article/2010/01/21/AR2010012104590.html.

2. Ginia Bellafante, "'Spartacus: Gods of the Arena' on Starz—Review," *New York Times*, January 20, 2011, http://www.nytimes.com/2011/01/21/arts/television/21spartacus.html.

3. Christopher Vitale, "A New Queered Gaze? Reading 'Spartacus: Blood and Sand' as Symptom of a Shift in the Male Gaze," *Orbis Mediologicus*, March 22, 2010, http://orbismediologicus.wordpress.com/2010/03/22/a-new-queered-gaze-reading-spartacus-blood-and-sand-as-symptom-of-a-shift-in-the-male-gaze/.

4. Bellafante, "Spartacus."

5. For the discourse around "quality cable drama," see for example Janet McCabe and Kim Akass, ed., *Quality TV. Contemporary American Television and Beyond* (New York: I.B. Tauris, 2007); Marc Leverette, et al., eds., *It's Not TV: Watching HBO in the Post-Television Era* (New York: Routledge, 2008); Michael Newman and Elana Levine, *Legitimating Television* (New York: Routledge, 2012).

6. Tim Goodman, "For Starz to Go Places, It Might Have to Rebrand—Or Remind Its Subscribers to Watch," *The Hollywood Reporter*, August 6, 2013, http://www.hollywoodreporter.com/bastard-machine/starz-original-programming-lags-behind-600503.

7. Jane Feuer, "HBO and the Concept of Quality TV," in *Quality TV: Contemporary American Television and Beyond*, eds. Janet McCabe and Kim Akass (New York: I.B. Tauris, 2007), 145.

8. Annie Leibowitz and Sam Kashner, "The Family Hour: An Oral History of The Sopranos," *Vanity Fair*, March 15, 2012, http://www.vanityfair.com/hollywood/2012/04/sopranos-oral-history; also Allen St. John, "Why Breaking Bad Is the Best Show Ever and Why That Matters," *Forbes*, September 16, 2013, http://www.forbes.com/sites/allenstjohn/2013/09/16/why-breaking-bad-is-the-best-show-ever-and-why-that-matters/#938f2804d93d.

9. *Spartacus: Blood and Sand*, "The Red Serpent," written by Steven S. DeKnight, first aired January 22, 2010, on Starz.

10. Thomas J. West III, "How STARZ Perfected the Lowbrow," *The Outtake*, June 2, 2015, https://theouttake.net/how-starz-perfected-the-lowbrow-9264cbe3a391#.euy3wn9rk.

11. See Marc Leverette, "Cocksucker, Motherfucker, Tits," In *It's Not TV: Watching HBO in the Post-Television Era*, ed. Marc Leverette, et al. (New York: Routledge, 2008), 123–151.

12. Miles McNutt, "Game of Thrones—'The Night Lands' and Sexposition," *Cultural Learnings*, April 8, 2012, https://cultural-learnings.com/2012/04/08/game-of-thrones-the-night-lands-and-sexposition/.Starz.

13. Linda Williams, "Film Bodies: Gender, Genre and Excess," in *Feminist Film Theory: A Reader*, ed. Sue Thornham (Edinburgh: Edinburgh University Press, 1999), 140–158.

14. *Spartacus: Blood and Sand*, "Sacramentum Gladiatorum," written by Steven S. DeKnight, first aired on January 29, 2010, on Starz.

15. For an analysis of the different representation of male and female nudity in "quality cable drama," see Hannah Mueller, "'At Least Let Us See Them Before You Cut Them All

Off!' The Gendered Representation of Nudity in Contemporary Quality TV," In *Auteur TV*, edited by Ralph Poole and Saskia Fürst (Heidelberg: Universitätsverlag Winter, 2017).

16. For film theory's most influential discussion of the cinematic male gaze, see Laura Mulvey, "Visual Pleasure and Narrative Cinema," *Screen* 16:3 (1975), 6–18.

17. *Spartacus: Gods of the Arena*, "Missio," written by Maurissa Tancharoen and Jed Whedon, first aired January 28, 2011, on Starz.

18. *Spartacus: Gods of the Arena*, "Paterfamilias," written by Aaron Helbing and Todd Helbing, first aired February 4, 2011, on Starz.

19. *Gods of the Arena*, "Missio."

20. See Mulvey, "Visual Pleasure."

21. Peter Lehman, *Running Scared: Masculinity and the Representation of the Male Body* (Detroit: Wayne State University Press, 2007), 178.

22. *Blood and Sand*, "Sacramentum Gladiatorum."

23. *Spartacus: Gods of the Arena*, "Reckoning," written by Brent Fletcher, first aired on February 18, 2011, on Starz.

24. Ryan McGee, "Sexposition, 'Spartacus,' and the Male Gaze," *Boob Tube Dude*, June 5, 2012, http://boobtubedude.com/index.php/2012/06/05/theories/sexposition-the-male-gaze-and-spartacus/.

25. Lehman, *Running Scared*, 118.

26. Ibid.

27. Ibid., 117.

28. *Spartacus: Blood and Sand*, "Shadow Games," written by Miranda Kwok, first aired on February 19, 2010, on Starz.

29. *Spartacus: Vengeance*, "Fugitivus," written by Steven S. DeKnight, first aired on January 27, 2012, on Starz.

30. Dickson and Cornelius, 170.

31. It might be relevant to consider in this context that some *Spartacus* actors chose to wear a prosthetic penis during the shoot, while others didn't. ANI, "Kirk Douglas to Make Cameo on New Spartacus as Prosthetic Penis," *ZNews*, August 6, 2009, http://zeenews.india.com/entertainment/idiotbox/kirk-douglas-to-make-cameo-on-new-spartacus-as-prosthetic-penis_37388.html.

32. Dickson and Cornelius argue that the penis on Spartacus is eroticized and sexualized because it is always shown "preceding, during, or just after acts of coitus" (Dickson and Cornelius 180), but a closer look at the respective occurrences contradicts this argument: in fact, male genitals are often shown in scenes of casual or forced nudity that are not linked to a sexual act.

33. *Blood and Sand*, "Shadow Games."

34. *Spartacus: Vengeance*, "Monsters," written by Brent Fletcher, first aired on March 23, 2012, on Starz.

35. *Spartacus: Blood and Sand*, "Revelations," written by Brent Fletcher, first aired on April 16, 2010, on Starz.

36. *Spartacus: Blood and Sand*, "Legends," written by Brent Fletcher, first aired on February 5, 2010, on Starz.

37. *Spartacus: Blood and Sand*, "The Thing in the Pit," written by Aaron Helbing and Todd Helbing, first aired on February 12, 2010, on Starz.

38. *Spartacus: Gods of the Arena*, "Beneath the Mask," written by Seamus Kevin Fahey and Misha Green, first aired on February 11, 2011, on Starz.

39. *Spartacus: Vengeance*, "A Place in This World," written by Brent Fletcher, first aired on February 3, 2012, on Starz.

40. Avi Santo, "Para-Television and Discourses of Distinction: The Culture of Production at HBO," In *It's Not TV: Watching HBO in the Post-Television Era*, ed. Marc Leverette, et al. (New York: Routledge, 2008), 34.

41. Consider for example shows like HBO's *The Sopranos*, *Oz*, *Rome*, *Deadwood*, *Boardwalk Empire*, *Generation Kill*, *Band of Brothers*, and *True Detective*; AMC's *Breaking Bad* and *Mad Men*; FX's *Shield*, *Rescue Me*, and *Sons of Anarchy*; Showtime's *The Tudors* and *Ray Donovan*; or Netflix's *House of Cards*.

42. Lynne Joyrich, "Critical and Textual Hypermasculinity," in *Logics of Television: Essays in Cultural Criticism*, ed. Patricia Mellencamp (London: BFI, 1990), 165.
43. *Blood and Sand*, "Sacramentum Gladiatorum."
44. *Blood and Sand*, "The Thing in the Pit."
45. *Spartacus: Gods of the Arena*, "Missio," written by Maurissa Tancharoen and Jed Whedon, first aired on January 28, 2011, on Starz.
46. Williams, "Film Bodies," 144.
47. *Ibid.*, 143.
48. *Vengeance*, "The Greater Good."
49. See for example Catharine MacKinnon, *Toward a Feminist Theory of the State* (Cambridge: Harvard University Press, 1989).
50. Williams, "Film Bodies," 140.
51. Ann Douglas, "Soft-Porn Culture," *The New Republic*, August 30, 1980, 26.
52. *Blood and Sand*, "The Red Serpent."
53. *American Horror Story: Murder House*, "Pilot," written by Ryan Murphy and Brad Falchuk, first aired on October 5, 2011, on FX.
54. *Spartacus: Blood and Sand*, "Mark of the Brotherhood," written by Aaron Helbing and Todd Helbing, first aired on March 19, 2010, on Starz.
55. Anise Strong, "Objects of Desire. Female Gazes and Male Bodies in *Spartacus: Blood and Sand*," in *Screening Love and Sex in the Ancient World*, ed. Monica S. Cyrino (New York: Palgrave McMillan, 2012), 173.
56. Lehman, *Running Scared*, 172.
57. *Spartacus: Vengeance*, "Empty Hands," written by Allison Miller, first aired on February 17, 2012, on Starz.
58. *Vengeance*, "Fugitivus."

BIBLIOGRAPHY

American Horror Story: Murder House. "Pilot." Written by Ryan Murphy and Brad Falchuk, first aired on October 5, 2011, on FX.
ANI. "Kirk Douglas to Make Cameo on New Spartacus as Prosthetic Penis." *ZNews*, August 6, 2009. http://zeenews.india.com/entertainment/idiotbox/kirk-douglas-to-make-cameo-on-new-spartacus-as-prosthetic-penis_37388.html.
Bellafante, Ginia. "'Spartacus: Gods of the Arena' on Starz—Review." *New York Times*, January 20, 2011, http://www.nytimes.com/2011/01/21/arts/television/21spartacus.html.
Dickson, Robert K., and Michael G. Cornelius. "(Re)Presenting the Phallus: Gladiators and Their 'Swords.'" In *Spartacus in the Television Arena. Essays on the Starz Series*, edited by Michael G. Cornelius, 170–185. Jefferson, NC: McFarland, 2015.
Douglas, Ann. "Soft-Porn Culture." *The New Republic*, August 30, 1980, 25–29.
Feuer, Jane. "HBO and the Concept of Quality TV." In *Quality TV: Contemporary American Television and Beyond*, edited by Janet McCabe and Kim Akass, 145–157. New York: I.B. Tauris, 2007.
Goodman, Tim. "For Starz to Go Places, It Might Have to Rebrand—Or Remind Its Subscribers to Watch." *The Hollywood Reporter*, August 6, 2013. http://www.hollywoodreporter.com/bastard-machine/starz-original-programming-lags-behind-600503.
Joyrich, Lynne. "Critical and Textual Hypermasculinity." In *Logics of Television: Essays in Cultural Criticism*, edited by Patricia Mellencamp, 156–72. London: BFI Books, 1990.
Leibowitz, Annie, and Sam Kashner. "The Family Hour: An Oral History of The Sopranos." *Vanity Fair*, March 15, 2012. http://www.vanityfair.com/hollywood/2012/04/sopranos-oral-history.
Lehman, Peter. *Running Scared: Masculinity and the Representation of the Male Body*. Detroit: Wayne State University Press, 2007.
Leverette, Marc. "Cocksucker, Motherfucker, Tits." In *It's Not TV: Watching HBO in the Post-Television Era*, edited by Marc Leverette et al., 123–151. New York: Routledge, 2008.
Leverette, Marc, et al., eds. *It's Not TV. Watching HBO in the Post-Television Era*. New York: Routledge, 2008.

MacKinnon, Catharine. *Toward a Feminist Theory of the State*. Cambridge: Harvard University Press, 1989.
McCabe, Jane, and Kim Akass, eds. *Quality TV. Contemporary American Television and Beyond*. New York: I.B. Tauris, 2007.
McGee, Ryan. "Sexposition, 'Spartacus,' and the Male Gaze." *Boob Tube Dude*, June 5, 2012. http://boobtubedude.com/index.php/2012/06/05/theories/sexposition-the-male-gaze-and-spartacus/.
McNutt, Miles. "Game of Thrones—'The Night Lands' and Sexposition." *Cultural Learnings*, April 8, 2012. https://cultural-learnings.com/2012/04/08/game-of-thrones-the-night-lands-and-sexposition/.
Mueller, Hannah. "'At Least Let Us See Them Before You Cut Them All Off!' The Gendered Representation of Nudity in Contemporary Quality TV." In *Auteur TV*, edited by Ralph Poole and Saskia Fürst. Heidelberg: Universitätsverlag Winter, 2017.
Mulvey, Laura. "Visual Pleasure and Narrative Cinema." *Screen* 16:3 (1975), 6–18.
Newman, Michael, and Elana Levine. *Legitimating Television*. New York: Routledge, 2012.
St. John, Allen. "Why Breaking Bad Is the Best Show Ever and Why That Matters." *Forbes*, September 16, 2013. http://www.forbes.com/sites/allenstjohn/2013/09/16/why-breaking-bad-is-the-best-show-ever-and-why-that-matters/#938f2804d93d.
Santo, Avi. "Para-Television and Discourses of Distinction. The Culture of Production at HBO." In *It's Not TV: Watching HBO in the Post-Television Era*, edited by Marc Leverette et al., 19–45. New York: Routledge, 2008.
Spartacus: Blood and Sand. "Legends." Written by Brent Fletcher, first aired on February 5, 2010, on Starz.
_____. "Mark of the Brotherhood." written by Aaron Helbing and Todd Helbing, first aired on March 19, 2010, on Starz.
_____. "The Red Serpent." Written by Steven S. DeKnight, first aired January 22, 2010, on Starz.
_____. "Revelations." Written by Brent Fletcher, first aired on April 16, 2010, on Starz.
_____. "Sacramentum Gladiatorum." Written by Steven S. DeKnight, first aired on January 29, 2010, on Starz.
_____. "Shadow Games." Written by Miranda Kwok, first aired on February 19, 2010, on Starz.
_____. "The Thing in the Pit." Written by Aaron Helbing and Todd Helbing, first aired on February 12, 2010, on Starz.
Spartacus: Gods of the Arena. "Beneath the Mask." Written by Seamus Kevin Fahey and Misha Green, first aired on February 11, 2011, on Starz.
_____. "Missio." Written by Maurissa Tancharoen and Jed Whedon, first aired January 28, 2011, on Starz.
_____. "Paterfamilias." Written by Aaron Helbing & Todd Helbing, first aired February 4, 2011, on Starz.
_____. "Reckoning." Written by Brent Fletcher, first aired on February 18, 2011, on Starz.
Spartacus: Vengeance. "Empty Hands." Written by Allison Miller, first aired on February 17, 2012, on Starz.
_____. "Fugitivus." Written by Steven S. DeKnight, first aired on January 27, 2012, on Starz.
_____. "Monsters," written by Brent Fletcher, first aired on March 23, 2012, on Starz.
_____. "A Place in this World." Written by Brent Fletcher, first aired on February 3, 2012, on Starz.
Strong, Anise. "Objects of Desire. Female Gazes and Male Bodies in *Spartacus: Blood and Sand*." In *Screening Love and Sex in the Ancient World*, edited by Monica S. Cyrino, 167–182. New York: Palgrave McMillan, 2012.
Stuever, Hank. "TV Preview: Starz's 'Spartacus' Offers up a Bloody, Good Time on Friday Night TV." *Washington Post*, January 22, 2010. http://www.washingtonpost.com/wp-dyn/content/article/2010/01/21/AR2010012104590.html.
Vitale, Christopher. "A New Queered Gaze? Reading 'Spartacus: Blood and Sand' as Symptom of a Shift in the Male Gaze." *Orbis Mediologicus*, March 22, 2010. http://orbismediologicus.wordpress.com/2010/03/22/a-new-queered-gaze-reading-spartacus-blood-and-sand-as-symptom-of-a-shift-in-the-male-gaze/.

West, Thomas J., III "How STARZ Perfected the Lowbrow." *The Outtake*, June 2, 2015. https://theouttake.net/how-starz-perfected-the-lowbrow-9264cbe3a391#.euy3wn9rk.

Williams, Linda. "Film Bodies: Gender, Genre and Excess." In *Feminist Film Theory: A Reader*, edited by Sue Thornham, 140–158. Edinburgh: Edinburgh University Press, 1999.

Sex, Lies and Denarii
Roman Depravity and Oppression in Starz's Spartacus

JERRY B. PIERCE

At its core, Starz's *Spartacus* series (*Blood and Sand*; *Gods of the Arena*; *Vengeance*; *War of the Damned*, 2010–2013) is a tale of the immoral and wicked relationship between wealth and power on the part of fictionalized Romans and how this wealth facilitates political, social, and sexual inequality. The series consistently emphasizes that the Roman political and social structure was dependent upon and perpetuated by the ruthless subjugation of others—including other Romans, but especially their slaves, who eventually revolt against their captors. This subjugation is shockingly demonstrated through various means of Roman exploitation, both physical (in the form of ownership of slaves and forced gladiatorial combat) and more importantly, sexual (which ranges from nudity and "simple" voyeurism to rape and torture). *Spartacus* makes an explicit connection between Roman wealth and (sexual) immorality in that as the former increases, so too does the latter. This association is made even more evident by its absence among the poor and powerless slaves, whose relationships are portrayed as purer, more genuine, and nothing like the exploitative sadism of the rich Romans. With few exceptions, the relationships between the slaves are depicted as ones of equality, love, and genuine caring, while the Romans, true to a long-standing trope found in numerous peplum and neo-peplum productions about Rome on the big and small screens, are both hedonistic and callous. The fact that Starz's *Spartacus* not only replicates this tired stereotype, but in fact exaggerates it further, is surprising given the series' nuanced depiction of homosexual relationships.

The Usual (Roman) Suspects

For close to a century, from the earliest twentieth-century cinematic forays into ancient Rome, such as Cecil B. DeMille's *The Sign of the Cross* (1932), right up through 2010's *Spartacus*, depictions of Rome (both its government and society) have almost universally presented an image of decadence, corruption, and oppression, whether the setting be the Republic or Empire. As Maria Wyke has noted, the frequent cinematic portrayals of Rome in this way has created what she termed a "historical consciousness" of this society which carries with it persistent audience expectations of more corruption and depravity than the historical record indicates.[1] Similarly, Sandra Joshel explains that cinematic Rome, especially the Empire, is usually depicted as "brutal, militaristic, and hypersexual" and is in fact "defined by its enjoyment of unrestrained power and moral corruption."[2] Moreover, the debauched scenes on display in these films (the grandeur, sexual excess, and acts of vivid sadism) function as an "exhibitionist spectacle" for the audience themselves, turning their viewing into a form of voyeurism that provides "the pleasure of gazing on the vividly realized vices and exoticisms" of ancient Rome.[3] As a general rule then, in the vast majority of these films all things Roman are suspect due to this perception of inherent corruption and moral decline, including not just the political and military leaders who direct the government but even the average Roman citizens attending gladiatorial matches and other public spectacles. As such, these cinematic tropes of Roman decline typically fall into three (sometimes overlapping) categories of representation: corruption, exploitation, and immorality.

Rarely shown in a positive manner, Roman politics on screen instead is portrayed as corrupted by power and money, a thoroughly compromised system that is on the verge of ruin. If set in the late Republic, the anachronistically "democratic" government of the people faces imminent collapse because of the greedy political maneuverings of men like Marcus Licinius Crassus (Lawrence Olivier) in *Spartacus* (1960, Stanley Kubrick) or Julius Caesar (Rex Harrison) in *Cleopatra* (1963, Joseph Mankiewicz). If set in the Empire, the selfish whims of an egotistical and often deranged emperor—Peter Ustinov's Nero in *Quo Vadis* (1951, Mervyn LeRoy) or Christopher Plummer's Commodus in *The Fall of the Roman Empire* (1964, Anthony Mann)—have created a dictatorial (typically fascist) and repressive regime. According to William Fitzgerald, the depiction of Rome in these films is "universally negative" and reveal that "oppression is the only possible consequence of power."[4] In both Republican and Imperial settings, corruption stems from greedy and self-serving elites, who are not coincidentally seen in luxurious and decadent settings that convey their privileged status and reinforce their degenerate and dangerous lifestyles. These include elaborate banquets, opulent palaces and villas, and lavish clothing. As wealthy Republican elites, both Crassus and Caesar are repeatedly seen enjoying sumptuous feasts and being doted on by slaves and attendants, while their ornate armor leaves no doubt about their affluence. In both cases, their wealth and influence is not put to the benefit of the Republic but to their own political fortunes, as Crassus tries to use the slave rebellion to cement his control over Rome while Caesar parlays his victories into an opportunity to become Rome's first king in five centuries. Similarly, during the Empire, Ustinov's Nero, as well as his cinematic predecessor in the same role, Charles Laughton in *The Sign of the Cross* are frequently seen banqueting in their palaces, attended by numerous slaves, dancers, and even exotic animals, dressed in elegant robes, and reclining upon gaudy thrones. As an expression of their selfishness, both emperors likewise have a callous disregard for their subjects and human life in general, as Laughton's bored Nero oversees executions of pious and simple Christians in the arena while Ustinov's Nero maniacally burns the city (and citizens) of Rome in order to rebuild it in his own image. Luxury becomes a clear visual marker of elite decadence, reinforcing the notion that power and wealth are both the sign and the cause of Roman political and moral corruption.

This imagery of decadent corruption is made all the more evident when Roman luxury is starkly contrasted with a film's plainly dressed, honorable protagonists, typically Christians or slaves. Thus a Christian martyr like *The Sign of the Cross*'s Mercia (Elissa Landi) is not only morally pure because she refuses the hedonism of the Romans, but her modest, unadorned attire physically reflects her inner moral purity. Likewise, the simple handmade clothing of the slaves in Spartacus' (Kirk Douglas) rebellion mirrors their grounded, humble desire for a peaceful and free existence out from under Roman shackles. Alastair Blanshard and Kim Shahabudin explain that the contrast can also be accomplished spatially as well, such as during Nero's decadent feast in *Quo Vadis*, where the innocent Christian Lygia (Deborah Kerr) is separated from the spectacle before her morally (through her repulsed reaction to the excess), physically (by her refusal to participate), and cinematically (literally distanced from the action by her placement in the frame).[5] According to Martin Winkler, these visual characterizations aid a film's narrative by allowing the audience "to identify emotionally with the meek and the persecuted and to root for the underdogs in their fight for liberation."[6] Such contrasts then heighten the moral distinction between the powerful and the powerless.

In such a corrupt system, it should come as no surprise that Romans are shown as exploitative and oppressive to the powerless, especially the multitude of slaves. These slaves exist in service to and often for the pleasure of elite Romans, with little regard for either their well-being or their lives. Romans as slave-masters is a visually recurring theme (and in this case, a historically accurate one) that reinforces the domineering nature of Roman society, even in films that do not feature slave uprisings as a central storyline. Slaves are thus tasked with anything from menial to degrading jobs, like serving wine to Crassus and his guests (*Spartacus*), filling the empress' bath with asses' milk or feeding fruit to the emperor (*The Sign of the Cross*), or trimming Nero's toenails (*Quo Vadis*), with the ever-present threat that they could be beaten (or worse) for the slightest failure. In addition to their labor, slaves are often required to offer themselves sexually to the desires of their Roman masters, with no regard for, and sometimes directly in spite of, their personal wishes. Of course, the most obvious example of slave exploitation is the very existence of gladiators, who are forced to fight and often die for the viewing pleasure of their Roman overlords.

Although instances can be found in various films, Kubrick's *Spartacus* provides several memorable examples of the exploitation and dehumanizing of slaves that not only encapsulates Roman on-screen oppression but also served as fodder for Starz's *Spartacus* series a half-century later. The opening scene of Kubrick's film informs the audience of the terrible nature of Roman slavery with an arid and treacherous mine, where slaves are literally worked to death and beaten for showing anything less than a callous disregard for their fellow slave. When Batiatus (Peter Ustinov), the owner of the Capuan *ludus* (gladiator school), arrives on scene, he is richly dressed, arrogantly dismissive, and accompanied by his personal slaves (one of whom he derides for holding a sun shade ineffectively). He inspects the slaves as if he were investing in livestock by examining their teeth and assessing their muscle tone, choosing those (like Spartacus who hamstrung a guard with his teeth) that seem to have some fighting potential. Upon returning to Capua, the entire *ludus* is one sprawling example of exploitation as the slaves are told they will be pampered like "stallions" but also trained to fight and die in the arena as expendable assets for "ladies and gentlemen *of quality*."[7] Although they retain their names, the slaves are essentially stripped of their former identities as they are remade as Roman gladiators and are kept from forming their own community within the *ludus*, forbidden from communicating with one another let alone forming bonds of friendship (lest they face a beating).[8] Female slaves are likewise objectified and used, not simply as domestic servants that cook and clean, but they are also randomly assigned to the male gladiators as a reward and to sate their sexual appetites. According to Elena Theodorakopoulos, both the stallion speech and the distributing of the women reveal that these slaves are seen as "sexual objects" and that "there is an erotic dimension to the power wielded over them by the Romans."[9] Batiatus' dehumanizing of these slaves is overshadowed by a visiting group of Roman patricians, including Marcus Crassus, who demand that the *lanista* (owner of a gladiatorial school) provide a showing of matched pairs of gladiators to fight to the death, something that is contrary to even the *ludus'* harsh rules. Cowed into submission by the wealthy Crassus, Batiatus reluctantly agrees and the audience is treated to a scene where the female Romans giggle as they select gladiators, not based on their abilities but simply on their physical and sexual attributes, indicating both their "inappropriate" sexual desires and "another sign of the corruption that will doom them."[10] Finally there is Crassus' infatuation with the slave girl and love interest of Spartacus, Varinia (Jean Simmons), who he purchases for his own desire, inadvertently sparking the entire gladiator and wider slave rebellion. All of these examples highlight the arrogant and brutal attitudes of the Romans toward their slaves, who they see simply as commodities to be bought, sold, abused, and killed for their own fickle pleasure.[11]

The third trait that is common to and expected of Romans on screen is moral depravity. This immorality often can take the form of decadence, such as the sumptuous banquets and dinner parties mentioned above which emphasize the gluttonous and wicked character of the Romans, especially in films that feature Christians, or to serve as a stark, moralizing contrast with the simple and poor lifestyle of their slaves. The immorality of the Romans can also be seen in virtually every film through their strong and consistent penchant for violence and brutality not only to slaves but also to their fellow citizens. The former category includes the execution or torture of Christians in *The Sign of the Cross*, *Quo Vadis*, and *The Robe* (1953, Henry Koster), as well as rebel gladiators and slaves in *Spartacus*. Examples of the latter trend can be found in Julius Caesar's murder by his own countrymen and former friends in *Cleopatra* and Commodus' ascension to the imperial throne via his father, Marcus Aurelius' (Alec Guinness) murder, and his subsequent massacre of his enemies, including burning several of them alive in the Roman Forum in *The Fall of the Roman Empire*.

Perhaps the most consistent and frequently seen form of Roman depravity is sexual immorality, an easy (sometimes lazy) means to vilify the Romans through their supposed penchant for "deviant" sexuality. The most common expression of this deviance is the ubiquitous Roman orgy, which had become so commonplace and accepted by audiences by the 1960s that it was mocked in the parody *A Funny Thing Happened on the Way to the Forum* (1966, Richard Lester) as something one would request like a dinner reservation, while its absence in the neo-peplum *Gladiator* (2000, Ridley Scott) was lamented by numerous reviewers.[12] According to Stacie Raucci, because orgy scenes were so prevalent in the heyday of Roman epic films from the 1930s to 1960s, the choreography and conduct at these seemingly frenzied scenes came to "offer the audience a subtle, yet effective means of appreciating the virtue and morality of the different characters."[13] On the one hand, orgies emphasize the hedonism, sexual excess, and perverse appetites of the Romans who are eager to participate, but they also usually include unwilling victims whose presence underlines the predatory and non-consensual aspect of the orgy. For example, both *The Sign of the Cross* and *Quo Vadis* feature orgies in which the lecherous Romans use the hyper-sexualized setting to seduce and corrupt the "pure" Christian protagonists, Mercia and Lygia. In both cases the orgies are attended by the emperor and empress, indicating to the audience that such acts are condoned from the top down and thus indicative of the thoroughness of Roman immorality. These orgies also allude to another deviant aspect of Roman sexuality: voyeurism. In contrast to private, monogamous relationships, Roman sexual excess is on display for all to see whether the participants wish it or not. Thus in *The Sign of the Cross*, the many Romans engaged in sexual frolicking pause to stare intently at the chaste Mercia, hoping their erotic activities will break her resolve and moral reservations, converting her to their ways. In similar fashion, Batiatus and Marcellus (Charles McGraw) are shown leering down at Spartacus and Varinia through a ceiling grate, encouraging them to indulge their desires while they watch. When Spartacus refuses, Batiatus chides him saying, "Come, come. Be generous. We must learn to share our pleasures," clearly indicating that sexual gratification is not something to be kept private, but should be visible and on display for the pleasure of others, especially other Romans for whom it is apparently a typical practice.[14]

As a final example of immorality, directors often suggest the Romans have homosexual desires (which would be seen as aberrant and in some cases criminal by audiences throughout the twentieth century), in contrast with the protagonists who are shown to practice heteronormative sexuality. As a general rule, since the adoption of the Hayes Code in 1930 that regulated on-screen morality, many cinematic villains have been coded with stereotyped traits that hint at their queer sexuality (usually homosexuality) without actually explicitly identifying them as such (dress, feminine mannerisms, or even simply the lack of a heterosexual partner), which is then linked to their status as antagonists. In fact, their queer identity is typically portrayed as both an expression of and also the direct cause of their (often murderous) deviance, a trend which can be seen in Roman and non–Roman films alike.[15] In the former camp, coded queer villains can be found in *The Sign of the Cross*, including a naked Poppaea (Claudette Colbert) ordering her female friend to disrobe and join her in the bath, an erotic dance by Ancaria (Joyzelle Joyner) as she attempts to seduce Mercia (at the aforementioned orgy no less), and the not-so-subtle homosexuality of Nero himself, who is almost never without his nearly-naked, smooth-skinned and exotic young male attendant (who also feeds him fruit from a platter). Though he lacks the obvious male consort, Ustinov's Nero in *Quo Vadis* is likewise coded as homosexual from his dramatic and flamboyant demeanor to his elegant and feminine robes and his complete disinterest in his empress. Perhaps the most famous example of deviant and threatening Roman sexuality is Crassus, which is made evident in the then-scandalous "Snails and Oysters" scene in *Spartacus*. Not only does Crassus threaten the success of the slave revolt (while ironically its cause), but he is also a predatory menace to the seemingly powerless slaves under his control, such as Antoninus (Tony Curtis), who he selects as his personal body servant out of intense sexual desire. The homoerotic "Snails and Oysters" scene has a naked Crassus being bathed by a nearly naked Antoninus, as the former asks his slave if a taste for snails (men/homosexuality) is immoral, while a taste for oysters (women/heterosexuality) is moral. In his attempt to seduce Antoninus, Crassus argues that his taste for snails (men) is not a question of appetite (exclusive homosexuality) and is therefore "not a question of morals."[16] After trying to subtly reason with Antoninus that such a relationship between them would not be immoral, Crassus uses the opportunity of the heavily armed Roman garrison marching nearby to demonstrate that despite any reservations, the slave will have no choice but to submit to his stronger and more powerful master. This approach is typical of Crassus (and the Romans in general) because he wants to make it appear as though Antoninus (and later Varinia) willingly chose to be with him, when in fact it is his superior status and threat of force that would make it so, not any actual affection on their part. Unfortunately for Crassus, Antoninus escapes to join Spartacus and the rebel slaves while his back is turned. Like his other queerly coded Roman counterparts, and because of an irrational fear of non-heterosexual relationships on the part of most twentieth-century audiences, Crassus' implied deviance and "lack of moral fiber and self-control" is indicative of the immorality and depravity at the heart of Rome.[17]

Romans in Starz's Spartacus

The Starz series *Spartacus* continues and in fact explicitly enhances this pattern of negative representation begun during the heyday of sword and sandal films. In fact, in the more than thirty speaking roles for Romans in the series, many of them with significant screen time and repeated appearances, only four Roman characters can be considered redeemable. The rest not only exhibit the main failings of their on-screen predecessors, but in fact take these abominable traits to new depths. The Romans in the series are excessively violent, exploitative, thoroughly untrustworthy, and so devoid of any moral compass that the flaws of their earlier counterparts pale in comparison.

The corrupt nature of these Romans is mainly linked to their overly ambitious and self-serving attitudes as they seek social and often political advancement. Roman society (represented mainly by Capua where two of the four seasons takes place) is presented as a hypercompetitive one where getting ahead and making a name for oneself can apparently only be accomplished at the expense of another in quite literally a cutthroat way since many of the main characters resort to violence, bribery, and murder. Because of this propensity for backstabbing, the Romans in *Spartacus* cannot be trusted, either by their slaves or their fellow citizens. The dishonest and deceitful nature of the Romans is evident in the premier episode, "The Red Serpent," which establishes their duplicity and sets in motion virtually all of the events connected to the gladiator rebellion and widespread slave revolt over the following two seasons. In this episode Thracian soldiers under Spartacus (Andy Whitfield, later Liam McIntyre) agree to help the Romans, led by Claudius Glaber (Craig Parker), against Mithridates (an eastern enemy of Rome), and in return Glaber promises to use his troops to defeat the Getae, vicious barbarians that threaten the Thracians. Despite these pledges of loyalty and assistance, Glaber reneges on his oath, causing the auxiliaries to desert in the hope of saving their village from the Getae. The loss of the Thracian troops causes Glaber to suffer a humiliating defeat at the hand of Mithridates, and he then seeks revenge by capturing and enslaving the fugitive Spartacus and his wife Sura (Erin Cummings). Glaber's decision to enslave Spartacus and send him to be executed in the Capuan arena, presumably to have this public death restore his honor among his fellow Romans, unexpectedly results in Spartacus' eventual success as a gladiator and his ultimate leadership of the massive slave rebellion that will engulf the Republic. This betrayal by Glaber is important not only because it immediately establishes Roman duplicity, but also because it shows the significant impact of a single Roman betrayal has wide ranging consequences that will affect thousands of slaves and Romans alike.

After the rebellion breaks out, the self-serving nature of the elite Romans and their intense competition with one another is on display as Glaber and his rivals jockey for prominence and favor in their attempts to end the revolt, rather than simply do what was best for Rome. Glaber's main rival is Publius Varinius (Brett Tucker), a wealthy member of the Senate who would prefer that Glaber fail so that he himself could claim victory and thus more prestige and honor by defeating Spartacus. Although Glaber attempts several times to join forces with Varinius, the latter refuses and instead works to undercut Glaber and embarrass him by lending his support to another local noble, Seppius (Tom Hobbs), who has assembled his own private forces to deal with the rebellion (and likewise make himself popular). To make matters worse, Glaber's father-in-law, Senator Albinius (Kevin J. Wilson), has no faith in Glaber and believes his daughter, Ilithyia (Viva Bianca), made a grave error by marrying such a failure. Ilithyia herself was likewise convinced of her husband's ineptitude and became so certain his incompetence would hinder her own social advancement that she began to conspire with Varinius to get her father to dissolve her marriage so they could marry instead. Although Albinius is initially opposed to the divorce because Glaber still holds rank and Ilithyia is pregnant with his child, he is nonetheless convinced to change his mind after being seduced and bedded by her friend Lucretia (Lucy Lawless). Unfortunately for them, just prior to publicly announcing the divorce (and remarriage) in the *Vengeance* episode "Libertus," Albinius is trapped by debris in the Capuan arena when Spartacus and the rebels attack to free their friends. Although still alive, Albinius is found in all the chaos by Glaber who, rather than rescuing him, smashes his skull in with a large beam, effectively ending any threat of divorce since the father's permission was needed for it. With Albinius out of the picture, and Varinius deciding to vacate Capua immediately, Glaber also eliminates his rival Seppius by raiding his villa, killing his entire household, and crushing Seppius' throat under his foot. This entire situation clearly highlights the devious nature of the Roman elite as they are willing to betray, deceive, and even murder members of their own family if they stand in the way of their own social and political advancement. Despite holding political offices, none of the actions of Glaber, Varinius, or Albinius are done in service to Rome, and in fact most of their decisions are harmful to the Republic since they are undertaken right in the middle of a massive slave rebellion that threatens its very survival.

As Ilithyia's active involvement in seeking a new husband better suited to her ambitions indicated, Roman women could be just as untrustworthy, corrupt and violent as their male counterparts. In addition to the divorce, Ilithyia also worked behind Glaber's back during her stay at Batiatus' (John Hannah) *ludus* to satisfy her many desires throughout *Blood and Sand*. When she saw the arrival of a new set of slaves in season one's "Mark of the Brotherhood," and on the advice of Lucretia, she purchased a gladiator for herself based on nothing more than the fact that he had an exceptionally large penis, objectifying him much like her predecessors did in Kubrick's *Spartacus*. Once she discovered that Spartacus, the supposed cause of her husband's humiliation, was also at the *ludus*, she promised her new slave his freedom if he would secretly murder Spartacus. Fortunately for Spartacus, the attempted murder is thwarted but Ilithyia's slave is gruesomely mutilated and then crucified and she coldly fails to intervene. Her violent ambitions are not limited to slaves as she, like most of the other Romans, has no qualms eliminating her fellow citizens if it suits her needs. For example, in "Whore" (*Blood and Sand*: episode 9) when Ilithyia finds out from Lucretia that the gladiators in the *ludus* can be used for sexual gratification, she decides on the champion of Capua (and Lucretia's secret love interest), Crixus (Manu Bennett) as her illicit sexual partner. Thinking that she is being pleasured by Crixus, Ilithyia is shocked to find out that it is actually Spartacus himself at the same moment her elite friend, Licinia (Brooke Harman), arrives to witness the "scandal." Although Lucretia engineered both the switch and Licinia's surprise arrival to gain leverage over Ilithyia, she was not prepared for Ilithyia's reaction to her friend's mockery and laughter. Clearly distraught, Ilithyia grabs Licinia and repeatedly smashes her face into the marble floor, killing her. Although initially shaken and dazed by what she has done, Ilithyia ultimately comes to embrace her violent streak, orchestrating the death of Spartacus' close friend, Varro (Jai Courtney), by Spartacus himself, closing the doors of the *ludus* during the revolt and trapping numerous Roman elites within to be slaughtered, executing a tortured slave at a celebration for Varinius to prove her worth and win his admiration, and even slitting the throat of her rival, Seppia (Hannah Mangan-Lawrence), as she tried to seduce her husband Glaber. According to Antony Augoustakis, all of these terrible acts stem from her "thirst for power."[18] Ilithyia's brutality, which far outstrips anything seen in peplum productions, is nevertheless on par with that of her fellow Romans in the series and like theirs is an outgrowth of the hypercompetitive corruption and ruthlessness that is associated with all Romans.

Even among non-elite Romans like Batiatus and his fellow *lanista* Solonius (Craig Walsh-Wrightson), competition, corruption, and success at any cost are seemingly inescapable aspects of Roman nature. In the first season of *Spartacus* (*Blood and Sand*), the *ludus* of Batiatus has fallen on hard times in part because his rival, Solonius, has curried favor with wealthy elites and nobles. Batiatus tries to change his fortunes and advance his standing first by appealing to Glaber (by purchasing Spartacus in the arena) and then improve public opinion of Titus Calavius (John Bach), the Capuan magistrate overseeing the games, by providing better gladiatorial entertainment than his competitor, Solonius. Thinking he has impressed the magistrate, Batiatus continues to try and earn his favor, hoping that perhaps he can become more than a *lanista*, even a senator, with Calavius' help. To help this dream of political advancement, in the tenth episode "Party Favors," Batiatus throws a lavish birthday party for Calavius' son, Numerius (Liam Powell), complete with a gladiatorial match between Spartacus and his friend Varro, that ends with Spartacus' victory but also with Numerius demanding Varro's death at Spartacus' hand for his loss. Batiatus protests that gladiators do not fight to the death in his *ludus*, but Calavius insists that his son be allowed his wish. When Batiatus reluctantly decides to acquiesce and violate his own policy, he does so in the hope of ingratiating himself to Calavius and furthering his political career. After Varro's death at the hand of Spartacus (an event that will trigger the rebellion), Batiatus discovers that it was all for naught when Calavius dismissively refuses to offer his patronage, telling Batiatus to "leave politics for the men who have the breeding for it."[19] This betrayal itself sets off a whole series of events orchestrated by Batiatus which will see Calavius kidnapped, tortured, and ultimately murdered, with blame conveniently placed on Batiatus' rival, Solonius. This exchange between Batiatus and Calavius is important for the viewer's understanding of Roman nature, proving once again that Romans in the series not only have a callous and violent disregard for the lives of others, but also will corruptly go against their own personal standards and rules if it means even the slightest hope of advancement. Calavius' dismissal of Batiatus and his lack of pedigree also reinforces the notion that elite Romans are depicted as jealous and covetous of their social and political position, using lesser men like Batiatus to satisfy their needs and appeal to their egos, while offering nothing in return unless they can see some way to profit or benefit.

Like their predecessors in earlier films, the Romans in the *Spartacus* series repeatedly exploit their slaves for their own gain, amusement, and especially for their own sexual pleasure. As in Kubrick's *Spartacus*, the mere presence of numerous slaves and gladiators is an immediate indication of how thoroughly abusive Roman society is. Especially in the house of Batiatus, domestic slaves are typically shown wearing collars to indicate their submissive and animal-like status, often with far less clothing than their Roman masters which in itself is a clear sign that they are not in control of their own bodies. The ubiquitous beatings and whippings, often for even the slightest transgression, further indicates how little the Romans regard their slaves. Likewise the very existence of the *ludus* itself and the arena to which gladiators are sent to fight and die for the amusement of their Roman overlords underscore the fact that the Romans see their slaves as expendable commodities that exist simply to serve their needs, however despicable or violent they may be. The fact that Batiatus would throw a party for Varinius at which the highlight was the torture and execution of captured slaves, and that all the other Romans accepted and encouraged it, exposes the depravity at the heart of Roman identity.

Similarly, the repeated sexual exploitation of the slaves reinforces the notion of Roman debauchery and degeneracy. Numerous examples of this abuse can be found throughout the series, particularly in the house of Batiatus where slaves are frequently forced to provide sexual pleasure for both Batiatus and Lucretia, not to mention the many other powerful Romans to whom they offer their slaves' bodies. In fact, some of the earliest scenes introducing Batiatus and his wife Lucretia involve sex together with several slaves. In one scene, a naked Lucretia is being bathed and primped by three equally naked female slaves when Batiatus arrives. He quickly strips down, grabs one of the slaves and spins her around before taking her from behind. The demeanor of the two is indicative of the exploitation and the imbalance of power at play, as she grimaces and clenches her lips together, while Batiatus roughly grabs her slave collar and thrusts into her with a twisted smile on his face until he finishes and pushes her away. His dismissiveness is compounded by the fact that both he and Lucretia continue to talk business and politics during their copulation, showing that they are at best indifferent to their slaves' well-being, to say nothing of the complete lack of consent. The voyeuristic element of Roman deviance is also apparent in this and other similar scenes, since these sexual encounters typically take place in wide-open rooms where their spouse or other member of the household, slave or free, can witness the action. A similar scene has Lucretia being manually pleasured by her female slave, Naevia (Lesley-Ann Brandt), in order to arouse Batiatus, who himself is in the process of receiving oral sex from yet another female slave, all of which is their version of foreplay for their own lovemaking. As Anise Strong has demonstrated, since both Batiatus and Lucretia engage in this sexual exploitation of their slaves, "what fundamentally matters in these relationships is not gender, but power."[20] Thus, none of these encounters are consensual or enjoyable for the slaves, as seen in their dour expressions, precisely because, as slaves, they have no say or control over their lives or even their own bodies. Everything about them, including their sexuality, is thoroughly controlled, measured, and put to use as dehumanized objects for the pleasure of the Roman masters.[21]

This sexual exploitation is also prevalent among several of the elite Roman women, who secretly use the enslaved male gladiators to satisfy their lust. While Batiatus has sex openly with female slaves in front of his wife with her consent, Lucretia has a long running secret affair with Crixus, the champion of the *ludus*. Unlike Batiatus and his encounters, Lucretia is actually enamored of Crixus and frequently summons him to her chambers for heated bouts of sex, even hoping to become pregnant by him, since her husband seems infertile. However, these encounters are similar to the exploitative ones mentioned above, not because she physically abuses, belittles, or dominates Crixus (as Batiatus did his female slaves), but because their sexual liaisons are compulsory and clearly against his will. Moreover, when one takes into account that Crixus is actually in a loving relationship, albeit prohibited, with Lucretia's own personal slave, Naevia, then Lucretia's sexual demands become even worse because she ends up forcing him into infidelity. Lucretia's affair with Crixus becomes even more problematic when she privately suggests to Ilithyia, in an attempt to win the latter's favor and patronage, that the gladiators in her house can be used to satisfy their own adulterous desires. Unfortunately for Lucretia, when Ilithyia chooses a gladiator for herself, she decides on Crixus, sending Lucretia into a jealous fit that is only remedied when, with the help of masks, she is able to swap Spartacus for Crixus. This "accidental" mix up, and its discovery by the well-timed, and clearly orchestrated arrival of Ilithyia's friend, Licinia, in the episode "Whore," becomes part of Lucretia's plan to blackmail Ilithyia with the threat of exposing her adultery, but also results in Ilithyia murdering Licinia. Such incidents illustrate the deceitful nature of these elite Romans who, once again, appear to act only in their own self-interest and to satisfy their illicit and immoral desires at the expense of their slaves and even other Romans.

As Lucretia attempted to do with Ilithyia, the Romans in the series frequently engage in sexual exploitation of their slaves to appease their more powerful superiors and gain favor or achieve political success. This exploitation can be as simple as the orgies held for various Roman elites or the more private sexual encounters that combine dominance and voyeurism made famous by Ustinov's Batiatus when he chided Douglas' Spartacus that pleasures had to be shared. For example, in order to appeal to Ilithyia's perverse tastes, Lucretia shows her the possible pleasures of the house of Batiatus by ordering the gladiator Varro, who is married, to openly have sex with a female slave who is not his wife as they and others watch closely, becoming viably aroused as they comment on his sexual prowess. Similarly, in *Gods of the Arena* episode "Paterfamilias," Batiatus and Lucretia need to secure the patronage of Quintilius Varus (Peter Feeney), a wealthy patron of the upcoming games, in order to get a better showing for his gladiators. Brought back to the *ludus* by seductive offers of Lucretia and her close friend, Gaia (Jaime Murray), Varus is first treated to a private duel between Crixus and Gannicus (Dustin Clare). Sensing Varus' attraction to Gannicus, Batiatus orders his gladiator to satisfy whatever sexual desire he may have, so that they may retain his favor. Despite Varus' fawning over Gannicus' nearly naked body, he decides to sit back and simply watch as Gannicus has sex with another female slave, Melitta (Marisa Ramirez). His desires satisfied, Varus grants Batiatus his favor, improving his standing at the upcoming games. Unfortunately, Batiatus' attempt to gratify Varus has the unintended consequence of spreading the word of the pleasures that await other powerful Romans at the house of Batiatus. Soon enough, others Romans arrive unannounced at the villa expecting the same treatment as Varus with the implication that, if they leave unsatisfied, they can always find a way to hinder Batiatus' goals and cause him to lose favor. One of those individuals is Cossutius (Jason Hood), a noble who easily has the most perverse, violent, and degrading sexual desires of all the Romans. For his pleasure, he chooses the young, virgin slave, Diona (Jessica Grace Smith), who naively thinks her first sexual encounter with a Roman noble will be pleasurable. Instead, Cossutius chooses the dirtiest, most animalistic gladiator, Rhaskos (Ioane King) to violently rape Diona, while he himself rapes her anally, much to her shock and dismay. His systematic abuse of Diona serves no other purpose than to satisfy his perverse and corrupt desire to defile slaves in the most degrading of ways. Cossutius' "degradation" of Diona is thus "represented as the result not of individual evil deeds but as the inevitable consequence of the Roman system of slavery and the gross inequality between elites and other citizens."[22] Despite the misgivings that both Batiatus and Lucretia initially have about letting men like Varus and Cossutius have their way with their slaves, they nevertheless allow these activities to take place because they believe they can exploit such vices for their own gain, with no concern for the physical and mental impact on their slaves. These scenes also reinforce the notion that such base and sordid desires are endemic to Roman identity as a whole, since Romans do not appear to be able to resist such debauchery.

Interestingly, Roman sexual immorality in *Spartacus* is not limited to their interactions with slaves as it occurs with and impacts their fellow Romans as well. There are the obvious and expected orgies that occur even in the first episode of *Blood and Sand*, most of which take place as a means for someone, usually Batiatus, to satisfy the hedonistic desires of their economic or political superiors in order to gain favor. These orgies, and the various public spectacles of debauched pleasure, are also examples of the voyeuristic aspect of Roman sexuality found in Batiatus' (Ustinov) aforementioned scolding of Spartacus (Douglas) to "share" his pleasures (but depicted in a much more explicit fashion). Likewise, as noted above there is also rampant adultery among the Romans, such as Lucretia's ongoing affair with Crixus, Ilithyia's disastrous liaison with Spartacus, Seppia's short-lived seduction of Glaber, and Marcus Licinius Crassus' (Simon Merrells) lengthy affair with his slave and lover, Kore (Jenna Lind), among others. While still adultery, only the Crassus/Kore relationship comes close to a mutually affectionate relationship and in order for it to last it must be kept secret since a Roman of Crassus' standing could never marry one of his own slaves. However, in typical Roman fashion it does not endure long, as Crassus decides to cast aside their relationship in order to pursue his career and to defeat Spartacus and his army. Yet another example of immorality intrinsic to the Romans is their penchant for sexual manipulation as a means to an end. The orgies and other pleasures of the house of Batiatus mentioned above are clear cases of Romans openly exploiting the vices of other Romans for their own advantage, but other secretive examples exist, such as Ilithyia's private seduction of the young Numerius at his birthday party in order to convince him to call for Varro's death in the match with Spartacus as well as Lucretia's bedding of the senator Albinius in her successful attempt to convince him to annul Ilithyia's marriage to Glaber. Both examples are rife with expected Roman debauchery: Ilithyia's enticement of Numerius is murderous in its intent (Varro's death) and smacks of pedophilia (Numerius has just turned fifteen), while Lucretia's bedding of Albinius is both adulterous and intended to make the audience uncomfortable with their vast age difference, not to mention her intent to dissolve a marriage.

Two final examples round out the lengthy list of Roman sexual deviance: incest and rape. The case of incest occurs between the elite brother and sister pair of Seppius and Seppia. After the party for Varinius where slaves are tortured and executed, Seppia is upset that she did not have the nerve to stab the slave, Acer (Alex Way) (who Ilithyia happily dispatched), and her brother comforts her with talk of his "warm embrace" and a passionate kiss on her lips.[23] Although an actual on-screen scene of incest between the two does not take place, their dialogue and actions strongly suggest not only that it will but also that, based on his lack of hesitation and her lack of surprise, it has in fact occurred before. In terms of rape, the majority of cases occur between a Roman perpetrator and a slave victim, such as the scene with Cossutius and Diona or virtually any sex between master and slave. But there is Roman on Roman rape as well; above all the instance in the *War of the Damned* episode "Separate Paths," where Crassus' son Tiberius (Christian Antidormi), an impetuous and mostly disgraceful soldier, attacks his bitter rival Julius Caesar (Todd Lasance), using his father's military guard to subdue Caesar (who he could not otherwise defeat) while he rapes him. Interestingly, as will be discussed below, Tiberius' rape of Caesar has little to do with the earlier stereotype equating homosexuality with deviance, since the sodomizing is not a case of sexual desire, but rather domination and humiliation. The incident between Tiberius and Caesar is actually similar to the ubiquitous Roman sexual assaults on their slaves in that it is a power dynamic of dominance, control, and forced sexual submission. Such examples reveal that in the series, Roman sexual deviance does not simply occur in interactions with their slaves, but something that transpires between Romans as well and almost always in conjunction with selfish, ulterior motives.

Despite the overwhelming majority of Romans being duplicitous, crassly exploitative, and morally flawed, there are a handful of redeemable Romans who stand out precisely because they lack the terrible traits of their fellow citizens. Only four Romans appear to fall into this category and, significantly, all of them have lost their wealth and status (those defining Roman characteristics) and three of them are actually reduced to slavery. The first two are the husband and wife pair Varro and Aurelia (Brooke Williams), who both become the slaves of Batiatus. Varro's loss of freedom and turn as a gladiator resulted from his debts, which he sought to pay off through debt slavery. After Varro's death due to Ilithyia's scheming, Aurelia is forced to continue paying the family debt and thus becomes a slave of Batiatus. Unlike other Romans, Varro is a good friend to Spartacus, is trustworthy and dependable, and not at all conniving or self-centered. Aurelia is also portrayed as a good person who loves her husband, is not corrupt or duplicitous, and even avenges his death by stabbing Numerius during the initial revolt in the finale of *Blood and Sand*. After fleeing Capua, the rebel slaves encounter another Roman,

Lucius Caelius (Peter McCauley), at an abandoned temple near Vesuvius that they use as a hideout in the "Libertus" episode of *Vengeance*. Caelius is also a man who despises his fellow Romans, since he lost his family, his home, and all wealth on account of the proscriptions of the Roman dictator Sulla. He proves his worth by providing sanctuary to the rebels, training some of them in archery, and even helping broker a deal with Glaber to acquire weapons for the slaves (in exchange for Ilithyia who was captured by Spartacus), losing his life in the process. It is important to note that despite Ilithyia's attempt to bribe Caelius with the possible restoration of his lost status if he frees her, he refuses to betray the rebels and maintains his honor. The final redeemable Roman is Laeta (Anna Hutchison) who is the noble wife of a wealthy magistrate in Sinuessa en Valle, a city ultimately taken by the rebel army. In her first appearance in the *War of the Damned* episode, "Wolves at the Gate," Laeta is seen trying to get more grain to her fellow citizens as well as protesting the treatment of slaves in general, claiming that if they were treated more humanely, they would not have cause to rebel. After the city falls to the rebels, her humanitarian nature is further enhanced as she hides women and children from massacre and even risks her life to bring them food. Ultimately, Spartacus allows Laeta to return to the Romans outside the city where she is taken to Crassus for questioning, but the Roman general ends up betraying her by handing her over to a Cilician pirate as a slave to punish her for aiding the rebels. Although she is rescued from the pirates by Gannicus, it is not before she is branded as a slave, a mark that eventually helps ingratiate her to the rebels when she rejoins them. What redeems these four is that they share none of the nasty traits of their fellow Romans but instead are akin to the rebel slaves, especially since three of the four actually become slaves themselves. All of them have lost power, wealth, and influence on account of other Romans but what makes them anti–Roman are the qualities they share with the slaves and rebels, including authentic friendship, communalism, and selflessness.

Gladiators and Slaves: The Anti-Romans

The community of slaves and gladiators provides a convenient counterexample to Roman decadence and immorality, a similarity the *Spartacus* series shares with its peplum predecessors. Like the persecuted Christians in *The Sign of the Cross* and *Quo Vadis*, or the rebel slaves in the 1960 *Spartacus* film, both the slave community and their interpersonal relationships are reliable, trustworthy, and altruistic, a sharp and noticeable contrast with their self-centered and corrupt Roman masters. In the *Spartacus* series the slaves work as a whole for the common good and their mutual survival, especially after the initial revolt in Capua. Although prior to the revolt many of the gladiators, including the leaders Spartacus and Crixus, were hypercompetitive and jockeyed for power and influence in the *ludus* and the arena, they were only able to achieve their freedom once they worked together against the Romans. This cooperation is best represented at the immediate outbreak of rebellion at the *ludus* in the *Blood and Sand* finale, "Kill Them All," when Spartacus wishes to attack Batiatus and the other Romans on a balcony above the training ground, but can only do so with the assistance of Crixus. Despite his initial reluctance, Crixus ultimately decides to help and Spartacus is able to leap off of Crixus' shield and lay waste to the Romans, thus precipitating the revolt. The gladiators also risk their lives for one another, not for personal glory but out of friendship and camaraderie, such as when Crixus and several others are captured and sentenced to death in the arena, Spartacus and the rebels concoct a bold and dangerous, but ultimately successful, plan to rescue them. Other examples include a raid on a Roman mine to free Naevia and other imprisoned slaves and even the mostly suicidal attack by the gladiators on several massive Roman armies, in order to allow the women, children, and non-combatants a successful chance to escape the clutches of Rome. This communalism is reinforced by Spartacus himself when he tells his comrades that in order to beat the Romans they must stand together as one, or divided they will fall. As in the 1960 version, the community of slaves as a collective is elevated above personal self-interest which shows that, as Alison Futrell has demonstrated, "the viability of the system is measured not by profit but by the benefit to its parts."[24] All of these examples are something the cinematic Romans would never do since they involve selfless sacrifice and no discernible personal advantage.

Interpersonal relationships among the slaves are also dramatically different than those of the Romans in part because they are monogamous, mutually affectionate, and above all consensual. The relationship between Spartacus and his wife Sura is just such an example as most of their screen time in the premier episode shows them in loving embraces, hugging, kissing, making love, and pledging undying fidelity to one another. Like the relationship between Spartacus and Varinia in Kubrick's version, the scenes between Spartacus and Sura are ones of "tenderness and delicacy," completely unlike those with their Roman masters.[25] Their marriage is not based on exploitation, lies, or dominance and submission, but genuine and true affection. Even after they are separated by Glaber's treachery, Spartacus does everything in his power to try and reunite with Sura, while after her murder by Batiatus' command he continues to honor her memory by plotting revenge. Crixus and Naevia likewise have a consensual and loving relationship that begins secretly in the *ludus*, yet they continue their contact despite the threat of discovery and punishment by Lucretia. When their affair is discovered and

Lucretia banishes Naevia first to sexual slavery and ultimately to a death sentence in the mines, Crixus stops at nothing to find and rescue her, putting his own life at risk to do so. After they are reunited it is a long while before Naevia can come to terms with her traumatic experience, but Crixus remains by her side offering her encouragement throughout. She eventually warms to him and learns fighting skills from the former gladiator, becoming one of the best fighters in the rebel army. The two remain together even when they split from Spartacus to attack Rome itself, although Crixus falls to Tiberius and Caesar in a pitched battle in *War of the Damned*'s "Separate Paths." Allowed to return to the rebels with Crixus' head as a warning, Naevia honors Crixus by chanting his name with the crowd of slaves at funeral games held in his honor, showing that their relationship continued even after death.

In a stark change from its peplum predecessors, Starz's *Spartacus* also develops several positive homosexual relationships among the slaves, without any of the previous negative stereotyping that demonized queer relations as aberrant and threatening. As Thomas J. West has convincingly argued, the series has made "a concerted effort to ensure that the viewer does not understand these characters as ... the deviant and pathological, often explicitly queer coded, characters encountered in many epic films set in antiquity."[26] These relationships, like those of the heterosexual slaves, exhibit the same collaborative, affectionate, monogamous, and consensual traits that differentiate them from their Roman counterparts. In the *Blood and Sand* episode "Sacramentum Gladiatorum," Spartacus and Varro are eating in the mess hall, when Spartacus asks about Barca (Antonio Te Maioha), the best gladiator in the *ludus* after Crixus. Varro then tells the story of Barca's enslavement and significant victories in the arena, even being forced to fight and kill his own father. What is significant about the exchange are not the details of his prowess but that while Varro tells the story, the scene depicts the fit, muscular and traditionally masculine Barca sitting affectionately with his male partner, Pietros (Eka Darville), in a clearly homosexual relationship yet no one reacts negatively or is appalled by their love. In a break with peplum tradition, this non-reaction is telling because queer relationships are in fact treated no differently than their heterosexual counterparts, as Barca is neither shunned nor villainized on account of his sexuality. Instead, Barca's relationship with Pietros is shown as one of mutual respect, genuine affection, and consensual sex, as they are often shown relaxing with one another, raising birds together, or otherwise enjoying each other's company. A similar relationship exists between the gladiators Agron (Daniel Feuerriegel) and Nasir (Pana Hema Taylor) who slowly fall in love with one another and eventually become inseparable. Like Barca and Pietros, no one derides the two for their love nor is it styled as immoral or depraved, as they are both highly valued members of Spartacus' army and in fact are essentially the only two of the original fighters to survive the rebellion. The crucial aspect is that, as West has argued, the relationships are "mutually desired and indeed a source of pleasure *for both parties*."[27] Unlike the depiction of Laughton's and Ustinov's Neros or Olivier's Crassus, queer relationships are no longer an automatic indicator of deviance nor a threat to the sexuality and safety of heterosexual protagonists.

As a general rule, the slaves and gladiators are overall depicted as more honest, trustworthy, and moral than their Roman adversaries but there are a handful who do not meet these standards, primarily due to their selfish and corrupt behavior. At several points in the series, certain slaves run afoul of Spartacus and his view that the rebels should put aside their own desires for the collective good. Rhaskos, the slave used by Cossutius to rape Diona, is typically seen engaging in excessive hedonism (drinking, public nudity, and sex with any available woman) and often acts impetuously to satisfy his own needs over that of others. For example, after the initial rebellion when the slaves are hiding in the sewers of Capua, Rhaskos and his fellow Gauls are reprimanded by Spartacus for taking extra rations, believing they have earned it because of their fighting skills. Although a minor infraction, this incident reveals the tension between selfless and selfish acts among the rebels. A more violent example occurs in the rebel camp when a group of German slaves joins but one of them decides to defy Spartacus, attempts to rape Naevia, and attacks Agron. After a massive brawl among the slaves, Spartacus fights and kills the ringleader by literally slicing his face off with his sword. Commanding everyone's attention, Spartacus tells the rebels that they can remain only if they work together, put their differences aside, and commit to the well-being of the group as a whole, once again asserting the primacy of communalism over crass self-interest.

A much more definitive example of a slave defying the collective good is the former gladiator turned personal servant of Batiatus, Ashur (Nick Tarabay). Unlike his brethren, Ashur is consistently portrayed as scheming, deceitful, and underhanded, always looking out for his own gain especially if it can come at the expense of someone else. Some examples of his treachery include orchestrating the death of Barca, to whom he owed a large debt, using his favor with Batiatus to demand sexual access to Naevia and foul her relationship with his immediate rival, Crixus, attempting to assault the widow Aurelia, cowardly and dirty fighting techniques, and habitually mistranslating for a fellow Assyrian to get him into trouble. Ashur is also the main slave selected for nefarious plots such as beating a rival *lanista* and murdering Solonius. Batiatus allows Ashur to receive the brand of the brotherhood of gladiators not through fighting prowess, but through murder and treachery. Even more egregious, after the initial rebellion Ashur allies himself with Glaber in order to seek revenge on his fellow slaves for never fully accepting him into their fold. To prove his loyalty to Glaber and Rome, Ashur slices off the mark of the brotherhood, tortures his former trainer Oenomaus (Peter Mensah) for information about Spartacus' whereabouts, and leads an assault on the rebels. With Glaber's protection, Ashur blackmails Lucretia since he was privy to her plan to help Ilithyia abort her child, and then repeatedly rapes and beats her in the champion's quarters he now undeservedly inhabits. He even goes so far as to demand Lucretia marry him in his new bid to become a great *lanista*. Ultimately his many double-dealings backfire on him, he loses Glaber's favor and is sent to Spartacus' camp ostensibly to get the rebels to surrender, but Glaber's real motive is to see them kill Ashur, which Naevia ultimately does in *Vengeance*'s "Wrath of the Gods."

Ashur's continual struggle for power, his treachery, and his selfish nature is important because it sets him apart from his fellow slaves and makes him like many of the Romans. Ashur lacks power and influence but wants to acquire them by any means possible, even if it means selling out or even murdering his fellow slaves. The only way Ashur can achieve his goals is through treachery, deceit, and sexual assault. In fact, Ashur does not simply exhibit Roman traits, he essentially becomes Roman through his actions, his aspirations, and even his attire, which becomes rich and decadent. Ashur's transformation appears to be a throwback to a key scene in the 1960 *Spartacus* where Kirk Douglas' titular character discovers the rebel slaves forcing captured Roman patricians to fight one another in their old training arena. Upon seeing this inverted spectacle where the slaves are now the masters, instigators and voyeurs of gladiatorial violence, Spartacus is enraged at their transformation, shouting, "What are we becoming? Romans? Have we learned nothing?"[28] He then chastises his fellow gladiators for swapping places with their former Roman masters and even adopting their disdain for human life, telling them that they could be a great and powerful army that could fight for their freedom, if they work together to free other slaves and not selfishly act like drunken thieves. Confronted with the reality of their actions, the slaves rally behind Spartacus and abandon their short-lived Roman traits of selfishness, hedonism and bloodlust. Yet in the new *Spartacus* series, such communalism is lost on Ashur who apparently learned nothing from his plight as a slave and instead transforms into the deviant, corrupt enemy that the rebels have struggled against for so long.

Conclusion

As part of the twenty-first century resurgence of neo-peplum film and television, many of the traditional and expected tropes of ancient Rome have been resurrected. Over four seasons, Starz's *Spartacus* series revisited the age-old themes of corruption, exploitation, and immorality that have been used to characterize Romans and their world cinematically for decades. The debauchery of the Romans is seen not just in their corrupt political system that relies on power, connections, and favors, but is enhanced and expressed on an interpersonal level by their illicit desires, their depravity, and their aberrant sexual behavior at levels that far surpass even the most explicit scenes of decadence from twentieth century films. These desires are typically fulfilled through their dominance, subjugation, and even blackmail of others, especially their so-called inferiors that includes not only slaves but even their fellow Romans. The selfish and depraved Romans are also starkly contrasted with the slaves and gladiators, who are represented as altruistic, selfless, and caring towards one another as they work toward their common goal of liberation from Roman oppression. That such qualities of the slaves are critical to their identity can be seen not just in their contrast with Romans, but especially with anyone who would "become Roman," such as the treacherous Ashur. To become Roman then is to betray the altruistic communalism of the slaves by selfishly putting one's own needs before that of others and instead embrace Roman corruption, hedonism and sadism, complete with its toll in human life and dignity. Interestingly, despite such oft-repeated examples of Roman deviance, a significant development is that, unlike the stereotyping inherited from earlier films, the *Spartacus* series breaks new ground in its refusal to perpetuate earlier tropes that pathologized queer sexuality by linking it with villainy and corruption. Alone among peplum and even neo-peplum epics, *Spartacus* normalizes queer relations by divesting them of their previous deviant overtones. Nevertheless, the *Spartacus* series continues to present a system that relies on the sexualized expression of dominance and mirrors that of the supposed larger, oppressive social and political Roman world made famous in earlier epic films.

NOTES

    1. Maria Wyke, *Projecting the Past: Ancient Rome, Cinema and History* (New York: Routledge, 1997), 3.
    2. Sandra R. Joshel, Margaret Malamud, and Donald T. McGuire, Jr., *Imperial Projections: Ancient Rome in Modern Popular Culture* (Baltimore: Johns Hopkins University Press, 2001), 3. See also Martin Winkler's argument that American films set in imperial Rome emphasize power leading to corruption as a "fundamental theme," Martin Winkler, "The Roman Empire in American Cinema after 1945," in *Imperial Projections*, ed. Joshel, et al., 51–52.
    3. Wyke, 25.
    4. William Fitzgerald, "Oppositions, Anxieties and Ambiguities in the Toga Movie," in *Imperial Projections*, ed. Joshel, et al., 26.
    5. Alastair Blanshard and Kim Shahabudin, *Classics on Screen: Ancient Greece and Rome on Film* (London: Bristol Classical Press, 2011), 47.
    6. Winkler, 54.
    7. *Spartacus*, directed by Stanley Kubrick (1960; Universal City, CA: Universal, 1998, DVD), emphasis mine.
    8. Alison Futrell, "Seeing Red: Spartacus as Domestic Economist," in *Imperial Projections*, ed. Joshel, et al., 100.

9. Elena Theodorakopoulos, *Ancient Rome at the Cinema: Story and Spectacle in Hollywood and Rome* (Exter: Bristol Phoenix Press, 2010), 60.
 10. Anise K. Strong, "Objects of Desire: Female Gaze and Male Bodies in *Spartacus: Blood and Sand*," in *Screening Love and Sex in the Ancient World*, ed. Monica Cyrino (New York: Palgrave Macmillan, 2013), 173.
 11. See Blanshard and Shahabudin's discussion that "the ultimate horror of slavery was not the inevitable cruelty that attended it, but the fact that it objectified humans to the point where they became nothing but lumps of meat," 91.
 12. Stacie Raucci, "The Order of Orgies: Sex and the Cinematic Roman," in Cyrino, ed., *Screening Love and Sex in the Ancient World*, 143.
 13. *Ibid.*, 144.
 14. *Spartacus*, directed by Stanley Kubrick.
 15. See Vito Russo, *The Celluloid Closet: Homosexuality in the Movies* (New York: Harper and Row, 1987), 61–123, and Jerry B. Pierce, "Gays of the Arena: Positive Reimagining of Homosexuality in Starz' *Spartacus*" (presentation, *Film and History Conference*, Milwaukee, September 28, 2012).
 16. *Spartacus*, directed by Stanley Kubrick.
 17. Theodorakopoulos, 67.
 18. Antony Augoustakis, "Partnership and Love in Spartacus," in Cyrino, ed., *Screening Sex and Love in the Ancient World*, 163.
 19. *Spartacus: Blood and Sand*, produced by Steven S. DeKnight (2010; Meridian, CO: Starz, 2014, Blu-ray).
 20. Strong, "Objects of Desire," 175.
 21. *Ibid*.
 22. *Ibid.*, 179.
 23. *Spartacus: Vengeance*, produced by Steven S. DeKnight (2010; Meridian, CO: Starz, 2014), Blu-ray.
 24. Futrell, 79. For further discussion on the difference between the slave and Roman armies, see Wyke, 65, Theodorakopoulos, 64–65, Joanna Paul, *Film and the Classical Epic Tradition* (Oxford: Oxford University Press, 2013), 207 and Jon Solomon, *The Ancient World in the Cinema* (New Haven: Yale University Press, 2001), 53.
 25. Jeffrey Richards, *Hollywood's Ancient Worlds* (New York: Continuum, 2008), 86. See also Strong, "Objects of Desire," 176.
 26. Thomas J. West, III, "Brothers in Arms: Spartacus, Historical Television and the Celebration of Queer Masculinity," in *Queer TV in the 21st Century: Essays on Broadcasting from Taboo to Acceptance*, ed. Kylo-Patrick R. Hart (Jefferson, NC: McFarland, 2016), 143.
 27. West, 148 (emphasis mine). See also Augoustakis, 161 and Pierce, passim.
 28. *Spartacus*, directed by Stanley Kubrick.

Bibliography

Augoustakis, Antony. "Partnership and Love in *Spartacus*." In *Screening Love and Sex in the Ancient World*, edited by Monica S. Cyrino, 157–165. New York: Palgrave Macmillan.
Blanshard, Alastair J.L., and Kim Shahabudin, *Classics on Screen: Ancient Greece and Rome on Film*. London: Bristol Classical Press, 2011.
Cleopatra. Directed by Joseph Mankiewicz. 1963. Los Angeles: 20th Century Fox, 2006. DVD.
Cornelius, Michael G. *Of Muscles and Men: Essays on the Sword and Sandal Film*. Jefferson, NC: McFarland, 2011.
Elliott, Andrew B.R. *The Return of the Epic Film: Genre, Aesthetics and History in the 21st Century*. Edinburgh: Edinburgh University Press, 2015.
The Fall of the Roman Empire. Directed by Anthony Mann. 1964. Hollywood: Paramount Pictures, 2008. DVD.
Fitzgerald, William. "Oppositions, Anxieties and Ambiguities in the Toga Movie." In *Imperial Projections: Ancient Rome in Modern Popular Culture*, edited by Sandra R. Joshel, et al., 23–49. Baltimore: Johns Hopkins University Press, 2001.
Futrell, Alison. "Seeing Red: Spartacus as Domestic Economist." In *Imperial Projections:*

Ancient Rome in Modern Popular Culture, edited by Sandra R. Joshel, et al., 77–118. Baltimore: Johns Hopkins University Press, 2001.
Joshel, Sandra R., Margaret Malamud, and Donald T. McGuire, Jr., ed. *Imperial Projections: Ancient Rome in Modern Popular Culture*. Baltimore: Johns Hopkins University Press, 2001.
Paul, Joanna. *Film and the Classical Epic Tradition*. Oxford: Oxford University Press, 2013.
Pierce, Jerry B. "Gays of the Arena: Positive Reimagining of Homosexuality in Starz' *Spartacus*." Presentation at the *Film and History Conference*, Milwaukee, September 28, 2012.
Quo Vadis. Directed by Mervyn LeRoy. 1951. Burbank, CA: Warner Brothers, 2008. DVD.
Raucci, Stacie. "The Order of Orgies: Sex and the Cinematic Roman." In *Screening Love and Sex in the Ancient World*, edited by Monica S. Cyrino, 143–155. New York: Palgrave Macmillan, 2013.
Richards, Jeffrey. *Hollywood's Ancient Worlds*. New York: Continuum, 2008.
The Robe. Directed by Henry Koster. 1953. Los Angeles: 20th Century Fox, 2014. DVD.
Russo, Vito. *The Celluloid Closet: Homosexuality in the Movies*. New York: Harper and Row, 1987.
The Sign of the Cross. Directed by Cecil B. DeMille. 1932. Universal City, CA: Universal, 2011. DVD.
Solomon, Jon. *The Ancient World in the Cinema*. New Haven: Yale University Press, 2001.
Spartacus. Directed by Stanley Kubrick. 1960. Universal City, CA: Universal, 1998. DVD.
Spartacus: The Complete Series. Produced by Steven S. DeKnight. 2010. Meridian, CO: Starz, 2014. Blu-Ray.
Strong, Anise K. "Objects of Desire: Female Gaze and Male Bodies in *Spartacus: Blood and Sand*." In *Screening Love and Sex in the Ancient World*, edited by Monica S. Cyrino, 167–181. New York: Palgrave Macmillan, 2013.
_____. "*Vice Is Nice: Rome* and Deviant Sexuality." In *Rome, Season One: History Makes Television*, edited by Monica S. Cyrino, 219–231. Malden, MA: Blackwell, 2008.
Theodorakopoulos, Elena. *Ancient Rome at the Cinema: Story and Spectacle In Hollywood and Rome*. Exeter: Bristol Phoenix Press, 2010.
West, Thomas J., III. "Brothers in Arms: Spartacus, Historical Television and the Celebration of Queer Masculinity." In *Queer TV in the 21st Century: Essays on Broadcasting from Taboo to Acceptance*, edited Kylo-Patrick R. Hart, 142–158. Jefferson, NC: McFarland, 2016.
Winkler, Martin M. "The Roman Empire in American Cinema After 1945." In *Imperial Projections: Ancient Rome in Modern Popular Culture*, edited by Sandra R. Joshel, et al, 50–76. Baltimore: Johns Hopkins University Press, 2001.
Wyke, Maria. *Projecting the Past: Ancient Rome, Cinema and History*. New York: Routledge, 1997.

In the Green Zone with the Ninth Legion
The Post-Iraq Roman Film

KEVIN J. WETMORE, JR.

Witney Seibold refers to Zack Snyder's 2007 film *300* as "American peplum" and locates the film in its political context: "It seemed, to many, that a film about brave, white military 'lager louts' getting the best of an army of dark-skinned Persians rang loudly of pro-imperialism, pro-military violence, and outright pro-fascism."[1] In other words, a neo-peplum about the Battle of Thermopylae from 480 BCE was widely read as reflecting, echoing and commenting upon contemporary events in the Middle East, specifically the ongoing wars in Iraq and Afghanistan, positing a small group of "half naked WWE wrestlers" fighting for freedom to protect the Spartans back home.[2] The rhetoric of the characters matched the rhetoric coming from the Bush administration concerning ongoing hostilities. This film was following in the footsteps of a long cinematic history of peplum America.

It is not unusual for American peplums to reflect the American military/political identity of the period. In particular, Rome is the model by which Hollywood measures, and constructs through a classical lens, America. In the introduction to *Imperial Projections: Ancient Rome in Modern Popular Culture*, Sandra Joshel, Margaret Malamud and Maria Wyke write, "Imperial Rome provides a screen onto which concerns about contemporary international relations, domestic politics and cultural tensions can be projected."[3] The mid-twentieth century American films concerning Rome, for example, *Quo Vadis* (1951, Mervyn LeRoy), *The Robe* (1953, Henry Koster), *Ben-Hur* (1959, William Wyler), *Spartacus* (1960, Stanley Kubrick), and *The Fall of the Roman Empire* (1964, Anthony Mann), present Rome and her soldiers as modeled after Nazis, fascists and/or communists. At best, they are a stand in for the British Empire, a declining imperial power run by effete morally and politically corrupt monarchs.

Maria Wyke notes that such films set up a "linguistic paradigm" in which British actors play the decadent Romans and Americans are "their virtuous Jewish or Christian opponents."[4] "In such narratives," she continues, "a hyperbolically tyrannical Rome stands for the decadent European Other, forever destined to be defeated by the vigorous Christian principles of democratic America."[5] Rebelling against such power are the colonies of the Roman Empire, often but not always the Holy Land, identified by performers and the sentiments they speak as being similar to the United States. Judah Ben-Hur (Charlton Heston), Spartacus (Kirk Douglas), and the men who follow them are rock-jawed, freedom-loving American Christians who fight back against the decadence and violence of Rome. Per Joshel, Malamud and Wyke, these films construct Rome as the recently defeated Germans or the (then) current threat from the Soviet Union and nations behind the Iron Curtain, and the Christians from the provinces as the Americans. Indigenous fighters are good; soldiers of the empire are servants of evil, just like in the real world.

Interestingly, in the period following the American invasion of Iraq in 2003, a reversal of this construction has begun to emerge in American cinema. As with *300*, it is the small group of freedom loving soldiers that prove synecdoche for the United States. American peplum post- Iraq identify as pro–Roman soldier, constructing their opponents are insurgents so hate-filled that they cannot even be quelled—only survived. The Americans are now the Roman soldiers in the far reaches of the empire. In films such as *The Last Legion* (2007, Doug Lefler), *Centurion* (2010, Neil Marshall), and *The Eagle* (2011, Kevin Macdonald), Roman soldiers attempting to establish the Pax Romana (Pax Americana?) in the far-flung provinces are confronted by violent, animalistic insurgents from the local population and must fight to protect themselves and each other, even as they are betrayed by the ruling class at home. While *Gladiator* (2000, Ridley Scott) arguably began the trend of critiquing the empire while romanticizing the imperial soldier who demonstrates the hollowness of the empire's ideals, it was after 9/11 and the invasions of Iraq and Afghanistan that American cinema set films in the provinces and featured Roman soldiers as protagonists. *The Eagle* has far more in common with *The Hurt Locker* (2009, Kathryn Bigelow) than with *Spartacus*.

Indeed, the post–Iraq peplum film echoes the experience of American soldiers in such films as *Redacted* (2007, Brian De Palma), *Stop-Loss* (2008, Kimberly Peirce), and *Green Zone* (2010, Paul Greengrass), all of which feature scenes of small groups of American soldiers in Iraq—guarding checkpoints, on patrol, engaging with locals and surviving attacks, from both weapons fire and IEDs. The soldiers are the "good guys" in enemy territory, sent to fight by politicians who avoided combat themselves, fighting mostly for their lives and to protect each other. As a result, post–Iraq War Roman films identifies itself with the Roman military, a complete reversal of identity. Cinema about ancient Rome in the twentieth century is "Epic Rome"; whereas films about Rome after 9/11 are "Iraq Rome." Interestingly, the three films that use this construction, *The Last Legion*, *Centurion* and *The Eagle*, all employ the popular history of the Ninth Legion of Rome as a background to explore the issues soldiers face when defending the empire from far away.

The Ninth Legion, also known as *Legio IX Hispana* in Latin (Ninth Spanish Legion), was sent to Britannia as part of the invading group sent between 43 and 60 CE. *Legio IX* was fortifying York by 107 but then vanished from the records between 108 and 120 CE. Guy de la Bédoyère reports, "During the Agricolan campaigns, the IX Legion had been ambushed in Scotland, and the culprits had escaped by vanishing into the forests and marshes."[6] The absence of the Ninth from any official records after this period gave rise to the theory that it vanished in Scotland as a result of the ambush. However, as de la Bédoyère also reports, "the old idea that it had been lost in Britain is no longer considered credible."[7] Most likely the legion was disbanded or sent elsewhere, actually vanishing in Parthia or Judea. Nevertheless, in popular culture, the Ninth vanished in Britannia under mysterious circumstances, most likely a Celtic ambush. The idea of an imperial legion ambushed by local insurgents and defeated in such a way that it "vanished" with the attackers also disappearing into the local landscape lends itself to depiction of later, similar, circumstances, most notably the wars in Iraq and Afghanistan.

The transition actually began with *Gladiator*, which "simultaneously invited American audiences both to distance themselves from and identify with the spectacle of Roman power, luxury and superiority."[8] The gladiators' coliseum is a site for mocking warriors and for citizens to take pleasure in violence; whereas the military scenes in the film show support and sympathy for the soldiers, many of whom are not Roman citizens and, in fact, are from other conquered peoples. This aspect reflects the U.S. military at the time of the film, in which some 65,000 foreign born individuals were on active duty in the military, or approximately five percent of active duty personnel, a much higher presence that in the general population.[9]

Yet, as Margaret Malamud points out, *Gladiator* is predicated on the idea that "there are no external enemies left to conquer ... the enemy is internal."[10] The terror attacks of 9/11, declaration and waging of the theoretical "War on Terror" and the actual wars in Iraq and Afghanistan, however, reaffirmed the idea of external enemies without giving up on the problem of internal enemies. The insurgents in Iraq, the Taliban and Al-Qaeda in Afghanistan were purely Other in American media and popular culture. Then-attorney general John Ashcroft remarked, "the attacks of September 11 drew a bright line of demarcation between the civil and the savage."[11] Administration officials described the enemy as hateful, barbarous, monstrous, perverted, without faith, inhuman, and evil, contrasting these depictions with the construction of Americans as under attack, in danger, brave, peace-loving, strong, resourceful and heroic.[12] American soldiers were portrayed by the administration as heroes going to live among those "savages," and while we might not be able to bring civility and civilization to them, they would respect our power and military might. But the insurgencies in each war began to cause damage and erode morale. American soldiers in Iraq mostly stuck to the Green Zone, the heavily fortified center of Baghdad with access controlled by American troops. In contrast, the Red Zone was the area outside, unsecured and a place of potential attack or IED use.

Through the media, the language and designations of the Iraq War became familiar to many Americans who understood the narrative of a small group of volunteer professional soldiers who split their time between a safe, fortified area and the larger nation, which was full of the aforementioned barbarous savages, given to attacking Americans.

Further problematizing the deployment of troops abroad is the deeply conflicted sense of Americans back home. Distrust of politicians, particularly "chicken hawks," those who deferred or avoided military service themselves such as the president and vice president, but were perceived as strongly in favor of military action when others would have to carry it out. There was a sense of the ruling class being hypocritical and corrupt, while all agreed, both the right and left sides of the political spectrum, to "support the troops." In other words, morally corrupt politicians sent professional soldiers to fight battles they themselves would not, and the soldiers not only faced risks that soldiers have before, but also had to face new challenges in the face of insurgencies.

Therefore, both Epic Roman films and Iraq Roman films posit what Monica Silveira Cyrino in her study of post–World War II Roman films terms "the moral corruption of the Romans."[13] They key difference is that the Epic Roman films focus on the "luxury, glamour and eroticism" of the Roman aristocracy but also on the luxury, violence and decadence of the Roman soldiers, while Iraq Roman films present the corrupt ruling class as being yet another enemy of the common foot soldier, who is the salt of the earth.[14]

All three films discussed here feature a small group of Roman soldiers "behind enemy lines" in Celtic Britain/Scotland. All three films depict the soldiers as good, honest, working class warriors put into untenable positions by the politicians back in Rome. All three films depict not the generals, but the midrank and foot soldiers of the military that must move out from the safety of the Roman-pacified areas into the Celtic-controlled countryside. Latin is represented in these films as conversational English; Celtic and Pictish characters use the actual languages and are subtitled. The British characters are thus presenting linguistically, visually, ethnically as Other. They are not Roman, do not share Roman values, and are savage and dangerous. They are monolithic, interchangeable and "the Enemy."

Conversely, the Ninth Legion itself is presented in these films as a multi-ethnic, multi-cultural force—soldiers from different cultures who work together on behalf of Rome. They may not have chosen to come to Britain, but whilst there will defend each other and Roman values to the last man. Emphasis in all three films is on camaraderie, the brotherhood of the soldiers themselves, the danger to them from the locals and the neglect, contempt for, and exploitation of the legion by the politicians "back home." Thus, this essay posits that all three films align with a construction of the wars in Iraq and Afghanistan more than they do with previous constructions of Rome. The focus on the soldiers, the contempt for the politicians, the concern for "our boys" occupying a foreign nation and threatened by insurgents who melt into the local population frame these films as peplum that echo the current wars, not the previous or Roman ones. All three employ the same structures, character types, narrative tropes and fight scenes in order to establish this construction, although the degree to which they do so varies. *The Last Legion* begins the association with the Iraq War that *Centurion* makes obvious and *The Eagle* finalizes.

The Last Legion

Released in 2007 and based on Valerio Massimo Manfredi's 2002 novel *L'ultima legione* (*The Last Legion*), the film's timeline does not resemble anything approaching historical reality. Set in Rome, Capri and then Britain in 460 CE, nearing the end of the empire, the film narrates how Rome fell through the machinations of its politicians in league with foreign barbarians, but the true legacy of Rome was transported to Britain in the form of the child emperor, guarded by a group of soldiers and joined by a remnant of the Ninth Legion (somehow mysteriously still around in 460) in order to install Romulus Augustus as the new ruler of Britain.

The film opens by asserting that the "Sword of Caesar" was passed down through the Roman emperors until it was lost to history. Yet still Rome sends her army far and wide to spread Roman rule and civilization. "Now a threatened Rome was calling back her bravest and her best to defend her boundaries," proclaims the text on a title card.[15] The audience is introduced to a group of soldiers, led by Aurelius (Colin Firth), who have returned to Rome in order to guard the young emperor. Romulus Augustus (Thomas Sangster), a boy of ten, is crowned emperor, but the Goths, betrayed by his father, invade

Rome, dethroning Romulus Augustus and placing their king, Odoacer (Peter Mullen) on the throne, who orders the death of his young predecessor.

Aurelius leads his soldiers to Capri to rescue Romulus, where they meet with Mira (Aishwarya Rai), an Indian warrior recruited to the service of Constantinople. Betrayed by the rulers and aristocrats of both Eastern and Western empires, including Nestor (John Hannah), a senator and the boy's uncle who wishes to hand him over to Odoacer in order to increase his own power, the small group of soldiers seemingly have nowhere to go until Ambrosinus (Ben Kingsley), born in Britain, but a Roman citizen and tutor to Romulus Augustus, suggests they go to Britannia. His reason: "The Ninth Legion is in Britannia," located at Hadrian's Wall, and will remain faithful to the boy emperor.[16] (We might note at this point we have left history thoroughly behind in the service of a larger adventure story with lots of sword fighting!)

The small group of soldiers arrives at the wall only to find it abandoned. "We've come a long way for a legion of ghosts," Aurelius laments.[17] A local farmer reveals, "I am Flavius Constantinus Marcellus, general of the Ninth Legion."[18] He and his men have gone to live among the Celts, as "Rome abandoned us."[19] Further trouble appears in the form of Vortgyn (Harry Van Gorkum), a local warlord in league with Odoacer, who seeks the sword Aurelius carries as it has a special inscription on it: "One edge to defend, one edge to defeat. In Britannia was I forged for the hand of he who is destined to rule." This is revealed to be the Sword of Caesar, and Vortgyn seeks it to drive the last Romans out of Britain and rule the nation, undivided.

Flavius Constantinus Marcellus summons his fellow former Ninth Legionnaires, who arrive at the wall with their old armor and weapons, pledging to fight to the death to protect the boy emperor. Aurelius speaks to the combined Roman unit:

> You men of the Ninth Legion, all of us, together we have fought all our lives for the empire our ancestors created, and together we have watched that empire crumble to dust. And with its fall we have lost two friends. I can tell you that in the darkest moments, I came to believe that there was nothing left to fight for. But I've been shown, through the wisdom of others, that there is one more battle to be waged, against tyranny and the slaughter of innocents. Let us defend to the last breath this island of Britannia, against those who would tear out its heart and soul! And then those who come after us l remember that there was such a thing as a Roman soldier, with a Roman sword, and a Roman heart![20]

We find in this speech a few important elements. First, the eponymous last legion is the Ninth, ostensibly vanished three hundred years before, but still somehow near Hadrian's Wall. Second, Aurelius' argument is that even with the fall of Rome, its corrupt politicians, its rule now by enemies from within, the soldiers still owe a duty to defeat evil in the form of the Celts who would "tear out [Britain's] heart and soul."[21] What makes this claim so extraordinary is that Aurelius just set foot in Britannia a few days before saying this. It is the local ruler, Vortgyn, the Celtic tribal chief, who is the threat to the "heart and soul" of the Celtic people in this speech, not the small group of Roman invaders. The local leader is "tyranny" who slaughters innocents, while the Ninth Legion and the newly arrived Roman bodyguard of the boy emperor are the true defenders of Britannia. Such rhetoric, of course, echoes the speeches given during the War on Terror, that America was the defender of freedom, truth and the rights of the indigenous people whose lands we had invaded and we were noble enough to fight their enemies within for them.

The climactic battle, as is usual for such films, features the heroic death of several of the supporting soldiers, and the eventual victory of Aurelius over Vortgyn, Odoacer, and the savage Celts. The Celts alive after the battle accept their new Roman rulers and the film then reveals that Augustus Caesar, the boy king of Britain, takes the name Pendragon, and fathers a son named Arthur. The Sword of Caesar, whose inscription becomes obscured over time, is revealed to be the sword Excalibur, and Ambrosinus is Merlin, now tutor to young Arthur. The entire film has been a story told to the young prince by the old wizard. The Romans took over Celtic Britain and transformed it into Camelot.

Both this film and the novel it is based upon plays fast and loose with history, mythology and even logic, but employs the language and narrative of American military action in Muslim nations to tell the story of the founding of Arthurian England. The Ninth Legion returns from retirement in order to battle for the freedom of the Celtic people to be ruled by Rome.

Centurion

As with *The Last Legion*, Neil Marshall's original narrative film *Centurion* opens with a contextualizing text: "The Roman Empire stretched from the African desert to the Caspian Sea, but its farthest, most untamed frontier was Northern Britain. In this unforgiving land, the Roman army encountered fierce resistance from a people known as the Picts. Using guerilla tactics and the landscape to their advantage, they brought the invasion to a halt. The stalemate has lasted almost 20 years. Now Rome has given orders to end the deadlock by any means necessary."[22] The language used to describe the indigenous people again echoes the rhetoric of the War on Terror: "untamed," "unforgiving land," "fierce resistance," etc. The Picts use "guerrilla tactics" and their superior knowledge of the area to fight the invading Romans, bringing the invasion "to a halt." There is no critique of empire or imperialism here. The soldiers are doing a job; the insurgents are trying to stop them.

The text may as well say the Picts hate the Romans for their freedoms. Lastly, the situation is now a "stalemate," also echoing the war in Iraq by 2010, which had been waged for seven years, through a number of commanders and "the surge," but no real victory or pacification, resulting in a drawdown of troops by President Obama. In this film, the Romans are fatigued of occupying their Iraq–Britannia.

The next image is of Quintus (Michael Fassbender), the titular centurion, running bound and shirtless through the snow. The film then cuts to two weeks earlier, when the Ninth Legion was posted to Inch-Tuth-Il, the northernmost Roman garrison in Britannia. They are in the Red Zone of Scotland, outside the protection of Hadrian's Wall. Inch-Tuth-Il is heavily fortified, heavily armed, and heavily guarded. A voiceover states, "This place is the asshole of the world. Even the land wants us dead."[23] Quintus is frustrated by the fact that the Picts will not be drawn into an open battle but rely upon insurgency to kill Romans and destroy parts of the fort. "This is a new kind of war, a war without honor, without end,"[24] echoing sentiments heard from Vietnam through Iraq. When the Picts do attack, it is a night raid that kills both several Romans and several Picts.

Julian Agricola (Paul Freeman), the Governor of Britannia in Carlyle, orders Quintus to guide General Titus Flavius Virilus (Dominic West) and the Ninth Legion north to defeat the Picts. The politician is indifferent to the fate of the soldiers but is desperate to report to Rome success at defeating the enemy. Agricola introduces them to their guide, Etain (Olga Kurylenko), a mute Pict whom they are told will lead them to the enemy. Instead, she leads them into an ambush and most of the legion is killed immediately. Seven Roman survivors live through the battle and must now move through Pict territory to return to the Green Zone on the other side of Hadrian's Wall.

The seven see two Roman soldiers hunted by the Picts, now led by Etain, who decapitates one of the soldiers with a knife. This action calls to mind the videos of Westerners being decapitated by Muslim extremists, such as American journalist Daniel Pearl, beheaded with a knife in Pakistan in 2002, American Nick Berg, decapitated with a knife in Iraq in May 2004 by a masked person claiming to be Abu Musab al-Zarqawi, American contractor Owen Eugene "Jack" Armstrong, also decapitated with a knife by Abu Musab al-Zarqawi in Iraq in September 2004, and British engineer Kenneth Bigley, decapitated with a knife in October 2004. All of these victims had their murders videotaped and placed on the web by their killers. Etain's decapitation of the Roman soldier specifically with a knife, followed by her lifting his head and looking directly at the camera (representing the point of view of the surviving Roman soldiers in hiding) directly evokes these videos.

The Romans attempt to rescue the captured Virilus, but are unable to free him. In their escape, they kill the young son of Gorlacon (Ulrich Thomsen), the ruler of this band of Picts, who then sends Etain, Aeron (Axelle Carolyn) and a group of Pict hunters to capture and kill the Romans, who themselves must run for the garrison at Hadrian's Wall. One by one the Roman soldiers are killed by Picts until only Quintus and Bothos (David Morrissey) arrive at the wall where the latter is killed by "friendly fire," the guards mistaking him for a Pict and shooting him with arrows.

Quintus faithfully reports what happened, but the governor is deeply disappointed, since the defeat is a disgrace. He announces the fate of the Ninth "will be struck from the record" in order to preserve Roman power, so that the tribes will not know Rome can be defeated. He insists that Quintus' story be struck from the record and Quintus himself silenced.[25] Instead, Quintus returns to the north of the Wall to be with Arianne (Imogen Poots), a Pict witch whom is the only person he trusts in the entire country now that his men are dead. As with *The Last Legion*, we are shown a small group of professional soldiers, betrayed by the politicians, fighting against an insurgency that wants to see them dead, and whose allegiance is to each other. Added to this film are the echoes of hostage decapitations and the presentation of Hadrian's Wall dividing Britannia into the Green Zone of the south, safe and comfortable for Romans, and the Red Zone of Scotland, in which the Pictish insurgents murder soldiers.

The Eagle

Based on the novel *The Eagle of the Ninth* by Rosemary Sutcliffe, this film is arguably the clearest demonstration of the echoes of Iraq in contemporary American pepla. Indeed, the differences between the novel, published in 1954, and the film, released in 2011, are markers that demonstrate the presence of the Iraq War in the film. The novel had been adapted before: in 1957 by BBC Radio and again in 1963 and 1996. It was adapted for television in 1977. None of the earlier versions have any of the major changes the film version made to the narrative.

At heart, both original novel and its filmic adaptation concern Marcus Flavia Aquila, the son of a well-known member of the Ninth Legion, who after being injured in battle and invalided out of the army, decides to go north and find the Eagle standard that had been carried by the Ninth. In the book, Marcus disguises himself as "Demetrius of Alexandria," a Greek eye doctor, who travels through Scotland, healing Picts and Celts of eye diseases, learning their languages, and living among them until he finds the Eagle. He decides he will take it, and will fight for it, but he has learned to admire and appreciate the people who have treated him well: "In the matter of the Eagle, they were the enemy, an enemy worthy of his steel. He liked and respected them; let them keep the Eagle, if they could."[26] None of this is in the film version. There is no liking or respecting the Picts and Celts. There is no disguise and living among them, only enemies to kill or be killed by.

The film begins with another title card text: "In 120 AD the Ninth Legion of the Roman Army marched into the unconquered territory of Northern Britain. They were never seen again. All 5000 men vanished, together with their treasured standard: The Eagle. Shamed by this great loss, the Emperor Hadrian ordered the construction of a giant wall to cut off the North of Britain forever. Hadrian's Wall marked the end of the known world."[27]

Again, the audience is told about the end of the Ninth, and that the land above Hadrian's Wall is always and forever Other. In this case, Hadrian's Wall marks the end of the world as known by Romans while the Celts and the Picts know the world beyond it very well. We are clearly meant to identity with the Romans and to understand the need of Marcus to remove a military shame (defeat), by taking a symbol of that defeat away from the enemy.

Twenty years later, Marcus Flavius Aquila (Channing Tatum) arrives at a fortification to assume command of the Fourth cohort of Gaul, Second Legion. He is greeted by Lutorius (Denis O'Hare), the acting commander, who explains Marcus' predecessor could not wait for him to arrive in order to take his leave. To the dismay of the soldiers, Marcus insists the fort be repaired, further fortified, and the men begin training daily. They are further mystified that he asked to be sent to the north of Britain. "To this shithole?" one asks incredulously.[28]

The accents are American, the conversations casual but in contemporary American military language. Lutorius is played as an NCO greeting the new commander; the new commander wants discipline reinstalled in his men, obviously not kept up by the previous commander, whose breaking of protocol by leaving before his replacement arrived indicates his lack of military virtue. Marcus, on the other hand, recognizes the danger from the local environment. In particular, he sees the threat posed by the local religion.

In the novel, Marcus befriends the local druid and goes hunting with him, recognizing that the newly repaired war weapons in the druid's collection indicates the locals might be planning to attack the Romans. Forearmed with this observation, he is able to prepare his men to fight. The film's Marcus does no such thing—he befriends no locals, he prepares his men to fight because he knows they are in a hostile environment, an occupying army surrounded by thousands of indigenous people who hide the insurgents among them.

The film's druid calls on the Celts to attack. He leads a suicide run in a chariot. He tells them, "God will bring us a great victory today."[29] A patrol has been captured by the Celts, so the insurgents bring the captives to Marcus' fortification. At a distance but in clear view of the other soldiers, the druid

188   Part Three: The "Glory" of Rome

decapitates a Roman soldier with a knife, once again, as with *Centurion*, evoking knife decapitations of hostages in Iraq and Afghanistan. Marcus leads a mission to rescue the other Roman prisoners and the Celts attack en masse. Using Roman battle tactics, they are able to get to and rescue the prisoners. The druid, however, is in a chariot and uses it to pursue and cut down Roman soldiers in a chariot version of a drive by. In an inversion, Marcus is able to use another chariot as an IED, causing the druid to wreck his chariot but not without seriously injuring Marcus.

There are two important things to observe from this battle sequence. First, the Celts are not just the enemy and the Other—they are being led by religious extremists in this film. It is the religious leaders who use the faith of the locals to generate animosity towards Rome and Romans. Second, the Roman soldier is injured when a vehicle is employed to distract and then injure him. Both of these aspects are further evocations of patrols in Iraq.

Marcus is given a citation and an honorable discharge. He then goes to live with his uncle in the South of Britain and rescues a brave slave who is going to be killed in a gladiator fight. The slave is Esca (Jamie Bell), a Celt that Marcus buys because he admires his bravery. Esca loathes Marcus, but because Marcus rescued him from the arena he feels a debt of honor: "I hate everything you stand for, everything you are. But you saved me. And for that I must serve you."[30] Esca, against his will, becomes a comprador—an indigenous person working with and for the Romans. In his case, out of obligation.

Marcus is invited to dinner by his uncle where he meets the politicians. Tribune Placidus (Pip Carter) is the same age as Marcus, but being born in a wealthy family, he is destined for politics. He tells Marcus he would have volunteered to fight as a soldier, "but my father insists I go into politics."[31] The contempt the film wants the viewer to feel for him is obvious. He is young, privileged and contemptuous of those below him socially. His family's wealth and connections kept him out of the military and allowed him to join the ruling class. He is the photo negative of Marcus—the opposite of everything the soldier is.

Marcus begs the senators to allow him to retrieve the Eagle. "Rome would love to get the Eagle back," he is told, "but politics being politics, no senator is going to risk thousands of lives on a tainted legion. My hands are tied."[32] His uncle Aquila (Donald Sutherland), a retired soldier, tells him, "The politicians have no notion of how you and I lived our lives."[33] Marcus responds that he is proud to be a soldier: "Can you imagine anything more magnificent than to be a soldier and serve Rome with courage and faithfulness?"[34] Far more than in Sutcliffe's book, the film juxtaposes the privileged elite in the safe areas versus the soldiers who risk everything to preserve freedom and the empire.

Esca and Marcus set out alone to go to the north coast of Scotland to find and retrieve the Eagle. "How can a piece of metal mean so much to you?" Esca asks.[35] "The Eagle is not just a piece of metal," Marcus counters. "The Eagle is Rome. It is a symbol of our honor, every victory, every achievement. Everywhere the Eagle goes we can say, 'Rome did that.'"[36] For Marcus, it is not simply a matter of restoring his family name, the Eagle is a symbol of Rome itself (and by extension, a symbol of America as well).

Esca, the voice of the conquered, however, reminds him of the other point of view. Esca's father was killed by Romans after slitting his own wife's throat (Esca's mother) so that the Roman soldiers could not rape her. "Rome did that, too," he softly states.[37] An interesting dynamic is developed by this exchange. There is mutual respect and friendship between the Celt and the Roman, but there is also a recognition of the culpability of Rome in what it does to the lives of the Celt. Rome is its victories and achievements, but it is also all the negative things it does too. America is the defeater of Saddam Hussein; yet also the perpetuators of Abu Ghraib and other atrocities against Iraqis.

The film suggests that Marcus' pride is acceptable, so long as it is kept within bounds. The film also suggests that the negative attributes of Rome will not be laid at his feet. The troops are doing what they were sent to do; if problems emerge, the soldiers are not held responsible for the negative actions.

As in the novel, they meet a hunter named Guern (Mark Strong), who is revealed to be a former soldier of the Ninth, a survivor of the slaughter by Picts and Celts two decades before. Guern describes the ambush by "rogue warriors" of the Seal People, who systematically and barbarically slaughtered the Ninth, including Marcus' father, and took the Eagle.[38] His description is accompanied by slow motion images of the slaughter. Marcus asks where the Seal People can be found. Guern tells him to ask Esca, since he is one.

Here Marcus learns his slave, his translator, his local guide, is, in fact, related to the people who killed his father. Angry though he is about this revelation, he believes they can use this to find the Eagle. Instead, the Seal People find them. Immediately, Esca tells them who he is and that Marcus is his slave. He physically abuses Marcus, as does the Seal Prince (Tahar Rahim), who invites Esca to come visit their people. Marcus is forced to walk bound behind the horses. He is abused by the Seal People and threatened multiple times with death. He sits outside in the rain while they sit inside, warm and eating. Marcus is arrogant and ethnocentric. Being Esca's slave finally teaches him humility and sympathy/empathy for the enemy whose land he has invaded.

When the Seal People reveal they have the Eagle during a celebration, Esca frees Marcus after the celebration and the two escape with the Eagle. Pursued by the Seal Prince and his men, they run for the Green Zone south of Hadrian's Wall, but Marcus is too weak to make it. He hides while Esca runs for help.

The help Esca returns with are the surviving members of the Ninth, including Guern. "When I ran from your father," he tells Marcus, "I ran from myself."[39] (Given how Guern is presented, alongside his older, fellow former soldiers who all have long hair and beards and are wearing battered, decrepit armor, it is not a stretch to see them as emblematic of the Vietnam veterans who have now come back to fight on behalf of America after all.) Guern tells Marcus his father died a hero.

The Seal People arrive at the place where the Romans have set up a defensive line and a battle follows. Forged Roman weapons and armor are employed against the obviously hand-made weapons of the Seal People. Yet in this fight they begin fairly well matched. Eventually, Marcus and the Seal Prince face off and weapons are lost. Marcus kills him by holding his head under water until he drowns and the stream washes off his makeup, revealing him as a young man, like Marcus and Esca themselves.

In the epilogue, Esca and Marcus barge into a smug meeting of senators and politicians in Southern Britain. They place the Eagle on the table in front of them. The politicians smile, ready to take credit for the recovery of the Eagle and the return of Roman honor, even though it was the soldier who actually did it against their wishes and advice. "The senate will want to reform the Ninth," they tell Marcus, who informs them he is not interested in fighting for Rome anymore.[40] When Tribune Placidus mocks Esca, Marcus tells him, "He's not a slave. And he knows more about honor and freedom than you ever will."[41] The film closes with the two friends walking out together, smiling. The narrative and the image suggesting the bonds of those who worked together in the Red Zone are stronger than national or ethnic bonds. Those who have gone to war together transcend other identities.

The Eagle does not match its literary source on many levels. As noted above, the lengthy period of disguise and subterfuge is lost. The Celts are not interested in having any foreigners in their land and they will kill or enslave anyone not Celtic. In addition, Marcus could never pass for Greek or Celtic, he is obviously a Roman soldier. He rides north of the wall as himself, there to take back what was taken.

Gone as well is the learning of their languages (as Esca provides all the translations for Marcus, similar to local Iraqis and Afghanis translating for American troops), the romance with his Roman neighbor Cattia, his training of a wolf pup named Cub, and any depiction of the Celts as a likable, respectable people. In *The Eagle*, the Celts are savage, barbarous, perverted people whose religion drives them to slaughter. While Roman politicians are craven, self-serving, hypocritical moral cowards, Roman soldiers are honorable servants of Rome and the true embodiment of the spirit of Rome. Much like *The Hurt Locker, The Eagle* has no time for generals or politicians. It is the soldiers who are the heart of Rome/America and the war effort.

All three films take the story of the Ninth Legion and use it to construct a Britain that looks and acts much like Iraq during and after the war, and posit the soldiers as honorable warriors fighting a savage, religiously-driven, inhuman enemy. If, as Joshel, Malamud and Wyke suggest, that in films about ancient Rome, "the [American] audience identifies with the colonized of the Roman Empire," that model ends with the invasions of Iraq and Afghanistan.[42] That is because America shifts from being the former colonized of Europe defending freedom against Europeans (as in the American Revolution and the two world wars) to being self-appointed world policeman spreading the Pax Americana. In doing so, we are no longer resisting the empire, we are the empire. Our soldiers are Roman soldiers, no longer persecuting Christians but fighting pagan insurgents who stand against everything America and the UK see themselves as standing for. In all three films, Roman soldiers find themselves in the Red Zone of Britain, running to get to the Green Zone in which Romans can no longer be harmed by local insurgents. These American neo-peplum films use the narrative of the Ninth Legion to reflect upon the reality of America as occupying force in the Middle East, as imperial power in the world, and as a nation meeting resistance in these efforts. Regardless of the corruption at the government levels, the moral turpitude and the contempt of the elite for the common soldiers, those common soldiers attempt to honorably protect one another, defend the local innocents and maintain some sort of order in the chaos. This is reimagining the American solider as noble warrior of the past, and identifying not with the imperial power itself, but with the brave souls who defend it and do its military work.

NOTES

1. Witney Seibold, "Ten Years Later, Zack Snyder's '300' Is Uglier Than Ever." *CraveOnline*, March 8, 2017, http://www.craveonline.com/entertainment/1227459-ten-years-later-zack-snyders-300-uglier-ever, accessed March 17, 2017.
2. The description is Seibold's. *Ibid.*
3. Sandra Joshel, Margaret Malamud and Maria Wyke, "Introduction," in *Imperial Projections: Ancient Rome in Modern Popular Culture* (Baltimore: Johns Hopkins University Press, 2006), 6.
4. Maria Wyke, *Projecting the Past: Ancient Rome, Cinema and History* (New York: Routledge, 1997), 23.
5. *Ibid.*
6. Guy de la Bédoyère, *Roman Britain: A New History* (New York: Thames and Hudson, 2006), 64.
7. *Ibid.*, 59.
8. *Ibid.*, 239.
9. Jeanne Batalova, "Immigrants in the U.S. Armed Forces," *Migration Policy Institute.com*, May 15, 2008, http://www.migrationpolicy.org/article/immigrants-us-armed-forces, accessed March 17, 2017.
10. Margaret Malamud, *Ancient Rome and Modern America* (Malden, MA: Wiley-Blackwell, 2009), 254.

11. Quoted in Richard Jackson, *Writing the War on Terrorism: Language, Politics and Counter-Terrorism* (Manchester: Manchester University Press, 2005), 8.
12. *Ibid.*, 60–80.
13. Monica Silveira Cyrino, *Big Screen Rome* (Malden: Blackwell, 2005), 3.
14. *Ibid.*
15. *The Last Legion*, directed by Doug Lefler (2007; New York: The Weinstein Company, 2008), DVD.
16. *Ibid.*
17. *Ibid.*
18. *Ibid.*
19. *Ibid.*
20. *Ibid.*
21. *Ibid.*
22. *Centurion*, directed by Neil Marshall (2010; Dallas: Magnolia Home Entertainment, 2011), DVD.
23. *Ibid.*
24. *Ibid.*
25. *Ibid.*
26. Rosemary Sutcliffe, *The Eagle of the Ninth* (Oxford: Oxford University Press, 1954), 174.
27. *The Eagle*, directed by Kevin McDonald (2011; Universal City, CA: Universal Studios Home Entertainment, 2011), DVD.
28. *Ibid.*
29. *Ibid.*
30. *Ibid.*
31. *Ibid.*
32. *Ibid.*
33. *Ibid.*
34. *Ibid.*
35. *Ibid.*
36. *Ibid.*
37. *Ibid.*
38. *Ibid.*
39. *Ibid.*
40. *Ibid.*
41. *Ibid.*
42. Joshel, Malamud, and Wyke, 8.

Bibliography

Batalova, Jeanne. "Immigrants in the U.S. Armed Forces" Migration Policy Institute.com. May 15, 2008. http://www.migrationpolicy.org/article/immigrants-us-armed-forces. Accessed March 17, 2017.
Ben-Hur. Directed by William Wyler. 1959. Burbank, CA: Warner Home Video, 2011. DVD.
Centurion. Directed by Neil Marshall. 2010. Dallas: Magnolia Home Entertainment, 2011. DVD.
Cyrino, Monica Silveira. *Big Screen Rome.* Malden, MA: Blackwell, 2005.
de la Bédoyère, Guy. *Roman Britain: A New History.* New York: Thames and Hudson, 2006.
Joshel, Sandra, Margaret Malamud, and Donald T. McGuire, eds. *Imperial Projections: Ancient Rome in Modern Popular Culture.* Baltimore: Johns Hopkins University Press, 2001.
The Eagle. Directed by Kevin Macdonald. 2011. Universal City, CA: Universal Studios Home Entertainment, 2011. DVD.
The Fall of the Roman Empire. Directed by Anthony Mann. Montreal: Alliance Home Entertainment, 1964. DVD.
Gladiator. Directed by Ridley Scott. 2000. Universal City, CA: Dreamworks, 2000. DVD.
Green Zone. Directed by Paul Greengrass. 2010. Universal City, CA: Universal Studios Home Entertainment, 2010. DVD.

Jackson, Richard. *Writing the War on Terrorism: Language, Politics and Counter-terrorism.* Manchester: Manchester University Press, 2005.
The Last Legion. Directed by Doug Lefler. 2007. New York City: The Weinstein Company, 2008. DVD.
Malamud, Margaret. *Ancient Rome and Modern America.* Malden, MA: Wiley-Blackwell, 2009.
Manfredi, Valerio Massimo. *The Last Legion.* Trans. Christine Feddersen Manfredi. New York: Washington Square Press, 2005.
Quo Vadis. Directed by Mervyn LeRoy. 1951. Burbank, CA: Warner Home Video, 2008. DVD.
Redacted. Directed by Brian De Palma. 2007. Los Angeles: Magnolia, 2008. DVD.
The Robe. Directed by Henry Koester. 1953. Los Angeles: Twentieth Century Fox Home Video, 2014. DVD.
Seibold, Witney. "Ten Years Later, Zack Snyder's '300' Is Uglier Than Ever." *CraveOnline.* March 8, 2017. http://www.craveonline.com/entertainment/1227459-ten-years-later-zack-snyders-300-uglier-ever. Accessed March 17, 2017.
Spartacus. Directed by Stanley Kubrick. 1960. Universal City, CA: Universal Home Entertainment, 2015. DVD.
Stop-Loss. Directed by Kimberly Peirce. 2008. Los Angeles: Paramount Home Video, 2008. DVD.
Sutcliffe, Rosemary. *The Eagle of the Ninth.* Oxford: Oxford University Press, 1954.
Wyke, Rosemary. *Projecting the Past: Ancient Rome, Cinema and History.* New York: Routledge, 2007.

PART FOUR: SCULPTED IN MARBLE:
GENDER AND REPRESENTATION

Laughing at the Body
The Imitation of Masculinity in Peplum Parody Films

TATIANA PROROKOVA

Comedy and/in the (Neo-)Peplum Film

The peplum movie genre flourished during the 1950s–60s. With its revival in 2000, the neo-peplum has arguably become even more popular than the peplum was. The prolonged interest of both the audience and directors in the peplum and later neo-peplum genre can be easily explained with the nature of the genre. Basing its plots on various biblical and mythological tales, the peplum film does not only always surprise its viewer with an interesting heroic story and valiant characters, but it also amazes one with a large scale of narrated events. Each peplum film includes vast masses of characters, which underlines the grandiosity of the project that is aimed at narrating a story that encompasses nations and lands rather than limited groups of people. Indeed, the use of special camera angles only reinforces this idea: the frequent inclusion of bird's-eye and panoramic views plunge the audience into the world of sublime ancient (mythic) history, revealing both the grand architecture and the bloody battles of the time. The scale of the plot is also intensified by the duration of a peplum film that is hardly similar to a regular one-and-a-half-hour film.

The seriousness and complexity of the plots hardly allows any space for comedy in the peplum and neo-peplum film. Yet a number of peplum *parodies* were indeed released, and all of them largely comment on the issue of male masculinity. Before proceeding to specific cinematic examples, it is significant to examine to what extent peplum films provide the material that can be converted into the object of mockery. In principle, there are no specific rules on what can be made fun of, as well as there are no strict limitations on creating a mockery. The mockery or parody is, however, always based on those particularities that characterize the film genre and thus are especially recognizable for the audience. For peplum and neo-peplum films, these are the characters and their actions which vary little between the films. For example, in these films the main character is a male whose particular deeds either turn him into a hero or simply reinforce his heroic nature. Significantly, portraying presumably ancient wars, these films are filled with male characters who are ready to fight and die for their families, friends, and lands. One of the most vivid attributes that construct the authenticity of the peplum and neo-peplum film is the warrior's clothing, i.e., the peplum and sandals, as well as his only weapon—the sword. This heroic manliness or masculinity that is determined by the hero's appearance and actions as well as the predominantly male environment in the film are the two chief elements that become the core components of the peplum parody. Before moving to the analysis of peplum parodies, however, it is important to examine the issue of parody in general.

Scholars provide various definitions of the term "parody"; yet this essay employs a rather neutral one given by Nil Korkut who claims that "parody is *an intentional imitation*—of a text, style, genre, or discourse—which includes an element of humor and which has an aim of interpreting its target in one way or another."[1] The pivotal aspect of this definition is that of an "intentional imitation," i.e., humor in the parody never happens to be an accident, rather, all the comedic moments are carefully thought over. Although the scholar laments that a parody is frequently "associated [only] with simple mockery or ridicule" once there is "too much emphasis on the comic in a definition of parody,"[2] in relation to the peplum parody film it is exactly the "mockery" and "ridicule" that become the central characteristics.

One can also argue that such films are not really parodies, but rather they employ the elements of pastiche. Defined as "an imitation or forgery which consists of a number of motives taken from several genuine works by any one artist recombined in such a way as to give the impression of being an independent original creation by that artist,"[3] pastiche can be called the core technique in many parody films, including the peplum and neo-peplum parodies. Here it not only facilitates the mix of various elements, but also, most importantly, helps the comedy and the peplum genres blend altogether and produce the *imitation* of the peplum film. It is crucial to understand that the peplum parody does not necessarily imitate a particular film, although as the analysis below will demonstrate, some of them do attempt to mock a specific text. For example, *Meet the Spartans* (2008, Jason Friedberg and Aaron Seltzer) focuses on imitating the genre itself, paying close attention to the details that would eventually make the parody recognizable as that related to the peplum film. As scholars have already pinpointed: "The pastiche in general does not imitate a text ... [because] *it is impossible to imitate a text ... one can imitate only a style: that is to say, a genre.*"⁴

Jonathan Gray, Jeffrey P. Jones, and Ethan Thomson argue that "parody attacks a particular text or genre, making fun of how that text or genre operates." The scholars proceed: "Pastiche merely imitates or repeats for mildly ironic amusement, whereas parody is actively critical."⁵ Linda Hutcheon considers parody "inter-art discourse" and claims that while pastiche imitates, parody employs "ironic transcontextualization"⁶ and thus, in the words of Amber Day, "provide[s] critical distance from the original."⁷ In the context of this essay, the term "parody" will be used to indicate the special sub-genre of the peplum and neo-peplum film. Yet the peplum parody film, as it will be argued further, also actively employs pastiche. Therefore, this essay suggests considering pastiche a technique that the parody peplum film uses to achieve a greater comedic effect.

The comedic elements of the peplum parody film are generally derived from the representation of male masculinity that is crucial in every peplum film. To understand how the issue of masculinity transforms, or rather, from which perspective it is tackled in the peplum parody film, it is pivotal to analyze the problem of male masculinity in ancient Greece and Rome that is a fundamental element in the peplum and neo-peplum film.

Male (Homo)Sexuality of Greek and Roman Warriors: Transitions from Historical Past to Cinematic Present

The peplum parody film bases most of its humor on the portrayal and interpretation of the male body and masculinity. To understand the reason for this particular choice, it is significant to trace the historical representation of Greek and Roman warriors that the peplum film arguably relies on.

Historical and cultural artifacts that were preserved till nowadays in the form of physical objects or literature reveal the cult of the male body in ancient Greece: "Ancient manhood was ... marked by an interest in the excellence of the male body and an indicative connection to soldierly endeavor, both literally and metaphorically."⁸ This is proved by statues and various other depictions that remained intact and allows modern audiences to learn ancient history through them. Scholars pay particular attention to ancient sports and note: "Nudity was a highly distinctive feature of ancient Greek athletics. Greek male athletes, at all ages and levels, trained and competed completely naked."⁹ The classical art historian and archeologist John Boardman comments on the issue of nudity in ancient Greece: "In Classical Greece the nude (men only) *was* acceptable in life. Athletes at exercise or competition went naked and it was possible to fight near-naked. Youths and even the more mature took no pains to conceal their private parts on any festive, and no doubt many more ordinary, public occasions.... In Greek art, therefore, the nude could carry no special 'artistic' connotation, nor could it exclusively designate a special class, such as hero or god."[10] Masculinity, therefore, was strongly body-oriented and maleness was defined by the body: "To show a male figure without clothes was certainly to invoke the beautiful body of the young athlete and to claim the athletic body as the model of all it was to be a man."[11]

It is quite apparent that such a strong focus on the body has drawn attention to the issue of male sexuality. It is clear that exposed male genitals reveal the body as a gendered, sexualized object, and arguably, provokes sexual attractiveness. To borrow from Nick Fisher: "[N]aked athletics had a powerful erotic appeal on the thousands of spectators at the games: men believed that nakedness, worn proudly as a 'costume,'[12] should reveal the perfection of the trained body and that an erotic response to muscular, bronzed bodies gleaming with olive oil, like statues was a natural part of the admiration elicited by divinely gifted beauty and skills."[13]

This is an interesting point to examine in relation to the question of the audience: whom exactly was that "erotic appeal" directed to? Knowing that only men were allowed to watch competitions, one can affirmatively state that it was an appeal from a man to another man. Although some scholars underscore the power of "the emotional desire [that can be] generated by gazing at a beautiful body ... regardless of one's sexual orientation,"[14] it seems plausible to claim that such viewings encouraged and eventually evoked homosexual desires in men. To borrow from Michel Foucault, "the Greek practiced, accepted, and valued relations between men and boys"; and even the interpretation of such sexual "freedom" by Greek philosophers reveals that "[t]hey never imagined that sexual pleasure was in itself an evil or that it could be counted among the natural stigmata of a transgression."[15]

Homosexuality, hence, was considered part of the Greek culture. Interestingly, while nakedness turned into "a defining element of Greek [sport] culture," it was "regarded with suspicion or ambivalence by foreigners, including many Romans."[16] Yet it is crucial to underline the fact that homosexuality by no means undermined male masculinity. On the contrary, the two literally existed in harmony as both athletes and warriors, who were involved in homosexual relations, were not considered outsiders or emasculated, but rather they constructed a majority and thus dictated a norm. Nonetheless, Thomas Hubbard makes a pivotal remark, claiming that male homosexuality (and specifically the relations between two males of different ages) of those times is incomparable to the modern understandings of homosexuality, and the multiple references to male homosexuality in literature and the art of that period "have more to do with discursive and artistic preoccupations with adolescent beauty and development than with any accurate demographic index of who was doing what with whom."[17]

The strong focus on the male body is inevitably noticed in the both the peplum and neo-peplum film. One can argue that most of such films present hypernormality and heterosexuality as the only option for male characters; thus they hardly ever put traditional male masculinity and sexuality into question. This tendency has generated a relatively strong response from the parody film genre, where the male body, either implicitly or explicitly, turns into the object of mockery and thus becomes the ground element in the humor.

History of the World: Part I (1981, Mel Brooks) mocked the representation of Romans, and particularly that of Caesar (Dom DeLuise), displaying him as an obese hedonist, thus questioning his masculinity and heterosexuality. His appearance contradicts that of the real Julius Caesar, who is known as an important figure in the Roman history for many achievements, including the military ones. The portrayal of Caesar in *History of the World: Part I*, however, hardly displays Caesar as anyone but a lazy man who is used to the luxurious life in his palace that guarantees him rich clothes, regular meals, and a soft place to rest. His yawning, while being greeted with a "Hail Caesar!"[18] reveals his explicit disinterest in the life of Rome. The heroic masculinity of the real Caesar is not only undermined visually through the representation of the body, but it is also put into question as Brooks' Caesar is apparently homosexual. Although he has a wife, he is absolutely indifferent to her. His attention is obviously drawn to one of his courtiers, an old man who, in quite a sleeky manner, announces Caesar's name and is eventually playfully touched with a scepter at his genitals by Caesar. The courtier is later flattered to receive a piece of jewelry that was stuck in Caesar's posterior while the governor was 'bathing' in his treasures. The old man receives the jewelry with awe and adoration rather than disgust. Caesar's later reference to the courtier as a "faggot"[19] only proves the orientation of the man to be homosexual. Inevitably, Caesar's multiple—approving—responses to the man portray him as a homosexual, too. Interestingly, the implied sexual relations between the old man and Caesar somewhat reflect the real situation during antiquity, when sex between men of different ages (specifically men and boys) was a regularity.

As Caesar walks along the chanting crowd, he sticks out his tongue and imitates kisses with his lips. His eventual question to his visitor (Marcus Vindictus [Shecky Greene], a Roman warrior who commanded the army in the fight against the Spartans)—"What's under the sheet?"[20]—obviously has a double meaning in this context and is meant to insist on Caesar's primary interest on male genitalia. Yet the question is soon clarified—although not without a hesitation—and the visitor reveals a bath (that is covered under the sheet) that he wants to present to Caesar. Caesar in *History of the World: Part I* is demasculinized. First, this is due to his appearance and behavior that is accompanied with multiple vulgar acts such as belching, farting, and genital scratching. Second, because he is a homosexual. It is interesting that Roman soldiers are also portrayed in the film as clumsy and inept, whereas their physical appearance can hardly be distinguished from that of civilian men in the Roman Empire.

Another important moment in the film takes place when Caesar orders his soldiers to kill the comedian whose performance apparently was a failure. When Caesar's visitor, screaming, "Cease him!"[21] takes out his sword, there is no blade in his scabbard, but only the handle. Considering the sword an explicit reference to the phallus, one can speculate that its absence demasculinizes the warrior, who is symbolically deprived of the male organ and thus appears castrated. The eventual fight between the comedian and Josephus (Gregory Hines)—who pretends to be a servant in the palace, and after having accidentally spilled a jar of wine on Caesar, falls into Caesar's disgrace and is sentenced to fight till death—serves to mock the gladiator fight, as the audience observes the two clumsily trying to hurt each other. The fight finishes quite soon, when one of the "warriors" slips on a banana peel that was discarded by Caesar. The "gladiators" are not only morally weak as they cannot wound each other, but they are also physically impotent. Thus, the unlimited strength of real gladiators that the peplum film always explicitly displays is mocked in *History of the World: Part I* to underscore a somewhat feminized nature of the warriors. The male body turns into the object through which masculinity can be put into question. A somewhat oxymoronic effect is achieved: the Roman warrior, when viewed from a current perspective, does not personify male masculinity but instead, becomes the object of mockery, whereas his heroic potency is clearly undermined.

A somewhat similar depiction of the Roman warrior can be found in *Hail, Caesar!* (2016, Joel and Ethan Coen). First, the mockery in this film is achieved in an early scene through the appearances of two actors who eventually contribute to the kidnapping of the main character—another actor, Baird Whitlock (George Clooney). The men caricature the ancient Romans as one of them is short and fat whereas the other one is high and slim. Their physical disproportions clearly accentuate the body parameters that are far from those of ideal Roman soldiers. Although the two men portray courtiers instead of soldiers, their appearance arguably draws attention to the general depiction of the Roman man, indicating the possibility of imperfection. Second, the character played by Whitlock in the film within the film (a historic epic called *Hail, Caesar! A Tale of the Christ*), is portrayed as a "real" man; however, when the actor is not playing this part, he is proving quite the opposite. It is interesting that Whitlock remains in his Roman uniform through the course of the film, including scenes when he is not performing as his character. In so doing, he conveys the image of a Roman into the real life in the U.S. in the middle of the twentieth century. While Whitlock's masculinity is not questioned visually, his actions, specifically his clumsiness and overt silliness, undermine his appearance as a masculine soldier, ridiculing the image of the Roman warrior.

Thus, whereas historically the naked and perfectly shaped male body was considered an aesthetic object and unveiled how masculine the man could be, the peplum parody film reverses this perception and demonstrates that the exaggerated focus on the appearance of the male body can reveal male homosexuality or/and ineptness. However, while *History of the World: Part I* and *Hail, Caesar!* only scratch the surface of this poignant issue, *Meet the Spartans* overtly suggests that the lack of clothes and tight relations between male warriors are not just aesthetics and historic cultural norms respectively but rather are the manifestations of homosexuality.

Artificial Body and Demasculinization in Meet the Spartans

The mockery of male masculinity in these rare peplum parody films is apparent; yet in *Meet the Spartans*, it is brought to the limit. Questioning masculinity of the main characters, the film overtly portrays the warriors as homosexuals not only through their behavior, but also most problematically, through the depiction of their bodies. The body becomes a vulnerable object that reveals the result of demasculinization of the men through various means: the male body is deprived of genitals and waxed, it is obese, or simply made out of plastic (i.e., artificially created). The acts of fighting are compared to dancing, (both are body movements), which represents queerness of the warriors as well. This imitation of masculinity mocks peplum film warriors, whose minimal clothing along with the demonstration of muscular bodies raise the issue of homosexuality. Such an aesthetic approach aims to ridicule the male body, presenting it as a physical object that can be artificially created either by developing muscles, like in case of the characters of (neo-)peplum films, or by mutilating and feminizing it, as it is illustrated in peplum (and even more vividly in neo-peplum) parody films.

Meet the Spartans overtly displays the male body as the object of mockery, shame, and artificiality, thus only proving the following contention of the gender studies scholars: "The body itself, once natural, had now come to be seen as a kind of cultural plastic. It is no longer imagined as merely an object requiring fixing, but has become a commodity like others—a car, appliances, a house, a personal computer—which needs to be updated and upgraded to reflect changing fashions and personal desires."[22]

The idea of the perfect body entwines the film. It is unsurprising then that as the film introduces the world of Sparta to its audience, the voiceover informs about the strict selection process when choosing infants into their ranks: "If any imperfections were found, the baby was rejected."[23] "[T]he perfect Spartan"[24] was eventually the (male) baby, who was physically strong from the infancy. Such is the main character Leonidas (Sean Maguire) who, despite being a baby, already possesses the features of a grown-up man, namely perfectly shaped abdominal muscles and a beard, both of which exhibit his maleness. As a grown man, he has a huge penis, which reinforces his male potency. Yet this nicely-shaped body also needs to be improved, and the audience can observe Leonidas wearing braces to make his teeth perfect.

The homosexuality of the Spartans is reinforced in a later scene, when Leonidas, meeting with a messenger, kisses him on his mouth. The newcomer is clearly disgusted with such behavior, yet Leonidas does not see anything perverted in the act and explains: "This is how men of Sparta greet one another. High fives for the women and open-mouth tongue kisses for the men."[25] The camera immediately focuses on random couples of men around Leonidas and his guest: the males are depicted stroking each other while their bodies are practically fully exposed. The messenger "get[s]" the idea, saying that there is "a free society"[26] in Sparta, which is virtually his euphemism for homosexuality. Leonidas and the messenger then discuss the important business concerning a coming war by holding hands with each other and swinging them in the air. It is important to note that the military stratagem is being discussed by two warriors who have been depicted in a homosexual fashion. This has the undertone that the ability to protect the land is compromised because of this depiction.

Sometime later in the film, Leonidas is referred to as a "douche bag" and "chest waxer,"[27] which clearly undermines his traditional male potency. More than that, in the scene that follows, a naked Leonidas is laughed at by a group of women, who discuss the size of his penis. Leonidas looks down, and the camera reveals the absence of any male genitals on his body. He embarrassingly covers himself with his hands, explaining his lack of genitalia with the fact that "it's cold."[28] The scene finishes with Leonidas lifting his wife as if she was a barbell. This sport activity substitutes actual sex with a woman, thus once again underlining that he is not sexually involved with females. It also arguably illustrates that Leonidas is more interested in making his body perfect, i.e., in exercising, than in spending time with his wife or making love to her. Aptly, the scene that follows starts with Leonidas kissing one of his warriors on the mouth.

Homosexuality of Leonidas and his Spartans is further reinforced and their masculinity is questioned in subsequent scenes that supposedly depict the actual battles that these men participated in. To specify, the combat is substituted with dancing. Once the 'fighting' is over, the men are shown having a drink. When what is supposed to be a commercial interludes, the viewing audience along with the Spartans hear two male voices singing/narrating:

> Real men of genius! Real men of genius! Today we salute you. Mr. Warmongering Latent Homosexual! Mr. Warmongering Latent Homosexual! Wearing nothing but leather underwear and a cape, you charge your enemy like an oiled-up hairless wonder. Spray-on tan! Sure, there's danger—charging rhinos, stampeding elephants and that cute toga-wearing guy named Chad. Uh! You only went out on one date but you'll remember it forever. Take your daily Valtrex! Your keen instincts tell you to cut, slice, and chop every man you see. But enough about your career as a hair stylist, let's talk war. Ow! That curling iron is hot! So this Butt's for you, King Leonidas because when the going gets tough, the tough go antiquing. Mr. Warmongering Latent Homosexual. Yeah.[29]

This commercial and the background song does not only explicitly articulate the homosexuality of the Spartans, but it stresses the desire of these men to have perfect bodies, accentuating the color of their skin that needs to be tanned and their hair that remains nicely styled. Discussing the desire of the Spartans to "cut, slice, and chop" the men around them, the commercial accentuates that this is not the warrior's "instincts" but rather the "instincts" of "real homosexuals," since the acts of "cut[ting], slic[ing], and chop[ping]" are referred to hairstyling. More than that, the mentioning of the antiviral drug Valtrex, which is used to treat herpes, might stand for the men's promiscuity. Finally, as the Spartans eventually start the real fight, they do so with their comrades sitting on their backs, which is arguably a metaphor for a sexual act between two males.

An important character who serves to underscore both the gay nature of the Spartans and the objectification of the body that the film literally builds its humor on is Dilio (Jareb Dauplaise), the only obese warrior in the unit. Unlike all the other warriors who are presumably the best and carefully chosen warriors of Sparta, Dilio is the only one who is not obsessed with the shape of his body. For example, in a scene where the exhausted Spartans drink beverages, Dilio instead greedily consumes donuts. It is important to note that historically, "[t]he young Spartans were bound to appear every tenth day naked before the ephors, who, when they perceived any inclinable to fatness, ordered them a scantier diet."[30] In *Meet the Spartans*, however, Dilio does not go on a diet. So that he could visually fit in with his comrades, his muscles are painted on his stomach, yet this obviously does not make him any stronger. When he runs, the camera intentionally lingers on his obese stomach that quivers like jelly. Dilio is the only man who is beaten up by a girl—one of the so-called warriors whom the Spartans encounter on their way. His body, therefore, becomes the main signifier of his absent warrior masculinity since physically he is not strong. On the other hand, it is the physical unattractiveness of his body that makes Dilio 'less' homosexual of all the Spartans. The absence of muscles and a nicely tanned, oiled skin makes him the black sheep when compared to the perfectly created, practically manufactured bodies of the other Spartans that are as similar to each other as clones.

Towards the end of the film, the body is celebrated as an absolutely artificial, plastic object. Whereas at first, one can observe multiple manipulations one can perform in order to harm the body (such as squeezing their nipples or hurting one with their own stretched underwear), the body of a Spartan eventually turns into a mannequin. Thus, when one of the Spartans is killed with a strong punch by the boxer Rocky (Dean Cochran), the audience witnesses the head of the warrior being separated from his neck without any traces of blood. Interestingly, Rocky is eventually killed with an injection of Botox that makes his already stiff body even stiffer. As a result, just like a plastic dummy, he falls down dead. Rocky's murderer is immediately killed with a spear that penetrates his body, breaking the skin and tissues as if he is a stuffed dummy rather than a living human being. The Spartan is ultimately reprimanded by Leonidas for not dying "attractive[ly]."[31] Indeed, his saliva oozes from his mouth, thus spoiling his appearance. Outraged, Leonidas runs to avenge the death of his comrade. This scene is filmed as if it were a *Grand Theft Auto*-esque video game, as one witnesses Leonidas running in an unnatural way with a faux gaming HUD on the screen. When he gets into a car, he dances to Aqua's "Barbie girl," of which the lyrics of the song which say that living a plastic life is fantastic. The reference here is explicitly to the bodies of the warriors that, being constantly worked on and literally abused, have lost their vitality and turned into artificially created objects without hair, wrinkles, or any other natural 'drawbacks.' This contention is partially illustrated in a later scene, when Leonidas, still in a video game, hits his enemy with a crowbar numerous times—the action is accompanied with a dull metallic sound—yet the body of the enemy remains intact. Finally, during a mid-credits sequence, the Spartans clean the post-fight mess up, putting trash into various containers. Significantly, the dead bodies go into a special blue container, the inscription on which reads "recycle bodies only,"[32] which once again underlines the artificiality of the bodies that from living organisms turn into self- or medically-created objects.

Through the multiple elements of pastiche, *Meet the Spartans* overtly proposes to consider the body the object that is being abused—cut, reshaped, tanned, waxed, castrated—in order to fit in particular standards. While this idea can be further developed in relation to beauty and fashion studies (especially due to the presence of several obese and disfigured characters, such as the aforementioned Dilio and the hunchback Paris Hilton [Nicole Parker]), this essay analyzes it in the frames of gender studies, particularly in the formation of male masculinity. *Meet the Spartans* makes it apparent that an artificially created male body hints at the owner's femininity and homosexuality, depriving him of the status of a potent male, especially in the context of the peplum and neo-peplum film genre, where the only masculinity of a man that is celebrated is a heroic one. *Meet the Spartans* rethinks the idea of male hyperheroism in these films, obviously considering it as unnatural as its complete lack presented in the parody itself.

Conclusion

With its predominantly male characters and multiple scenes of war and heroism, the peplum is arguably one of the most vivid examples of a cinematic genre that explicitly deals with the issue of masculinity. Strong male heroes who risk their lives for their beloved ones and the well-being of the people, skillfully fighting with swords, being able to endure any pain and overcome all the obstacles, vividly create an image of the absolute conventional male masculinity. The hard, muscular body in such films becomes the physical object that determines masculinity of the warrior.

Although not replete with examples, the peplum parody film overtly mocks this heroic masculinity—also through the portrayal of the body. While in peplum films the muscular body is the core element, in the peplum parody the body is frequently depicted as being physically untrained, as in *History of the World: Part I* and *Hail, Caesar!*. When the body is portrayed as muscular, which is obviously the case of most of the characters in *Meet the Spartans*, its exaggerated strength and almost unbelievable invulnerability are mocked and presented as unnatural. Thus, the body becomes an artificial object that, despite its visual potency, demasculinizes its owner. The comic effect that the peplum parody film achieves is, therefore, largely based on the portrayal of the male body that is either so weak or unnaturally strong that it can only *imitate* traditional masculinity.

NOTES

1. Nil Korkut, *Kinds of Parody from the Medieval to the Postmodern* (Frankfurt am Main: Peter Lang, 2009), 21, my emphasis.
2. *Ibid.*
3. Peter and Linda Murray qtd. in Margaret A. Rose, *Parody: Ancient, Modern, and Post-modern* (Cambridge: Cambridge University Press, 1993), 72.
4. Genette qtd. in Korkut, *Kinds of Parody*, 17, emphasis in original.
5. Jonathan Gray, Jeffrey P. Jones, and Ethan Thompson, "The State of Satire, the Satire of State," in *Satire TV: Politics and Comedy in the Post-Network Era*, ed. Jonathan Gray, Jeffrey

P. Jones, and Ethan Thompson (New York: New York University Press, 2009), 17.

6. Hutcheon qtd in Amber Day, "And Now. .. the News? Mimesis and the Real in *The Daily Show*," in *Satire TV: Politics and Comedy in the Post-Network Era*, ed. Jonathan Gray, Jeffrey P. Jones, and Ethan Thompson (New York: New York University Press, 2009), 94.

7. Amber Day, "And Now. .. the News? Mimesis and the Real in *The Daily Show*," in *Satire TV: Politics and Comedy in the Post-Network Era*, ed. Jonathan Gray, Jeffrey P. Jones, and Ethan Thompson (New York: New York University Press, 2009), 94.

8. Mark Masterson, "Studies of Ancient Masculinity," in *A Companion to Greek and Roman Sexualities*, ed. Thomas K. Hubbard (Malden, MA: Blackwell, 2014), 28.

9. Nick Fisher, "Athletics and Sexuality," in *A Companion to Greek and Roman Sexualities*, ed. Thomas K. Hubbard (Malden, MA: Blackwell, 2014), 244.

10. Boardman qtd. in Robin Osborne, "Men Without Clothes: Heroic Nakedness and Greek Art," in *Gender and the Body in the Ancient Mediterranean*, ed. Maria Wyke (Oxford: Blackwell, 1998), 81.

11. Robin Osborne, "Men Without Clothes: Heroic Nakedness and Greek Art," in *Gender and the Body in the Ancient Mediterranean*, ed. Maria Wyke (Oxford: Blackwell, 1998), 100.

12. Bonfante, qtd. in Fisher, "Athletics and Sexuality," 246.

13. Fisher, "Athletics and Sexuality," 246.

14. Mark Stansbury-O'Donnell, "Desirability and the Body," in *A Companion to Greek and Roman Sexualities*, ed. Thomas K. Hubbard (Malden, MA: Blackwell, 2014), 41.

15. Foucault qtd in Joseph Bristow, *Sexuality* (London: Routledge, 1997), 184–185.

16. Fisher, "Athletics and Sexuality," 244.

17. Thomas K. Hubbard, "Peer Homosexuality," in *A Companion to Greek and Roman Sexualities*, ed. Thomas K. Hubbard (Malden, MA: Blackwell, 2014), 128.

18. *History of the World, Part I*, directed by Mel Brooks (1981; Century City, CA: 20th Century Fox, 2006), DVD.

19. *Ibid.*

20. *Ibid.*

21. *Ibid.*

22. Anne Cranny-Francis, Wendy Waring, Pam Stavropoulos, and Joan Kirkby, *Gender Studies: Terms and Debates* (Basingstoke: Palgrave Macmillan, 2003), 202.

23. *Meet the Spartans*, directed by Jason Friedberg and Aaron Seltzer (2008; Century City, CA: 20th Century Fox, 2008), DVD.

24. *Ibid.*

25. *Ibid.*

26. *Ibid.*

27. *Ibid.*

28. *Ibid.*

29. *Ibid.*

30. Osborne, "Men Without Clothes," 81.

31. *Meet the Spartans*, directed by Friedberg and Seltzer.

32. *Ibid.*

Bibliography

Bristow, Joseph. *Sexuality*. London: Routledge, 1997.

Cranny-Francis, Anne, Wendy Waring, Pam Stavropoulos, and Joan Kirkby. *Gender Studies: Terms and Debates*. Basingstoke: Palgrave Macmillan, 2003.

Day, Amber. "And Now ... the News? Mimesis and the Real in *The Daily Show*." In *Satire TV: Politics and Comedy in the Post-Network Era*, edited by Jonathan Gray, Jeffrey P. Jones, and Ethan Thompson, 85–103. New York: New York University Press, 2009.

Fisher, Nick. "Athletics and Sexuality." In *A Companion to Greek and Roman Sexualities*, edited by Thomas K. Hubbard, 244–264. Malden, MA: Blackwell, 2014.

Gray, Jonathan, Jeffrey P. Jones, and Ethan Thompson. "The State of Satire, the Satire of State." In *Satire TV: Politics and Comedy in the Post-Network Era*, edited by Jonathan

Gray, Jeffrey P. Jones, and Ethan Thompson, 3–36. New York: New York University Press, 2009.
Hail, Caesar! Directed by Joel and Ethan Coen. 2016. Universal City, CA: Universal Pictures. 2016. DVD.
History of the World, Part I. Directed by Mel Brooks. 1981. Century City, CA: 20th Century Fox. 2006. DVD.
Hubbard, Thomas K. "Peer Homosexuality." In *A Companion to Greek and Roman Sexualities*, edited by Thomas K. Hubbard, 128–149. Malden, MA: Blackwell, 2014.
Korkut, Nil. *Kinds of Parody from the Medieval to the Postmodern*. Frankfurt am Main: Peter Lang, 2009.
Masterson, Mark. "Studies of Ancient Masculinity." In *A Companion to Greek and Roman Sexualities*, edited by Thomas K. Hubbard, 17–30. Malden, MA: Blackwell, 2014.
Meet the Spartans. Directed by Jason Friedberg and Aaron Seltzer. 2008. Century City, CA: 20th Century Fox. 2008. DVD.
Osborne, Robin. "Men Without Clothes: Heroic Nakedness and Greek Art." In *Gender and the Body in the Ancient Mediterranean*, edited by Maria Wyke, 80–104. Oxford: Blackwell, 1998.
Rose, Margaret A. *Parody: Ancient, Modern, and Post-modern*. Cambridge: Cambridge University Press, 1993.
Stansbury-O'Donnell, Mark. "Desirability and the Body." In *A Companion to Greek and Roman Sexualities*, edited by Thomas K. Hubbard, 31–53. Malden, MA: Blackwell, 2014.

Queering the Quest
Neo-Peplum and the Neo-Femme in Xena: Warrior Princess

HAYDEE SMITH

"In a time of ancient gods, warlords, and kings. A land in turmoil cried out for a hero. *She* was Xena, a mighty princess forged in the heat of battle. The power. The passion. The danger. *Her* courage will change the world."[1] These opening credits to the phenomenally rated television series *Xena: Warrior Princess* (1995–2001) starkly point to the inherent masculinity of the (hero's) quest and centrally place the eponymous heroine, Xena (Lucy Lawless), as the harbinger of world change. From the moment that Xena is introduced on-screen, her character development indelibly reconstructs traditional western tropes of femininity, female empowerment, and feminist media.

This series aired during a cultural moment of the 1990s that marked a revival of queerly gendered icons, such as the femme lesbian, in the fields of gender and sexuality studies and feminist media studies. By blending the classical genre of the hero's journey with feminist ideology, *Xena: Warrior Princess* exemplifies how the neo-peplum genre subverts restrictive gendered ideologies through imaginative re-tellings of mythologized gender roles. The most apparent change to the classical hero's quest is the series' emphasis on the individual and collective journeys of two closely-bonded women—Xena and Gabrielle (Renee O'Connor). By tracing the intricate and intimate relationship between two women, *Xena* queers the standard format of the male-dominated heroic epic. Further, an analysis of the show's allusive narrative structure and elusive lesbian subtexts reveal how *Xena* critiques the constructed nature of romantic relationships, expected gender roles, and the aesthetics of culturally coded gender presentations.

Autolycus (Bruce Campbell), the king of thieves and a recurring character in the series, describes Xena in a tongue-in-cheek manner typical of the show's campy tone: "Xena is this warrior. She goes around saving people and righting wrongs. It's all pretty sappy, but she seems to get her kicks out of it."[2] The typical quest involves an unquestionably "good," usually male, lone hero. Elyce Rae Helford, acclaimed media scholar, argues that *Xena* "offers an antidote for fans of the traditionally male-supremacist superhero genre. Heroes tend to be men in historical accounts and popular texts, yet Xena demonstrates the traditional traits of a hero, from courage and selflessness to intelligence and displays of physical strength"[3] Xena's embodiment of these "traditional traits" unsettles the patriarchal notion that males are strong saviors and females are damsels in distress. The popularity of the series in the mid-1990s portrayed a shift in mainstream ideas of gender roles: "by the end of its second season, *Xena: Warrior Princess* had become the highest rated of all syndicated action series."[4] The quest was no longer a predominantly male sphere. The placement of a heroine in a usually male role is the first indicator of the show's queer nature; the format and content of the series provide more examples of how *Xena* has queered the quest.

The character of Xena is first introduced as a villain in the first season of *Hercules: The Legendary Journeys* (1995–1999). In the episode "The Warrior Princess," Xena fulfills the traditional role of the femme fatale—an alluring figure whose intelligence, skill, and sensuality are employed in order to destroy the hero.[5] In this episode, Xena is cast as a blood-thirsty warlord whose sole passion is to murder Hercules (Kevin Sorbo) and take on the mantle of the greatest warrior alive. In order to achieve this nefarious goal, Xena seduces Hercules' companion, Iolaus (Michael Hurst). She manipulates the besotted Iolaus into believing that Hercules deserves death, but by the end of the episode, Hercules convinces Xena to use her powers for the greater good. This containment of Xena's dangerous nature panders to patriarchal ideals of male-centric narratives. Xena is allowed to live at the end of the series because Hercules has deemed her a subject worth saving.

The popularity of this villain turned gold-hearted vixen launched *Xena: Warrior Princess* as a spin-off and saved Xena from her initially planned death in *Hercules: The Legendary Journeys*. As creator Robert Tapert explains: "we were going to have Xena killed. We kept her alive so she could go on."[6] This decision to create a spin-off series, instead of simply killing off Xena, refused the gendered limit set by other producers in 1995 who claimed: "You just can't do a female superhero show. It's not gonna work!"[7] By situating Xena's redemption narrative as part of "the legendary journeys" of Hercules, the creators of both series contained Xena's dangerous feminine power, yet enabled *Xena: Warrior Princess* to infiltrate mainstream network television with its subversive programming.

By taking up shelter in the shadow of patriarchal ideals, *Xena* functions similarly to the productive instability of what this paper establishes as the neo-femme icon—a veritable queer wolf in seemingly straight sheep's clothing. In a May 1997 interview with *TV Guide* magazine, Lucy Lawless, the actress who brings Xena to life, states: "my personal goal is to totally infiltrate popular culture."[8] The reporter quips back: "In other words, world domination."[9] This lighthearted exchange between two influential participants of mass culture—a reporter for *TV Guide* magazine, arguably one of the foremost curators of popular televisual tastes since its official debut in 1953,[10] and Lawless, a popular television actress of a hit syndicated show—marks the extreme importance of the success of *Xena* on mainstream television. By gaining access to a large and devoted audience, the producers of *Xena* were able to "totally infiltrate popular culture" and disseminate progressive social messages through the use of camp, subtext, and the historical distance and appeal of classical mythology. This triad of camp performances, covert sexuality, and classical antiquity mirrors the triumvirate of strategies employed by the neo-femme—performing feminine mimicry, disguising oneself with passing privilege, and queerly retelling social stories about hegemonic feminine gender roles.

The femme aesthetic relies on inference, coded signifiers, and queer subtext—all narrative strategies that saturate *Xena*. While the characters Xena and Gabrielle have been productively theorized as a butch/femme pairing,[11] this essay argues that they function as a neo-femme dyad. By intentionally deploying an excessive performance of the feminine: appearing vulnerable, emphasizing stylized beauty, and facilely engaging emotion, Gabrielle offers a pacifist femme aesthetic that contrasts against the aggressive femme sensuality of Xena. Whereas Helford provides an excellent discussion of the polysemic nature of *Xena: Warrior Princess* and the violent dynamic at play in the arguable butch/femme relationship between Xena and Gabrielle,[12] this essay posits *Xena* as the harbinger of the neo-femme. The 1940s and 50s crystallized butch/femme as mutual constructions in American culture,[13] but the revival of butch and femme lesbian identities in the 1990s began to unravel this classic dyad into more nuanced participants—instead of mutually (co)dependent identities.[14] While butch and femme folks often appear represented together, *Xena* offers the initial space in mainstream television for femme/femme relationships to be showcased and explored. Whereas sex/gender can be divided, so too can aesthetic/behavior.

The neo-femme is primarily defined by her aesthetic choices and her self-identification as a femme, regardless of her behavior. The femme lesbian has been theorized: in terms of her relationship with the butch lesbian,[15] as embodying the passing threat undergirding Cold War anxieties,[16] and "as bent, unfixed, unhinged, and finally unhyphenated."[17] In the essay "A Fem(me)inist Manifesto," Lisa Duggan and Kathleen McHugh provide a complicated commentary on the contradictory theoretical and historical formations of femmes. They argue that "[i]n her inscription—fem(me)—we find the enclosure of an ego ('me'), a fundamental challenge to the category, the slot, the ideal of the feminine. Historically, the feminine arises apparently ego-less, bereft of active drives, agency, mobility, thought."[18] Here, "ego" becomes the fundamental tool for individual identity claims, and self-aggrandizement becomes a necessary tactic for survival. Xena's physicality—her power and sensuality—becomes a touchstone through which to understand the political implications of Duggan and McHugh's formulation, where femme is "an anti(identity)body, a queer body in fem(me)inine drag" and "not an identity, not a history, not a location on the map of desire."[19] The attention to performance and contradiction in Duggan and McHugh's definition of femmes relies upon a political deployment of gendered mimicry. The same kind of mimicry that enables Xena to be labeled both a warrior and a princess.

In *The Sex Which Is Not One*, Luce Irigaray claims that "mimicry" allows for the "conver[sion of] a form of subordination into an affirmation, and thus to begin to thwart it."[20] This invocation to "play with mimesis"[21] directly follows the call for "an examination of the *operation of the 'grammar'* of each figure of discourse, its syntactic laws or requirements, its imaginary configurations, its metaphoric networks, and also, of course, what it does not articulate at the level of utterance: *its silences.*"[22] Mimicry allows the femme to assume the problematic mantles of feminine trappings, without actually becoming ensnared in the service of the patriarchy: "to play with mimesis is thus, for a woman, to try to recover the place of her exploitation by discourse, without allowing herself to be simply reduced to it."[23] Xena weaponizes femininity through a conscious deployment of sensuality.

Sensuality is another form of power. As Jeffrey A. Brown argues: "Perhaps the real liberating and stereotype-breaking potential of female characters in action roles is that they can assume positions of power while also being sex symbols."[24] By exploiting her aesthetic appeal, Xena commands attention wherever she travels, and the series' captivated audience is increasingly open to internalizing the more subtle messages of the show. Brown further argues that "this has subversive potential because it mocks masculine presumptions and undeniably illustrates that even the most cartoonishly feminine of heroines can also be tough, self-reliant, and powerful."[25] The intent of *Xena* was the same as all syndicated shows: to earn ratings and profit; the impact of the series is far greater than could be measured by a Nielson box. The depiction of a ferocious feminine figure on primetime television imparts the lesson that strength and heroism is no longer monopolized by masculinity.

Xena's strength and sexuality are not the only queer aspects of the show; her feminized appearance juxtaposed against her masculinized manner revises binary gender roles and regulations. Common critiques of sex/gender/sexuality alignments (such as femme-presenting, cisgendered women) often include accusations of passing privilege and complicity with heterosexually oriented patriarchal ideals of womanhood. Stereotypically, feminized characteristics include: a focus on physical beauty, sensitive emotions, a predisposition to caregiving, and the manipulation of sexuality in the service of social status achievements. Whereas the aesthetic and identitarian choices of the femme lesbian has been criticized by some feminist scholars,[26] a queer reading of *Xena: Warrior Princess* reveals the subversive and potentially politically productive stakes of purposefully assuming and enacting a femme identity.

Within the worlds and world-making of television and celebrity, femininity and feminized gendered performance are the axis on which power and desire pivot. Femme icons within mass media narratives reveal the precarity and suffering inherent to the purposeful taking up of a feminized desirability within patriarchal economies of capital—material, cultural, social, and erotic. Femininity here may signify variable projects, but it is always highly visible and *must* be seen. Chris Holmlund argues that "for most observers, the assumption of heterosexuality is so strong that the femme is easily seen as just another woman's friend. But for those who know where, when, and how to look, the femme's sexual preference is as unmistakable as her gender. With the femme, far more than with the butch, then, it is obvious that images can be misleading, and clear that reception and context are key."[27] Moreover, Holmlund theorizes that in "femme films, three specific strategies are used to foster a diversity of audience responses: (1) making the female lead a femme, which allows both heterosexual and lesbian responses/identifications; (2) focusing on the exchange of female looks that can be variously read as erotic (especially when the looking turns into a love scene) or 'just friendly'; and (3) referring ambiguously and allusively to what may or may not be lesbianism and/or lesbian lifestyles."[28] By "focusing on the exchange of female looks," the relationship between Xena and Gabrielle becomes indicative of same-sex desire.

The relationship between Xena and Gabrielle resists easy classifications and an examination of the series' lesbian content reveals that before lesbian identities and actions can be understood as simply standard deviations, they must no longer be recognized as strikingly deviant. In an episode where Xena willingly descends into Hell to save a kidnapped Gabrielle, she articulates her feelings towards her damned damsel: "Gabrielle, the love that we have, it's stronger than Heaven or Hell. It transcends Good or Evil. It's an end in itself. Our souls are destined to be together."[29] This intense proclamation of devotion exemplifies what Adrienne Rich calls "an electric and empowering charge between women."[30] The "soul mate" status of Xena's and Gabrielle's love typifies how "lesbian existence comprises both the breaking of a taboo and the rejection of a compulsory way of life. It is also a direct or indirect attack on male right of access to women."[31] The bond between Xena and Gabrielle is under incessant attack from Ares (Kevin Smith), God of War and former paramour of Xena. The battle between Gabrielle and Ares is analogous to the internal struggle between Xena's dark past and her reformed life. A queer reading of the situation, however, places Gabrielle as the icon of lesbian existence, and Ares as the dispossessed patriarchy which is vainly trying to suppress the transcendent love between two women back into an ill-fitting heterosexual model. In addition, Rich posits that the "erasure of lesbian existence (except as exotic or perverse) in art, literature, [and] film" is a "fairly obvious form of compulsion," which is part of an "idealization of heterosexual romance and marriage."[32] Rich's argument is demonstrated by the episode "Seeds of Faith" where Xena's mother attempts to find a husband for the pregnant warrior princess:

> ARES: I wish I had known you were looking for a father.
> XENA: I'm not.
> ARES: Oh? Well, somebody clearly got the job.
> XENA: Yeah—Gabrielle.
> ARES: I would have *paid* to see that.[33]

Ares' reaction to the allusion of amorous activity between Xena and Gabrielle represents the typical objectifying response to lesbianism. Xena's mother's efforts to find her a husband and Ares' prurient interest in the lesbian relationship reflect the perceived lack of legitimacy that relationships outside of the heterosexual, monogamous norm face. Despite the light-hearted nature of this fantasy-epic, the themes portrayed in *Xena* skillfully address problems facing lesbian relationships without alienating a mainstream audience. It is precisely the series' ability to subtly naturalize a same-sex relationship that rectifies Rich's point of lesbian invisibility in historical and mainstream narratives. The show not only empowers a lesbian audience, it also deconstructs the patriarchal binary of men as active saviors and women as passive victims.

Xena and Gabrielle's resistance against the linkage of reproductive heterosexuality to a gendered power disparity conveys how these characters have both queered the fundamental elements of the masculine quest and appropriated optics of the male gaze. As queer theorist and artist Nayland Blake notes: "from the margins, queers have picked those things that could work for them and recoded them, rewritten their meanings, opening up the possibility of viral reinsertion into the body of general discourse."[34] In the pilot episode, "Sins of the Past," Gabrielle desperately tries to escape her mundane village life: "I won't stay home. I don't belong there, Xena. I'm not the little girl that my parents wanted me to be."[35] Gabrielle's plea to join Xena on her quest marked the beginning of their relationship; their relationship marked the beginning of the end of unyielding heterosexuality and gender roles on mainstream television. "The very visibility of lesbianism on the screen seems to unsettle the rigidity of sexual categorizations and the maintenance of patriarchal, heterosexist hegemony."[36] Television representations have the intent of entertainment, but often have the impact of providing role models. The message conveyed by *Xena: Warrior Princess* is one of self-reliance, self-definition, and a resistance to normative values. The effect of Xena's strength in inspiring Gabrielle to leave the doldrums of domesticity mirrors the efficacy of the show in relating self-sufficiency and reclaiming agency. In the same episode, after Xena rescues Gabrielle's village from slave traders, Gabrielle displays a remarkable sense of independence (given her social position as a rural woman in ancient Greece):

> PERDICAS: Let's go, Gabrielle.
> GABRIELLE: Hey. Just because we're betrothed, doesn't mean you can boss me around. I want to stay and talk to Xena. (turns to Xena)
> GABRIELLE: You've got to take me with you and teach me everything you know. You can't leave me here.
> XENA: Why?
> GABRIELLE: Did you see the guy they want me to marry?
> XENA: He looks like a gentle soul. That's rare in a man.
> GABRIELLE: It's not the gentle part I have a problem with; it's the dull, stupid, part.[37]

Later in the episode, Gabrielle confesses her plan to join Xena to her sister:

> GABRIELLE: Lila, you know I'm different from everybody else in this town.
> LILA: I know you're crazy.
> GABRIELLE: Well, call it whatever you like. The point is I don't fit in here. And the idea of marrying Perdicas...[38]

Gabrielle's fiery spirit and determination to follow Xena marks an important split in the usual lessons taught by fairy tales and epics; the image of Gabrielle riding off into the sunset with Xena queers the stereotype of the adventure ending in heterosexual marital bliss. Gabrielle's defiant remark to her betrothed defies the patriarchal tradition of the husband as the omnipotent head of household, and the word choice of "dull" and "stupid" reflects on the way that heterosexual institutions have escaped critique and scrutiny. Gabrielle's restlessness, belief that she doesn't "fit in" and revelation that she is "not the little girl that [her] parents wanted her to be" subverts the standard expectation that a female's future contains marriage to a male.

Whether or not the relationship between Xena and Gabrielle is lesbian, it is undeniably queer; the queer nature of such a bond offers almost limitless possibilities once the heterosexual marital track has been derailed. Xena's and Gabrielle's affiliation is not the only empowering aspect of the show;

Xena herself defies conventional Western notions of femininity and her character offers an authoritative androgynous alternative to other popular representations of women.

Xena: Warrior Princess is a revolutionary illustration of the power in polysemy. For example, in the episode "You Are There" Xena and Grabrielle refuse to answer the prurient questions of the invasive, investigative reporter, Nigel (Michael Hurst):

> NIGEL: Wait! Hold it! ... [to camera] ... And now, ladies and gentlemen, a world exclusive—for the first time anywhere, Xena and Gabrielle reveal the true nature of their relationship.... Gabrielle, Xena, are you two lovers?
> XENA: You want the truth?
> NIGEL: That's right, Xena, we want the truth. The whole world wants the truth.
> XENA: It's like this, technically ... [the camera begins to fade in and out].³⁹

Nigel's insistence on the "truth" reveals the tendency of the modern world to classify bodies and behaviors into categories. As a reporter with modern day clothing and technology—such as video cameras and microphone equipment—Nigel stands in for the contemporary audiences of the 1990s. Xena's use of "technically" denotes that her relationship with Gabrielle remains productively ambiguous. This elusive answer portrays the progressive potential of queer readings. Annamarie Jagose posits: "by refusing to crystallize in any specific form, queer maintains a relationship of resistance to whatever constitutes the normal."⁴⁰ Further, as Helford notes, Xena and Gabrielle's lack of jealousy regarding the other's relationships with men "illustrates well an alternative relationship pattern to traditional heterosexual monogamy within a system of male supremacy."⁴¹ The portrayal of a relationship between women that is often described within the show as "soul mates" is revolutionary in and of itself; the lack of emphasis on monogamy is another queer facet of the show.

Xena: Warrior Princess enables a rewriting of classic mythology in the service of "queering the discourse": "Rather than submitting ourselves to another cycle of marginalization and cultural amnesia, we should continue to learn from the past and keep queering the discourse."⁴² The lasting legacy of Xena will not be her fighting skills or her lethal beauty, but the revelations that masculine and feminine are aspects and not identities, and most importantly, love and fulfillment are not the sole property of monogamous, married, heterosexual couples. By providing a queer site for discussion, *Xena* has reinvented the heroic epic and reclaimed female agency.

This multifaceted depiction of a ferocious, femme figure on primetime television imparts the lesson that strength and heroism are not contained within gendered dichotomies. By queering the quest, and contributing to mainstream television's visual culture through showcasing the boundless depths of a same-sex relationship, *Xena* provides a playful alternative history, establishes an empowering androgynous role model, and evokes critical thought on the political implications of gendered narratives. *Xena: Warrior Princess* plays with the conventions of the hero's quest—by providing a queer site for discussion—and ultimately reinvents the heroic epic by reviving the classical origins of power feminism. The ability to be read in various contexts—as a lesbian show, as an action-adventure, as a journey intimately shared by female companions, and as a fantastical farce—imbues the series with polysemic richness. Xena's aesthetic, strength, and sexuality defy feminine/masculine demarcations and reconfigure gender roles and regulations. Her character offers an authoritative androgynous alternative to the traditional yoking of femininity to passivity. Both the show and the eponymous heroine highlight the subversive potential of neo-femmes—agents of change who are able to crossover into regulated mainstream spaces while providing role models and imaginative spaces for queer communities.

NOTES

1. *Xena: Warrior Princess-The Complete Series*, performed by Lucy Lawless (1995–2001; Universal City, CA: Universal Studios Home Entertainment, 2016), DVD.
2. "The Key to The Kingdom," *Xena: Warrior Princess-The Complete Series*, directed by Bruce Campbell (11 Jan. 1999; Universal City, CA: Universal Studios Home Entertainment, 2016), DVD.
3. Elyce Rae Helford, "Feminism, Queer Studies, and the Sexual Politics of Xena: Warrior Princess," in *Fantasy Girls: Gender in the New Universe of Science Fiction and Fantasy Television*, ed. Elyce Rae Helford (Oxford: Rowman & Littlefield, Inc, 2000), 136.
4. K. Stoddard Hayes, *Xena: Warrior Princess: The Complete Illustrated Companion* (London: Titan Books, 2003), 12.
5. "The Warrior Princess," *Hercules: The Legendary Journeys-Season 1*, directed by Bruce Seth Green (13 Mar. 1995; Universal City, CA: Universal Studios Home Entertainment, 2010), DVD.
6. Robert Tapert, interview by Bret Ryan Rudnick, *Whoosh* 52 (Jan. 2001), accessed March 27, 2017, http://www.whoosh.org/issue52/itapert1.html.
7. Ibid.
8. "The Woman Behind the Warrior," Lucy Lawless, interview by David Rensin, *TV Guide* 45 no. 18 (May 3, 1997), accessed March 27, 2017, http://www.warriorprincess.com/Lucy/lucytvg0597.html.
9. Ibid.
10. Ibid.
11. Helford, "Feminism, Queer Studies…," 135–161.
12. Ibid.
13. Elizabeth Lapovsky Kennedy and Madeline D. Davis, *Boots of Leather, Slippers of Gold: The History of a Lesbian Community* (New York: Routledge, 2014).
14. Chloë Brushwood Rose and Anna Camilleri, introduction to *Brazen Femme: Queering Femininity* (Vancouver: Arsenal Pulp Press, 2002), 11–15.
15. Joan Nestle, "The Fem Question," in *Pleasure and Danger: Exploring Female Sexuality*, ed. Carole S. Vance (Boston: Routledge & K. Paul, 1984), 232–240.
16. Robert J. Corber, *Cold War Femme: Lesbianism, National identity, and Hollywood Cinema* (Durham: Duke University Press, 2011).
17. Rose and Camilleri, "Introduction," 12.
18. Lisa Duggan and Kathleen McHugh, "A Fem(me)inist Manifesto," *Women & Performance: A Journal of Feminist Theory* 8, no. 2 (1996): 154, doi:10.1080/07407709608571236.
19. Ibid., 154.

20. Luce Irigaray, *The Sex Which Is Not One* (Ithaca: Cornell University Press, 1985), 76.
21. *Ibid.*, 76.
22. *Ibid.*, 75; emphasis in original.
23. *Ibid.*,76.
24. Jeffrey A. Brown, "Gender, Sexuality, and Toughness: The Bad Girls of Action Film and Comic Books," in *Action Chicks: New Images of Tough Women in Popular Culture*, ed. Sherrie A. Inness (New York: Palgrave Macmillan, 2004), 72.
25. *Ibid.*
26. Nestle, "The Fem Question," 234.
27. Chris Holmlund, "When Is a Lesbian Not a Lesbian: The Lesbian Continuum and the Mainstream Femme Film," in *Impossible Bodies: Femininity and Masculinity at the Movies* (London: Routledge, 2002), 35.
28. *Ibid.*, 33.
29. "Fallen Angel." *Xena: Warrior Princess-The Complete Series*, directed by John Fawcett (27 Sept. 1999; Universal City, CA: Universal Studios Home Entertainment, 2016), DVD.
30. Adrienne Rich, "Compulsory Heterosexuality and Lesbian Existence," in *The Lesbian and Gay Studies Reader*, ed. Henry Abelove, Michèle Aina. Barale, and David M. Halperin (New York: Routledge, 1993), 245.
31. *Ibid.*, 239.
32. *Ibid.*, 234.
33. "Seeds of Faith," *Xena: Warrior Princess-The Complete Series*, directed by Garth Maxwell (10 Jan. 2000. Universal City, CA: Universal Studios Home Entertainment, 2016), DVD.
34. Nayland Blake, "Curating in A Different Light," in *In a Different Light: Visual Culture, Sexual Identity, Queer Practice*, ed. Nayland Blake, Lawrence Rinder, and Amy Scholder (New York: City Lights Books, 1995), 12.
35. "Sins of the Past," *Xena: Warrior Princess-The Complete Series*, directed by Doug Lefler (4 Sept. 1995. Universal City, CA: Universal Studios Home Entertainment, 2016), DVD.
36. Karen Hollinger, "Theorizing Mainstream Female Spectatorship: The Case of the Popular Lesbian Film," *Cinema Journal* 37, no. 2 (1998): 11, doi:10.2307/1225639.
37. "Sins of the Past."
38. *Ibid.*
39. "You Are There," *Xena: Warrior Princess-The Complete Series*, directed by John Laing (5 Feb. 2001; Universal City, CA: Universal Studios Home Entertainment, 2016), DVD.
40. Annamarie Jagose, *Queer Theory: An Introduction* (New York: New York University Press, 1996), 99.
41. Helford, "Feminism, Queer Studies and...," 151.
42. Blake, "Curating in a Different Light," 42–43.

BIBLIOGRAPHY

Blake, Nayland. "Curating in a Different Light." In *In a Different Light: Visual Culture, Sexual Identity, Queer Practice*, edited by Nayland Blake, Lawrence Rinder, and Amy Scholder, 9–43. New York: City Lights Books, 1995.
Brown, Jeffrey A. "Gender, Sexuality, and Toughness: The Bad Girls of Action Film and Comic Books." In *Action Chicks: New Images of Tough Women in Popular Culture*. Edited by Sherrie A. Inness. New York: Palgrave Macmillan, 2004. 47–74.
Duggan, Lisa, and Kathleen McHugh. "A Fem(me)inist Manifesto."*Women & Performance: A Journal of Feminist Theory* 8, no. 2 (1996): 153–59. doi:10.1080/07407709608571236.
"Fallen Angel." *Xena: Warrior Princess-The Complete Series*. Directed by John Fawcett. 27 Sept. 1999. Universal City, CA: Universal Studios Home Entertainment, 2016. DVD.
Hayes, K. Stoddard. *Xena: Warrior Princess: The Complete Illustrated Companion*. London: Titan Books, 2003.
Helford, Elyce Rae. "Feminism, Queer Studies, and the Sexual Politics of Xena: Warrior

Princess." In *Fantasy Girls: Gender in the New Universe of Science Fiction and Fantasy Television*, edited by Elyce Rae Helford, 135–161. Oxford: Rowman & Littlefield, 2000.

Hollinger, Karen. "Theorizing Mainstream Female Spectatorship: The Case of the Popular Lesbian Film."*Cinema Journal* 37, no. 2 (1998): 3–17. doi:10.2307/1225639.

Holmlund, Chris. "When Is a Lesbian Not a Lesbian: The Lesbian Continuum and the Mainstream Femme Film." In *Impossible Bodies: Femininity and Masculinity at the Movies*, 31–50. London: Routledge, 2002.

Irigaray, Luce. *The Sex Which Is Not One*. Ithaca: Cornell University Press, 1985.

Jagose, Annamarie. *Queer Theory: An Introduction*. New York: New York University Press, 1996.

Kennedy, Elizabeth Lapovsky, and Madeline D. Davis. *Boots of Leather, Slippers of Gold: The History of a Lesbian Community*. New York: Routledge, 2014.

"The Key to the Kingdom." *Xena: Warrior Princess-The Complete Series*. Directed by Bruce Campbell. 11 Jan. 1999. Universal City, CA: Universal Studios Home Entertainment, 2016. DVD.

Lawless, Lucy. "The Woman Behind the Warrior." By David Rensin, *TV Guide*, 45 no. 18 (May 3, 1997). Accessed March 27, 2017. http://www.warriorprincess.com/Lucy/lucytvg0597.html.

Nestle, Joan. "The Fem Question." In *Pleasure and Danger: Exploring Female Sexuality*, edited by Carole S. Vance, 232–40. Boston: Routledge & K. Paul, 1984.

Rich, Adrienne. "Compulsory Heterosexuality and Lesbian Existence." In *The Lesbian and Gay Studies Reader*, edited by Henry Abelove, Michèle Aina Barale, and David M. Halperin, 227–54. New York: Routledge, 1993.

Rose, Chloë Brushwood, and Anna Camilleri. Introduction to *Brazen Femme: Queering Femininity*. Edited by Chloë Brushwood Rose and Anna Camilleri, 11–15. Vancouver: Arsenal Pulp Press, 2002.

"Seeds of Faith." *Xena: Warrior Princess-The Complete Series*. Directed by Garth Maxwell. 10 Jan. 2000. Universal City, CA: Universal Studios Home Entertainment, 2016. DVD.

"Sins of the Past." *Xena: Warrior Princess-The Complete Series*. Directed by Doug Lefler. 4 Sept. 1995. Universal City, CA: Universal Studios Home Entertainment, 2016. DVD.

Tapert, Robert. "An Interview with Robert Tapert." By Bret Ryan Rudnick. *Whoosh* 52 (Jan. 2001). Accessed March 27, 2017. http://www.whoosh.org/issue52/itapert1.html.

"The Warrior Princess." *Hercules: The Legendary Journeys-Season 1*. Directed by Bruce Seth Green. 13 Mar. 1995. Universal City, CA: Universal Studios Home Entertainment, 2010. DVD.

Xena: Warrior Princess-The Complete Series. Performed by Lucy Lawless. 1995–2001. Universal City, CA: Universal Studios Home Entertainment, 2016. DVD.

"You Are There." *Xena: Warrior Princess-The Complete Series*. Directed by John Laing. 5 Feb. 2001. Universal City, CA: Universal Studios Home Entertainment, 2016. DVD.

Afterword

Steven L. Sears

I'm humming a song in my head. You have no idea what it is, and there is little chance you could. Even if you know me, you wouldn't be able to guess it. It's an echo from my childhood, when I was no more than seven or eight, when I would sit in front of that glowing box called "television" and watch a series of movies call *The Sons of Hercules*.

If you, like me, watched those old movies, I can guarantee you, you are smiling right now. And, just as certainly, you are having a rush of nostalgic memories. You're hearing it in your head, you're humming along as well. Your chest might have swelled a bit in reaction, a call back to when you would stand in front of that TV and, for a moment, you were a son of Hercules. If you were like me, anyway.

Culled from a collection of old Italian movies, *The Sons of Hercules* was exactly what you might think. Powerful, muscly, daring, courageous and handsome men wearing tunics and robes, fighting on behalf of the oppressed, defending liberty and, at times, love from evil warlords, emperors and powerful despots.

I didn't care about the graininess of the films, or that the stunts seemed a little too choreographed, or that the words didn't seem to match the movements of their lips. These were HEROES! I couldn't wait to see them. Other movies, such as *Jason and the Argonauts* and *Son of Samson* also drew me in. Yes, yes, the rest of the world was smitten with Westerns at that time, but not me. I liked some of them but, sorry Dad, I never really got into *Gunsmoke*. Togas, tyrants and gladiators, that was the ticket for me.

My heroes were Mark Foster, Steve Reeves and Kirk Morris. And pretty much anyone else who swung a sword and collapsed buildings with bulging muscles, whether they played Hercules, Jason, Pericles or Samson. The stars of the peplum films of old.

I had a rich fantasy life as a child and the peplum genre fulfilled my classic mythological niche, just as Captain Kirk later held sway over the science fiction section of my mental amusement park.

But things change, movies change, television changes. With the exception of a few attempts at the sword and sandal format, it was unlikely we would ever see the golden age of Italian mythological films again.

I grew up (as much as I could) and moved on to my career as a television writer in Hollywood. It was there that, one day, I was asked to meet with a man named David Eick at Renaissance Pictures. I didn't know a lot about Renaissance Pictures except that it was owned and run by Sam Raimi of *Evil Dead* fame with his partner, producer Rob Tapert. David had read a script of mine and wanted to meet. The bungalow was on the Universal lot. "This is our development office," he said, sweeping his arm to take in the closet space filled with books and scripts that was his office.

The meeting was just what we call a "meet n' greet," to get to know each other in case something comes up later. I asked him what Renaissance was working on. He said that they had this little idea they were putting together, a retelling of Hercules. I brightened and told him I was a fan of the old Italian movies. I remember him smiling and saying, "Well, we're going to do it a bit differently...."

That became the hit series *Hercules* debuting in 1995 and lasting six seasons. Starring Kevin Sorbo as a congenial and more accessible Hercules (Kevin was a perfect casting choice), and Michael Hurst as Iolaus (another talented find), this new series single handedly launched a decade of fantasy action hero programming across the board as every studio wanted to capture the flame that Renaissance had lit. And, of course, my beloved *Xena* was a direct result. Starring Lucy Lawless, *Xena* has had a huge popularity, but it was a spin-off from its big brother, *Hercules*. Without that series, *Xena* would not have existed (a quick tip o' the hat and thank you to everyone involved with *Hercules*!).

Oh, did I mention another spin-off of *Hercules* was *Young Hercules*? Yeah. Starring a little known actor named Ryan Gosling. But I digress...

Surprisingly, my meeting with David Eick wasn't the reason I ended up working on *Xena*, but that's another story for another time. What did matter is that I did end up working on a series that took on the peplum legacy.

Obviously, like our big brother *Hercules*, *Xena* couldn't repeat the old Italian movies. The taste of the public had moved on. The audience had changed. What was once seen as heroic and adventurous had become quaint, melodramatic and contrived. But the idea and allure of the hero ... yes, that still endured, as it does today. We always need heroes. Greater than life heroes, flawed heroes, honest heroes, dark heroes, something that we can try to see in ourselves that tells us that, in the right circumstance with the right situation, we, too, might be a hero.

Truth is, fictional heroes are often too perfect. That's what makes them exceptional. Even when we see their flaws at the beginning, we know they will rise above it and do the right thing. They are born to it; it is their destiny. Alas, the best we can hope for ourselves is that, if not born a hero, we can at least be heroic when the time comes.

That's something we kept in mind when we wrote *Xena*. It wasn't enough for Xena to be a hero, she had to be heroic. It was reflected best in the path of her partner, Gabrielle, played by Renee O'Connor. They didn't stand confident and brave, fists on hips whenever danger approached as Mitchel Gordon did with the Cyclops, or Richard Harrison had done when confronted by Medusa. No, the audience was more sophisticated, more aware of themselves. Our heroes had to be as well.

So with Xena, you had a hero who was born from darkness. A character who had done truly evil things in her past, justifying her actions, as all villains do. Someone who realized the bad that she had done and wanted to change. She wanted to do good, not necessarily to balance karmic books that could never be rewritten, but because it was the right thing to do. Her challenge, her struggle, wasn't against monsters and warlords, it was against herself. Her mission was to find herself again. In her partner, Gabrielle, the audience saw themselves as her; wide-eyed and innocent, traveling along for adventure but finding the hero in herself along the way. Exactly what we all want to believe about ourselves, disguised as entertainment. Kevin's Hercules took a similar tract with a different approach. A demi-god who is good by nature trying to do right in a world of evil.

That sparked something. We saw it in our ratings, we saw it in our fans. We weren't just a sword and sorcery series. Our characters had meaning. They had depth. They touched on the feeling that we all have purpose, and the fear that we might die without knowing it.

And we had swords. And chicks in leather. Let's not forget, this is television after all.

Hey, here's a trivia question: What does Lucy Lawless, Stanley Kubrick, Kirk Douglas and Dalton Trumbo have in common? Answer: *Xena*. We did an episode where we used a clip of the movie *Spartacus* as a major resolution. Moving on.

What about film? Did the peplum of old return? Yes. And no. The huge adventure theme of big pictures was already established. *Indiana Jones*, *Star Wars*, and others proved the concept of big budget adventure. And it could be argued that they borrowed some elements from peplum themes or that they merely adapted themes that have endured throughout the history of cinema. But even with the popularity of our two TV shows, no one could see a gladiator based movie being successful.

Except for a movie titled *Gladiator*. Huh. Where did that come from?

Afterword

Written by David Franzoni, John Logan, William Nicholson, directed by Ridley Scott and starring Russel Crowe, it took people by surprise. Finally, a peplum movie for the mind! Yes, it was gladiator based. But it was more, much more. It was a call back to the old Italian movies, but it was everything it needed to take it to the next level. I'd love to say that our *Hercules* and *Xena* paved the way, but truth is, it was remarkable in its own right. Although if we didn't pave the way, I like to think we had a little bit to do with the concrete. When I saw it, it reminded me of my childhood watching those old movies. I heard *The Sons of Hercules* theme in my head again. The characters were larger than life, but they were real. No superhuman strength involved, no gods to ordain the warriors. Real people.

But certainly *Gladiator* was a one-off. What else could be done?

A TV series about the aforementioned *Spartacus*? Well ... yes. Brought to you by many of the people who worked on *Xena*, and including Lucy Lawless in the first season, *Spartacus* came to Starz network and had three very successful seasons, despite the tragic death of its talented star, Andy Whitfield. And it was, like *Gladiator*, a very thoughtful series. It had a lot more of the action of the old peplum movies, but it was not a series with a clear cut sense of right. It was about people, characters, and their own destinies.

Which brings me back to *The Sons of Hercules*. The heroes we have now are flawed, they struggle, they sometimes miss the mark in their redemption. That's a reflection of us, the audience. But at the core, we have to believe that our heroes are good. Their intentions are good. They truly do have a moral compass that might be hidden to themselves, but are revealed as they move forward. The peplum heroes not only had all that, it wasn't disguised. It was open, it was obvious. They were heroes from beginning to end. The audience knew it from the moment they saw them, saving someone or a group of people who could not ever pay back his efforts. Their message was that we could all be heroes if we looked deep enough inside ourselves.

That's why it's relevant to look back on those movies now. Yes, campy. Yes, dated. Yes, the villains are arch and over acted. Yes, the anachronisms are obvious (what's with the fifties hairstyles?). But they make you want to stand in the middle of the room, a towel around your waist, hands on hips, and believe that YOU can be Hercules too.

And if you have a chance, google *The Sons of Hercules* and listen to the theme. Awesome...

Steven L. Sears has worked for three decades as a writer, story editor, producer and creator in television, film, digital media and animation. His career encompasses fifteen separate television series, including the original *A-Team* and the cult classic *Xena*.

About the Contributors

Djoymi **Baker** teaches screen studies at the University of Melbourne and Swinburne University of Technology. She is the co-author of *The Encyclopedia of Epic Films*. Her articles on topics including the sword-and-sandal epic, television stardom and spectatorship have appeared in journals and edited collections.

Nicholas **Diak** is a pop culture scholar whose research has focused on Italian genre films (particularly spy films), exploitation cinema, post-industrial and synthwave music, and H.P. Lovecraft. He has contributed essays on a variety of topics including James Bond to journals and edited collections.

Kevin M. **Flanagan** is a visiting lecturer in English and film studies at the University of Pittsburgh. His essays have been published in *Critical Quarterly*, the *Journal of British Cinema and Television*, *Framework*, *Adaptation*, and in numerous edited collections and reference books.

Valerie Estelle **Frankel** is the author of about fifty books on pop culture. Many of them focus on women's roles in fiction, including *From Girl to Goddess*, *Buffy and the Heroine's Journey*, *Women in Game of Thrones* and *The Many Faces of Katniss Everdeen*. She teaches at Mission College.

Paul **Johnson** is an independent researcher. His work has investigated aspects of visual effects and compositing throughout cinema's history and its application into concealing, and conversely visually releasing, certain physical structures within films' images and their production.

Hannah **Mueller** teaches television and media studies at New York University and Hunter College. Her research focuses on participatory and fan culture, transmedia storytelling, media representations of nudity and sex, popular representations of prisons and incarcerated people, and the construction of "high" and "low" cultures/audiences.

Steve **Nash** lectures in literature and media at Leeds Beckett University. His research has focused on rhizomatic approaches to narrative across Victorian fiction, poetry, television, film, and videogames. His published creative works include two poetry collections.

About the Contributors

Jerry B. **Pierce** is an assistant professor of history at Penn State, Hazleton. His scholarly research focuses on portrayals of masculinity and homosexuality in ancient film. He has published on heteronormativity in *Gladiator*, *Troy*, and *300*, masculinity and sexuality in *Alexander*, and the revival of classical epic film after the year 2000.

Nick **Poulakis** is a staff member of the Ethnomusicology and Cultural Anthropology Laboratory at the National and Kapodistrian University of Athens (Greece), where he teaches film music, ethnographic cinema and applied ethnomusicology. He is the author of *Musicology and Cinema*.

Tatiana **Prorokova** holds a PhD in American Studies from the University of Marburg, Germany, and is an academic editor at Pod Academy, United Kingdom. Her research interests include war studies, ecocriticism, gender studies, and race studies. She is a co-editor of *Cultures of War in Graphic Novels: Violence, Trauma, and Memory*.

Haydee **Smith** is a doctoral candidate at the University of California, San Diego. Her research focuses on intersectional identity formations and the representations of divas, femmes, disability, and queer sexuality in modernist literature and women's films.

Kevin J. **Wetmore**, Jr., is a professor at Loyola Marymount University. He is the author of several books and he has contributed more than four dozen essays on various topics to numerous edited collections. He is also an actor, director and stage combat choreographer.

Index

The Abyss 8
Achilles 36, 45, 46
adaptation 2, 10, 15, 21, 22–23, 24, 25–26, 34, 39, 40, 44, 45, 47, 48, 51, 53, 87, 186
Addai-Robinson, Cynthia 137
Africanus 100
Age of Empires 11
Agricola 180, 185
Agron 138, 142, 143, 144, 172–173
Albinius 162–163, 168
Alcmene 44, 121
Alias 7
Altman, Rick 22–23, 32
al-Zarqawi, Abu Musab 185
Amazons 11, 49, 116, 119, 124–125, 128
American Horror Story 146
American peplum 178, 179
Amphiaraus 52
Andersen, Alex Høgh 82
Anderson, Paul W.S. 14
Antigone 120
Antoninus 161
Antonioni, Michelangelo 33
Aphrodite 115, 129
Apocalypto 13
Apollodorus 47
Ares 123, 124, 127, 129, 213
Argento, Dario 33
Armstrong, Owen Eugene 185
Arquilla, John 72, 73
Artemisia 73
Ashur 173–174, 175
Asterix 10
Atalanta 118, 120
Atkins, Rachel 100
Atlantis 100, 118
Atlantis: End of a World, Birth of a Legend 15, 95, 100–101, 102, 103–104, 105, 108–109
Attacker 10

Attali, Jacques 97
Attila the Hun (television series) 12
Auctus 142, 143
Augoustakis, Antony 164
Auguet, Roland 65, 66
Aurelia 169, 173
Aurelius 182, 183, 184
Autolycus 54, 121, 122, 208
automated key frame animation 35
Avatar 8

Baahubali: The Beginning 13
Baahubali 2: The Conclusion 13
Baird Whitlock 13, 70, 200–201
Bakare, Ariyon 35
Bakhtin, Mikhail 46, 47, 65
Bakshi, Ralph 13
Balem Abrasax 26, 27, 29, 30, 33, 35, 37
Barbarians Rising 7
Barca 141–142, 143, 172, 173
Barsoom 5
Batiatus 137, 139, 141, 147, 158–159, 160, 163, 164–166, 167, 168, 171, 173
Battle of Artemisium 73
Battle of Cannae 71, 76
Battle of Marathon 73, 125
The Battle of Olympus 11
Battlestar Galactica 7
Bava, Mario 69, 118
Bay, Michael 15
BBC 7, 15, 95, 99, 101, 104, 107, 109, 110, 186
Beard, Mary 45, 54
The Beastmaster (1982) 5, 9
BeastMaster (television series) 7
Bekmambetov, Timur 14
Bell, Jamie 188
Ben-Hur (1959) 5, 14, 63, 178
Ben-Hur (2016) 14
Benjamin, Walter 110

226 Index

Bennett, Manu 137, 163
Beowulf (character) 12, 116, 126
Beowulf (2007) 8
Beowulf & Grendel 12
Berg, Nick 185
Bhabha, Homi 96
Bianca, Viva 139, 162
Bigley, Kenneth 185
Black Sails 7, 136
Blackstar 6
Blake, Nayland 213
Blanshard, Alastair 31, 35, 157
Blood Axis 10
blood eagle 82, 88–89
Boardman, John 197–198
body genres 136, 144, 145, 149
Bondanella, Peter 4, 34
Booth, Douglas 25
Borchard, Gregory A. 66
Bound 26
Boxleitner, Bruce 31
Bragaglia, Carlo Ludovico 36, 64, 69
Brandt, Lesley-Ann 137, 166
Brass, Tinto 67
Bridges, Jeff 30, 35
Brill, Lesley 67, 68
British Cultural Studies 1
Brooks, Mel 16, 199
Brooks, Peter 28
Brouwers, Josho 45
Brown, Jeffrey 211
Brown, Josef 142
Bruce, Victoria 100
Buffy the Vampire Slayer (character) 123
Buffy the Vampire Slayer (television series) 7
Buhler, James 97
Burdick, Alan 96
Burke, Frank 29
Burke, Liam 53
Burroughs, Edgar Rice 5
Butler, Eamonn 34
Butler, Gerard 12, 36, 71

Cabiria (1914) 63, 68–69
The Caesars (1968) 6
Cain, Dean 117
Caine Wise 27, 29, 31, 38–39
Caius Julius Polybius 100
Caligula 66–67
Caligula (1979) 67
Camelot 7
Cameron, James 8
camp 29, 36, 118, 209
Campbell, Bruce 117, 121, 208
Campogalliani, Carlo 4
Canetti, Elias 64, 67–68

Capua 146, 158, 162, 163, 164, 169, 171, 173
Capuano, Luigi 24
Carano, Gina 38
Carter, Jim 100
Catena, Carolina 69
Cavallini, Eleonora 45
Cavill, Henry 74
Celadus 100
Centurion 15, 179, 180, 182, 184–186, 188
Cerberus 51
Ceryneian Hind 52, 129
CGI 8, 64, 68, 72, 101, 102, 103, 107, 110, 136
Chaffey, Don 8
Cheurfa, Anis 31
Christie, Julie 45
Church, Thomas Haden 34
Cicero 66
Cimber, Matt 5
cinema of attractions 53
CinemaScope 8
Cinemax 9
Clare, Dustin 143, 167
Clark Kent 117
Clarke, Rebecca 100
Clash of the Titans (1981) 8
Clash of the Titans (2010) 5, 8, 45, 51, 73
Cleopatra 115, 116, 125
Cleopatra (1963) 5, 156
Clooney, George 13, 70, 200
Cloud Atlas 26
Clu 30, 31, 35, 36–37, 40
cluster concept 30
Coen brothers 13, 70, 200
Collins, Jim 47
Collins, Lynn 28
The Colossus of Rhodes 4, 25
Columbus, Chris 13
comic book 2, 4, 6, 9, 10–11, 14, 15, 44, 48–50, 51, 53, 129; *see also* graphic novel
Commodus (*Fall of the Roman Empire* character) 156, 159
Commodus (*Gladiator* character) 36, 72
Conan: Adventures in an Age Undreamed Of 14
Conan the Adventurer 7
Conan the Barbarian (1982) 5, 14, 38
Conan the Barbarian (2011) 8
Cool World 13
Cornelius, Michael G. 5, 140, 151
Coscarelli, Don 5, 9
Cossutius 167–168, 169, 173
Cottafavi, Vittorio 21, 23, 26
Cotterill, Chrissie 100
Cotys 52
Cretan Bull 52
Crixus 137–138, 139, 141, 143, 144, 149, 163–164, 166, 167, 168, 171–172

Croton, Andrea 120
crowds 15, 32, 63–64, 65–74, 75, 172, 199
Crowe, Russell 36, 72, 222
Crystal Viper 10
cultural memory 47, 90
Cummings, Erin 162
Cupid 120
Curtis, Tony 161
Cyrino, Monica Silveira 181

DaCosta, Ya 26
Dafoe, William 34
Daft Punk 27, 30, 37
D'Aquino, John 121
Dark Angel 7
Dark Horse Comics 14
Darkest of Days 11
Darville, Eka 141, 172
David 126
Davies, Sam 33
Davis, Desmond 8
Day, Amber 197
DC 10, 49
The Death Song of Ragnar Lodbrog 81, 82, 83, 87
Deemer, Rob 97
Dejah Thoris 28, 29
de la Bédoyère, Guy 180
Deleuze, Gilles 79, 80–81
Demeter 120
DeMille, Cecil B. 21, 68, 156
deviant 36–39, 159–161, 172, 174–175, 212
Dewey, John 96
Dhandwar, Tarsem Singh 45, 64
Dickson, Robert 140
Dilio 203–204
Dilios 71–72
Diona 167–168, 169, 173
Disney 29, 118
docudrama 15, 95, 98, 99, 100, 101, 102, 103, 104, 105, 106, 107, 108, 109, 110
Dominici, Franco 70
Donen, Stanley 52
Douglas, Ann 145
Douglas, Kirk 157, 167, 168, 174, 179, 221
Dowden, Ken 46
Downey, Roma 119
dubbing 33–35, 39
duBois, Page 72
Duggan, Lisa 210, 211
Dyer, Richard 53
Dynamite Entertainment 10

Eades, Caroline 5
The Eagle 15, 179, 180, 182, 186–191
The Eagle of the Ninth 186
Eastmancolor 7

Echidna 121
Eddas 15, 79–80, 81, 83, 84, 86, 91
Edward, Mike 147
Eick, David 220
Elfquest 11
Elliott, Kamilla 26
Elsaesser, Thomas 28
Emmerich, Roland 13
Empire 7
Empire of the Wolf 10
Ensiferum 10
Ephialtes 73
Epidia 100
Ergenia 52
Erymanthian Boar 45
Esca 188–190
Etain 185, 186
Euripides 47, 116, 126
Evans, Luke 74
Everson, Corrina "Cory" 118, 120
The Evil Dead 115
Ex Deo 10
exploitation cinema 136, 144, 149

Fabius Maximus 70
Facebook 12
Falafel 121–122
Falero, Sandra 126
The Fall of the Roman Empire 70, 156, 159, 178
Fandom 3, 11, 16
Fassbender, Michael 185
Feld, Steven 101
feminism 16, 115, 116, 117, 123, 125, 145, 208, 212, 216
femme fatale 138, 209
Ferguson, Rebecca 52
Ferri, Anthony J. 66
Ferzetti, Gabriele 70
Feuer, Jane 51
Feuerriegel, Dan 138, 172
Fiennes, Ralph 73
Filie, Dan 19
Filmation 6
Fimmel, Travis 81, 87
Firth, Colin 182
Firth, Jonathan 100
Fisher, Nick 198
Fiske, John 1
Fitzgerald, William 156
Fitzherbert, Henry 48
Fortunata 100
Foster, Meg 119
Foucault, Michel 88, 198
Frain, James 37
Francisci, Pietro 4, 25, 48, 63, 118
Frank, Roberta 86, 87–88, 90, 91

Franzoni, David 222
Freudenthal, Thor 13
Friedberg, Jason 16, 196
Futrell, Alison 171

Gabrielle 115, 116, 124, 125, 126, 127, 128, 129, 208, 210, 212–214, 215, 221
Galtar and the Golden Lance 6
Gannicus 143, 167, 170
Gardner, Jane F. 66
Garrett, Beau 26
gaze 26–27, 136–137, 138–139, 140–141, 143, 144, 145, 146–147, 148, 150, 213
gender 2, 16, 26, 37–38, 89, 124, 136–137, 138, 143, 144, 166, 198, 201, 205, 208, 209, 210, 211–212, 213, 214, 215, 216
Genette, Gérard 48
Gentilomo, Giacomo 6
giallo 4, 33
Gibson, Mel 13
girl power 123
Glaber 141, 148, 162–163, 164, 168, 170, 171, 173, 174
Gladiator 5, 7, 10, 14, 36, 38, 63, 72, 159, 179, 180, 221, 222
Gladiators of Rome 8
Gledhill, Christine 39
Goddard, Gary 5
Gods of Egypt 12, 14
God of War (video game series) 11
Gold Key Comics 50
Golden Fleece 10, 25
Goldstein, Gary 48
Goliath 126
Goliath Against the Giants 36
Gor 5
Goscinny, René 10
graphic novel 2, 9, 10, 44, 47, 48, 50, 51, 53, 56; *see also* comic book
Gray, Jonathan 48, 197
Greeghan 35
Green, Eva 73
Green, Karen 11
Green Zone 181, 185, 186, 189–190, 191
Green Zone (2010) 179
greenscreen 8
Griffith, D.W. 69
Gruendemann, Eric 128
Guattari, Felix 79, 80–81, 90
Gunnarsson, Sturla 12
Gunning, Tom 53

Hades 51, 73, 120, 129
Hadrian 66, 187
Hadrian's Wall 183, 185, 186, 187, 190
Hail, Caesar! 13, 16, 70–71, 200–201, 205
Hall, Stuart 1

Hannah, John 137, 163, 183
Hannah-Barbera 6
Hannibal (character) 70, 71
Hannibal (1959) 64, 69–70, 71
Harlin, Renny 8, 45
Harper, Jessica 33
Harryhausen, Ray 8
Hatcher, Teri 117
Haywire 38
He-Man and the Masters of the Universe 6
Hedlund, Garrett 26
Helen of Troy 116, 125–126
Helen of Troy (1956) 69
Helford, Elyce Rae 209, 210, 215
Helgeland, Brian 13
Hera 44, 45, 47, 119, 121, 128
Heracles *see* Hercules (mythological character)
Hercules (Dwayne "The Rock" Johnson) 15, 44–45, 48, 50, 51, 52, 43, 54, 59
Hercules (*Le fatiche di Ercole*, 1958) 4, 6, 7, 25, 36, 48, 52, 118
Hercules (Italian pepla character) 7, 24, 30, 36, 37, 38, 52, 69, 219, 220
Hercules (Kevin Sorbo) 116, 117, 118–121, 122–123, 129, 209, 220, 221
Hercules (mythological character) 10, 15, 44, 46, 47–48, 49, 50, 51, 52, 53, 54, 55, 58, 129, 222
Hercules (2014) 15, 38, 44–46, 47, 48, 49, 50–51, 52, 53, 54
Hercules Against the Moon Men 6
Hercules and the Amazon Women 119, 121
Hercules and the Black Pirates (*Sansone contro il corsaro nero*) 24
Hercules at the Centre of the Earth 118
Hercules in the Haunted World 69
Hercules: The Legendary Journeys 6–7, 115–123, 209, 220–222
Hercules Unchained 63
The Herculoids 6
Hermann, Pernille 84, 85, 86, 90
Hermes 27
Higgins, Scott 28, 30, 31
Hippolyta 10, 119
historic epic 4, 5, 6, 8, 9, 12, 13, 14, 21, 32, 118, 172, 175, 200
History Channel 82, 90
History of the World, Part I 16, 199–201, 205
Hodgson, Martin 100
Hoffman, Bridget 121
Hollander, Lee 85, 86
Holloway, Liddy 121
Holmlund, Chris 212

Index 229

Homer 21, 27, 45, 46, 47, 116, 126
homosexuality 142–143, 149, 150, 155, 160–161, 169, 172, 198, 199, 200, 201, 202–203, 204, 205
Hrossharsgrani 10
Hubbard, Thomas 198
Hughes, Howard 69, 76
Hugo Hercules 49–50
Hulu 9
Hundra 5
Hurst, Michael 119, 122, 209, 215, 220
Hurt, John 52
The Hurt Locker 179, 191
Hutcheon, Linda 197
Hyperion 74

I, Claudius 6
Ibson, John 118
Idyll 47
Iliad 45, 46, 126
Ilithyia 139, 140, 141, 146–147, 162–164, 166, 167, 168, 169, 170, 174
IMAX 8
Immortals 45, 51, 64, 74
internet 2, 11–12
intertextuality 2, 9, 44, 46, 47, 48, 50, 52, 54, 85, 98
Intolerance 69
Iolaus 45, 51, 119, 121, 122, 209, 220
Iraq War 15, 178, 179–182, 185–186, 188, 190–191
Irigaray, Luce 211
Isenberg, Noah 71
Ivar the Boneless 82, 88, 89

Jack of All Trades 7
Jack Reacher 38
Jagose, Annamarie 215
Jarvis 37
Jason 25, 116, 219
Jason and the Argonauts 8, 219
Jenkins, Henry 46, 48, 55, 56
Jenkins, Patty 14
Jenkins, Sam 119
John Carter (character) 5, 27–28, 29, 31, 38–39
John Carter (2012 film) 8, 15, 21, 27–28, 29, 30–31, 34, 38, 40
Johnson, Dwayne "The Rock" 15, 38, 44, 48, 50, 53–54, 59
Johnston, Sarah Iles 46, 47, 55, 57
Jones, Jeffrey P. 197
Jones, Leigh 100
Joshel, Sandra 156, 178, 179, 191
Joxer 115
Joyrich, Lynne 142
Julia 100

Julius Caesar 115, 116, 122, 125, 128, 156–157, 159, 169, 172, 199–200
Jupiter Ascending 15, 21, 25–26, 27, 29, 30, 31, 33, 35, 36, 37–38, 39, 40
Jupiter Jones 26, 27, 29
Juran, Nathan H. 8
Jurassic Park 23

Kalique Abrasax, 33
Karlin, Fred 109
Kassabian, Anahid 104
Kelly, Gene 52
Kevin Flynn 30, 32, 35, 36
Kiersch, Fritz 5
King Arthur: Legend of the Sword 14
Kipling, Rudyard 10
Kirby, Jack 49
Kitsch, Taylor 27
Klecker, Cornelia 51
A Knight's Tale 13
The Knives of Kush 10
Kogge, Michael 10
Korkut, Nil 196
Körner, Wilhelm H.D. 49
Kosinski, Joseph 15, 21
Koster, Henry 159, 178
Kronos 74
Kubrick, Stanley 5, 54, 156, 158, 163, 165, 171, 178, 221
Kunis, Mila 26
Kurylenko, Olga 185

Laeta 170
Lagertha 89
Landi, Elissa 157
Lasseter, John 8
The Last Days of Pompeii 6
The Last Legion 15, 179–180, 182–184, 186
L'Atlantide 69, 76
Lawless, Lucy 115, 119, 124, 139, 163, 208, 210, 220, 221, 222s
Lawlor, Leonard 80
Layton, Bob 49
Lee, Stan 49
Lefler, Doug 15, 128, 179
The Legend of Hercules 8, 14, 45
Lehman, Peter 138, 140
Leitch, Thomas 22
Leone, Sergio 4, 25
Leonidas 12, 36, 71, 202–203, 204
Leonisas, Stephanie 100
Leprohon, Pierre 21
Lernaean Hydra 45, 51, 52
LeRoy, Marvyn 69, 156, 178
Leterrier, Louis 5, 8, 45, 73
Létoublon, Françoise 5
Licinia 164, 167

Liebesman, Jonathan 8, 45, 64
Lipkin, Steve 95, 110
Lisberger, Steven 39
Logan, John 222
Lois & Clark: The New Adventures of Superman 117–118
Lois Lane 117–118
Loren, Sophia 70
The Loves of Hercules / Hercules vs. the Hydra 36
Lucanio, Patrick 23, 28
Lucilla 70
Lucius Caelius 170
Lucretia 139, 140, 163–164, 165–167, 168, 171–172, 174
Lupi Gladius 10
Lutz, Kellan 74
Lygia 157, 160
Lysia 119

Macdonald, Kevin 15, 179
Maciste 30, 69
Magic Mike 39
Malamud, Margaret 178, 179, 180, 191
Malatesta, Guido 36
male body 36, 38–39, 53–54, 137, 138, 139, 140, 143, 144, 147, 149, 197–198, 199, 200, 201–202, 203, 204, 205
Mallory Kane 38
Manfredi, Valerio Massimo 182
Mankiewicz, Joseph 5, 156
Mann, Anthony 70, 156, 178
Marcus Flavia Aquila 186, 187, 188–190
Marcus Licinius Crassus 156, 157, 158–159, 161, 168, 169, 170, 173
Marshall, Neil 15, 179, 184
Marvel 10, 49
Marvel Boy 49
Masada 6
masculinity 14, 16, 38, 39, 82, 106, 142, 147, 195, 196, 197, 198, 199, 200, 201, 203, 204, 205, 208, 211
Masters of the Universe (1987) 5
The Matrix 8, 26, 38, 53
matte painting 8, 68
Mature, Victor 70
Maximus Decimus Meridius 36, 37, 38, 72
McArthur, Colin 40
McDowell, Malcolm 66
McGee, Ryan 140
McGlynn, Mary Elizabeth 125
McHugh, Kathleen 210, 211
McIntyre, Liam 137, 162
McQuarrie, Christopher 38
McRobbie, Angela 1
McShane, Ian 52

Megara 47, 56
Meet the Spartans 16, 196, 201–205
Meister, Melissa 125
Melitta 137–138, 167
melodrama 28, 29, 30, 35, 39, 98, 99, 101, 103, 107, 118, 136, 137, 144, 145, 146, 149, 220
Mensah, Peter 137, 174
Mercia 157, 160
Meyer, Stephen 105
Middleton, Tuppence 33
Milius, John 5, 38
Miller, Frank 9
Minitius 70
Minkowitz, Donna 122
Mitchell, Tony 15, 95
Moore, Steve 10, 47, 48–49, 50, 51, 53, 54, 55, 56
Mori, Masahiro 35
Morton, Samantha 34
Morwood, James 66
Moss, Paige 120
motion-capture 34–35, 68
motor-only shooting 33, 35
Mount Tartarus 74
Mount Vesuvius 11, 100, 103, 170
Mulvey, Laura 26
Murro, Noam 8, 64
music 6, 9, 10, 15, 27, 30, 70, 95, 97–98, 99, 101–105, 106, 107–110
musical 51–52
Muybridge, Eadweard 52–53
Mystery Science Theater 3000 6

Naevia 137–138, 141, 143, 144, 166, 171–172, 173, 174
Nasir 138, 142, 143, 172
Nemean Lion 45, 51, 52
Neo 38
neo-femme 210, 216
neomythological 4, 21
neo-noir 5
neo-peplum 1, 2, 3, 5–6, 8, 9, 10, 11, 12, 23, 24, 15, 16, 21, 22, 23, 24, 25, 30, 34, 38, 39, 40, 45, 51, 52, 64, 70, 71, 72, 73, 74, 79, 88, 95, 99, 101, 107, 110, 155, 159, 174, 178, 191, 195, 196, 197, 199, 201, 205, 208
Nero 156, 157, 158, 160, 173
Netflix 7, 9, 26, 136
network warfare 72, 73
Neumeyer, David 97
Newby, Zahra 65
Newell, Kate 22
Newell, Mike 8
Nicholson, Peter 15, 95
Nicholson, William 222

Index 231

Nielsen, Brigitte 10
Ninth Legion 180, 182, 183, 184, 185, 186, 187, 189, 190, 191
Nispel, Marcus 8
Norell, Paul 121
Norse 1, 15, 49, 80, 83, 84, 85, 87, 88, 89, 90, 116, 122
Norton, Bill L. 119, 121
nudity 136, 137, 138, 140, 149, 150, 155, 197–198
Numerius 164, 168, 169

O'Brien, Daniel 24
O'Connor, Renée 115, 125, 208, 221
Odysseus 28, 47
Odyssey 27, 28, 47, 126
Oedipus 25–26, 120
Oenomaus 137–138, 174
Oksner, Bob 49
Olivier, Lawrence 156, 173
The Olympian 10
Other 73, 98, 104, 105, 108, 179, 180, 182, 187, 188

Pagano, Bartolomeo 69
Pandora 125
paratext 15, 44, 46, 48, 49, 50, 53, 54
Park, Reg 69
Parker, Craig 141, 162
parody 13, 16, 70, 159, 195–196, 197, 199, 201, 205
pastiche 196–197, 204
Pastrone, Giovanni 63
Pausanias 47
Pearl, Daniel 185
penis 140–141, 147, 151, 163, 202
peplum 4, 5, 6, 7, 8, 10, 11, 13, 16, 21, 22, 23, 24, 25, 27, 28, 29, 30, 31, 32, 33, 34, 35, 36, 37, 38, 40, 52, 53, 54, 63, 64, 68, 69, 70, 71, 72, 74, 75, 99, 155, 164, 170, 172, 175, 178, 179, 182, 195, 196, 197, 199, 200, 201, 205, 219, 220
Percy Jackson (film series) 13
Persephone 120–121
Petersen, Wolfgang 36, 45
Phoenix, Joaquin 36, 72
Picts 184–186, 187, 189
Pierce, Jerry 15, 36, 37, 39, 155
Pietros 141–142, 143, 172
Pigott-Smith, Tim 100
The Pillars of the Earth 7
Pinaruti 100–101, 103
Pini, Wendy 11
Pitt, Brad 36
Plato 100
Plinia 100
Pliny the Elder 100

Pliny the Younger 100, 103
Poetic Edda 79, 84, 86, 91; *see also Eddas*
Pompeii (city) 100, 102, 103, 108
Pompeii (2014)
Pompeii: The Last Day 15, 95, 100, 101, 102–104, 105, 107–109
Pompey 125, 128
Poole, Russell 85
popular culture 1, 11, 12, 15, 44, 97, 142, 180, 210
pornography 136, 137, 138–139, 140, 144, 145, 146, 148, 149
Poseidon 74, 129
Price, Neil 79, 80, 86, 90
Prince of Persia 11
Prince of Persia: The Sands of Time 8
Prodicus 47
Prose Edda 79, 84; *see also Eddas*
Proyas, Alex 12
Psyche 120
Publius Varinius 162, 163, 164, 165, 169

Quintilius Varus 138, 167, 168
Quintus 185, 186
Quo Vadis (1951) 69, 156, 157, 158, 159, 160, 170, 178
Quo Vadis? (1985) 6
Quorra 30, 31, 39

Ragnar Lothbrok 80, 81–82, 83, 87, 88, 89, 91
Ragnar's Saga Loðbrókar 79, 81
Ragnarssona þáttr 79
Raimi, Sam 115, 117, 220
Raimi, Tes 115
Rajamouli, S.S. 13
Ramirez, Marisa 137, 167
Rankovic, Slavica 83, 90
rape 81, 89, 116, 137, 149, 150, 155, 167–168, 169, 173, 174, 189
Ratner, Brett 15, 38, 44, 45, 46, 48, 49, 50, 52
Raucci, Stacie 159
Reardon, John 30, 35
Red Sonja (1985) 10
Red Sonja (character) 10–11
Red Sonja: Queen of the Plagues 10
Red Zone 181, 185, 186, 190, 191
Redacted 179
Redmayne, Eddie 26, 29
Reeves, Keanu 38
Reeves, Steve 5, 7, 36, 38, 48, 52, 118, 219
Renaissance Pictures 7, 115, 220
representation 2, 15, 36, 38, 39, 46, 52, 67, 71, 83, 87, 89, 95–96, 97, 98–100, 101, 102, 103–104, 105, 106, 107, 108, 110,

127, 136, 137, 138–139 142, 150, 156, 161, 197, 199, 215
Reynolds, Richard 50
Rhaskos 167, 173
rhizome 79, 80–81, 82, 83, 86, 91
Rich, Adrienne 212–213
Richardson, John 110
Rinzler 31
Rippon, Todd 126
Rise of the Argonauts 11
Ritchie, Guy 14
Ritchie, Reece 45, 100
Rix, Robert 81, 82, 83, 87
The Robe 159, 178
Rogers, Holly 107
Roman Mysteries 7
Rome (television series) 7, 135, 136
Rome: Total War 12
Ronfeldt, David 72, 73
Rourke, Mickey 74
Ruby-Spears 6
Rushing, Robert A. 5, 52, 53, 71, 75
Ryse: Son of Rome 11

Sabinus 100
saga 15, 79–80, 81–82, 83, 84, 85–90, 91
Salmoneus 118, 122
Sam Flynn 26, 27, 30, 32, 36–37, 38, 39
Samson 24–25, 30, 49, 219
Sanders, Julie 24, 25, 26
Sandow, Eugen 53
Santoro, Rodrigo 36
Sawyer, Phil 103
Schnurbein, Stefanie von 83–84, 89
Schulian, John 120
Schwarzenegger, Arnold 38
Scott, Ridley 5, 36, 63, 159, 179, 222
Sears, Steven L. 115, 219–222
Segovax 147
Seibold, Whitney 178
Seltzer, Aaron 16, 196
Sense8 26
Seppia 141, 164, 168, 169
Seppius 162, 163, 169
September 11th terrorist attacks 179, 180
The 7th Voyage of Sinbad 8
Sewell, Rufus 54
sex 16, 136, 137–138, 139, 141, 142–143, 145, 150, 155, 156, 158, 159–160, 163–164, 165–166, 167, 168, 169, 172, 173, 198, 202
Shadix, Glenn 121
Shadow of Rome 11
Shahabudin, Kim 31, 35, 157
Shapiro, H.A. 54
Sharif, Omar 70
She-Ra: Princess of Power 6
Shepherd, Chad 100

Siegel, Jerry 49
The Sign of the Cross 156, 157, 158, 159, 160, 170
Sigurdson, Erika 81, 87, 88, 89
Simmons, Jean 159
Simon, Joe 49
Singer, Ben 30
Singin' in the Rain 52
Sirens 26–27, 126
skaldic verse 79, 82, 83–84, 85–86
Smith, Kevin 123, 213
Snyder, Zach 5, 36, 51, 64, 178
Soderbergh, Steven 38, 39
Sohamus 70
Sola 34
Solomon, Max 35
Solonius 164, 165, 173
Son of Zorn 7, 13
The Sons of Hercules 6, 219, 222
Sorbo, Kevin 115, 116, 117, 118, 119–120, 122–123, 209, 220, 221
Spartacus (1960) 5, 54, 72, 156–159, 160, 161, 163, 165, 167, 168, 170, 171, 174, 178, 179, 221
Spartacus (film character) 157, 158, 159, 160, 161, 167, 168, 171, 179
Spartacus (television series) 7, 12, 15, 135–151, 155–156, 158, 161–175, 222
Spartacus (television series character) 137–138, 141, 143, 145, 146, 147, 162, 163, 164, 166, 168, 168, 169, 170, 171, 172, 173, 174
Spartans 73, 178, 199, 202–204
Spielberg, Steven 23
Stafford, Emma 47
Staiff, Russell 108
Stanton, Andrew 8, 21
Stapleton, Sullivan 73
Star Trek 11
Star Wars 11, 55, 221
Starr, Anthony 126
Starz 15, 135–136, 149, 155, 158, 161, 172, 174, 222
Steel, Alan 24–25
Stephanus the Fuller 100
Stephenson, John 65
Stewart, R.J. 126
Stop-Loss 179
Straffi, Iginio 8
Strong, Anise 147, 166
Sturluson, Snorri 79, 84, 86
Sundmark, Björn 80, 81
superhero 10, 14, 15, 44, 46, 48–50, 53, 54, 55, 57, 104, 123, 124, 209
Superman 48, 49, 117, 123
Sura 162, 171
Suspiria 33

Sutcliffe, Rosemary 186, 188
swarms 64, 68, 72–74
sword and planet 5, 6, 10, 15, 21, 22, 25, 27, 28, 29, 30, 31, 34, 35, 36, 38, 39, 40
sword and sandal 4, 5, 6, 7, 8, 13, 14, 16, 21, 36, 44, 48, 50, 52, 53, 54, 63, 68, 69, 70, 99, 135, 161, 220
sword and sorcery 5, 6, 10, 13, 14, 63, 99, 115, 125, 221
Szymczak, Karolina 44

Tal Hajus 34
Talos 8
Tapert, Rob 115, 116, 123, 209, 220
Tars Tarkus 34
Tatum, Channing 27, 39, 187
Taylor, Pana Hema 138, 172
Taylor, Timothy 101
Te Maioha, Antonio 141, 172
The Ten Commandments 68
10,000 B.C. 13
Terminator 2: Judgement Day 8
Thark 31, 34
Themistocles 73
Theocritus 47
Theodorakopoulos, Elena 158
Thera 100, 101
Therns 30, 38
Theseus 74, 116
Thetis 45
Thomson, Erik 120
Thomson, Ethan 197
Thor 49, 50
Thor: Ragnarok 14, 15
Thorne, Frank 11
The Thracian Wars 10, 44, 47, 48, 55
3D 8, 68
300 (film) 5, 8, 9, 10, 12, 14, 36, 51, 53, 58, 64, 71, 73, 74, 178, 179
300 (graphic novel) 9, 10, 51
300: March to Glory 9
300: Rise of an Empire 8, 64, 73
Thundarr the Barbarian 6
Tiberius 169, 172
Tiernan, Andrew 73
Titans 74
Titus Abrasax 25–26, 37–38
Titus Calavius 164–165
Titus Flavius Virilus 185
Townend, Matthew 83–84
Toy Story 8
trailers 15, 48, 50, 51
Transformers: The Last Knight 15
transmedia 6, 9, 11, 13–16, 44, 46, 47, 48, 50, 55, 56
Trebor, Robert 118
Tron 39

Tron: Legacy 15, 21, 26–27, 29, 30, 31, 32, 35, 36–37, 40
Troy (2004) 36, 45, 51
Troy: Fall of a City 7
Tucker, Brett 162
The Tudors 7
Twitter 12, 15, 54
Tydings, Alexandra 115
Tykwer, Tom 26
Typhon 121

Ulmer, Edgar G. 64, 69, 71
Ulysses 116, 121, 126
uncanny valley 35
Universal 115, 123, 220
Unwin, Ty 101, 108–109
Urban, Karl 120, 122
Ursus 4
Ustinov, Peter 156, 157, 158, 160, 167, 168, 173

Valiant Comics 10
Varinia 159, 160, 161, 171
Varro 164, 167, 168, 169, 172
Veeram 13
video game 2, 6, 9, 11, 14, 74, 96, 99, 105, 204
Vikings 79–84, 87–91
Vikings (television series) 7, 15, 79–81, 83–85, 87–89
violence 87–89, 136, 137, 138, 142, 144, 145, 147, 148, 149–150, 161, 162, 163, 173, 174, 180
Vitale, Christopher 135
voyeurism 137, 138, 140, 141, 143, 145, 146, 147, 148–149, 150, 155, 156, 160, 166, 167, 168

The Wachowskis 8, 15, 21, 26, 38, 53
Waititi, Taika 14
Wanner, Kevin 85, 90, 91
War on Terror 184
Ward, Susan 120
Wax, Murray 84
Wax, Rosalie 84
Weisbrot, Robert 117
West, Dominic 185
West, Thomas J. 172, 173
Whissel, Kristen 68, 72
Whitburn, Katherine 100
White, Hayden 98
Whitelock, Robert 100
Whitfield, Andy 137, 162, 222
Who Framed Roger Rabbit 13
widescreen 7, 8
Wijaya, Admira 53
Wilde, Olivia 30

Williams, Christian 118
Williams, Linda 99, 136, 144
Wilson, Sarah 120
Winkler, Martin 21, 22, 25, 26, 27, 45, 46, 157, 175
Winnick, Katheryn 89
Wise, Robert 69
Wonder Woman (character) 10–11, 49
Wonder Woman (2017) 11, 14
Wong, Douglas 116
Woola 29
Wrath of the Titans 8, 45, 64, 74
Wright, Rayburn 109
Wuilleumier, Pierre 66
Wyke, Maria 52, 156, 178, 179, 191
Wyler, William 5, 63, 178

Xena (character) 115, 116, 120, 122, 123–124, 125–127, 128, 129, 208–209, 210, 211, 212–215, 216
Xena: Warrior Princess 7, 12, 16, 115, 116, 121–122, 123–129, 208–210, 211, 212–216, 220, 221, 222
Xenaphon 47
Xerxes 36, 74
xkcd 4
X-Men 46
X-O Manowar 10

Yishharu 100–101
Young, Cathy 124–125

Zalbenal 48
Zemeckis, Robert 8, 13
Zeus 44, 52, 73, 74, 121, 129

www.ingramcontent.com/pod-product-compliance
Lightning Source LLC
Chambersburg PA
CBHW051220300426
44116CB00006B/651